D0881272

The
LATIN AMERICAN ECONOMIES

This volume was produced as the result of a collaborative project sponsored by the Joint Committee on Latin American Studies of the Social Science Research Council and the American Council of Learned Societies.

The

LATIN AMERICAN ECONOMIES

Growth and the Export Sector 1880–1930

Edited by

Roberto Cortés Conde and Shane J. Hunt

Contributors

João Manoel Cardoso de Mello
Carmen Cariola
Roberto Cortés Conde
Shane J. Hunt
William McGreevey
Osvaldo Sunkel
Maria da Conceição Tavares

HOLMES & MEIER
New York   London

First published in the United States of America 1985 by
Holmes & Meier Publishers, Inc.
30 Irving Place
New York, N.Y. 10003

Great Britain:
Holmes & Meier Publishers, Ltd.
Hillview House
One Hallswelle Parade
London NW11 ODL, England

Book design by Stephanie Barton

Library of Congress Cataloging in Publication Data
Main entry under title:

The Latin American economies.

Bibliography: p.
Includes index.
Contents: The transition to economic growth in
Colombia / by William Paul McGreevey—The capitalist
export economy in Brazil, 1884–1930 / by João Manoel
Cardoso de Mello and Maria da Conceição Tavares—
The growth of the nitrate industry and socio-economic
change in Chile, 1880–1930 / by Carmen Cariola and
Osvaldo Sunkel—[etc.]
1. Latin America—Economic conditions—Addresses,
essays, lectures.   2. Latin America—Commerce—Addresses,
essays, lectures.   I. Cortés Conde, Roberto.
II. Hunt, Shane J.   III. Mello, João Manoel Cardoso de.
IV. Joint Committee on Latin American Studies.
HC125.L349   330.98′003   82-1007
ISBN 0-8419-0771-4

CONTENTS

Tables & Figures

Chapter 2

Tables

Figures

Chapter 3

Tables

Chapter 4

Tables

Appendix A

Appendix B

Chapter 5

Tables

Chapter 6

Tables

PREFACE

The collaborative effort which produced this volume was organized and supported by the Joint Committee on Latin American Studies of the Social Science Research Council and the American Council of Learned Societies. The Joint Committee's project on economic history consisted of two phases. The first attempted a sum·nary of the state of knowledge regarding Latin America's economic h'story since Independence, and resulted in the publication of *Latin America: A Guide to Economic History, 1830–1930*, edited by Roberto Cortés Conde and Stanley J. Stein (Berkeley: University of California Press, 1977). That volume presented annotated bibliographies and historiographic essays on Argentina, Brazil, Chile, Colombia, Mexico, and Peru.

The second phase, devoted to substantive studies of the same countries, is the genesis of the present volume. The number of countries is in fact reduced by one, since it was not possible to bring the Mexican study to completion.

Both phases of this project have emphasized cooperative effort and integrative approaches. The cooperation has joined North Americans and Latin Americans in common effort. It has also sought, successfully we think, to unite historians and economists in a search for common viewpoints. In this way the studies have atempted to integrate the quantitative approaches associated with economics and the broader integrative view which is the tradition of history.

R.C.C.
S.J.H.

Acknowledgements

We express our great appreciation to the various scholars who have served on the Joint Committee during the gestation of the project. Our debt to Bryce Wood and Joseph Grunwald is particularly great; their organizational talents were essential to the initiation of this project, as well as to its predecessor bibliographic survey.

We also thank Heraclio Bonilla, Enrique Florescano, Tulio Halperin, Stanley Ross, and Stanley J. Stein, who formed an advisory committee which assisted greatly in defining the project's scope and focus. Tulio Halperin, Albert Hirschman, Fernando Rosenzweig, and Stanley Ross attended a conference of participating authors held when the project was in mid-passage and assisted greatly with their comments on the drafts presented. At a later stage, each manuscript was given a careful critical reading by an expert on the country in question. We express our thanks for this to Richard Mallon (Argentina), Flavio Versiani (Brazil), Frank Safford (Colombia), Tom Davis (Chile), and Rosemary Thorp (Peru). We also thank Stanley Stein and Richard Graham for a critical reading of special sections.

At the SSRC, four generations of Staff Associates have pushed the project along with firmness tempered by patience: Michael Potashnik, Louis Wolf Goodman, Reid Andrews, and Brooke Larson. Finally, a special debt of gratitude is owed to Diana Brown, whose editorial talents eliminated the roughest edges and brought the manuscript to publishable form. In this effort she was ably assisted by María Onestini.

R.C.C.
S.J.H.

1
Introduction

This book represents the culmination of a project on the Economic History of Latin America sponsored by the Joint Committee on Latin American Studies of the American Council of Learned Societies and the Social Science Research Council. The first phase of the project led to the publication of critical bibliographic studies on the economic history of Latin America.[1] The project's objectives were also described in that volume. In this volume we close the project by presenting substantive studies on a period in the economic history of five countries (Argentina, Brazil, Colombia, Chile, and Peru).*

Despite the different cases studied, and the varied approaches, theoretical perspectives, and interpretations, there has been from the outset a common concern with the debate over the problems of Latin American economic growth. More precisely, we wished to know if exogenous forces stemming from the growing demand for exports (from the middle of the nineteenth century until the 1930s) had positive long-term effects on the economic development of these countries, and if so, to what degree; or, alternatively, whether they represented an obstacle to development.

The authors generally agreed that one way to address this question was to examine aspects of economic history between 1880 and 1930.** We found that many of the previous studies and interpretations of this period suffered from scarce data, data of poor quality, or an absolute lack of data on many of the period's most relevant aspects. We wished, therefore, not only to undertake new interpretive studies but also to include new and more reliable information on basic aspects of Latin American economic history. We trust that at least some cases we present here

---

*Unfortunately the essay on Mexico was not finished in time to be included in this volume.
**The study on Peru covers a somewhat earlier period, from about 1840 to about 1900.

3

contain in addition to new perspectives on the issues discussed new and relevant information that will improve our understanding of them.

The authors also agreed that during the period in question, there was important economic growth in primary production for export within the framework of an open world economy into which the Latin American market became integrated. Our accord on the theme extended to several principal questions: How did growth in the export sector extend to the rest of the economy? Did it have multiplying and cumulative effects that permitted sustained growth, or were the effects lost with the decline of external demand? In cases of sustained growth, what were the specific mechanisms for the transmission of this growth? All the authors agreed on the importance of developing an approach that accounted for internal factors, such as describing the original conditions existing at the time of the external impact, and those conditions that developed from it.

Agreement on the questions does not imply agreement on the answers, as will become apparent in those essays in which partial answers were attempted. The authors agreed there could be no attempt to reach unanimity or to develop complete or final answers in a project that was to some extent limited by its resources. Our more modest intention was to contribute to the understanding of the period and its problems by bringing more and better information to bear and by attempting to develop an analytical sketch that would take into account our shared concerns.

THE PROBLEMS

The central question, then, was to discover how economic growth took place.

The tentative replies suggest that, first, in the export sectors, and then, in the other sectors of the domestic economies, growth resulted partly from an aggregation of factors of production—land, capital, and labor—and partly from a more efficient use of the available factors of production. The latter entailed changes, adaptation, or technological improvements as well as the entrepreneurial ability to implement them. In fact, economic growth almost always resulted from a combination of all of these factors, although what distinguishes the Latin American export sectors at this time was the availability of previously unused natural resources (land or mineral resources). The reasons these resources had been idle were:

1. There were no markets because of lack of population, low income, and the absence of transportation networks.
2. The lack of other resources, either capital or labor, prevented the development of production.

3. Finally, the entrepreneurial ability to mobilize missing resources, and to use other abundant and idle resources, was lacking. To a certain extent the study of the growth of the export sectors of Latin American economies during this period concerns the *mobilization* of these factors, as well as determining whether the mobilization occurred as a result of a domestic decision or as the automatic response to an external impulse.

Argentine cattle raising appears to provide an example—rare for the rest of Latin America—of the use of a resource for which there was no outlet other than export (Cortés Conde). The only domestic factor of production that was generally scarce was labor. It is important to remember, though, that while there was almost no supplement to the domestic labor force in Peru (Hunt), labor was supplied by immigrants in the Brazilian and Argentine cases and apparently by natural population increase in the case of Chile.

The second problem has to do with whether, and under what circumstances—once the factors of production had been mobilized and had resulted in increased production of primary goods for export—this increase in economic activity limited itself to the export sector or extended into other sectors.

In order to deal with this problem, the authors generally used the concept of linkages developed by Hirschman.[2] This concept assumes that investments are reoriented, or resources are reallocated, when backward linkages to other activities appear as the result of the development of the initial export activity, thus raising prices and profits. Alternatively, it assumes a lowering of costs in the increased supply of export products, which generates other activities. Such "forward linkages" are rare among the exports developed in Latin America during the period in question, but cattle raising in Argentina is a case in point that merits attention.

Hirschman's original concept of linkages was supplemented by the concept of demand linkages[3] and fiscal linkages.[4] The importance of demand linkages is developed in this volume especially in the studies on Chile (Cariola and Sunkel) and Argentina (Cortés Conde), and the importance of fiscal linkages in the study on Peru (Hunt).

What seems outstanding in these studies is that as a result of various linkages, the development of primary activities for export had effects that were transmitted to the rest of the economy. Thus there was no single pure "enclave" among these cases. Some of the effects occurred as a result of market expansion in response to population growth and increased income (demand linkages); others occurred as a result of demand for other inputs (backward linkages), especially transportation, or as a result of the establishment of an administrative structure that reallocated resources (fiscal linkages). In the economies that were able to respond with increased supply—Chile, Brazil, and Argentina—the demand linkages had notable effects. In the Peruvian case, on the other hand, the response was slower and the demand linkages generated significant inflationary phenomena. The results of public-sector investments also differed; in Chile (Cariola and Sunkel) and Peru (Hunt) investments made with public funds seem to have failed. Nevertheless, the central questions continued to concern how demand was generated for new products or inputs, and how the necessary savings or surpluses were generated to respond to the increased demand with increased supply. This is to say that the problem of linkages, which is generally approached from the demand side, in fact requires equal attention from the supply side.

The capacity to produce surpluses was determined by the level of income and the earnings ratio, including earnings generated by the exploitation of natural resources. The earnings ratio, in turn, depended on the price-cost relationship, which was determined by various factors of technology, efficiency, and market structure. In some cases, the earnings ratio resulted from monopolistic quasi rents, where there were no cost considerations because of monopolistic control of the resources. In other instances, there were near-monopolistic situations where exporters controlled the supplies (for example, coffee production in Brazil during several years under the valorization policy). In yet other cases, prices were internationally fixed and the exporters were price takers. Since there were many suppliers on the market, the new suppliers had to adapt and become competitive by reducing their costs (using fertile lands, cheap labor, or even devaluation policies, which contributed to reducing labor costs). In almost all the export sectors and the sectors affected by the various linkages, the cost of labor had an important inverse relation to the rate of earnings, and while there was nothing as formal as a wage policy, various government measures did affect wage levels. Without doubt, the most important measure was the pro-immigration policy common to all these countries. Also important were government policies regarding land and the development of labor unions.

Once it was established how surplus was generated, the next question consisted in discovering the rate at which surpluses were saved and reinvested. This rate depended on the consumption patterns established by the entrepreneurial and rent-collecting class. There is an abundance of anecdotal material but almost no data on this matter. With regard to the portion of surplus that was saved and not consumed, it is important to point out that a significant part was retained by the state to pay for the infrastructural works.

This was the case in Chile and Peru, where fiscal linkages *adversely affected* export activity (Cariola and Sunkel). In the Argentine case, exports permitted a sustained influx of imports. These provided the financial resources on which the government counted in order to pay its foreign debt, to which investments in infrastructure had contributed in an important way (Cortés Conde).

Another part of the surplus was reinvested in material and equipment (to a large degree, imported) for the individual firms, or was deposited in the banking system.

As a result of the development of export activities, markets were broadened by the construction of transportation networks and the importation of capital goods for industry, and, therefore, investment alternatives developed in other industries which could produce goods that were previously imported (Brazil, Argentina, Chile). This was especially true where the profit rate on export activities declined because of a deterioration in the terms of trade.[5] There were two important limitations in the process of reallocating surplus: (1) the availability of, and knowledge of, other technology; and (2) entrepreneurial specialization in the primary sector, which made it difficult to initiate activity in the secondary sector.

The five essays in this volume reveal an early process of industrial development that was much more significant than previously suspected. They discuss the economic effects on five Latin American countries of resource-intensive production for export based on an abundant factor of production: land, including mining. Two of the cases deal with mineral resources: Peruvian guano and Chilean nitrates. The other studies discuss the use of land for agrarian production. The authors have sought to determine the production functions involved, so as to specify their effects on the economy as a whole.

In each case, production was intensive in the use of natural resources (land or minerals), and required different and specific proportions of the other factors of production, labor and capital. Nitrates (Cariola and Sunkel), for example, had more intensive labor requirements than copper, and this accounts for the different effect that its exploitation had on the Chilean economy. The effects of exploiting nonrenewable minerals also differed from those of exploiting a nonperishable resource like land.[6] In the case of non-perishable resources, the effects differed because of the elasticity of supply: in Brazil, for example, coffee plants reached maturity in five years, whereas Argentine grain was an annual crop. Compared to previous work on the subject, these essays are noteworthy in their emphasis on the technological nature of resources (production functions) and their effects on the national economies.

The writers attempt to specify the mechanisms by which increased income from the export sector was transmitted to other economic sectors. They question the commonly held view in Latin America that since Latin American production found its market abroad and made use of foreign factors of production (principally capital), the export sectors formed enclaves that were separate from the national economies. This view further holds that the increased income generated by the export sector did not remain in the Latin American countries, but was, to a significant extent, transferred abroad (toward both markets and capital), partly by means of profit remittances in the form of luxury imports for upper-income groups.[7]

What these essays attempt to do is to determine empirically the degree to which revenues from the export sector were transmitted to the domestic economy by means of various linkages, in particular by means of payments to domestic factors of production.

Although in many cases the role of foreign capital was important—albeit less so than previously supposed (Hunt, Cariola and Sunkel)—the authors go beyond the question of remittance of profits abroad and develop a more comprehensive concept to determine what proportion of income generated by the export sector remained in the national economies. To an extent they use a concept similar to that of "returned value"[8]; that is, the total sum of payments made to the domestic factors of production. In the cases of guano in Peru and nitrates in Chile, the conclusion reached was that the proportion of income that remained in the respective countries was relatively high, which contradicts the more popular view.

The authors assume in almost every case, although not always explicitly, that a more efficient allocation of resources, through the exploitation of "untapped" resources, generated an important economic surplus, significant proportions of which were saved and contributed to high rates of capital formation and economic growth.

Investment incentives did not appear simply because there was a sudden increase in demand that raised prices and assured high profits. Increased demand through the price mechanism may have operated in the case of guano and even nitrates, but this was not so with Argentine grain production (Cortés Conde), where the expansion in cultivation occurred during a period of price declines. However, investment incentives did develop because of significant reductions in costs that kept profit rates high. In Brazil, for example, lower costs permitted an expansion in the market for coffee (Mello and Tavares), and in Argentina lower costs allowed exports to compete in foreign markets during the 1890s—a period of sharply declining prices. In both countries lower costs were made possible by the incorporation of abundant and fertile lands by the extension of railroads into the interior. In Brazil, moreover, there was an important gap between international prices and production costs (wages), which ensured high profits, an explanation that correlates with the well-known Hamilton-Keynes thesis. In Argentina (Cortés Conde), this gap only existed for a short period between 1888 and 1894, but nonetheless provided a strong push for grain cultivation. To a large extent, what characterized the agricultural development of Argentina was not only lower costs but the constant effort to reduce costs yet further by means of more efficient organization, including increased production scale and the introduction of crop rotation. These efforts resulted in greater productivity and more rapid, and less costly, adjustments to market fluctuations. As a result, profits were maintained at a high level and the real income of workers increased, as, consequently, did domestic demand.

THE ESSAYS

Colombia

McGreevey's essays proposes to determine how, where, and when the transition between a state of low economic activity and one of economic growth developed in Colombia.

He deals first with population growth: its greater increase in urban than in rural areas, and the displacement of labor from the rural to urban areas beginning at the end of the nineteenth century. Then he examines the growth in coffee exports and the construction of the railroad network that allowed the incorporation of new lands for coffee production. He maintains that it was during the twentieth century, precisely from 1905 on, that a spurt in economic activity began.

The impulse for developing new coffee lands and increasing coffee exports came from rising coffee prices (the result of Brazil's valorization policy) and the presence of a railroad network that moved populations to new areas beyond the Magdalena River. McGreevey is concerned with the factors that led to the transition and acceleration of growth. He finds his answers in increased profit rates, due not only to rising prices but also to a lowering of real wages among coffee workers. In order to support his argument he presents tables showing the evolution of income from coffee production. Again, his results are consonant with the well-known Hamilton-Keynes thesis. In addition, he points out that the end of the War of a Thousand Days also ended disorder, anarchy, and the destruction of property and resources. The government was then able to impose a stabilizing policy that permitted a real increase in fiscal revenues and protected nascent industries. At the same time, it repressed working-class aspirations and prevented an increase in labor costs.

Brazil

Mello and Tavares's essay argues that in view of international market conditions at the time, the factors that ensured high profitability to coffee production, and provided a strong incentive for coffee cultivation, were the incorporation of new lands by way of railroad expansion and the availability of an abundant labor force. The increase in coffee exports resulted in an increased importing capacity that allowed (1) the acquisition of capital goods by the coffee production complex as well as by the urban sector and related services, and (2) imports of consumption goods at low prices, which kept the cost of labor low. They argue that when industrial activities grew, wages were provided for the working class from within because the industrial sector had previously been able to import the capital goods necessary for the growth of domestic industries.

With regard to specific aspects of production, Mello and Tavares point out that the coffee cycle depended not only on demand on the world market, but also on the domestic supply situation, which was conditioned by the five-year period required for the coffee plants to mature. In the short run the supply of coffee was inelastic to changes in demand in the world market. However, the supply was also affected by the deliberate intervention of the Brazilian government.

The cycle was characterized, first, by a period of high prices, expansion in production and productive capacity, and the incorporation of new lands under cultivation. This period was followed by one of oversupply and a consequent decline in prices, culminating in economic crisis and a fall in profits. The crisis of coffee extended to the urban sector of the coffee complex and thus affected the economy as a whole.

The government adopted different strategies to contain these unfavorable effects. In some cases, it instituted devaluationist policies that maintained high profits when international prices were falling. This was possible because wages lagged behind the rise of the exchange rate. At other times, it held back and accumulated stocks (a valorization and defense policy) when the oversupply in Brazil threatened to unsettle the markets. This was possible because of Brazil's quasi-monopolistic position as a world supplier of coffee (in contrast to the situation with grain in Argentina). The two policies—which were successful in maintaining profit margins—had different consequences.

Devaluationist policies increased the cost of importing capital goods for industries, but thanks to the protection offered by the exchange rate, they increased the cost of locally produced articles even more, resulting in an expansion of the domestic sector. These policies then, according to Mello and Tavares, were not contrary to the interests of the urban and industrial sectors.[9] Nonetheless the excess of monetary issues that followed devaluation led to a severe inflation and the 1899 crisis, to which the government responded with tough monetary stabilization policies and with reductions in government expenditures.

When, during the next cycle of expansion, the increase in productive capacity again was translated into an oversupply of coffee the government responded with the valorization policy, which tried to cut production and accumulate stocks of coffee. The valorization policy was intended to reduce exports and to avoid a greater overvaluation of the Brazilian exchange rate. It also acted to maintain the profit rate. Nonetheless, Mello and Tavares write, citing Delfím Netto,[10] the valorization policy, followed by policies of defense, led to an increase in international prices, and consequently intensified competition, thus threatening Brazil's quasi-monopolistic position. Moreover, as prices rose, so did the amount of land under cultivation, and the oversupply of coffee became even greater—until the dramatic end in 1929. In fact, government policies tended to lessen the effects of international demand by acting on the exchange rate or controlling the supply by accumulating stocks. Mello and Tavares point out that there was no conflict of interest between the export and the industrial sectors, and that the latter emerged as a result of the expansion of the former. The expansion of coffee provided the industrial sector with:

1. The ability to import capital goods at low prices during periods of revaluation. This also happened in periods of devaluation because the prices of industrial goods rose faster than did the exchange rate.
2. The development of a labor market and the availability of a surplus that the coffee sector did not completely absorb.
3. Protection by means of devaluation.

In the final analysis—and this is central to Mello and Tavares's argument—the industrial sector benefited because the coffee sector could not absorb all the surplus it produced and the extra surplus was invested in the industrial sector. The coffee sector could not absorb all the surplus partly because of the length of time needed for coffee plants to mature, partly because of the time involved in developing new lands, and partly because the supply of land was limited. The labor force involved in coffee production generated a demand for foodstuffs and clothing; at first, this demand was supplied from abroad, but later it was supplied domestically. Because foodstuffs and clothing did not require much capital and used only simple technology, what developed was a light consumer goods industry, not heavy industry.

The industrial sector imported capital goods during coffee boom periods, when it had underutilized capital, which it subsequently used when exchange restrictions were in effect and imports became more expensive.

Chile

The essay by Cariola and Sunkel examines the view commonly held in Chile that the expansion of nitrate mining for export did not contribute to the economic development of the country.[11] This thesis maintains that the income from nitrate exports did not remain in Chile but flowed out to foreign countries through profit remittances of foreign corporations, or was spent by and among a small group of upper-income Chileans on luxury consumption. It holds, moreover, that the opening of the country to international trade flooded Chile with imports, which hindered the development of local manufactures, and that the specialization in mining produced an agricultural crisis that affected the whole economy.[12] The same view asserts that the exploitation of nitrates was an enclave, isolated from the rest of the Chilean economy. Cariola and Sunkel refute these affirmations and maintain that the expansion in nitrate exports—although controlled to an important extent by foreign capital—far from creating an enclave, contributed to a significant degree to Chilean development. The formation of a national market, the consolidation of the state, the growing demand for consumer goods and for production inputs, were some of the mechanisms by which the growth was transmitted.

Their essay demonstrates that the general increase in income resulting from exports had a positive effect on the economy for the following reasons:

1. It contributed to the formation of a national market linking the Norte Grande and its nitrate deposits with the old Valle Central and the recently conquered lands in the south (Watkins's demand linkages).
2. It precipitated the building of a transportation network.
3. It provided a rapidly expanding market in the Norte Grande for the agriculture of the Valle Central and the new southern territories.

Cariola and Sunkel examine the technological nature of the resource in question, nitrates, and study the effects that its exploitation had on the economy as a whole (a concern common to many of the essays in this volume). Nitrates are more labor intensive than copper, they point out, but since the deposits are less concentrated, mining nitrates had distinctive consequences.

The need for labor in the Norte Grande stimulated migration to previously deserted areas, thus creating urban centers and generating demand for activities and services that would support the new population. The special demand for foodstuffs—produced elsewhere, since agriculture was unproductive in these deserted mining regions—led to a specialization of the domestic market.

Cariola and Sunkel also examine the role of government as collector and redistributor of the income generated by the export sector. The government received a tax on nitrates exports; it was fixed at 8 percent in 1880, but rose to 43 percent by 1890, with an average over the whole period of 33 percent. They estimate that the Chilean government may have received about 55 percent of the nitrate revenues and played a central role in distributing this surplus (the fiscal linkages of Hirschman).[13]

In sum, they argue that the expansion of nitrates works for export in the Norte Grande after the War of the Pacific meant:

1. The development of a previously deserted area.
2. Growth in population and employment.
3. The construction of urban and transportation networks.
4. An increased national income.

All these factors translated into a strong stimulus for the development of manufacturing, to which the devaluation of the peso also contributed.

Peru

Hunt's essay also challenges the popular enclave thesis. He argues precisely the opposite case for guano in the Peruvian economy: the income generated by guano exports was transmitted to the economy as a whole through an increased demand for goods and services. In view of the rigidity of domestic supply, however, this produced a strong increase in prices that slowed down local production and favored imports. This change, argues Hunt, led to the eclipse of the handicraft sector, and its eventual replacement by modern manufacturing.

In support of the first proposition—that the income from guano was transmitted to the rest of the economy—Hunt estimates the returned value,[14] that is, the share of income paid to the domestic factors of production. Since the share of labor in the total output was very low (4 percent of the cost), the returned value was limited to government revenues and the income of the contractors, which he estimates at 70 percent of the final sale value. Thus, he maintains, one simply cannot describe the guano economy as an enclave. Quite the contrary, the government received the largest share of guano revenues and was the principal reallocator of these revenues.

Guano posed few problems of extraction: it required very little capital and only rudimentary technology. The nation, which owned the resources according to Spanish juridical tradition, maintained a monopolistic control over the exploitation of the fertilizer for forty years. The intervention of foreign capital in the guano business had to do with the fact that the government not only wished to maintain its monopoly but also sought to control the worldwide distribution network. Whereas guano extraction required little capital or technology, the distribution network, on the other hand, required both in great quantities. Moreover, control of the distribution network required access to, and knowledge of, European markets, which gave European capital a great advantage.

As the principal collector of guano incomes, the government went through a period of fiscal bonanza. Government revenues increased five times, and expenditures grew even faster, by eight times. The government was able to pay off all its domestic and foreign debts, though some were tainted by suspicion of fraud, and to abolish taxes on the indigenous population by a modification of the tax system, which from then on rested primarily on guano revenues. Increased government expenditures resulted principally from extending outlays on railroads (20 percent), welfare (abolishing levies on the indigenous population—7 percent), increases in the civil bureaucracy (30 percent), and in the military (25 percent). Thus the outlays on the civil and military bureaucracy contributed primarily to an extension of services and personnel (particularly military personnel) rather than to an increase in the incomes of a limited group of functionaries. The remaining 18 percent was transferred to Peruvians and foreigners to pay off outstanding debts. Thus distributed, revenues from guano generated a significant demand for goods and services. However, the potentially transforming effect of these revenues on the national economy was eroded by the increased prices of domestic goods.

Hunt's central thesis is that although guano provided an adequate surplus, it also impeded the rise of social and entrepreneurial attitudes necessary for economic growth. It was not a case of guano bypassing the Peruvian economy, but rather of its effects on the cost-price structure of the economy.

Hunt's conclusions are also consonant with the Hamilton-Keynes thesis with regard to the effect of price inflation on rates of profit and rates of growth.

The increase in internal prices produced by the guano revenues dealt a death blow to handicraft industry. The factors of production that were thus freed in the handicraft industry could not be absorbed by guano production; paradoxically, this resulted in both an underutilization of factors of production, and in chronic unemployment.

Hunt appears to be arguing that demand linkages alone are not sufficient for self-sustained growth, and that the economic structure should be flexible enough to respond appropriately to increased demand and to expand in sectors that absorb employment. In fact, the positive gains that guano exports made possible led to an overvaluation of the Peruvian sol, which lowered protective measures and affected domestic production. On the other hand, investments that were made in infrastructure generally failed. In contrast to what happened in Chile, Brazil, and Argentina, the Peruvian railroads failed to play a pioneer role in the development of markets.

Argentina

The essay on Argentina attempts to show the workings of two distinct patterns of primary production for exports.

The first one, extensive cattle raising for hide exports during the first half of the nineteenth century, generated limited surpluses and had few linkage effects. Cattle raising developed according to the resources available at the time, and did not require large amounts of capital or labor. For precisely these reasons, extensive cattle raising had limited accumulative and multiplying effects. The second was agricultural production (as well as the production of meat), which appeared toward the end of the nineteenth century. Although this pattern of production also involved a primary product with an outlet on the foreign market, its effects on the economy were very different from those of the first type. The essay focuses on the different intensity with which resources were exploited in the first and second patterns of production, and describes how scarce or nonexistent resources (capital or labor) were mobilized to place into production resources that were potentially abundant. The result of this combination was translated into a more efficient use of resources and the generation of important surpluses, which provided a base for significant economic growth.

After discussing how factors of production were mobilized (the sources of financing for capital, the incorporation of labor, etc.), the essay analyzes the relation of the export sector to the rest of the economy. It emphasizes that growth in the former was transmitted to the economy as a whole. The essay points out that exports not only generated an important surplus but also led to the economic integration of the country (transportation, communication), the population of rural areas, an increase in the number of wage earners and in the amount of wages, and the generation of domestic demand. Finally, export revenues permitted imports of capital goods for local production of manufactured goods when comparative advantage and new circumstance made their production within the country more profitable.

The role of entrepreneurs, in both the public and the private sectors, in mobilizing and combining resources was very significant from the early period. Later on, private entrepreneurs made greater growth possible by developing new techniques and improving the organization of productive processes.

ISSUES AND PROBLEMS

In the preceding pages we have described the expansion of the export sectors of Latin America and their principal characteristics. We turn now to some of the issues and problems as they occurred in the economic histories of these countries. Several of the problems are more or less explicit in many of the essays; other problems are omitted because the nature of our project limited coverage. Therefore, in order to provide a general framework for each essay dealing with a specific country, we shall review here the historical problems that are most relevant. What we wish to do is to specify the problems or aspects of the evolution of these five economies that produced rigidities or inelasticities and that led to imperfect markets. We believe that these rigidities and imperfections correspond to situations in which different sectors of the economy are of different degrees of backwardness (which implies that the market does not completely work), and where the state is not yet consolidated. It is our argument that these factors had important consequences for growth and the allocation of resources.

External Vulnerability

It has been argued that economic growth based on the expansion of the export sector was extremely vulnerable to fluctuations on the international market, especially when each country's supply individually had very limited effects.

Changes in market prices were especially serious when income from exports comprised a high proportion of national income. Specific references to this difficulty are made in the essays on the problem of coffee prices in Brazil and Colombia and the prices of copper, nitrates, and agricultural produce in Chile and Argentina. Yet another manifestation of this vulnerability is the way in which price fluctuations affected the availability of foreign exchange. This was especially problematic in cases when, in order to encourage exports, it was necessary to finance the importation of capital goods—before the revenues to pay for them became available from the exports—with credits obtained from abroad. Then, when export prices declined, the service and amortization of the external debt represented a large proportion of foreign exchange revenues. Finally, a third aspect of vulnerability is related to problems of growth. If the growth rate depended on capital formation, and this, in turn, was determined in the concrete situations described by capital goods imports, the availability of foreign exchange fixed the limits of the growth rates. Therefore the fluctuation of prices determined the course of growth.

Price variations affected the countries studied differently because of the inelasticity of supply in response to prices. Thus when a change in relative prices occurred, it did not affect the allocation of factors of production because either there were no alternative markets or the factors could not be allocated to the production of a different commodity. Changes in the international price of copper did not mean that Chile could then sell its copper at home; there was no internal demand for it. Neither was there any alternative use for the capital and the labor working in copper, since there was no demand for either factor in other sectors of the economy. This was so precisely because in most of the countries discussed, the situation was one of a surplus for which no other outlet existed besides exports (vent for surplus). Coffee production, or meat production, where there was not sufficient domestic demand, faced similar problems.

This was particularly important with respect to the mechanisms of adjustment of the gold standard. When price variations reflected changes in comparative advantage, the disequilibria in the balance of payments—with effects on the flight of gold and on domestic prices—did not lead to automatic adjustments since, in view of the inelasticity of substitution, there were no alternative uses for the factors of production. This was a fairly general pattern in Brazil and Argentina.

Stabilization Policies: Contradictory Goals

The disequilibrium in the balance of payments resulting from international price variations made it necessary to adopt measures that would restore equilibrium. Regardless of short-term financial measures, credits, etc., reduced imports and increased exports were the only solutions. An adjustment in the gold standard was produced automatically, since the outflow of gold made imported goods more expensive (thus reducing imports) and exports more attractive, since they were paid for in gold.* In the situations specific to Latin American countries in the nineteenth century this had an additional effect: reduced imports produced a significant drop in government revenues.

In most cases, government revenues were derived from foreign trade, especially from taxes on imports. Therefore all policies attempting to stabilize the foreign sector through import reductions produced unbalancing effects on public finances by diminishing the revenues of the government.

To be sure, the fiscal structures in effect were not the most appropriate. However, replacing the most backward structures that still existed (Indian tribute in Peru and the sale or granting of lands in Argentina) with a modern tax system (e.g., an income or sales tax) required a labor market and consumption levels that did not exist in any of the countries under consideration. On the other hand, if export products had become routine

---

*Since guano was a "free" resource, its export was not responsive to the exchange rate.

items of family consumption, the price increases would have affected the cost of living. These stresses produced recessive situations with strong inflationary pressures.

When this situation became generalized, the whole world wagered against the ability of the governments to achieve monetary stability. This translated into a greater demand for strong currencies—principally gold—which further increased the price of gold and tended to deplete the reserves held by the state. Under these circumstances pressures to abandon the gold standard and its fixed exchange rate were inevitable. Such pressures were common in Chile, and they led to the 1878 devaluation. What devaluation meant was an increase in export revenues, without affecting the protection afforded local industries. During periods this was also the case in Brazil and Argentina.

Abandoning the gold standard solved the problem of delivering gold at the established rate and permitted these countries to maintain their reserves. Local currency—the currency in which the government received its revenues—was devalued as a result of inconvertibility. Consequently, foreign liabilities became even greater and more burdensome. This situation tended to diminish the government's ability to pay its debts and created a generalized distrust in its administrative capacity, which had a negative effect on private enterprise. In addition, such a climate favored speculation and administrative corruption.

Those who were responsible for adopting political decisions were faced with contradictory alternatives:

1. All development goals aimed at economic growth led in the end—especially if there were unfavorable price fluctuations—to a growing deficit in the balance of payments and to a crisis in the foreign sector.
2. All policies aimed at stabilizing the foreign sector not only entailed great austerity measures (no simple matter) but also a reduction in revenues and a diminished ability to pay debts abroad—precisely what the governments wished to avoid.

It would seem that whichever path was chosen, the consequences would necessarily be adverse. Under these circumstances, states were often forced to adopt measures that were not consonant with a goal of national development.

Imperfections in the Capital Market

The international market for capital in the nineteenth century was almost entirely limited to the city of London. Thus, whereas the demand for capital came from various places and regions, this demand converged on the London market, where the Bank of England's decisions on local interest rates affected the supply of English capital, practically the only source of supply for foreign bonds.

Nevertheless, it is well known that the most important factor affecting the cost of money for the debtor countries was not the evolution of interest rates but rather the discounts on the face value with which bonds were negotiated at the London banks.

Still, the discount below par—which was the risk price as perceived by the buyers—was fairly sensitive to the behavior of the debtors. In fact, interest rates were considerably higher when there was a general impression—arising out of the default into which most Latin American countries had fallen after the independence wars—that these were high-risk investments. In the late nineteenth century, when the debtor nations appeared to meet their obligations more strictly, interest rates began to decline. This was clear in the case of Argentina.

Another factor that increased the risk price was related to the fluctuation of the external sectors of these Latin American economies and the ways in which they attempted to maintain their ability to pay foreign debts while maintaining equilibrium in the foreign sector. We have seen that these objectives, taken simultaneously, had contradictory effects.

Investors were more willing to invest in foreign bonds when the prices of the exported products were high, and the debtors were more willing to pay high interest rates when they were experiencing boom periods. Conversely, during periods of low prices the cost of the debt relative to the ability to pay (export earnings plus credits) was lower, not only because export earnings diminished as a result of the price declines, but also because investors were less enthusiastic about those bonds. Thus, again, there were cumulative tendencies toward disequilibrium.

The Accumulation of Inequalities

The backward and forward linkages of the export sector led to investments in specific sectors of the economy and in specific regions (those linked to export production). These were very important to the development of infrastructure, particularly railroads, in São Paulo and Argentina, for example. When relative price changes indicated that production in other sectors or other regions might be more profitable, the fact that the preexisting investments had been made implied that in the areas linked to the export sector there were external economies that did not exist in other economic areas or regions; lower transportation costs, the availability of labor, and the existence of markets were critical in this regard. This difference in costs made the transfer of factors of production to other regions, where they might have been more profitable, less likely.

The profit rate was influenced by markets with very different costs. This led to continual reinvestments in the same sector or region, and a consequent accumulation of inequalities between these regions and other areas with less capital accumulation. In the long run, it led to a decline in the profit rate of the favored regions.

The Limits of Administrative and Entrepreneurial Capacity

One of the noneconomic aspects that affects the process of development is the existence of a group possessing the ability and the skills to undertake public administration and efficient private enterprise. It would seem that in the face of all the difficulties we have discussed, such groups were important in the development and training of personnel who would have to make decisions on the basis of experiences that were contradictory, not always rational, and frequently apparently insoluble. We have discussed some of the challenges faced by government administrations in most of the cases discussed here during the nineteenth century: for example, the effort to attain balance in the foreign sector, while maintaining ability to pay debts; or to promote exports—that is, to grow—while avoiding disequilibrium. And the governments faced the problem of how to achieve all of these goals while presenting an orderly administration that would inspire confidence in the European creditors. The problem was whether (or how) to adopt political measures, or to limit themselves to simply depending on the fluctuation of international prices. The latter is in fact what ultimtely took place in almost all the cases presented in this book. The most severe measures adopted by some countries were generally of limited effect. The way out of disequilibrium was made possible by changes in international prices, which did not depend at all on the supply of the exporting country (except in the case of Brazilian coffee, where Brazil maintained a quasi-monopolistic control of supply).

The temptation to await changes in international prices, the roulette game of price (which has been so commented on in the Cuban case), may appear to have been irrational. In some cases, however, though a seemingly desperate strategy, it was the only possible path. How else would we expect the individual entrepreneur to behave, in view of the characteristics we have described? In an economy composed of sectors at different stages of development, and an imperfect market? With a recently emerged and still very weak state? In such a situation is it not logical to expect the entrepreneur to bet against monetary stability and attempt to profit from a quasi-monopolistic position? Under these circumstances, individual benefit does not necessarily coincide with social benefit.

The entrance of Latin American countries into the world market occurred in historically concrete situations, with different and specific consequences for each in its attempt to adjust to market requirements, as well as for its power and ability to negotiate. Although the perfect market has never existed, the European countries in the nineteenth century had reached a development level and had institutional structures that allowed far greater fluidity in their market mechanisms. The historical backwardness of Latin American countries translated into situations in which there were various degrees of market imperfection. Transportation costs were varied, as were political and economic risks in countries that were just recently recovering from wars for independence and civil strife, and forming incipient states. These constraints resulted in very different experiences with regard to economic growth, depending on the particular sectors and regions.

NOTES

1. R. Cortés Conde and S. J. Stein, eds., *Latin America: A Guide to Economic History, 1820–1930* (Berkeley and Los Angeles: University of California, 1977).

2. Albert O. Hirschman, *The Strategy of Economic Development* (New Haven: Yale University Press, 1958).

3. Melville H. Watkins, "A Staple Theory of Economic Growth," *Canadian Journal of Economics and Political Science* 29, (May 1963): 141–58.

4. Albert O. Hirschman, "A Generalized Linkage Approach to Development, with Special Reference to Staples," in Manning Nash, *Essays on Economic Development and Cultural Change* (Chicago: University of Chicago Press, 1977). Published as supplement to *Economic Development and Cultural Change,* 25 (1977); (Spanish version: "Enfoque generalizado del desarrollo por medio de enlaces, con referencia especial a los productos basicos," *El trimestra, económico,* 44, no. 1 (enero–marzo 1977).

5. Guido Di Tella and Manuel Zymelman, *Los ciclos económicos argentinos* (Buenos Aires: Paidós, 1973); and Guido Di Tella and Manuel Zymelman, *Las etapas del desarrollo económico argentino* (Buenos Aires: Eudeba, 1967).

6. Francisco A. Encina, *Nuestra inferioridad económica* (Santiago: Editorial Universitaria, 1955).

7. Celso Furtado, *The Economic Growth of Brazil* (Berkeley and Los Angeles: University of California Press, 1963); and Aníbal Pinto Santa Cruz, *Chile, un caso de desarrollo frustrado* (Santiago de Chile: Editorial Universitaria, 1962).

8. Clark Reynolds, "Development Problems of an Export Economy: The Case of Chile and Copper," in Markos Mamalakis and Clark Reynolds, *Essays on the Chilean Economy* (Homewood, Ill.: Richard D. Irwin, 1965), pp. 201–398.

9. Furtado, *The Economic Growth of Brazil.*

10. Delfím Netto, *O Problema do café no Brasil,* 2nd ed. (São Paulo: Universidade de São Paulo, 1966).

11. Encina, *Nuestra inferioridad económica;* Julio Jobet, *Ensayo crítico del desarrollo económico y social de Chile* (Santiago: Editorial Universitaria, 1951);

Hernán Ramírez Necochea, "The Economic Origins of Independence," in R. A. Humphreys and John Lynch, *The Origins of the Latin American Revolutions, 1808–1826* (New York: Alfred Knopf, 1967), p. 169; Pinto, *Chile, un caso de desarrollo frustrado.*

12. Encina, *Nuestra inferioridad económica.*

13. Hirschman, "A Generalized Linkage Approach to Development."

14. Reynolds, "Development Problems of an Export Economy."

2
The Transition to Economic Growth in
COLOMBIA

*William Paul McGreevey**

A principal issue in the economic history of Colombia centers on how to explain the timing of economic change in the late nineteenth and early twentieth centuries. Can the transition to regular growth (if there was such a transition) be explained by reference to identifiable changes in the parameters affecting growth possibilities? Is there some "extraeconomic" pattern of causation that explains events? The controversy arose in debate over the closing paragraphs of my book on this period:

> One is driven finally to a motivational rather than a mechanical explanation of how the transition occurred. . . . A complicated theory—Hagen's withdrawal of expected status, for example—has intuitive appeal, but a much simpler theory is possible: Colombians made the transition and began to develop because they wanted to. The population expansion was important and certainly innovations were essential. But the basic ingredient of the transition was the will to make it. Having recognized that element of motivation and will, the economist reaches the end of his own range of expertise.[1]

It is possible now to elaborate the factual detail on the period 1895–1915, when the transition probably occurred, to dispose of the issues of acceleration and timing and to reject alternative hypotheses explaining an acceleration, such as an increased role of the public sector or changing conditions for export demand. In place of these exogenously determined

*The views expressed in this paper are those of the author and should not be attributed to the World Bank.

causes of acceleration, one looks at the structure of the Colombian society and economy to seek internal evidence for, and causes of, change.

To say that Colombians developed at a certain period because they wanted to—a phrasing that might invite semantic rather than substantive debate—is simply to say that previously their attentions lay elsewhere, that events brought them to change their focus of concern, and that this change was not solely induced by such economic phenomena as different demand, prices, and market opportunities. The purpose of this essay is to demonstrate what economic conditions did affect economic decision making and to show the special role played by the War of a Thousand Days and the loss of Panama in shifting the attention of potential entrepreneurs to growth-producing economic activities.

How can one avoid tautology when making the suggestion that volition played a central role in the transition to growth? There is a fairly thin line between tautology and rejectable hypothesis. Lewis[2] showed that an expression such as "All swans are white" could be an empirical statement subject to refutation by the identification of a single black swan. If, however, the person making the statement refused to recognize a particular black bird as a swan because of its color, then the initial statement would have been a simple tautology. So also the statement "Colombians began to develop because they wanted to" may be merely tautologous, for how could it be proved false? The possibility of refutation is essential if it is to be taken as a scientific statement.

Lewis, an epistemologist, expresses the problem of knowledge and the role of hypothesis and theory cogently:

> The truth of the a priori [tautology] is formal only; but we cannot capture the truth of experience if we have no net to catch it in—that is its immense importance. But so far as the validity of all material truth depends upon the predictability of particular experience, the problem of our knowledge of it is that of the validity of our probability-judgements. That there may be no such valid knowledge because "there are no necessary connections of matters of fact," represents a problem which is still to be met.[3]

To have knowledge of the material world, one cannot escape theorizing. The design of theories may be more or less explicit, but the method of history, as of the social sciences, inevitably requires theory. When made explicit, theorizing is all the easier to separate from the formal and tautological.

This essay argues that an acceleration in the rate of economic development occurred in Colombia. Before that acceleration, many Colombians were concerned with other matters, particularly the political struggles between Liberals and Conservatives and the various ephemeral offshoots of those main party groupings. Thus "wanting to develop" could be interpreted as a new phenomenon that occurred when Colombians' attention shifted from politics to business.

One means to avoid tautology is to answer the following questions:

1. Is there any identifiable acceleration in the tempo of economic activity in the period under consideration?
2. Is that acceleration sufficient to warrant terming it a "transition"?
3. What proximate and more distant causes may be adduced to explain the acceleration in such areas as social overhead capital investments, coffee cultivation and export, manufacturing growth, urbanization, and rural change?
4. What remains to be explained by will; and what, in turn, explains the presence of such will at one date and not at an earlier or later one?

These are the questions this essay will answer. Subsequent periods of economic change had their special features that require analysis, but our concern is with an early period of transition—early, to be sure, but with implications that have continued to permeate the process of economic change in Colombia.

I

There are still no comprehensive indicators for economic activity in Colombia for the first quarter of the twentieth century, let alone for the nineteenth. There are no estimates of gross product, total labor force, productivity, the sectoral distribution of output, nor of such related indicators as income distribution by class or income level, the structure of industries by size and output of firms, the age and sex composition of the labor force in total and by industrial classification, and a host of other matters on which modern nations regularly collect ample data as a means of keeping track of their problems and progress. Without such basic data against which to check on the scattered data that are available, it is virtually impossible to confirm that the specific evidence is broadly consistent with larger trends and conditions. Thus in considering the quantitative data that follow, the reader must keep in mind just how limited the available data are. At best, they furnish clues to movements of the economy.

Consider how frequently in recent years the concept of gross national product has been criticized as a misleading indicator of economic conditions, both for international comparisons, as a guide to the welfare of specific groups (the working poor and the unemployed, for example), and even as a measure over time of a nation's progress. So serious have the criticisms been that some very good economists have asked, "Is growth obsolete?"[4] They have created a new series of Measured Economic Welfare (MEW), reaching many decades into the past, with a view to taking into account the negative effects of urbanization, pollution, and other costs of economic growth. In the present investigation, of course, we are not even so well off as to be able to criticize GNP figures for their failure to accurately represent the state of economic affairs.

For all the limitations, though, this era of transition is important enough to merit both effort and compromise in the search for information that will allow us to understand it better. To that end, we will consider those subjects on which there exist some data that give indications about the state of the economy. We begin with population.

Population

National censuses were taken in 1870, 1905, 1912, and 1918. Some regional population counts were also conducted in the 1890s, but, as with the national censuses, they must be used with care. The national censuses have been subjected to some analysis by competent demographers. Collver,[5] for instance, estimated that the census of 1905 undercounted the population by about 8 percent, a conclusion he reached by examining the age and sex structure and identifying undercounts in particular male and female cohorts. Accepting his adjustments, Table 1 indicates some main demographic characteristics of the total and urban population.

Once the Collver-suggested adjustment to the 1905 census is made, the resultant cumulative annual growth rates indicate a smooth acceleration from 1.4 percent per annum in the period 1870–1905 to 1.8 percent in 1905–1912, then an accelerated growth of 2.4 percent per annum in 1912–1918. The growth of urban population provides an indicator of the gradual transfer of population from agrarian to nonagrarian pursuits. Over the years 1870–1912 the population of the nineteen major *municipios* was growing at a rate somewhat higher than that of the total population, which indicates that there must have been some net migration to these cities, unless their birth rates were considerably higher than those in rural areas or their death rates much lower. The share of total population in those nineteen *municipios* rose from 7.6 percent in 1870 to 11.5 percent in 1912.

In the years after the 1912 census, the annual growth rate of the nineteen *municipios* accelerated to 3.9 percent, which was considerably greater than that for the total population. By 1918 the nineteen *municipios* held 12.5 percent of Colombia's population.

These data demonstrate accelerated rates of population growth, of urban growth, and of migration from countryside to city. The acceleration can be demonstrated for the period 1912–1918 over the previous intercensal period 1905–1912. However, these dates were determined arbitrarily by the availability of census data for the terminal years of the periods considered. The specific timing of acceleration may have been some years before or after 1912.

Exports

The timing of acceleration of Colombian exports is somewhat easier to date specifically than that of population because annual data on exports are available from published official sources. These data are analyzed in some detail in other works.[6] Figure 1 briefly summarizes long-term trends in total exports by value from 1835 to 1940. There was a strong upward movement from 1849 to 1875, based largely on expansion of tobacco exports. With the end of the tobacco boom, and despite some temporary success with other tropical products, there was until the turn of the century a downward trend, which was exacerbated by the War of a Thousand Days, 1899–1902. The downward trend appears even more emphatic for exports per capita, which reached a nineteenth-century peak of 8.40 dollars in the quinquennium 1875–1879 and declined to 4.10 dollars at century's end, 1895–1899.[7]

Despite the overall decline there were some signs of growth during that epoch in individual regions and for specific products. For example, exports of coffee on the Ferrocarril de Antioquia were expanding by about 25 percent per annum over the period 1888–1899.[8] During this epoch, however, the expansion of coffee in Antioquia was accompanied by a decline in some traditional export lines, including tobacco and straw hats. Until 1902 the export trade for Colombia as a whole was in decline. All the more remarkable, then, was the turnaround generated largely by the expansion of coffee exports, which permitted total exports to grow at the very high rate of 10.8 percent per annum for a full quarter century between the low point of 1902 and the peak year of 1928, the end of one phase of the coffee boom.

In large measure Colombia's success at export expansion was due to the country's enlargement of its share of world coffee exports. In 1905 Colombia produced about 3 percent of world consumption. By 1910 that share had expanded only slightly to 3.35 percent but by 1920 it had grown to 7.61 percent and it reached 14.57 percent in 1933.[9] This expansion must have owed something to the Brazilian scheme of valorization of coffee, a price-support mechanism designed to iron out short-term fluctuations in coffee prices that had the added fillip for Colombian producers of setting a floor price which guaranteed them good price expectations for expanded production.[10] The Brazilian federal government's decision to accept some responsibility for maintaining a price floor in 1907 may have encouraged Colombian growers. Since Brazilian policy also sought to limit production

FIGURE 1
COLOMBIAN EXPORTS, 1835–1940
(MILLIONS OF CURRENT DOLLARS)

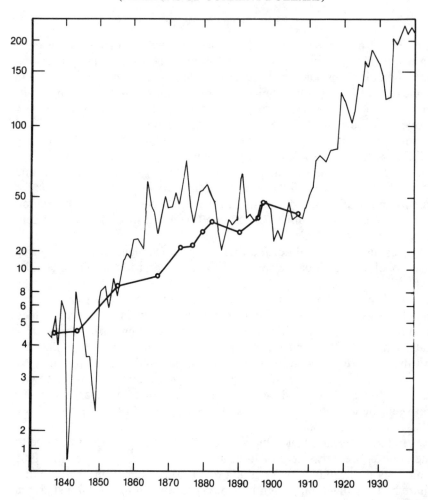

SOURCES FOR EACH CURVE: Solid line: M. Urrutia and M. Arrubla, eds., *Compendio de estadísticas históricas de Colombia* (Bogotá: Universidad Nacional de Colombia, 1970), pp. 108–110, and facing p. 208; Line with circles: José Antonio Ocampo, "Las exportaciones colombianas en el siglo XIX" in *Desarrollo y sociedad,* 4 (Bogotá: Facultad de Economía, Universidad de los Andes, 1980), Table 1, col. (1)a, p. 167.

in order to maintain prices, Colombian growers were able to expand their initially minuscule market share to a proportion sufficient to make Colombia the second largest coffee exporter by 1930.

Coffee exports formed only 7 percent of total exports in the 1870s; that share rose to 39 percent in the quinquennium 1905–1909 and reached 74 percent in the years 1920–1924. Other exports were also expanding. For example, banana cultivation, which was just beginning at the close of the nineteenth century, made up 4 percent of exports in the years 1905–1909, then peaked at 9 percent of the total exports in the years 1910–1914—i.e., before the continuing expansion of coffee swamped the slow growth of banana cultivation in the Santa Marta region. The export of hides increased as a share of total exports just when coffee was expanding most rapidly—from 9 percent in the years 1910–1914 to 12 percent for 1915–1919. However, the share of hides in total exports fell back thereafter and they never again constituted as much as 5 percent of total exports. The share of precious metals in total exports declined over the whole period under consideration and stayed down until the brief fluorescence of gold and silver during the Great Depression of the 1930s. Petroleum exports did not contribute significantly to exports until the late 1920s.[11]

The acceleration of exports, then, was obviously led by coffee, but other export products participated as well, bananas and hides being the most obvious examples. A recent feature of Colombian historiography is a deemphasis on the special role of the Antioqueños and their cultivation of coffee in favor of broader recognition of other regional groups as participants in the process of economic development.[12] Certainly the coffee export expansion was not *only* an Antioqueño phenomenon, though that regional group played a major part in coffee cultivation. The temperate zones of Cundinamarca, Tolima, and Valle del Cauca were also important locales for coffee production for export, and the north coastal area contributed to export expansion with hides and bananas, so the acceleration was not region specific.[13] But so little has been written about the economic history of the north coast of Colombia that one cannot be sure what impact the export acceleration had there—except for the banana zone. In a parallel fashion, the south (Cauca and Nariño) has also been ignored in the general analyses of Colombian economic history.

Railroad Expansion

The transport system expanded *pari passu* with exports. Railway building slowed in the years between 1880 and 1903 but rapidly increased thereafter.[14] The retardation is demonstrated by a comparison of trackage expansion in Colombia with that of Argentina, Mexico, and Brazil. By 1910 those countries had constructed between 58 and 84 percent of all the lines they would build. Colombia in that year had completed but 26 percent of some 3,000 kilometers in service in the country in the 1960s. By 1930 Colombia had matched the completion rates of the other three countries: all four had between 87 and 100 percent of their eventual trackage in service that year. Kilometers in use expanded at the cumulative annual growth rates indicated in Table 2.

The fastest expansion of trackage occurred in the period 1904–1909, during the presidency of Rafael Reyes. Reyes is remembered as an admirer of the scientific positivism of Porfirian Mexico, which in many ways he sought to emulate. In 1901 he represented Colombia at the Second Pan American Conference in Mexico, where he expressed his view of the railway in a speech:

> In times past it was the Cross or the Koran, the sword or the book that accomplished the conquests of civilization; today it is the powerful locomotive, flying over the shining rail, breathing like a volcano that awakens peoples to progress, well-being and liberty . . . and those who do not conform to that progress it crushes beneath its wheels.[15]

Once in power, Reyes reversed the stagnation of railway construction, which had been imposed by war and low coffee prices over the previous fifteen years.

Railway expansion was still proceeding quite rapidly in the 1920s, and, of course, from a much higher base of total construction in place by that time. The most rapid expansion of track in place appears to have anticipated the expansion of exports, which grew fastest in the period after 1910.

The coffee railways expanded most during the years 1904–1914. Over the whole decade coffee railways expanded from 279 to 783 kilometers, whereas other railways expanded from 87 to 122 kilometers.[16] The Ferrocarril del Pacífico and Ferrocarril de Antioquia were the two lines built up most substantially during that ten-year period. Both were coffee railways and both to some degree anticipated the opening of the Panama Canal in 1914, which would provide a new transport link so that coffee could be shipped through the Pacific port of Buenaventura for Atlantic markets.

Certainly the Pacific ports of Colombia were of minor importance in trade prior to the opening of the canal. A British consular report summarizing trade by custom house for the years 1894–1898 showed that during that five-year period only 3.1 percent of the volume of Colombian coffee exports was recorded at the custom house of Buenaventura (see Table 3). Prior to the opening of the canal, coffee exports passed through north coast ports and, via Cúcuta, through the Gulf of Maracaibo to the Atlantic. By the 1940s nearly 60 percent of Colombian coffee moved on the Ferrocarril del Pacífico and out of the port of Buenaventura.[17] Thus the acceleration in railway growth was generated by new opportunities to cultivate western lands previously too distant from the Magdalena River. That new opportunity arose, of course, because of the long-delayed completion of the canal.

Manufacturing Development

Several major industries got their start in Bogotá in the 1890s—the brewery Bavaria and its companion organization, Fenicia, a glassworks that made the bottles for the beer. Other new enterprises were started during that epoch, but the accelerated development of manufacturing came later, as data on the founding of manufacturing companies demonstrates. Table 4 shows the period of foundation of sixty-two companies listed in a survey published in 1916. Some 120 companies were included in the survey, but only sixty-two provided the date of foundation. Thus the data may be biased, although in which direction is unclear. New companies may have been reluctant to admit their newness, and old companies may have lost the record of when they were founded. The data on the sixty-two companies do indicate that few were founded before 1890 and that the starting up of enterprises accelerated between 1905–1909 and 1910–1915. A possible additional bias is that newly formed companies in the years just prior to the survey survived to be counted, whereas equally long-lived firms formed in the nineteenth century despite their importance during their epoch, may have ceased to exist by the time of the survey. This "survival factor" can be checked by looking at the *valor patrimonio* (roughly equivalent to paid-in capital) of manufacturing firms listed in the 1945 industrial census, by date of founding of those firms. The data appear in Table 5.

All firms founded before 1910 had the largest capital as of 1945, i.e., more than that of firms founded in other periods selected in Table 5. Although the industrial census did not identify individual companies, a very large share of the 135 million pesos total would be accounted for by Bavaria and Fenicia. Moreover, several of the textile mills of Antioquia, the forerunners of Coltejer and Fabricato, were founded between 1904 and 1909. The capital of firms founded in the years 1910 to 1920 was greater than that of firms founded in the 1920s and 1930s. The data do tend to confirm accelerated industrialization during the Great Depression; they also bring fresh emphasis to the importance of industrial growth in the years 1910–1920.

When Tables 4 and 5 are analyzed together, one sees that the most likely timing of accelerated industrial expansion was in the period after 1905 and before 1921. Company foundings were intensive between 1905 and 1915; the capital of firms founded before 1921 was 230 million pesos in 1945, as compared to 162 million pesos for firms founded between 1921 and 1935. These data can be tricky, however. A firm founded in 1912 may have remained quite small until the boom of the 1920s, and then added most of its size during that decade. Nonetheless, it would still be listed in the table as of its date of founding. Given the usual emphasis on the 1920s and 1930s as the epoch of manufacturing growth, these data may be somewhat misleading. Nonetheless, it may be useful to emphasize the early phase of manufacturing development and to specify somewhat better than was previously possible its timing and acceleration.

Causes of the War of a Thousand Days

The chances for economic progress were substantially improved after 1902 by the settlement of the conflict and disturbances known as the War of a Thousand Days. That period of civil war, lasting from the fall of 1899 until the middle of 1902, was perhaps the most violent in Colombian history. Not only was it important while it was going on; out of this conflict came the calm that prevailed until the 1930s. There were, of course, incidents of violence between management and workers, and between Liberals and Conservatives, in the years between 1902 and 1935, and they will be discussed briefly at a later point in this essay. However, peace was the rule—so much so that one labor historian wrote, "In the Conservative peace of the first decades of the twentieth century the most important events in Bogotá were the crowning of national poets and parades celebrating various national or religious dates."[18]

There is little to be gained here from a detailed examination of the causes and consequences of the War of a Thousand Days; that task has been admirably performed by Bergquist.[19] However, in addition to the political factors and intrigues that Bergquist examines, certain economic changes which occurred prior to the outbreak of conflict apparently played a major role in the decision of some elements to resort to open warfare. Chief among these was the decline in coffee prices, accompanied by an increase in the cost of imports. The effects on the terms of trade are shown in Table 6.

After the "good times" for potential coffee growers in the early 1890s, the price conditions of international trade began to work against coffee and its cultivators. The peak year was 1893, when coffee prices reached a level that would not be exceeded until 1919. Moreover, the terms of trade between coffee and the imported products that coffee was to buy were never again as favorable as they were in 1893 and 1894—at least not until the unusual boom of the 1950s and, later, the special conditions created by the Brazilian frost in the fall of 1975. Perhaps these conditions *should have* generated an export boom; indeed, Dickson's consular report does show a rapid growth in the volume of coffee exports between 1894 and 1898 as follows: for 1894, 27.98 million kilos; for 1895, 28.85; for 1896, 37.63; for 1897, 34.0; and for 1898, 37.67 million kilos exported.[20] Over the five-year period the cumulative annual growth rate in exports was about 7.7 percent. An export boom generated by extremely favorable terms of trade was under way.

The boom was aborted by the downturn of coffee prices. Because coffee is a perennial, the decision to plant it must be made long before the actual payout or harvesting. After plantings and expansion were encouraged in the early 1890s, harvesting did not get under way in earnest until three to five years later. Thus the growers may themselves have initiated a classic cycle in which high prices generate increased supplies, which, as they come on the market, depress prices. Certainly the big increase in the volume of exports was not matched in the years 1894–1898 by an increase in sales revenues. The data from Dickson's consular report demonstrating this relationship appear in Table 7. They indicate that prices per kilo were higher in 1895 than in 1894, whereas the data in Table 6 show higher prices in 1894 than in 1895. The difference is perhaps to be expected since the sources and methods of calculation are different. Both series do demonstrate a decline of coffee prices in the late 1890s from their peak in the earlier part of the decade. The Dickson data show that by 1898 prices had declined 29 percent from their 1895 peak; the data in Table 7 show a price decline of 31 percent between 1894 and 1898. Thus the data, though drawn from different sources, are roughly comparable: they show in increased coffee exports a substantial quantitative response to the high prices of the early 1890s, a downturn of prices (generated perhaps by the oversupply occasioned by the high prices), and a steady worsening of the terms of trade until the century's end. That worsening must be seen as one of the proximate causes of the War of a Thousand Days.

Except for the movement for independence (1810–1819) and the era of *violencia* (c. 1948–1963), no period in Colombian history comes close to approximating the death and destruction wrought during the War of a Thousand Days. The minister of government, Aristides Fernández, wrote in a letter of resignation dated May 10, 1903, that "pools of blood still flowed and the bones of more than one hundred thousand Colombians bleached unburied."[21] Since the population at the time was about 4 million, this suggests that some 2.5 percent of the total population was killed during this war. That percentage may be compared with the 2 percent of the population killed during the Civil War of 1861–1865 in the United States.[22] Not only was the Colombian conflict more tragic in its impact on human life than was the better known U.S. Civil War, but it was a singularly massive episode of violence in Colombian history. Thus it seems quite proper to emphasize its ending as a critical factor in the conditions necessary for accelerated development. The impact of the war on economic conditions for one hacienda in Cundinamarca is described by Deas,[23] who draws on letters written by Cornelio Rubio, *mayordomo* for the hacienda. The labor force, draft animals, cattle, and coffee were all subject to impressment or abuse by government or rebels. (Bergquist,[24] however, suggests that losses may have been exaggerated in some accounts.) Production and movement on public roads virtually ceased for long periods. Certainly the political leaders of the time were aware of the importance of ending the conflict for the possibilities of economic progress, as is indicated in the following quotation from President Jorge Holquin's presidential message: "If peace is a great asset to all countries, at the moment it is of supreme importance for Colombia because on it depends all hopes of economic redemption and of intellectual and material progress. . . ."[25]

In his review of political positions during the War of a Thousand Days, Bergquist found an interlocking of politics, economics, and the Panama question:

> Throughout the postwar period bipartisan export-import interests managed to use the Panama question for their political advantage. The issue of the canal and fear of United States intentions on the Isthmus had already served the political interests of moderate political factions within the two traditional parties by providing them with a face-saving way of ending a war over which they had begun to lose control. After the war the secession of Panama bolstered the political fortunes of bipartisan export-import interests by fostering a consensus among Colombian leaders that the nation must unite politically and develop itself materially if it were to avoid further dismemberment.[26]

The political elites clearly saw that the requirements for national identity included a development effort and economic growth. Given that for nearly a decade in the 1820s, Bogotá had putatively ruled an area that now includes Venezuela, Ecuador, and Panama as well as Colombia, and that Mexico, in mid-nineteenth century, had been shorn of substantial territory after the Mexican war with the United States, their fear and concern were certainly genuine.

The aborted coffee boom of the 1890s even suggests that the conditions for accelerated development may have existed in that decade, but development was thwarted by the combined effects of depressed coffee prices and civil war. The intricate interaction of these causal elements is one subject of Palacios's recent work.[27]

We turn now to other aspects of government policy that promoted economic development: the successful action to restabilize the Colombian currency, the establishment of tariffs protecting the nascent textile industry, and the increase of expenditures to promote the formation of social overhead capital.

Stabilization Policy

During the War of a Thousand Days the major factions printed money to pay expenses with the result that the value of paper currency plummeted. A paper peso had been worth nearly one U.S. dollar before 1880; at the close of the war in 1902 it was worth one-hundredth of a U.S. penny. Consular reports for the 1880s and 1890s indicate that multiple forms of currency were in use in Colombia during those decades—several kinds of paper money, metal coins of gold and silver, foreign currency, and debt instruments of the Colombian government. These last sold at a discount, but during certain periods could be used for partial payment of customs duties.[28] As a result, the real duties paid by importers were considerably lower than they might otherwise have been because the importers could pay with these depreciated bonds. These complicated price interrelationships between various means of payment make it difficult to interpret the data since the historian is never certain whether values are quoted in paper pesos, gold pesos, U.S. dollars, or some combination thereof.[29] One contemporary observed that in 1909, just prior to the enforcement of a stable currency and exchange rate against gold, the printed pesos exchanged at a rate of more than 13,000 per 100 U.S. dollars.[30] Stabilization made it possible to collect import duties with regularity and hence assisted in protecting the infant industries of that epoch. It must also have substantially lowered risk by removing one variable—the expected future value of money—from the calculus that businessmen had to employ in reaching their decisions. The Junta de Estabilización took in extant stocks of paper currency in exchange for revalued pesos tied in value to gold. From 1910 until the Great Depression that peso traded roughly at par with the U.S. dollar; thus stabilization was eminently successful.

Tariffs. Luis Ospina Vásquez presents a detailed analysis of tariff policy and tariff rates in his monumental work *Industria y protección.*[31] He emphasizes that the tariff established by the government of Rafael Reyes in 1905 served to protect the Medellín textile industry.

Another approach to estimating the level of tariffs (though not necessarily the structure of protection) is to examine the relationship over time between total imports and total tariff revenues. Pertinent data appear in Table 8, which includes two quite different series of data on imports. The old series was developed from a review of the statistics from Colombia's trading partners, and first appeared in a work edited by Urrutia and Arrubla,[32] and in somewhat different form in my own book.[33] Umaña showed certain significant errors in those calculations, particularly with respect to treatment of goods moving through Panama.[34] Ocampo has undertaken a thorough review of Colombian trade data and presents convincing evidence to support the new series, which take into account problems of double counting and treatment of colonial extensions of the European trading partners, among other things.[35] His new estimates appear here, for the years under consideration, under column 2 in Table 8. Tariff revenues were taken from annual ministerial reports.

The last two columns of Table 8 show distinctly different estimates of the weight of tariff revenues as a percentage of imports, particularly during the 1880s. Tariff rates, instead of being below 20 percent, as column 4 shows, were more likely above 40 percent, as the column 5 figures indicate. For the years 1888–1890 the tariff rate was apparently even higher than it proved to be after the Reyes tariff reform was established in 1905.

The calculations that produced the figures in the old series, calculations to which this author contributed, now appear to be in error.[36] Moreover, reliance on them may have led analysts to underestimate the serious intent of the policymakers, particularly successors to Rafael Nunez, to use government protectionist policy to encourage public-sector expansion for development purposes. Though the high tariff rates of the late 1880s may not have been sufficient to protect infant industries, they generated some public-sector funds for investment in transport and social overhead capital. All the more reason that an effective transition to growth was delayed until after 1905.

Public Sector Revenues. Tariffs on imports provided the bulk of public revenue. Since Colombia's foreign trade was so limited after more than a quarter century of decline from 1875 to 1902, revenues were also exiguous, especially when compared to those in other Latin American countries. The annual report of the minister of finance for 1911 offered the comparison presented in Table 9. Tax revenues per capita for the central government were lower than in the six other countries included in the survey. Including both departmental and central government revenues would raise Colombia's ranking somewhat; but it must be noted that data on local government revenues from the other countries are not included. With such limited revenues, the Colombian government was hardly in a position to foster economic development.

Because import duties constitute a significant share of total government revenues, one would expect to see a systematic relationship between revenues and total imports. Moreover, since imports may constitute a regular supply of inputs for economic activities from which the public sector absorbs some tax revenues, the trends in imports might explain movements in total public-sector revenues.

The data that appear in Figure 2 provide only a partial confirmation of

FIGURE 2.
SCATTER DIAGRAM OF VALUE OF IMPORTS AND
CENTRAL GOVERNMENT REVENUES FOR 1880–1929
(MILLIONS OF CURRENT DOLLARS)

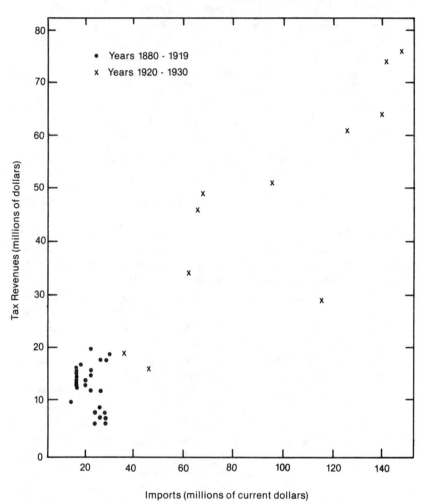

SOURCES: Imports: Urrutia and Arrubla, eds., *Compendio de estadísticas históricas de Colombia,* pp. 108–110. Central government revenues: annual ministerial reports.

these propositions. For the period 1880–1920 there appears to be no systematic relationship between the two variables, as indicated by the clustering of all points in the lower-left-hand quadrant bounded by a maximum of 20 million dollars in central government revenues and 40 million in total imports. In some years (e.g., 1888, 1891, and 1897), revenues seemed fairly high; in others (1881–1884) they were considerably lower, though imports were at practically the same level. The lack of any systematic relationship is in itself worth remarking, for the fact that revenues could vary so much with so little difference in imports suggests that import duty rates were not being systematically applied.

For the period of 1920–1930 the relationship between central government revenues and imports is quite pronounced. A linear regression of revenues on imports produces the following relationship:

$$R = 8.18 + 0.44\,M \qquad (1921\text{–}1930)$$
$$r^2 = +0.91 \qquad n = 10$$

As the estimate of r^2 indicates, the relationship between the two variables for the 1920s is quite close.

One might therefore expect that for the same period the relationship between imports and revenues from imports would be at least as close. However, quite the contrary, there is no significant correlation between revenues from import duties and total imports for the period 1921–1930, which suggests that the relationship between total central government revenues and imports derives not from the fact that import duties constitute a significant share of revenues, but from other factors. These other factors might include the manner of which public-sector revenues affected the demand for imports in the 1920s. When the central government gained access to the 25 million dollars indemnity provided by the U.S. government for the loss of Panama, it also gained entry to Wall Street, permitting extensive borrowing for social overhead capital improvements—in railways, highways, and a variety of municipal building programs for water supplies, sewage, and public buildings. Since a significant component of these activities required imported inputs (particularly the railways, and perhaps secondarily the municipal facilities), the new central government revenues from the sale of publicly secured bonds and instruments of debt automatically gave rise to increased imports. A secondary question that cannot be answered here is the extent to which the foreign debt generated in the 1920s was tied to the presumption of imports provided by companies in the United States (and other countries) from which the loans had come. In this respect, one would wish to examine the relationships between major Wall Street investment houses and manufacturing concerns (particularly in heavy capital goods industries) that supplied the imports used during this period.

Expenditures. As the data in Figure 2 indicate, central government revenues did not change much between 1880 and 1919: in no year did they exceed 20 million pesos. (Revenues were very much higher in the 1920s.) Because revenues were limited, the role of the central government as a provider of such social overhead capital as transport, communications, education, and improved health services was also limited. Figure 3 displays the limited data that could be culled from official sources on the

FIGURE 3.
PERCENTAGE DISTRIBUTION OF CENTRAL GOVERNMENT–BUDGETED
EXPENDITURES BY FUNCTIONAL CLASSIFICATION, 1879–1930*

SOURCES: Annual ministerial reports.
*There are no data for 1883–1894, 1896, 1898–1909, and 1914. Social overhead capital includes post and telegraph services, public works, *benificencias,* and ministries of development, agriculture, and commerce, and industries. For the years 1895, 1897, and 1915–1923 post and telegraph and *beneficencias* were included under Administrative Expenses.

distribution of central government expenditures by functional classification. They indicate that expenditures on the formation of human
and social overhead capital constituted only about 10 percent of central
government–budgeted expenditures in 1895 and 1897, the only years in
that decade for which data could be located. Data are available on a more
regular basis from 1910 onward; by that date expenditures on social overhead capital were a more substantial share of total expenditures. The
share devoted to education remained in the 4–8 percent range. State governments devoted about 12 percent of their expenditures to schooling in
1873–1874.[37] Capital expenditures were particularly great in the mid-1920s
as a result of the railway and road-building programs and expansion of
municipal services (water, electricity, and sewage) financed by external
capital. But significant public-sector investments were being made from at
least 1910 onward. The somewhat earlier expansion of private-sector rail
construction (see Table 2) suggests that the intensification of such investment began around 1905, and hence contributed substantially to the transition and accelerated development, particularly in urban areas and as an
aid to agricultural exports.

Timing of Acceleration

Several measures of economic change support the argument that there
was an acceleration of economic activity beginning around 1905. The rate
of change of exports by value actually turned around from negative to
positive. Manufacturing development accelerated sometime after 1905, as
did railway facilities in use. Total population was growing faster after 1912
than before, and urban population growth also speeded up after 1912.
Specific dating of accelerated population growth is made difficult because
census data are so widely separated in time. Revenues for the public
sector did not pick up until after 1920, but tariff revenues were a much
higher percentage of imports in the years 1905–1915 than in most earlier
years. The rate of growth of coffee exports by volume and value in the
years 1910–1919 was higher than before or since. All these considerations
argue strongly for the proposition that there was a significant change in
the tempo of economic activity between 1905 and 1915.

Is there any evidence against the hypothesis of accelerated development in that decade? The backward projections from the 1925–1975
period that Urrutia[38] uses to show smooth growth rates from 1880 onward
do not take into account any of the evidence of acceleration after 1900
presented here. If anything, his data demonstrate how much poorer the
country was in the nineteenth century than it would become in the twentieth. The data presented cover but a small share of total economic activity. Traditional agriculture and stock raising, about which there is virtually

no reliable first-hand evidence, probably did not experience any dramatic change in the years 1905 through 1915. Estimates of cattle population over the years between 1890 and 1940 assembled by Wylie[39] indicate no significant change from the tempo of growth of about 2.5 percent per year. The rapid growth of exports—particularly coffee, which was being sown and grown on previously uncultivated lands that had to be cleared—may have generated enough demand for labor to cause an actual decline in production of subsistence crops, though there do not appear to be data that permit verification of that possibility. Cropland devoted to export products expanded at the rate of 7.2 percent per annum over the period 1910–1925; that for domestic consumption (urban and rural) expanded at only 2.2 percent.[40] A good deal of labor must have shifted from domestic production to export production; that shift could have caused a decline in home production. During the first phase of accelerated export production the labor transfer may have been possible without a loss in home production. Wages in coffee production over the years 1880–1911 were stable— even falling at haciendas Santa Barbara[41] and Jónas.[42] It was only later—in the 1920s—that enough signs of labor scarcity appear to lead one to suspect that increased export production implied decreased home production.

This accelerated development probably did not touch the mass of Colombia's rural population. Only those who participated directly or indirectly in the expanding export sector, the more rapid growth of cities, and the nascent manufacturing enterprises experienced significant benefits from the acceleration of economic activity. Still, the number of such participants must have been far from insignificant. By the time of the first coffee census in 1932, nearly a fifth of all rural families in Colombia were coffee growers on their own account.[43] The share of total population living in the nineteen largest cities increased from around 11 to 12.5 percent in the years 1905–1918 (see Table 1). At a conservative estimate, a fifth to a quarter of the Colombian population may have participated directly in the benefits of accelerated development. What about the rest of the population?

There are few quantitative data on trends in real wages, income, and welfare for the other three-quarters or four-fifths of Colombia's population. Some data on the incomes of workers on haciendas in eastern Colombia appear in Ospina Vásquez,[44] and these demonstrate a decline in the purchasing power of rural workers' income from the late eighteenth to the late nineteenth centuries, with the decline particularly precipitous in the second half of the nineteenth century. A more recent publication by Alberto Pardo Pardo draws on data from the Beneficencia de Cundinamarca and a host of other sources to prepare long series on prices, wages, and real salaries.[45] The data base for this series is weak and limited in many respects, and preliminary efforts to replicate Pardo Pardo's procedures leave doubts about whether these data can be used to check on real trends in welfare. Nonetheless, his data do merit examination. To that end, his series of daily wages, the annual equivalent thereof, a cost-of-living index for Bogotá, and the resultant index of real wages are presented in Table 10. Pardo Pardo's commentary on secular trends in real wages covers a much longer period than that included in the table; his commentary places these data in the long-term context:

> The nineteenth century began with a decline, afterwards followed by a recuperation, associated with the war of independence, which continued until about 1850, and followed by another decline through 1860. In that year began a collapse, the consequences of which lasted sixty years. In 1921 began another period of progress that was more or less continuous, with the exception of a downturn between 1941 and 1950. From that latter date onward, progress has been spectacular, perhaps even too much so. . . .
>
> The most unfavorable period for the working class was between 1860 and 1926. The most favorable periods were 1650–1680, 1700–1865 and 1926–1966. By far the most favorable period has been the latest because the difference between price and wage changes has been substantial and growing.[46]

One way of estimating the trend of real salaries over the period 1888 through 1924 is to calculate the trend line by ordinary least squares for those years. The equation for that trend is as follows:[47]

$$\text{Real Salary} = -856 + 0.49 \text{ Time}$$

Following this trend, real wages over the whole period were rising at about 0.6 percent per annum. However, the trend was certainly not constant over the thirty-six-year period. There was a rise up to 1899 and a substantial fall through 1905, then another rise through 1915. The very wide movements of this index suggest that one should be cautious about placing too much faith in the numbers. Nonetheless, the upward movement of real salaries after 1905 would be consistent with the more rapid economic growth in those years. And the previous down trend from 1899 to 1905 could well be related to the effects of the War of a Thousand Days. Unfortunately, the occasional errors in Pardo Pardo's tables and the absence of background material that would permit identification of the groups to whom the indices apply (rural or urban? white-collar or blue-collar? employees or self-employed?) make it difficult to carry out a serious analysis.

Other indications of the conditions of life for the majority of Colombians during this period are more dramatic but also more difficult to interpret as aspects of long-term trends. Dr. Manual Cotes gathered data in 1893 on teamsters, stonecutters, and agricultural workers with special reference to diet.[48] He found that 78 percent of the daily food intake by weight of the male agricultural worker came in the form of *chicha,* a fermented beer of the highlands. On the average, men consumed 228 grams of alcohol daily, and as a result, alcoholism was the major health problem of the area. Cotes, in listing the principal maladies of teamsters, placed alcoholism first, followed by tuberculosis, ulcers, gastroenteritis, hepatitis, rheumatism, dysentery, and syphilis, with yellow fever and malaria important among those who entered the lowlands.[49] After reviewing the data on consumption in a sample of 350 Bogotá families in 1939, Socarrás estimated daily consumption of *chicha* at 2,250 grams daily among adult male workers.[50] He suggests that his estimate may be low; it is but 63 percent of the consumption of the workers studied forty-five years earlier by Cotes. In the 1930s Bogotá sample, *chicha* was estimated to account for about 50 percent of caloric intake.[51] Even into the 1960s the problem remained:

> One result of "dietary inadequacy is that much of the population relies for extra needed calories upon heavy alcohol consumption." Alcohol is also preferred to the unclean water usually available to workers and peasants. "A more adequate diet could lower the need for drink as an extra source of fuel. Nonetheless, until healthier social conditions in general are created, it is doubtful that the need for escape can be met without heavy resort to alcohol."[52]

An anthropologist who studied the function of alcohol in rural Colombia in the 1950s developed the theory that mestizo drinking was an outlet for frustration created by the discrepancy between high aspirations for success and limited chances for achievement. In his view, chronic insecurity derived from the uncertainty of rewards and the rigidity of the larger hierarchical social structure; alcoholism then became an escape.[53] This theory is interesting, but the longevity of the problem of alcoholism in rural Colombia suggests that some more fundamental cause—such as the need to consume enough calories at a low price—may be as important as the psychological dimension in explaining the syndrome of alcoholism. Palacios[54] presents estimates of caloric intake from several hacienda records. The ration on Hacienda Jónas in Antioquia, 1896–1917, was equivalent to 3,578 kcal. daily. Hacienda Buenavista provided 3,260 kcal. in 1930, Hacienda Florencia 2,510 kcal. in 1934, and Quipile 1,850 kcal. in the same year. Perhaps these data are too few to suggest any time trend, but the data from the Hacienda Jónas at least suggest that rations were well above adult daily requirements.

There may, however, be a conceptual error in Palacios's calculation with respect to his attribution of 324 calories to each 100 grams of maize, the food which was estimated to contribute 45 percent of total calorie intake. However, if the ration given was in the form of *mazamorra,* a corn-based gruel consumed in Colombia, the calorie content would have been substantially lower.

Applying the calorie-content rates used by Palacios to the diet identified by Cotes (600 grams of *mazamorra,* 360 grams of bread, 3,575 grams of *chicha,* and 40 grams of chocolate), one finds a per capita consumption of about 2,800 calories daily, nearly 20 percent above minimum daily requirements. Since Cotes believed the agricultural workers were virtually starving to death, it seems reasonable to conclude that their intake of calories via *mazamorra* were much lower than the Palacios figures imply.

In an alternative calculation based on U.S. Department of Agriculture estimates of food values, and assuming a calorie content (per 100 grams) of 51 kcal. for corn, 243 for bread, 42 for *chicha* (same as U.S. beer), and 511 for unsweetened chocolate, one finds daily calorie consumption to be 1,940 for agricultural workers of the Bogotá Sabana. That figure seems quite realistic, being just above 80 percent of current suggested minimum daily requirements.

The Palacios estimates for Hacienda Jónas are probably in error with respect to calorie content of the ration. The consumption levels identified by Cotes are consistent with the observations of Samper concerning declining consumption between the mid-nineteenth century and the 1890s.[55]

These considerations suggest the following conclusion: There was a transition from a period of virtual stagnation or decline to one of accelerated development which began sometime between 1905 and 1915. That development directly touched the lives of perhaps a quarter of the Colombian population, and affected a somewhat larger proportion indirectly, by raising their real welfare. However, much of the rest of the population experienced little, if any, real improvement in their conditions of life or standard of living for many years after the transition began. The result was a very uneven pattern of development.

II

What caused the transition to occur? What kept it from beginning sooner? These are difficult questions and the answers given here will not be entirely satisfactory or complete, not only because the data are incomplete and in some instances of questionable validity, but also because there is an epistemological problem of sorting out lines of causation from a web of interdependence. Though we exist in a circular world, we are forced to use the linear technology of writing one line at a time. Out of the many lines of causation one might pursue, this essay will first examine the role of real wages in stimulating coffee cultivation, then turn to the international market for coffee and its effect on profitability, and finally consider the overall impact of the War of a Thousand Days and the loss of Panama.

Trends in Real Wages

The transition from decline (or stagnation) to growth in the years between 1890 and 1915 may have been made possible by a Hamilton-like inflation effect on wages and profits—i.e., real wages fell, the potential for profits rose, and entrepreneurs began to invest substantially in coffee and export-related enterprises.[56] To test this hypothesis, one needs data on real wages, profits, and output. No complete data exist; however, two theses completed at the Universidad de los Andes do provide data on two coffee haciendas covering the period 1882 through 1911. Time series of real wages assembled by Dario Bustamante for a Cundinamarcan hacienda, 1882–1897[57] and by Fernando Lleras for the Antioqueño hacienda Jónas, 1897–1911[58] were spliced together at the only overlapping year to yield one series, which appears in Table 11.

A note of caution: The data examined here are unlike those presented elsewhere in this book on real wages. For example, Argentine data were gathered systematically from firms and analyzed at the time by competent statisticians to check for consistency and reliability. The data developed here are drawn from but two haciendas' records, have never been subjected to scientific scrutiny, and thus are a weak reed on which to build an analysis of trends in real wages. After the publication of Bustamante's work the Santa Barbara hacienda account books were reexamined by Palacios,[59] who produced some analyses that differ somewhat from those of Bustamante.

Obviously, there is considerable doubt about any conclusions reached from examination of such limited and potentially inconsistent data. However, a principal conclusion, equivalent to that reached by Urrutia,[60] seems warranted: Over the whole period from the early 1880s until the close of the first decade of the twentieth century, real wages in coffee production were sliding downward. This conclusion can be sustained without resorting to the splicing of the two data sources used, though such splicing permits a somewhat more analytical treatment. When a straight line is fit by regression to the real wage series, 1882–1911, the resultant relationship is as follows:

$$\text{Real Wages} = 11439.7 - 5.97\,T$$

$$N = 28 \qquad r^2 = 0.76$$

Averaged over the whole period, this relationship suggests that wages were falling some 5 to 6 percent per annum. Examining the short-term trends in more detail, one sees that wages were high in the years 1882–1885, then declined precipitously to a low point in 1889. Then they rose again until 1895 or 1896, when they began a fall that lasted until 1903. After a slight recovery in 1904 and 1905, the downward trend reasserted itself.

The data of Pardo Pardo[61] show a less steep but still noticeable decline in real wages. Of course, one must have reservations about these conclusions, given the meager evidence (one charitable institution and two haciendas) on which the two time series of Tables 10 and 11 are based. One would confide more in the reliability of the conclusion of wage decline if the two series moved together. Such a movement was examined. For the twenty-one years for which both the Pardo Pardo series (Table 10) and the Table 11 series are available (between 1889 and 1911), the coefficient of correlation was $r = +0.51$. Considering that the two indices are supposed to be measuring roughly the same thing, the coefficient of correlation is very low. Nonetheless, the Pardo Pardo data and conclusions are at the least broadly consistent with those of Table 11. It therefore seems reasonable to conclude that real wages did decline in the last decades of the nineteenth century and the first years of the twentieth. But one must consider the views of contemporary observers.

This declining-wage hypothesis seems not to be sustained in Vice-Consul Dickson's 1903 report on coffee. In a review of events leading up to the War of a Thousand Days he refers to "over-planting of coffee all over the country" and suggests that the "limited amount of labour available was not sufficiently taken into account."

> The result has been that a large number of coffee plantations have been abandoned in whole or in part because the available capital estimated for three years' expenses was all spent in the first year, owing to the unforeseen rise in wages caused by the rush. This was the condition of the coffee industry when the revolution broke out in October, 1899.[62]

Dickson did not ignore the possibility that as money wages rose, the exchange rate was also changing, so that coffee entrepreneurs may not have been worse off. Workers, however, could have been worse off if local prices rose more than wages. He remarks:

> At first the depreciation worked favourably for coffee exporters, because prices went up gradually, their expenses were in depreciated paper and their gains in gold. But this financial chaos has ultimately resulted to everyone's disadvantage. The price of transport has, like everything else, become exorbitant and, at the same time, the price of coffee in the markets of the United States and Europe is steadily going down.[63]

The vice-consul did not have at his disposal sufficient material to enable him to judge the specific movements of real wages. The combination of events during this epoch included a decline in the terms of trade for coffee, conflict that culminated in the War of a Thousand Days, and a sudden inflation caused by overactive printing presses. All these events were occurring simultaneously. Moreover, Dickson wrote in late 1903, perhaps the worst moment for coffee—and for Colombia—in this century.

> To-day the coffee plantations are, from want of labour, losing half their coffee. Only those who have the best machinery can pretend to do a profitable business. The greater part of the produce of the last three years is still stored in the river ports, as there are no adequate means of despatching it. The coffee which has been kept on the estates themselves, in rooms which were never intended to hold three years' produce, has greatly deteriorated and may tend to lower the market price of Colombian coffee.[64]

Malcom Deas found the U.S. consul in Bogotá reporting in equally pessimistic terms in 1903:

> A study of the industries of Colombia, past and present, impresses one with the fact that without an exception they have all risen to a height from which much was expected, and that when just approaching the zenith, for some cause such as war, overproduction or the like . . . they have begun to decline.[65]

These facts were surely sufficient cause for depression and trauma in the coffee industry, but their specific relation to the level of real wages is less certain. In Table 11, one sees a peak for the coffee real wage series in 1895, then a decline. The series elaborated by Pardo Pardo (Table 10) shows a peak in 1899 and a precipitous decline the following year. Thus, real wages may have stayed high right up to the advent of the War of a Thousand Days in October 1899 and hence may have pinched the aborted coffee boom of the early 1890s. This interpretation is consistent with both the observations of Vice-Consul Dickson and the limited available data. However, much more information on wage trends in this period ought to be sought out.

Bustamante was the first of at least three economic historians (Deas and Palacios used the data) to examine the account books for the Hacienda Santa Barbara in Cundinamarca owned by Roberto Herrera Restrepo. In an M.A. thesis directed by Miguel Urrutia at the Universidad de los Andes, Bustamante made the first effort to calculate the profitability of coffee investments in nineteenth-century Colombia. In one table he set out invested capital, net profits, and a presumed profit rate for the hacienda for selected years between 1886 and 1899.[66] Palacios, in a subsequent work, reports the results of his own examination of the original account books for the hacienda and summarizes these results in several tables, at the same time detailing certain information missed by Bustamante. Of particular importance is the difference between total capital[67] and fixed capital.[68] When the former is used, the apparent annual profitability (profits per unit of assets) is considerably lower than Bustamante's figures imply. For example, the peak year of profitability according to Bustamante was 1896 when profits were 72 percent of assets, whereas Palacios[69] found a profit rate of only 26.7 percent for that year.

Table 12 combines data from Bustamante and, primarily, Palacios to show the evolution of the presumed profit rate for the Hacienda Santa Barbara over the period 1886–1902. The combined figures indicate that profits as a share of invested capital reached a peak in 1895 and subsequently fell. Unfortunately, the series does not bridge the period of the War of a Thousand Days. Moreover, it is uncertain how well the original source, the account books of the hacienda, dealt with the problem of multiple currency values, exchange rates, and inflation. A check on the relationship between the profit rate and the real wage index in Table 11 indicates no significant correlation.[70] Nor is there any significant relationship between the absolute value of profits and the real wage index. These findings should not be interpreted as a rejection of the hypothesis that falling wages caused higher profits and hence induced increased investment. Rather, other factors were operating in the 1890s (particularly after 1897) to depress profits, the most important being the declining terms of trade for coffee, deriving mainly from falling international coffee prices.

To examine simultaneously the impact of international prices and that of domestic costs (principally labor), a somewhat more complicated method must be used. Again, the available data are limited and conclusions derived must be tentative. Moreover, it is essential to describe the assumptions used.

Data on three variables—physical volume of exports, real wages on coffee haciendas, and international coffee prices—were assembled in Table 13 for the years 1894–1899 and 1905–1911. The price series index is given, not for the year indicated, but for the year four years before. This displacement of the price series was done to take account of the lagged response of production to price by growers. Today's prices influence the decision whether or not to plant coffee (expand production), but the actual response in the form of increased exports takes about four years because of the long gestation period of coffee plantations. Thus coffee exports in 1894 are assumed to be responding to coffee prices in 1890. Obviously, a more complicated distributed-lag model would be desirable methodologically, but the simple model used here is easier to estimate and simpler to interpret once estimated.

Given the data in Table 13, one may estimate the simple correlation coefficients between the three series, then use these r values to calculate partial correlation coefficients. The values of r between pairs of variables are as follows:

$$r_{12} = -0.69$$
$$r_{13} = -0.76$$
$$r_{23} = +0.71$$

There is a significant negative correlation between the volume of exports and real wages, i.e., exports tended to go up when wages went down. The value of r_{13} is the highest of those derived from Table 13. Thus declining wages over the whole period appear to have encouraged increased production. Of course, one must take into account other variables as well. The relationship between the volume of exports and prices is more difficult to interpret because it is also negative ($r_{12} = -0.69$), implying that exports go up as prices go down—not the normally expected relationship. However, when the partial correlation coefficients are calculated as below, the measure of correlation is much lower. The relationship between international coffee prices and real wages is somewhat surprising ($r_{23} = +0.71$) because it suggests that local wages moved up (or down) with international prices. The transmission of international price movements to the local economy appears more direct than one might have anticipated. Remember, however, that wages are lagged four years behind coffee prices. The linear regression equation is as follows:

$$\text{Real Wage}_t = 36.8 + 0.23 \text{ Price}_{t-4}$$

This finding contrasts with Dickson's report that wages were high and yet workers could not be found. The explanation may lie in the fact that conditions were so disturbed by the War of a Thousand Days that what looked like a problem of high wages was really a problem of labor scarcity occasioned by the special short-term conditions of warfare and conflict.

These data indicate how the stage was set for the impressive increase in coffee planting and export beginning after 1905. As world prices went down, so did local wages; then as prices recovered, wages rose less rapidly. It was perhaps the preliminary experiences of the 1890s that taught the nascent coffee cultivators how to husband their resources and hence be more successful in the early twentieth century. Put another way, they learned how to exploit their capital and human resources.

The r values presented above may be used to calculate partial correlation coefficients, i.e., measures of relationship between a pair of variables when a third variable is held constant. Such a procedure permits one to see whether a strong relationship exists between two variables when a third is also taken into account. The partial correlation coefficients were as follows:[71]

$$r_{12.3} = -0.33$$
$$r_{13.2} = -0.53$$
$$r_{23.1} = +0.39$$

When one holds constant the international price of coffee, variations in real wages explain more of the variance of exports than do variations in international prices when wages are held constant.

The value of $r_{13.2}$ is the highest of those estimated in the exercise. The value of $r_{12.3}$ is, of course, still negative, and hence not entirely anticipated; however, it is very much lower than that of $r_{13.2}$, which does have the expected negative sign. Wages still appear to be closely linked to international coffee prices even when the volume of exports is taken into account. Wages respond positively to international coffee prices, then volume of exports responds negatively to increased wage costs. The result is that the volume of exports appears to respond negatively to an increase in international prices. When in the first decade of the twentieth century it became possible to delay the response of wages to international prices, a profit breach opened, so that profits must have shot up with the increased production of the post-1909 boom. The investment of those profits in expanded production could then fuel further growth.

We may have here a partial explanation for the timing of the coffee export boom—for both why it occurred when it did and why it did not occur earlier. The link between higher international prices and local wages was interrupted after the War of a Thousand Days—perhaps because workers were more restrained after those bloody events. Coffee prices reached a twentieth-century low in 1906, driving down local wages.[72] They had increased by 60 percent by 1911; during the same period Lleras's real wage index (see Table 11) declined by 20 percent. In the coffee zone of Cundinamarca, in which production expanded dramatically early in the twentieth century, there was a notable expansion of the labor force. In 1906, according to the *Revista Nacional de Agricultura,* there were 12,000 permanent workers in the coffee zone and more than 100,000 seasonal workers at harvest time. Those numbers had grown to 80,000 and 240,000, respectively, by 1914, as reported in the December issue of the same journal.[73] Therein lies the coffee grower's opportunity. In an earlier period of aborted expansion in the 1890s, wage increases prevented more rapid profit growth. Accumulation of a surplus was limited and expansion of production gave way to the problems described in Dickson's consular report. In 1903 Dickson did not foresee that an immense coffee boom was just a few years away. This lack of foresight is particularly notable in his mention of three departments as areas of coffee growing—Cundinamarca, Santander, and Tolima. Yet by 1913 the Antioqueño departments of Antioquia and Caldas—not even mentioned by Dickson—would be producing 384,000 bags of coffee, 35 percent of Colombia's total production. This incongruence is mentioned, not to impugn Dickson's excellent first-hand report, but rather to show how difficult it is to interpret contemporary evidence and anticipate long-term trends.

The Profitability of Coffee Cultivation

In making the decision to plant coffee the entrepreneur must take into account a future stream of income and expenses and balance the resulting present discounted value (PDV) of this stream against alternative uses for his resources. The formal presentation of this process can be reduced to the following equation:

$$\text{PDV} = \sum_{i=1}^{t} \frac{B_i - C_i}{(1 + r)^t}$$

One may evaluate this equation (once benefits and costs are established, obviously more than a trivial task) either in terms of a given r—for example, the rate of return on comparable investments—or one may determine the internal rate of return on the investment itself by finding the r that equates the present discounted value of the stream of benefits and of costs. That r is then the putative return on the investment being made.

Because the eventual returns with a perennial such as coffee are far in the future, the immediate costs of land clearing, preparation, and planting weigh very heavily in the entrepreneurial decision to plant or not. The small-scale family farm of the Antioqueños had a notable advantage in that they could interplant coffee with plantains, maize, and beans in early years and subsist on those products until the coffee bushes began to produce.[74]

A schematic version of the timing of costs and revenues (benefits) derived from coffee cultivation appears in Figure 4. The curves indicate high early costs for land clearing, preparation, and planting well before the commencement of revenues from coffee sales. Only in year 4 does the enterprise begin to show a profit (revenues greater than costs). Thereafter revenues may exceed costs by a substantial margin until the end of the economic life of the coffee plant. The time structure of investment over the first five years of a coffee plantation was estimated by Carrasquilla to be 48 percent of the total in the first year, and 16, 10, 8, and 18 percent in each of the succeeding four years.[75] Price expectations and the ability to transport the product to market also enter into the entrepreneurial deci-

FIGURE 4.
TIME SCHEDULE OF INPUTS AND OUTPUT IN COFFEE CULTIVATION

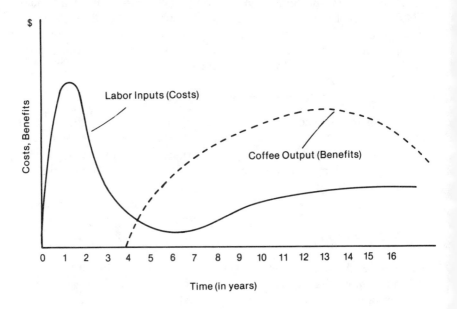

Time (in years)

sion. When the labor inputs curve shifts upward as a result of higher wages, there is less incentive to undertake production. Conversely, if the coffee output curve shifts downward as a result of lower prices for the volume produced and sold, then the incentive to produce will be weakened. Finally, because of the long gestation period for coffee growing, the cost of capital to invest (measured by both the rate of interest and the difficulty of securing investable funds) will have a significant effect on the production decision. These three variables are represented in the equation calculating PDV above. The interest rate or internal rate of return on capital provides the link between financial events (expenditures on labor and revenues from sales, for example) that occur at different points in time.

Three kinds of data make it possible to calculate the profitability of coffee cultivation: anticipated profits based on expected prices and costs as revealed by prospective coffee growers; an *ex post* calculation drawing on observed prices and costs; and an analysis of costs and resources for Hacienda Santa Barbara, 1885–1900. For the first kind of data, a publication of the Bureau of American Republics presents estimates of the costs of clearing and preparing land for coffee production as of 1893. These data were presented as follows:

The cost of the land for setting out and growing 100,000 coffee plants, and of implements and cultivation needed, is thus estimated by an intelligent American, who examined various localities and studied the question of coffee cultivation on the spot:

First Year	$ 5,567
Second Year	5,414
Third Year	1,754
Fourth Year	3,000
Machinery for cleaning the berries	2,000
Total	$17,735(dollars)

The same gentleman gives the yield of the coffee tree from the third year forward as from two and one-half to four pounds per tree each year. This estimate is probably too high, but even at one pound per tree the product of 100,000 trees would be worth 20,000 dollars for the fourth year at 20 cents per pound.

The cost of transportation from Bogotá to New York is estimated at 2.9 cents per pound, and the *Estadística Mercantil* puts the cost of production at 4.5 cents per pound. The profit is thus seen to be substantial. The price of labor is low, the wages of a day laborer being about 25 cents, and in some districts children are employed in gathering coffee at the low wages of 5 cents a day, according to the statement of the gentleman before alluded to.[76]

Perhaps the most serious problem with this assessment of the potential profitability of coffee growing is the absurdly high yield estimate that the "gentleman" in question offers. The functionary of the Bureau of the American Republics could not take it seriously; nonetheless, he accepted the estimates of costs of cultivation at face value.

These data on costs are complemented in the analysis below of profitability of investments at Hacienda Santa Barbara. Naturally, they are not entirely pertinent to the case of a small holder who may decide to sow coffee bushes along with subsistence crops such as corn, beans, and plantains. However, these small holders were probably led to their coffee-planting decisions by the bigger cultivators in their neighborhood; thus the decisions on whether or not to plant coffee, made by major cultivators, were simply copied by the "Juan Valdezes" of the countryside. In that sense, the decision-making process of the large cultivators may have been more influential than either their numbers or their control over production would indicate.[77] Hence the analysis of this decision-making process is broadly relevant to the expansion of coffee cultivation.*

To calculate the prospective internal rate of return, like the Bureau of the American Republics official, we will assume that the costs estimates are reasonable, but will lower coffee production per tree to one pound. Costs beyond the fourth year (which include the purchase of machinery) are assumed to be 0.075 dollars per pound. Production continues for twenty years. The resultant series of costs and revenues and the net return is presented in Table 14. Using the formula for present discounted value above, one may, by a process of iteration, calculate r, the internal rate of return.[78] Using the data in Table 14, r is found to be 48 percent.

This result emerges from what is merely a simulation exercise; however, it may be pertinent to real entrepreneurial decisions taken in the early 1890s because the information used is virtually the same as that which entrepreneurs were using as a basis for their decisions.

Further realism can be introduced into the calculations by examining the effects of using observed trends in wages and international prices in calculating costs, revenues, and the rate of return. Data for that calculation are presented in Table 15.[79] With the simultaneous fall in both wages and international coffee prices, the costs and revenues that the simulated 1893 entrepreneur would have experienced are generally lower than those on which the Bureau of American Republics' projections were predicated. The net return is generally lower in Table 15 than in Table 14. The resultant internal rate of return on the original 1893 investment is then 33 percent, still a quite high level, though in no year did revenues ever reach the 20,000 dollar level.

Further analysis can be carried out with this technique by checking how the rate of return would be affected by the shifting over time of expected costs and revenues.

Another means to check the rate of return on coffee investments is to use the data developed by Marco Palacios from the Hacienda Santa Barbara account books.[80] There are data indicating an initial investment of 36,703 pesos in 1885, subsequent changes in two assets series (capital and value of hacienda), a series of current annual costs, production, and prices. From these data one can elaborate two alternative series (see columns 1 and 2 of Table 16), using the two assets series on which Palacios places considerable emphasis, and estimate the internal rate of return under these two assumptions. The data for these calculations appear in Table 16.

Using the results of net return from column 5, one finds that the internal rate of return to investment in Hacienda Santa Barbara was 23.1 percent. Using the alternative capital costs implied by imputing all increases in the value of the hacienda to real costs of building up the estate, the internal rate of return was 34.4 percent. In either case the rate of return was clearly substantial, despite the considerable problems Herrera Restrepo faced in owning and managing the estate, and despite its eventual dissolution (described by Deas[81]). The second series produces a seemingly smoother growth of costs, revenues, and net returns to the estate, and therefore would appear to be a more accurate reflection of the real economic profitability of the estate, at least when viewed from the long-term perspective of the period in the 1880s when the decision was made to make the investment.

Expectations must have been much less encouraging in 1899 or 1900 when prices were down more than labor costs. In contrast, by 1910 the future must have looked very bright indeed. Even with the long delay between initial investment and eventual payout over the years of coffee production, it may have been possible to earn an annual rate of return of 40 to 50 percent. Profits of that magnitude obviously would encourage greatly expanded production.

By that time, however, another significant change had occurred in coffee cultivation that was to influence the size of holdings and the distribution of benefits from production. The first coffee estates set out in the 1880s and 1890s by Bogotá coffee speculators[82] depended critically on the availability of labor. At first, workers were readily available from the nearby highlands of Cundinamarca and Boyaca, some as *arrendatarios* who got usufructs in exchange for labor, and some as seasonal workers at harvest times. It was in this cheap-labor era that coffee looked so profitable to the speculators.

The *arrendatarios* readily picked up the techniques of growing coffee. Some managed to gain control of land simply by migrating to open areas of the Quindio across the Magdalena River; others participated in the dissolution of the estates after 1917. There was no way the speculators could hold down wages and hence continue the level of profits predicted by the foregoing simulation analysis. Instead, the small holders themselves enjoyed the advantages of the profitability of coffee cultivation and greatly expanded their numbers, even into the 1960s.[83] As production and cultivation became more and more the province of the small holder—first in Antioquia and Caldas, then in Cundinamarca, the Quindio, and Valle del Cauca—the powerful interests in the coffee business specialized in coffee buying, processing, and marketing. By the 1930s the Federación Nacional de Cafeteros had become the ideal vehicle to organize and rationalize the industry, while leaving production decisions to smallholders.

The War and Panama

Do the squeeze on real wages and the profitability of coffee cultivation successfully explain the transition? The profitability associated with expansion in the 1890s, coupled with the abortion of that expansion, suggest that some additional elements must have come into play in the years after 1900 that explain why the transition was delayed until after 1905. The War of a Thousand Days and its aftermath, combined with the impact of the loss of Panama, provide additional elements that explain why the transition did not occur earlier.[84]

The following discussion of the impact of the War of a Thousand Days and the events leading to the secession of Panama relies substantially on books by Lemaitre,[85] Bergquist,[86] and McCullough.[87] The first is a lengthy political history; the second provides an excellent review of the political life of Bogotá in the period leading up to and including the war; the last is a more general book that examines first the French and then the subsequent American interest in constructing a Panama canal. All rely on primary documents that their authors examined for purposes different from those of this essay. Nonetheless, these works make important contributions to understanding the role of the two major events they study in the subsequent phase of rapid economic change in Colombia. The War of a Thousand Days preceded, and was a major cause of, Colombia's loss of Panama.[88] North Americans, particularly President Theodore Roosevelt, perceived the Colombian civil war as evidence of instability in Bogotá and the isthmus, and of the inability of the Colombian government to make an effective agreement for proceeding with canal construction. Roosevelt perhaps even thought (McCullough suggests as much) that the civil war was merely a ruse to secure American support for Colombia's demand that it share in the proposed 40 million dollar payment to the French company that held the concession to build the canal.[89]

> Perhaps even more than their concern over potential developments in Panama, upper-class leaders of *all political parties* were preoccupied with signs that forces unleashed by the war had gotten beyond their control and were eroding their monopoly on economic, social and political power. . . .
> Peace Liberals, Historical Conservatives, and ultimately, Nationalists always stressed the growing "savagery" of the conflict and the threat the war posed to "civilization" in Colombia. Their language reflected their alarm over the breakdown of respect for private property and upper-class privilege which resulted from the forced loans and contributions, expropriations, and robberies practiced by both the government and the revolutionary forces as the war dragged on.[90]

A Liberal leader, Celso Román, quoted by Bergquist, expressed well the elite's hoped-for outcome of the struggle: "It is advisable that the tempest cease in order that people and things return to occupy the position and level to which, given their background and their conduct, they are suited."[91] The Conservatives' hegemony was not built on favorable attitudes toward their policies in that party alone. Political and economic elites, crosscutting political party lines as they have since the origin of party politics in the mid-nineteenth century, shared the desire to stop bickering and start building.

One does not speak of the loss of Panama in polite conversation in Colombia. A canny Colombian historian explains why:

> The Panama question is surrounded by special circumstances worth clarifying. In every family exists the blurred memory of a dispute, or of

some fabulous business deal, on which depended, at a critical moment, prosperity or collective ruin. About this dispute or deal exists a tacit agreement, neither to mention or allude to it publicly, as homage is paid in not mentioning the duodenal ulcer or cardiac flutters of living grandparents. For these same reasons the family of Colombians prefers not to speak of Panama.[92]

McCullough offers a clear picture of how the separation of Panama from Colombia came to be a national humiliation. On June 9, 1903, John Hay, U.S. secretary of state, sent a message through his ambassador to the Colombian minister of foreign affairs: "If Colombia should now reject the treaty [for U.S. construction of the canal] or unduly delay its ratification, the friendly understanding between the two countries would be so seriously compromised that action might be taken by the Congress next winter which every friend of Colombia would regret."[93] On June 14, 1903, an article appeared in the New York *World* that, McCullough shows, could reasonably be attributed to Roosevelt himself. It says in part:

President Roosevelt is determined to have the Panama canal route. He has no intention of beginning negotiations for the Nicaragua route. . . .

Advices received here daily indicate great opposition to the canal treaty at Bogotá. Its defeat seems probable for two reasons:

1. The greed of the Colombian Government, which insists on a largely increased payment for the property and concession.
2. The fact that certain factions have worked themselves into a frenzy over the alleged relinquishment of sovereignty to lands necessary for building the canal. . . .

The State of Panama will secede if the Colombian Congress fails to ratify the canal treaty. . . .

The citizens of Panama propose, after seceding, to make a treaty with the United States, giving this Government the equivalent of absolute sovereignty over the Canal Zone. . . .

In return the President of the United States would promptly recognize the new Government, when established, and would at once appoint a minister to negotiate and sign a canal treaty. . . .

It is intended to wait a reasonable time for action by the Colombian Congress, which convenes 20 June, and then, if nothing else is done, to make the above plan operative.[94]

McCullough closes his citation of this remarkable document with the comment, "The article was unsigned. The White House issued no denials."[95]

Events unfolded much as this article predicted. On August 12, 1903, the Colombian Senate rejected the Hay-Herran Treaty, which provided for transfer of the French concession to the United States and hence the building of the canal. By September a Panamanian leader was in contact with the U.S. State Department through third parties. In October the

Panamanians managed to buy the cooperation of the Colombia garrison based in Panama City and received assurances that U.S. sea power would be used to prevent Colombia from maintaining military control in the isthmus. With the cooperation of the U.S. manager of the Panama railroad, a contingent of five hundred Colombian troops in Colón was separated from its leaders, who were sent on to Panama City. After the arrest of the generals by the Panamanians, the troops were induced to board a ship and return to Barranquilla. By November 6 the threat of violence had passed. The United States immediately recognized the new government of the Republic of Panama.

The observation that a foreign power can and will impose its manifest destiny to the point of undermining territorial sovereignty must have weighed heavily on Colombian politicians. They had let a major part of the nation and an important economic resource slip from their control. Whatever their anger about Yankee perfidy, they must have been angry with themselves as well.[96] Perhaps in those events of 1903 one sees as much the denial of expected status, which Hagen[97] attributed to the Antioqueños, as the regional rivalries that characterized the eighteenth and nineteenth centuries. It may be no accident that the best novel Colombia has produced, *One Hundred Years of Solitude,* by Gabriel García Márquez, is a fictional evocation of mystery and guilt, a shroud of violence around a sensate core of impotence. The War of a Thousand Days, the imprecations of the foreigner, the sense of something lost in Macondo, these are central to García Márquez's novel, and, one would suppose, to Colombian attitudes as well.

The War of a Thousand Days and loss of Panama restrained the normal political competitiveness of the Liberal party, a faction of which was held responsible for the war and in part for the loss of Panama. The Conservatives, often in coalition with centrist Liberals, managed to remain in power virtually unchallenged for a quarter century. Thus they were able to adopt policies favoring business, manufacturing, trade, exporters, and foreign investment. Protest, which might have found some support among a faction of the Liberal party, simply found no outlet.

In an analysis of long-term trends in Colombian politics Solaun sought the parallels between reaction to the War of a Thousand Days and reaction to the *violencia* of the period 1948–1963:

> The tranquility of this perid [1905–1930] appears to have been a reaction to the Mil Días civil war, and its alleged consequences. . . . Above all there was a general feeling at the time that had Colombia not been divided and exhausted by the war, Panama would not have been lost. A strong consensus, reflected in the press of both parties, arose on the need to prevent civil wars at practically any cost in order to safeguard the national territory. Not even under maximum pressure for civil war, such as was provided by the 1922 presidential campaign, did the specter of Panama disappear.[98]

Just as external threats drove factions together, so did it mute the urgency for a larger share of the benefits of development. Certainly the working class did not experience rapid salary increases. Berry's data indicate that a peon at the Fenicia glass factory in Bogotá earned 29 centavos daily in 1905. Salaries increased moderately up to 1917, when a comparable peon earned 35 centavos.[99] The rate of increase was but 1.6 percent per annum. Wages rose much more rapidly thereafter—to 88 centavos in 1921 and a peak of 123 centavos in 1929. Real wages in rural areas between 1911 and the 1920s were probably stagnant, if not declining, as they had been in the previous decade. It was in the rural areas of export cultivation that the earliest evidence of twentieth-century agrarian protest appears.

The evidence developed by Pierre Gilhodes suggests that rural unrest was particularly centered in areas of export-crop cultivation. His work examines the origins of violence in Viotá, the rebellious coffee zone in southern Cundinamarca that held out as an independent Marxist state against the central government for several decades. He notes the following historical development:

> By the middle of 1917 and, above all, in 1918, the first peasant organizations appeared, and the first peasant demonstrations related to urban disturbances occurred. The two centers of rural agitation were the banana plantations of the United Fruit Company near Santa Marta . . . and the coffee plantations of the lower valley of the Bogotá River. A strike broke out on the banana and coffee plantations; the peasants burned the public buildings of Viotá, and refused to work without a raise in salary and an improvement in working and living conditions. The strike caused great alarm among the landlords who generally lived in Bogotá, where they were able to pressure for the intervention of public troops.[100]

As in Mexico, where sugar workers in Morelos along with displaced small holders supported the Zapatista movement, and where mine workers in the Guanajuato region also supported revolution, so in Colombia elements of rural unrest coalesced in areas where large plantations of coffee and bananas served to focus worker grievances.[101] These plantations were also intimately linked to the external sector and international trade. Thus along with the benefits of higher income (and profits) came protests against the manner in which those gains were being distributed.

In a recent work on peasant movements Tovar presents data on landholdings and landlessness by regional groupings.[102] Although the regional comparisons he makes are flawed by the failure to adjust for the age structure of the population and the obvious idiosyncrasies of the data in the censuses of 1912 and 1918, he does call attention to the fact that a large percentage of the rural population was landless. With respect to coffee growing this situation changed dramatically in the 1920s and 1930s (see Table 17). Between 1925 and 1932 the area planted in coffee increased by 120 percent, with much of that growth concentrated in properties of less than twenty thousand coffee plants. Over the same period the number of small properties grew from 43,629 to 146,477, an increase of 236 percent, whereas larger properties grew from 1,575 to 2,871, an increase of only 82 percent.[103] The continuation of this direction of change—from domination of large holdings to predominance of small ones—is demonstrated in Table 17, which shows a doubling of coffee farms in Cundinamarca in the period 1932–1940. During this period Law 200 of 1936 took effect and helped put the large coffee estates into the hands of the *arrendatarios* who had worked them since the late nineteenth century. However, the shrinkage in size of holdings was reversed in the late 1930s, so that in most coffee-growing departments of Colombia the average size of holdings increased up to the census of 1970.[104] The ratio of seasonal workers to landowners changed dramatically in Viotá between the 1938 and 1951 censuses. In 1938, there were about twenty-three workers for each landowner; thirteen years later, after reforms had been instituted, the ratio was 1.7:1.[105] In Viotá, possibly the most extreme case of agrarian change in Colombia, the era of the coffee speculator, begun not in the mists of the colonial past, but only in the last quarter of the nineteenth century, was brought to an end. Not surprisingly, however, this shift in the control of rural land had virtually no impact on the overall distribution of power and income within the economy as a whole.[106]

It was not possible to ascertain whether this process of peasant takeover of larger landholdings had begun earlier. Hirschman's essay on Colombian land reform does not refer to any significant changes before about 1928.[107] Conservative hegemony and the absence of tenure changes through the mid-1920s would be consistent. Tovar's review of newspaper accounts of rural protest and struggles on specific haciendas is devoted principally to actions in the 1930s.[108]

The war and the loss of Panama had the effect of ending protests against the accumulation of capital by the coffee cultivators and the nascent manufacturers, the beneficiaries and architects of the transition. These events may have played a role similar to that of the *ejido* system in post revolutionary Mexico: by diverting the peasants' attention from the enrichment of the large farms and their owners, the *ejido* system and its communitarian ideology assured that accumulation could go forward.[109] The war and the loss of Panama practically made political protest illegal.

From another point of view, the war and the loss of Panama may have made Colombians aware that their future control over their own fate as a nation required attention to development. Bergquist writes, "After the war, the secession of Panama bolstered the political fortunes of bipartisan export-import interests by fostering a consensus among Colombian leaders that the nation must unite politically and develop itself materially if it were to avoid further dismemberment."[110] The governments of Rafael Reyes (1904–1909) and Carlos E. Restrepo (1910–1914) were both bipartisan and favored export interests. Groups that had fought each other tooth and nail from the days of the Olimpo Radical (the Radical Olympus) in the 1860s were now willing and able to cooperate.[111]

The impact of foreign power thus generated a sense of urgency to develop. The loss of Panama and the tragedy of the War of a Thousand Days were signal events that could have caused the transition to occur when it did rather than sooner or later.[112] These events, then, are the ones which generated the special factor of *will* as a variable explaining the transition to economic growth.[113]

In concluding this essay we return to the questions with which we began. Was there an identifiable acceleration of economic activity? It seems clear that there was, beginning sometime around 1905; moreover, there are some signs that an earlier acceleration almost began in the 1890s, in coffee export and consumer-goods manufactures. That earlier acceleration was, however, aborted by weakened demand and lower prices for coffee, and more importantly, the diversion of effort to political conflict.

Was the acceleration of economic activity that began in 1905 sufficient to warrant the term *transition?* This term applied to the phenomena of economic history is no more or less precise than stages in the process of growth.[114] Nonetheless, it seems fair to associate the term *transition* with a reversal from decay to growth, i.e., from the stagnation of the late nineteenth century to rapid growth after 1905. Moreover, the expansion of exports at more than 10 percent per annum over two decades was much more rapid than the volume of world trade as a whole, which grew about 2 percent per annum over the period 1901–1905 to 1930.[115] The product of the Colombian modern manufacturing sector grew by at least 3.5 percent annually, and probably by as much as 9 percent annually over the score of years 1905–1925.[116] Industrial production for the world as a whole grew during the same period by about 3 percent per annum.[117] Obviously, then, the acceleration in Colombia during this period was great enough to be characterized as a transition.

What caused the acceleration, particularly in capital investments, export expansion, urbanization, and manufacturing growth? A wide range of factors played a role; they have been discussed in this essay and in previous works.[118] Here we need only recall the interactive effects of railroad building, export demand, the wage squeeze, and profitability as explanatory variables for the expansion of coffee cultivation. These several factors put into place most of the conditions for rapid growth as early as 1890, or perhaps even before. Nonetheless, the transition to growth was delayed.

What remains to be explained by will? The initial conditions for growth were present, yet growth did not occur until after 1905. The events of the War of a Thousand Days and the loss of Panama were proximate determinants of change in Colombia, a change from internal conflict to awareness of the need for cooperation to develop. If, after November 1903, Colombians wanted to develop, it was in some measure because they realized the costs to national sovereignty and self-determination of allowing internal conflict to create conditions so detrimental to national objectives. Development of the national economy was the only way out of an unhealthy dependence on a power that had put its own national interest ahead of its expressed obligations to Colombia.

The events of *fin de siècle* Colombia were the crucible in which the will to develop was tested and tempered. There was no way in which Colombians could impose their will on the United States. There seemed to be no way in which Liberals could resist the hegemony of the Conservative party. If politics no longer offered solutions to personal, regional, or national problems, growing coffee was the alternative. It remained only to heed the call of Rafael Uribe Uribe, the guilded exile: "Colombians! Sow coffee!"

TABLE 1

POPULATION OF COLOMBIA AND 19 MAJOR *MUNICIPIOS*, 1870–1918

Year	Total Population (in thousands)	Population of 19 Major *Municipios* (in thousands)	Urban Total (%)	Cumulative Annual Growth Rates Total (%)	Cumulative Annual Growth Rates 19 Major *Municipios* (%)
1870	2,708	206	7.6	—	—
1905	4,475*	490	10.9	1.4	2.5
1912	5,073	583	11.5	1.8	2.5
1918	5,855	733	12.5	2.4	3.9

SOURCE: National censuses; data on nineteen *municipios* from W. P. McGreevey, *An Economic History of Colombia, 1845–1930*, (New York: Cambridge University Press, 1971), p. 110.

*The figure for 1905 is adjusted according to Collver's contention (in *Birth Rates in Latin America*) that the 1905 census was underenumerated by 8 percent. Cumulative growth rates take account of this changed estimate of the 1905 population.

TABLE 2
CUMULATIVE ANNUAL GROWTH RATES OF KILOMETERS IN SERVICE
FOR SELECTED PERIODS, 1885–1934

Period	Rate of Expansion of km. in Service (%)
1885–1890	6.8
1890–1904	5.1
1904–1909	9.8
1909–1914	5.3
1914–1922	3.0
1922–1934	6.8

SOURCE: W. P. McGreevey, *An Economic History of Colombia, 1845–1930*, table 32, p. 256.

TABLE 3
EXPORT OF COFFEE FROM THE CUSTOMS HOUSES OF COLOMBIA,
1894–98

Customs House*	Quantity (millions of kilos)	Percent	Value (millions of dollars)[†]
Barranquilla	72.7	43.8	24.9
Cartagena	14.4	8.7	6.9
Buenaventura	5.2	3.1	2.2
Tumaco	0.6	0.3	0.2
Ipiales	—	—	—
Riohacha	1.0	0.6	0.3
Cúcuta	72.0	43.4	20.7
Meta	0.3	0.2	—
Total	166.1	100.0	55.2

SOURCE: Great Britain. Foreign Office, Diplomatic and Consular Reports: Miscellaneous Series no. 598. "Report on the Present State of the Coffee Trade . . ." (11 Sept. 1903), by Spencer S. Dickson (London: H.M. Stationery Office, 1903) p. 7.
*For Buenaventura, eight months of 1894 are missing; and for 1895, the value of 302,351 kilos is missing. With regard to Meta: in 1897 there are only data for January, February, and September to December; in 1898 from April to July.
[†]Values are in United States gold: 5 dollars = 1 pound sterling.

TABLE 4
PERIOD OF FOUNDING OF 62 COMPANIES INCLUDED IN REPORT ON INDUSTRIES, 1916

Period	No. of Companies Founded
Before 1870	2
1870–1879	0
1880–1889	2
1890–1899	7
1900–1904	5
1905–1909	14
1910–1915	32
Total	62

SOURCE: *Informe anual del Ministro de Hacienda, 1916* (Bogotá: Imprenta Oficial, 1916), pp. XCVI–CXIII.

TABLE 5
PERIOD OF FOUNDING OF MANUFACTURING COMPANIES AND *VALOR PATRIMONIO*, (MILLIONS OF PESOS), 1945

Period	*Valor Patrimonio*
Before 1910	135
1910–1920	95
1921–1925	28
1926–1929	57
1930–1931	16
1932–1933	32
1934–1935	29

SOURCE: Censo Industrial 1945; reported in Oscar Rodríguez Salazar, *Efectos de la gran depresión sobre la industria colombiana* (Medellín: Ediciones Tigre del Papel, 1973), Table B–1.

TABLE 6
INDICES OF COFFEE PRICES, IMPORT PRICES, AND TERMS OF TRADE, 1891–1921

Year	P_x (Coffee) (1920–1929 = 100)	P_m (Imports) (1923–1925 = 100)	$\frac{P_x}{P_m} \times 100$
1891	74	55	135
1892	73	51	143
1893	82	48	171
1894	72	44	164
1895	70	47	149
1896	68	48	142
1897	59	45	131
1898	50	44	113
1899	37	51	73
1900	30	57	52
1901	—	54	—
1902	47	53	89
1903	46	58	79
1904	49	58	84
1905	47	58	81
1906	46	64	72
1907	49	67	73
1908	50	59	84
1909	48	61	79
1910	66	65	102
1911	73	61	120
1912	—	67	—
1913	68	73	93
1914	68	62	109
1915	63	69	91
1916	62	94	66
1917	56	119	47
1918	71	130	55
1919	120	129	93
1920	93	143	65
1921	67	99	68

SOURCE: Urrutia and Arrubla, eds., *Compendio de estadísticas históricas de Colombia*, pp. 212–213.

TABLE 7
EXPORT OF COFFEE BY VOLUME AND VALUE, 1894–1898*

Year	Quantity (millions of kilos)	Value (millions of dollars)	Average Price per kilo (millions of dollars)
1894	27.98	9.98	0.36
1895	28.85	10.97	0.38
1896	37.63	13.22	0.35
1897	34.00	11.03	0.32
1898	37.66	10.02	0.27

SOURCE: Great Britain. Foreign Office, Diplomatic and Consular Reports, "The Present State of the Coffee Trade . . . ," p. 8.
*For certain minor qualifications concerning the data used, see footnote to Table 3. The final column was calculated for presentation here and does not appear in the original source.

TABLE 8
COLOMBIAN IMPORTS, TARIFF REVENUES, AND THEIR RELATIONSHIP, 1879–1890, 1905–1919

Year	Imports Old Series (1)	Imports New Series (2)	Tariff Revenues (Colombian pesos) (3)	$\frac{3}{1} \times 100$ (%) (4)	$\frac{3}{2} \times 100$ (%) (5)
1879	26.0	10.8	3.5	13.5	32
1880	23.5	10.7	4.3	18.3	40
1881	26.5	10.1	4.3	16.2	43
1882	26.9	12.4	4.4	16.4	35
1883	27.0	11.5	1.8	6.7	16
1884	25.3	9.9	1.7	6.7	17
1885	16.1	8.0	6.9	26.4	86
1886	20.9	7.4	1.6	7.7	22
1887	25.8	8.8	4.8	18.6	55
1888	26.1	10.0	6.9	26.4	69
1889	21.7	11.5	7.7	35.5	67
1890	25.1	12.7	8.6	34.3	68
1905	15.0	12.3	6.2	41.3	50
1906	16.7	10.6	7.4	44.3	70
1907	17.8	12.1	6.6	37.1	55
1908	17.4	13.5	6.2	35.6	46
1909	16.9	11.1	6.5	38.5	59
1910	17.4	17.4	8.7	50.0	50
1911	18.1	—	9.1	50.3	—
1912	24.0	—	10.1	42.1	—
1913	28.5	—	12.9	45.3	—
1914	21.0	—	9.8	46.7	—
1915	17.8	—	7.4	41.6	—
1916	29.7	—	—	—	—
1917	24.8	—	7.4	29.8	—
1918	21.8	—	4.7	21.6	—
1919	47.5	—	7.0	14.7	—

SOURCES: Old series of imports: Urrutia and Arrubla, eds., *Compendio de estadísticas históricas de Colombia,* pp. 205–206; New Series: Ocampo, "Las importaciones colombianas en el siglo XIX," in Urrutia (1980), p. 100; tariff revenues: ministerial reports.

TABLE 9
POPULATION, CENTRAL GOVERNMENT TAX REVENUES, AND
REVENUES PER CAPITA FOR 7 COUNTRIES, C. 1910
(MILLIONS OF U.S. DOLLARS AND DOLLARS PER CAPITA)

Country	Population	Tax Revenues	Taxes/Person
Argentina	7.0	116.8	16.70
Costa Rica	0.4	3.5	9.40
Ecuador	1.4	7.9	5.66
Brazil	17.3	98.3	5.60
Peru	4.0	20.0	5.00
Venezuela	2.7	9.6	3.60
Colombia	5.0	12.5	2.50
Colombia, with departmental revenues		19.4	3.88

SOURCE: Colombia, Ministerio de Hacienda y Crédito Público, *Informe del Ministerio de Hacienda y Crédito Público,* (Bogotá, 1912), p. lxxxvi.

TABLE 10

MONEY WAGES, A COST-OF-LIVING INDEX AND REAL SALARIES,
BENEFICENCIA DE CUNDINAMARCA, BOGOTÁ, COLOMBIA, 1888–1924

Year	Daily Wage (pesos)	Annual Wage (pesos)	Index (1923 = 100)	Cost-of-Living Index (1923 = 100)	Real Salaries (1923 = 100)
1888	0.40	116.80	74	88	84
1889	0.49	143.08	90	113	80
1890	0.48	140.16	88	109	81
1891	0.51	148.92	94	108	87
1892	0.59	172.28	109	108	100
1893	0.58	169.36	107	115	93
1894	0.58	169.36	107	128	84
1895	0.65	189.80	120	135	89
1896	0.82	239.44	151	154	98
1897	0.88	256.96	162	166	98
1898	0.70	204.40	129	159	81
1899	0.86	251.12	158	156	101
1900	0.85	248.20	157	215	74
1901	1.28	373.76	236	616	38
1902	4.80	1,401.60	884	2575	34
1903	17.50	5,510.00	3224	6917	46
1904	31.10	9,081.20	5730	7895	72
1905	24.40	7,124.80	4496	9271	48
1906	31.00	9,052.00	5712	7308	78
1907	30.00	8,760.00	5528	6356	86
1908	30.00	8,760.00	5528	7550	73
1909	—	—	—	82	—
1910	—	—	—	74	—
1911	0.30	87.60	55	70	78
1912	—	—	—	87	—
1913	—	—	—	106	—
1914	0.41	122.59	77	94	82
1915	0.44	131.56	83	85	98
1916	0.48	143.52	90	73	124
1917	0.46	137.54	87	84	104
1918	0.49	146.51	92	96	96
1919	0.50	149.50	94	117	80
1920	0.61	182.39	115	130	89
1921	0.66	197.34	124	113	110
1922	0.51	152.49	96	108	90
1923	0.53	158.47	100	100	100
1924	0.63	188.37	119	107	111

SOURCE: Pardo Pardo, *Geografía económica y humana de Colombia,* pp. 221, 234–35. The column heading *Reales* on pp. 234 and 235 in this work is a printing error; it should read *Pesos.* Pardo Pardo indicates days worked per annum. Real salaries for 1888 and 1890 were changed from the original because of what appear to be printing errors.

TABLE 11

REAL-WAGES INDEX FOR TWO COFFEE PLANTATIONS, 1882–1911

Year	Real Wages (1897 = 100)	Year	Real Wages (1897 = 100)
1882	204	1897	100
1883	210	1898	98
1884	241	1899	92
1885	239	1900	95
1886	173	1901	85
1887	—	1902	75
1888	—	1903	72
1889	96	1904	80
1890	108	1905	81
1891	169	1906	68
1892	169	1907	60
1893	185	1908	65
1894	134	1909	59
1895	202	1910	62
1896	163	1911	54

Sources: Bustamante, "Efectos económicos del papel moneda durante la regeneración," p. 620, based on data from Hacienda Santa Barbara account books; and Lleras, "El café, antecedentes generales y expansión hasta 1914," based on Hacienda Jónas account books. The two series cover 1882–1897 and 1897–1911, respectively, and appear in Urrutia, *50 años de desarrollo económico colombiano,* Tables 8 and 9, pp. 108, 110). Splicing the two series together at the overlap year ignores the important fact that Santa Barbara is in Cundinamarca and Jónas is in Antioquia, and hence were potentially quite different in their economic experiences and structures. No other sources, and no single source, permit bridging quantitatively across the War of a Thousand Days while including a significant prior period. Therefore this synthetic series must be used with great caution.

TABLE 12
CAPITAL INVESTED, NET PROFITS, AND PROFIT RATE ON A
CUNDINAMARCAN COFFEE HACIENDA, 1886–1900
(THOUSANDS OF PESOS)

Year	Fixed Capital	Total Capital (Thousands of pesos)	Net Profits	Profit Rate (%)
1885	—	36.7	—	—
1886	34.0	—	7.9	23
1887	45.2	—	8.0	18
1888	48.0	—	—	—
1889	51.1	76.6	10.8	14.1
1890	54.5	77.3	10.3	13.3
1891	57.8	83.8	11.9	14.3
1892	62.6	100.5	13.3	13.2
1893	68.0	110.1	13.0	11.8
1894	70.0	119.6	23.5	19.7
1895	70.0	165.0	46.5	28.2
1896	80.0	216.4	57.7	26.7
1897	78.2	205.5	47.4	18.4
1898	80.0	165.1	14.4	8.7
1899	80.0	141.3	32.1	11.3
1900	—	136.4	27.1	20.0*

SOURCES: Bustamante, "Efectos económicos del papel moneda durante la regeneración," p. 613; and Palacios, *El café en Colombia,* Tables 2.4 and 2.6 on pp. 68 and 72. Where numbers conflicted, Palacios was preferred. All data were derived from account books of the Hacienda Santa Barbara. The concepts of net profits, and hence of the profit rate, is not necessarily consistent with modern accounting concepts of profit.

*Hypothetical calculation made by Herrera Restrepo; there were no shipments that year to Europe.

TABLE 13

DATA ON 3 VARIABLES ASSOCIATED WITH COFFEE CULTIVATION AND EXPORT, 1890–1899, 1901–1911

Year	Exports (thousands of 60-kilo sacks)	Coffee Prices in New York 4 yrs. before (1923 = 100)	Real Wages on 2 Coffee Haciendas (1897 = 100)
1894	324	67	134
1895	344	74	202
1896	456	73	163
1897	441	82	100
1898	510	72	98
1899	371	70	92
1905	487	(38)	81
1906	610	47	68
1907	545	46	60
1908	582	49	65
1909	678	47	59
1910	548	46	62
1911	606	49	54

SOURCES: For exports: Diego Monsalve, *Colombia cafetera,* (Barcelona: Artes Gráficas, 1927), reproduced in Alvaro Tirado Mejía, *Introducción a la historia económica de Colombia* (Medellín: La Carreta, 1971), Third Edition. For coffee prices: Urrutia y Arrubla, eds., *Compendio de estadísticas históricas de Colombia,* p. 212; for real wages: see Table 11 of this text.

TABLE 14

**PROSPECTIVE COSTS AND REVENUES FROM A 100,000-TREE
COFFEE PLANTATION, BASED ON BUREAU OF THE AMERICAN
REPUBLICS ESTIMATE, 1893 (THOUSANDS OF DOLLARS)**

Year	Costs of Labor and Transport	Revenues	Net Return
1	6	0	− 6
2	5	0	− 5
3	2	0	− 2
4	12.5	20	+ 7.5
5	7.5	20	+ 12.5
.	.	.	.
.	.	.	.
.	.	.	.
.	.	.	.
20	7.5	20	+ 12.5

SOURCE: Bureau of the American Republics, "Coffee in America," *Monthly Bulletin of the Bureau of the American Republics,* October 1893, pp. 25–26. The cost of machinery has been added to fourth-year costs.

TABLE 15
SIMULATED COSTS AND REVENUES FROM A 100,000-TREE COFFEE PLANTATION BEGINNING OPERATIONS IN 1893 AND EXPERIENCING WAGE AND PRICE TRENDS AS OBSERVED, 1893–1911
(THOUSANDS OF DOLLARS)

Year	Costs of Labor and Transport*	Revenues[†]	Net Return
1893	6.0	0	− 6.0
1894	3.6	0	− 3.6
1895	2.2	0	− 2.2
1896	11.0	15.6	+ 4.6
1897	4.1	13.6	+ 9.5
1898	4.0	11.5	+ 7.5
1899	3.8	8.5	+ 4.7
1900	3.8	6.9	+ 3.1
1901	3.5	0[‡]	− 3.5
1902	3.1	10.8	+ 7.7
1903	2.9	10.6	+ 7.7
1904	3.2	11.3	+ 8.1
1905	3.3	10.8	+ 7.5
1906	2.8	10.6	+ 7.8
1907	2.4	11.3	+ 8.9
1908	2.6	11.5	+ 8.9
1909	2.4	11.0	+ 8.6
1910	2.6	15.2	+12.6
1911	2.2	16.8	+14.6

Sources: For land clearing and initial expense, the same as Table 14, except that costs were deflated by the real wage index of Table 11.

*This is the cost series in Table 14, deflated by real wage series in Table 11. Some distortion or bias may be introduced because of the difference in movements of wages and transport costs, which were not investigated.

[†]Revenues from Table 14, deflated by the coffee price index in Table 6, which is available for the years through 1911 in the same source as for the data in Table 6.

[‡]No price data are available for this year. The simulation thus assumes there were no sales.

TABLE 16
ESTIMATED COSTS AND REVENUES FOR HACIENDA SANTA BARBARA, 1885–1900 (THOUSANDS OF CURRENT DOLLARS)

Year	(1) Capital "Capital"*	(2) Costs "Value"[†]	(3) Current Costs[‡]	(4) Revenues[§]	(5) Net[‖]	(6) Return[¶]
1885	36.7	36.7	0	10.6	− 26.1	− 26.1
1886	—	(2.7)	6.5	9.2	+ 2.7	+ 5.4
1887	—	11.1	5.7	18.0	+ 12.3	+ 1.2
1888	—	2.9	10.3	23.6	+ 13.3	+ 10.4
1889	40.	3.1	11.3	26.0	− 25.3	+ 11.6
1890	0.7	3.4	11.1	28.0	+ 16.2	+ 13.5
1891	6.4	3.3	10.6	24.2	+ 7.2	+ 10.3
1892	16.8	4.8	14.4	24.7	− 6.5	+ 5.5
1893	9.6	5.4	15.4	24.7	− 0.3	+ 3.9
1894	9.5	2.0	19.8	51.9	+ 22.6	+ 30.1
1895	45.4	—	32.4	83.1	+ 5.3	+ 50.7
1896	51.4	10.0	30.5	60.6	− 21.3	+ 20.1
1897	(11.0)	(1.8)	37.7	98.6	+ 70.9	+ 62.7
1898	(40.0)	1.8	34.9	44.3	+ 49.4	+ 7.7
1899	(23.8)	0	22.1	52.1	+ 53.8	+ 30.0
1900	(4.9)	0	19.0	0	− 14.1	− 19.0

*Column 1 is based on col. 1 of table in M. Palacios, *Coffee in Colombia, 1850–1970: An Economic, Social, and Political History* (Cambridge: Cambridge University Press, 1980), p. 48, assuming no change in total capital for 1885–1888, and estimating additions to capital in subsequent years as the difference in capital for year *t* with that for year *t*-1.

[†]Column 2 is based on col. 2 of table in Palacios, *Coffee in Colombia*, p. 48, following the same method as used for column 1 here and assuming that total capital stays at 80,000 pesos to the close of the period.

[‡]Column 3 is the same as col. 10 of table in Palacios, *Coffee in Colombia*, p. 49, which includes wages, salaries, transport, insurance, and commissions.

[§]Column 4 is col. 11 times col. 13 of table in Palacios, *Coffee in Colombia*, p. 49, but using the 1886 price for that year as well as for 1885 since no data were given.

[‖]Column 5 is column 4 minus the sum of columns 1 and 3.

[¶]Column 6 is column 4 minus the sums of columns 2 and 3.

TABLE 17
CUNDINAMARCA'S COFFEE FARMS IN 1932 AND 1940

Year	No. of Farms	Production, in 60-kilo sacks
1932	13,812	364,379
1940	30,270	370,018

SOURCE: Ministerio del Trabajo, *Seguridad social campesina* (Bogotá: Editorial Cosmos, 1954); reprinted in Urrutia, *50 años de desarrollo económico colombiano*, p. 93.

NOTES

1. W. P. McGreevey, *An Economic History of Colombia, 1845–1930* (New York: Cambridge University Press, 1971), p. 304.

2. C. I. Lewis, *Mind and the World Order* (New York: Dover Publications, 1956, originally published 1929), p. 303.

3. Ibid, pp. 307–308.

4. W. D. Nordhaus and J. Tobin, "Is Growth Obsolete?" in *Economic Growth* (New York: National Bureau of Economic Research, 1972), pp. 1–80.

5. A. Collver, *Birth Rates in Latin America: New Estimates of Historical Trends and Fluctuations,* res. ser. no. 7 (Berkeley: Institute of International Studies, University of California, 1965).

6. M. Urrutia Montoya and M. Arrubla, eds., *Compendio de estadísticas históricas de Colombia* (Bogotá: Universidad Nacional de Colombia, 1970), pp. 106–108 offers a systematic presentation of data developed by this author in collaboration with Jorge Rodríguez and Michael Conniff in the period 1967–1969 when all three of us were at the University of California at Berkeley. These data were subjected to critical review by the Instituto de Estudios Colombianos, *Historia económica de Colombia: un debate en marcha,* (Bogotá: Biblioteca del Banco Popular, 1979), by F. Safford, *Aspectos del siglo XIX en Colombia* (Medellín: Ediciones Hombre Nuevo, 1977), and by M. Palacios, *El café en Colombia (1850–1970). Una história económica, social, y política* (Bogotá: Editorial Presencia, 1979); (English translation: *Coffee in Columbia, 1850–1970: An Economic, Social, and Political History* [Cambridge: Cambridge University Press, 1980]), for lack of critical attention to the shortcomings of the original sources. Subsequent scholars have returned to the original data, of both Colombian and trading-partner origin, in an effort to rebuild a statistical base as reliable as possible. J. A. Ocampo, "Las exportaciones colombianas en el siglo XIX," *Desarrollo y sociedad,* 4 (Bogotá: Facultad de Economía, Universidad de los Andes), pp. 163–226, has done a thorough job. A comparison of his Table 1, col. 1a, p. 167, with the data in Figure 1 of this essay does not bring to light any serious differences, except that the figure's current-dollar estimates, 1860–1880, appear somewhat higher than his.

7. McGreevey, *An Economic History of Colombia,* p. 104.

8. Calculated from data on Ferrocarril de Antioquia freight movements that appear in Diego Monsalve, *Monografía estadística del Departamento de Antioquia* (Medellín: Imprenta Oficial, 1929), p. 159. For machinery imports, see A. López and J. Rodríguez, *Estadística de Antioquia* (Medellín, 1914), pp. 150–152.

9. Mariano Ospina Pérez, "La industria cafetera en Colombia," *Boletín del Departamento de Contraloría,* 78 (Bogotá, March 1934), p. 252.

10. A scientific analysis of this period appears in two works by Vernon D. Wickizer: *Coffee, Tea and Cocoa* (Palo Alto, Calif.: Stanford University Press, 1951); and *The World Coffee Economy, with Special Reference to Control Schemes* (Palo Alto, Calif.: Stanford University Food Research Institute, 1943). Colombian interest in coffee cultivation, which began in the mid-nineteenth century, was undoubtedly stimulated by the "gilded exile," General Rafael Uribe

Uribe, who spent several years in Brazil and wrote a book titled *Por la América del Sur* (Bogotá, 1908) that extolled the virtues of coffee cultivation. The general was the model for a character in Gabriel García Márquez's novel *One Hundred Years of Solitude.*

11. These data and percentages are drawn from Banco de la República, *XXXVIII y XXXIX informe anual del gerente a la junta directiva,* part II (Bogotá, 1960), pp. 202, 203, 216. The data assembled by Ocampo, *Las exportaciones colombianas en el siglo XIX,* p. 176, differ somewhat from these figures.

12. Palacios, *El café en Colombia (1850–1970),* pp. 37–80.

13. Marco Palacios, "Las 'condiciones de la oferta' de café," Seminario sobre historia económica de Colombia (Bogotá: Instituto de Estudios Colombianos, 1979), offers an interesting commentary on non-Antioqueño aspects of economic change. He rejects in particular the unidirectional movement toward progress as an adequate description of economic events in Colombia in this century. Malcolm Deas "A Colombian Coffee Estate: Santa Barbara, Cundinamarca, 1870–1912," in Kenneth Duncan and Ian Rutledge, *Land and Labor in Latin America* (Cambridge: Cambridge University Press, 1977), pp. 269–298, reveals new perspectives on coffee cultivation in Cundinamarca.

14. Safford, *Aspectos del siglo XIX en Colombia,* pp. 270–276.

15. Reyes' speech quoted in *La Opinión,* 10, February 1902; cited in Charles W. Bergquist, *Coffee and Conflict in Colombia, 1886–1910* (Durham, North Carolina: Duke University Press, 1978), p. 221.

16. Data drawn from McGreevey, *An Economic History of Colombia,* table 32, p. 256. The distinction between coffee and other railways is explained on p. 261.

17. James J. Parsons, *Antioqueño Colonization in Western Colombia* (Berkeley: University of California Press, 1948), p. 146.

18. Miguel Urrutia, *The Development of the Colombian Labor Movement* (New Haven, Conn.: Yale University Press, 1969), p. 63.

19. Bergquist, *Coffee and Conflict in Colombia.*

20. Great Britain. Foreign Office, Diplomatic and Consular Reports, "The Present State of the Coffee Trade, to 1903," Vice-Consul Spencer S. Dickson, p. 8.

21. Aristides Fernández and José Joaquín Casas, joint letter of resignation submitted to President Marroquín; cited and discussed in detail by Bergquist, *Coffee and Conflict in Colombia,* p. 208.

22. This comparison was suggested by E. E. Hagen, *On the Theory of Social Change: How Economic Growth Begins* (Homewood, Ill.: Dorsey Press, 1962), p. 379, who cites it as evidence of "a people whose need for aggression was almost uncontrollable."

23. Deas, "A Colombian Coffee Estate," pp. 285–290.

24. Bergquist, *Coffee and Conflict in Colombia,* p. 203.

25. Colombia, Presidente, *Mensaje al Congreso Nacional, 1909* (Bogotá: Imprenta Nacional, 1909), p. 6. I am indebted to Carlos Arturo Marulanda Ramírez, formerly of Cambridge University, for making available to me a preliminary draft of a chapter from his thesis, from which this quotation is drawn.

26. Bergquist, *Coffee and Conflict in Colombia,* pp. 195–196.

27. Palacios, *Coffee in Colombia,* pp. 121–140.

28. British consular reports of the period sometimes offered comments on the degree to which paper and metallic currencies were used in calculating the value of exports and imports.

29. Some of the problems discussed in the chapter on foreign trade in Urrutia and Arrubla, eds., *Compendio de estadísticas históricas de Colombia;* see also Ocampo, "Las exportaciones colombianas en el siglo XIX"; and Miguel Urrutia, *Ensayos sobre história económica colombiana* (Bogotá: Fedesarrollo, 1980), p. 120, m. 1.

30. Antonio José Uribe, *Crédito, moneda y bancos* (Bogotá: Librería Colombiana, Camacho Roldán y Tamayo, 1926), p. 11; cited in C. Marulanda Ramírez, "The Pre–1923 Era: Years of Second Class Membership in the World System," ms., p. 53.

31. L. Ospina Vásquez, *Industria y protección en Colombia, 1810–1930* (Medellín: Editorial E.S.F., 1955).

32. Urrutia and Arrubla, eds., *Compendio de estadísticas históricas de Colombia,* pp. 205–206.

33. McGreevey, *An Economic History of Colombia,* pp. 99–210.

34. Instituto de Estudios Colombianos, *Historia económica de Colombia.*

35. In Urrutia, *Ensayos sobre historia económica colombiana,* pp. 99–142.

36. Analyses of persistent disequilibrium (McGreevey, *An Economic History of Colombia,* pp. 111–116) in Colombia's balance of trade would obviously require fundamental revision in light of Ocampo's data.

37. Research figures are Malcolm Deas', in Urrutia, *Ensayos sobre historia económica colombiana,* p. 57.

38. M. Urrutia Montoya, *50 años de desarrollo económico colombiano* (Bogotá: La Carreta, 1979), pp. 38–42.

39. Kathyrn H. Wylie, *The Agriculture of Colombia,* Foreign Agriculture Bulletin No. 1 (Washington, D.C.: U.S. Department of Agriculture, Office of Foreign Agriculture Relations, 1942). Wylie's data are presented graphically in McGreevey, *An Economic History of Colombia,* fig. 6, p. 134.

40. Estimates based on McGreevey, *An Economic History of Colombia,* table 17, p. 122. The rate of expansion of cropland for domestic consumption was assumed to be the same as that for the growth of population.

41. Bustamante, "Efectos económicos del papel moneda durante la regeneración."

42. Palacios, *Coffee in Colombia.*

43. Federación Nacional de Cafeteros de Colombia, "Censo cafetero levantado en 1932," *Boletín de Estadística,* 1 (1933): 117–156; McGreevey, *An Economic History of Colombia,* p. 198. Uribe Uribe, *Por la América del Sur,* had argued that as early as 1894 a quarter of the Colombia population depended on coffee. Palacios, *Coffee in Colombia,* p. 138, labels that assertion "a blatant lie."

44. *Industria y protección en Colombia,* p. 429. Data for selected years during the period 1727–1892, from Ospina Vásquez are supplemented with figures from 1962 in McGreevey, *An Economic History of Colombia,* table 18, p. 132.

45. A. Pardo Pardo, *Geografía económica y humana de Colombia* (Bogotá: Ediciones Tercer Mundo, 1972), pp. 221–236. Surprisingly, this work was not once

mentioned at the seminar held in 1975, despite the potential richness of the empirical data that it contains.

46. Ibid., p. 229.

47. The value of r^2 for this linear regression is only 0.07, not significant for the 32 observations (leaving out 1909–1910 and 1912–1913) in table 10. A correct interpretation might be that there was no discernible trend in real wages over the whole of this period. For the shorter period, 1889–1908, the regression equation is $RS = 3323 - 1.71T$, so that the real salary appears to be declining 2-3 percent per year. The instability of the sign of T and low r^2 suggest there was little or no trend.

48. M. Cotes, "Régimen alimenticio de los jornaleros de la sabana de Bogotá," *Anales de la Academia Nacional de Medicina*, I, no. 1 (Bogotá, 1893): 5–48. Cotes had a sample of about 200 families.

49. Ibid., pp. 28, 38.

50. José Francisco Socarrás, "Alimentación de la clase obrera en Bogotá," *Anales de economía y estadística*, 2, no. 5 (1939): 29.

51. Ibid., p. 32.

52. Maurice Zeitlin, "Camilo's Colombia," in M. Zeitlin, ed., *Father Camilo Torres' Revolutionary Writings* (New York: Harper Colophon Books, 1972), p. 14. Zeitlin has quoted in turn from Lyman H. Legters et al; *U.S. Army Area Handbook for Colombia*, 2nd ed. (Washington, D.C.: U.S. Department of the Army; U.S. Government Printing Office), pp. 263, 286–287.

53. William C. Sayres, "Ritual Drinking, Ethnic Status, and Inebriety in Rural Colombia," *Quarterly Journal for the Study of Alcoholism* (March 1956); cf. related papers in David J. Pittman and Charles R. Snyder, eds., *Society, Culture and Drinking Patterns* (New York: Wiley, 1962).

54. Palacios, *Coffee in Colombia*, p. 110.

55. Ospina Vásquez, *Industria y protección en Colombia*, p. 429; and M. Arango, *Café e industria, 1850–1930*. (Bogotá: Carlos Valencia Editores, 1977).

56. E. J. Hamilton, *American Treasure and the Price Revolution in Spain, 1501–1650* (Cambridge, Mass.: Harvard University Press, 1934).

57. D. Bustamante Roldán, "Efectos económicos del papel moneda durante la regeneración," *Cuadernos Colombianos*, 1, No. 4 (Medellín, 1974), pp. 559–660.

58. F. Lleras, "El café, antecedentes generales y expansión hasta 1914," I have not seen Lleras's work but rely on Miguel Urrutia, *50 años de desarrollo económico colombiano*, which I cite hereon as the source for the data originally presented in the Lleras thesis.

59. Palacios, *Coffee in Colombia*.

60. Urrutia, *50 años de desarrollo económico colombiano*, pp. 106–115.

61. Pardo Pardo, *Geografía económica y humana de Colombia*, p. 234.

62. Great Britain. Foreign Office, Diplomatic and Consular Reports, "The Present State of the Coffee Trade in Colombia," (1903), p. 6.

63. Ibid.

64. Ibid.

65. Deas, "Colombian Coffee Estate: Santa Barbara," p. 292.

66. Bustamante, "Efectos económicos del papel moneda," p. 613.

67. Palacios, *El café en Colombia*, p. 72, col. 1.

68. Bustamante, "Efectos económicos del papel moneda," p. 613.

69. Palacios, *El café en Colombia*, p. 68.

70. There are data for both series for 11 years between 1886 and 1899; the coefficient of correlation, $r = +0.097$, is not statistically significant.

71. $r_{12.3}$ is the symbol for the partial correlation between variables 1 and 2 when 3 is held constant.

72. Urrutia and Arrubla, eds., *Compendio de estadísticas históricas*, table 3, pp. 212–213.

73. J. A. Bejarano, "El fin de la economía exportadora y los orígenes del problema agrario," pt. II, *Cuadernos colombianos*, 7, (Medellín, 1975): 388.

74. Parsons, *Antioqueño Colonization in Western Colombia*, pp. 137–153; Palacios, *Coffee in Colombia*, pp. 180–197.

75. Palacios, *El café en Colombia*, p. 58.

76. Bureau of the American Republics, "Coffee in America," *Monthly Bulletin*, (Washington, D.C., October 1893), pp. 25–26.

77. At the time of the 1932 coffee census only 14 percent of producing farms had 60,000 coffee bushes or more, the size that Beyer used to distinguish large from medium and small holdings. Note that these units were producing units, not ownership units, so that the percentage of large-holding decision-makers may have been smaller still. Nonetheless, these large holders are believed to have dominated small producers in their neighborhood in the marketing of coffee. See Palacios, "Las 'condiciones de oferta' de café."

78. A simillar procedure was used in McGreevey, *An Economic History of Colombia*, pp. 271–277, to calculate the rate of return to investments in the railways of Colombia in the years 1922–1957. The estimated internal rate of return to rail investments was about 20 percent using the most likely estimates of costs and benefits.

79. Information is available for only 19 years, not 20. The effect on r of shortening the assumed payout period by one year is slight because of the high discount rate.

80. Palacios, *Coffee in Colombia*, pp. 48–49.

81. Deas, "A Colombian Coffee Estate."

82. Palacios, *Coffee in Colombia*, pp. 25–54.

83. Ibid., p. 229.

84. R. Cortés Conde and S. J. Stein, eds., *Latin America: A Guide to Economic History, 1820–1930* (Berkeley: University of California Press, 1977), pp. 370–381.

85. Eduardo Lemaitre, *Panamá y su separación de Colombia, una historia que parece novela* (Bogotá: Biblioteca Banco Popular, 1972).

86. Bergquist, *Coffee and Conflict in Colombia*.

87. David McCullough, *The Path Between the Seas: The Creation of the Panama Canal, 1870–1914* (New York: Simon and Schuster, 1977).

88. Lemaitre, *Panamá y su separación de Colombia*, p. 299.

89. McCullough, *The Path Between the Seas*, pp. 329–341.

90. Bergquist, *Coffee and Conflict in Colombia*, p. 188.

91. *El Nuevo Tiempo*, June 21, 1902, cited in ibid., p. 192.

92. Enrique Caballero, *Historia económica de Colombia* (Bogotá: Italgraf, 1970), p. 159, author's translation.

93. McCullough, *The Path Between the Seas,* p. 334.

94. Ibid., pp. 334–335.

95. Ibid.

96. Lemaitre, *Panamá y su separación de Colombia,* p. 546.

97. Hagen, *On the Theory of Social Change.*

98. R. Albert Berry, R. Hellman, and M. Solaum, eds., *Politics of Compromise: Coalition Government in Colombia* (New Brunswick, N.J.: Transaction Books, 1980), p. 10.

99. R. A. Berry, *Real Wage Trends in Colombian Manufacturing and Construction during the Twentieth Century* (research rept. no. 7403, Dept. of Economics, University of Western Ontario, 1974), table A–1, col 4.

100. Pierre Gilhodes, "Agrarian Struggles in Colombia," in Rodolfo Stavenhagen, *Agrarian Problems and Peasant Movements in Latin America* (New York, 1970), pp. 411–414.

101. John Womack, *Zapata and the Mexican Revolution* (New York: Knopf, 1969).

102. H. Tovar, *El movimiento campesino en Colombia durante los siglos XIX y XX* (Bogotá: Ediciones Libres, 1975), pp. 26–28.

103. Arango, *Café e industria, 1850–1930,* p. 163.

104. Palacios, *Coffee in Colombia,* p. 245.

105. Ibid., p. 229.

106. Ibid., p. 244.

107. Albert Hirschman, *Journeys Toward Progress* (New York: Twentieth Century Fund, 1963), pp. 101 ff.

108. Tovar, *El movimiento campesino,* pp. 35–88.

109. Cf. Clark Reynolds, *The Mexican Economy: Twentieth–Century Structure and Growth* (New Haven, Conn.: Yale University Press, 1970) and Roger Hansen, *The Politics of Mexican Development* (New York: Johns Hopkins University Press, 1971).

110. Bergquist, *Coffee and Conflict in Colombia,* p. 196.

111. Ibid., p. 256.

112. Cortés Conde and Stein, *Latin America,* pp. 376–381.

113. Safford, *The Ideal of the Practical,* p. 232.

114. Hagen, *On the Theory of Social Change.*

115. W. W. Rostow, *The World Economy: History and Prospect* (Austin: University of Texas Press, 1978), p. 669.

116. W. P. McGreevey, *An Economic History of Colombia* (Ph.D. diss., Massachusetts Institute of Technology, Cambridge, Mass., 1964).

117. Rostow, *The World Economy,* p. 662.

118. McGreevey, *An Economic History of Colombia;* and Cortés Condes and Stein, *Latin America.*

3
The Capitalist Export Economy in
BRAZIL
1884–1930*

*João Manoel Cardoso de
Mello
Maria da Conceição Tavares*

INTRODUCTION

This essay will analyze the formation and dynamics of Brazil's capitalist export economy. To do this, we must have in mind the origins of that system, or more precisely, the passage from a colonial to a capitalist export economy by way of a national mercantile-slave economy.[1] This historical process is best understood in light of the transformations undergone by world capitalism since the Industrial Revolution—changes that brought crisis to the old colonial order.[2]

Metropolitan commercial capital developed the colonial economy for the purpose of stimulating primitive accumulation at home during the transition from feudalism to capitalism. Significantly, in Latin America commercial interests did not limit themselves to the exploitation of pre-conquest modes of production; rather, they extended their normal range of activities to engage not only in trade but also in production itself. In so doing, they founded the colonial economy, and very early gave it a mercantile character by assuring the realization of production in the world market. In colonizing for capitalist ends mercantile interests asserted con-

*The authors would like to thank Rae Flory for her translation.

trol of the colonial economy by "reinventing" servile and slave labor. They effected the continual reproduction of slavery's intrinsic social relations through the slave traffic—a sector of colonial commerce and a principal source of accumulation. In sum, commercial capital mobilized Brazil's productive forces and implanted corresponding social relations of production to serve its own ends.

If at the outset the evolution of capitalism and the colonial economy constituted a single, unified process, and if this process stimulated capitalism in its early manufacturing stage, this same movement eventually led to the Industrial Revolution and the emergence of specifically capitalist modes of production. Thereafter accumulation relied on its own momentum for growth and ceased to require external props. The transition to industrial capitalism both foreshadowed and hastened the ultimate dissolution of the colonial economy, as mutual advantage turned into antagonism and what had once furthered development now obstructed it. From this point on, the relations between capitalism and the colonial economy became increasingly contradictory.

With its hunger for markets, the Industrial Revolution provoked crisis in the relatively complex precapitalist economies with which it came into contact. This was generally true in Latin America where, nonetheless, European industrial capitalism did not destroy the economic bedrock of forced labor. Rather, its major impact at this juncture was to contribute decisively to the demise of the colonial pact and to the formation of independent national states. The existing labor arrangement remained intact both because it was in no way affected by the entry of British manufactured goods and because the choice of substituting free for forced labor had become a *national* decision. In other words, the passing of one feature of the colonial economy—the dual political domination and commercial monopoly exercised by the metropolis—opened Latin American markets to British industrial capital. At the same time, however, the emergence of national states meant that Latin American development would cease to be a purely "reflexive" process. At best, free trade industrialism could use all the resources it could muster to exert pressure on the traffic in slaves; it could not, by itself, impose its objectives.

If competitive capitalism initially brought crisis to precapitalist economies, it soon created the conditions for their reorganization. In Britain the passage of the Corn Laws in 1846 roundly defeated agrarian protectionist interests, while the shift in the focus of accumulation from the textile industry to the capital goods industry (definitive with the Great Railway Mania of 1845–1847) encouraged the exportation of capital— defined as money capital and capital goods, but principally as the extension of capitalist social relations of production.[3]

It was at this point that British industrial capitalists promoted India's cotton export industry based on wage labor, thereby reorganizing the Indian economy to serve their own interests.[4] Circumstances were different in Latin America, however, where the British lacked both the power and the incentive to reorganize individual national economies. Here Britain was dealing not with its own colonies but with independent nations, albeit weak ones. Furthermore, in view of Britain's competition from her own colonies and from other industrialized nations such as the United States, investment opportunities in Latin America did not seem particularly attractive.[5] In other words, the weakness of capitalism's power of diffusion in this region ultimately derived not from the absence or instability of external demand but from the internal difficulties posed by mounting vigorous export economies. Where national mercantile capital proved capable of undertaking this task, as in Brazil, it became possible in a certain sense to create external demand. For their part, capital imports, although less visible, played a significant part in Brazil's transition from a colonial to a capitalist export economy.

It should be added, however, that during its competitive phase (from the Industrial Revolution to the beginning of the depression of 1873) capitalism's power of diffusion was itself limited; only England had advanced sufficiently to promote the extension of capitalism abroad. With the emergence of monopoly capitalism between 1880 and 1900, circumstances changed dramatically. Monopoly capitalism greatly accelerated the subversion of social relations and the global diffusion of capitalism by converting the exportation of capital—now directed chiefly at precapitalist areas—into a basic characteristic of the world market.[6]

We can identify three concrete historical situations in which capital from industrialized nations penetrated precapitalist economies. In the first, capital was invested in largely undifferentiated precapitalist systems that, for the most part, had not been incorporated into the world market. In such circumstances one can correctly refer to "imported capitalism" imposed entirely from without, inasmuch as internal factors had little to do with economic reorganization.

The second form of capitalist penetration consisted of the conversion of previously unoccupied colonial areas into large-scale producers of foodstuffs. Massive immigration made it possible to overcome the resistance of small private commercial producers and to implant capital as a social relation, while the importation of means of production permitted the installation of the infrastructure so vital to the operation of the food export business. In this case, which concerns a particular form of capitalist colonization, it is preferable to speak of the *transplantation* of capitalism.[7]

The experience of much of politically independent Latin America was substantially different. It is true that roughly between 1880 and 1900 both the extraordinary inflow of capital (whether channeled into the productive nuclei of the export sectors or into their supporting infrastructures) and mass immigration in some countries were crucial to the formation of capitalist export economies. Nevertheless, Latin American economic history cannot be categorized in terms of either the importation or the transplantation of capitalism, since development in this instance was not strictly a function of the actions of the industrial nations. To the contrary, any study of economic change in Latin America must necessarily begin with an analysis of the dynamics of the national economies themselves and then consider how immigration and the transfer of capital acted as catalysts to transform these economies from within.

In conclusion, the passage from a colonial to a capitalist export economy was a complex process that must be viewed from a broad perspective. Economic change was determined in the first instance by internal factors, and in the last instance by the evolution of world capitalism—that is, by the emergence of industrial capitalism, its development during a competitive stage, and the transition from competitive to monopoly capitalism.

This is precisely the perspective we adopt to outline the beginnings of the Brazilian capitalist export economy. Thereafter we examine the dynamics of that economic system in the period 1889 through 1932. Our analysis of this phase of Brazilian development begins with a study of the cyclical movement of coffee capital, the focal point of accumulation in these years. Next we offer an assessment of the relationship between official economic policy and capital accumulation in the coffee sector.

Once these fundamental issues have been addressed, we turn our attention to the establishment of large-scale industry in Brazil and, in doing so, attempt to clarify the relations between the Brazilian economy and the dominant monopoly capitalist economies. It is our contention that the subordinate position of Brazil in world capitalism was determined both on the side of realization of coffee capital and on the side of accumulation of industrial capital. This approach ultimately reveals how the development of monopoly capitalism determined the movement of the capitalist export economy, and how this movement translated internally into the hegemony of coffee capital—predominantly mercantile—over industrial capital.

We further propose to explain the industrial expansion that took place between 1895 and 1929 and to deal, finally, with the crisis of 1929. This critical period had a decisive impact on the coffee export complex and prepared the way for a change in the pattern of accumulation within the Brazilian economy that, from the 1930s on, initiated a new phase in the country's capitalist development.

I. COFFEE CAPITAL: THE DYNAMICS OF ACCUMULATION

There can be little doubt that the coffee export complex was the dynamic center of the Brazilian economy between 1886 and 1930. Accordingly, the expansion of coffee capital, an eminently cyclical process, is the logical point of departure for understanding the pattern of accumulation in this period.

Accumulation and the Cyclical Development of Coffee Capital

The coffee export complex consisted of a productive nucleus that included the processing industry, as well as an urban sector that provided transportation, commercial export-import, and financial services. In consequence, coffee capital, with its agro-industrial, commercial, and financial components, was multifaceted.

We can begin by explaining the reproduction of coffee capital as a whole. In the process of production, coffee agriculture incurred certain determined costs—the depreciation of fixed capital, wages, commercial and financial charges, transportation costs, and taxes—and also realized a profit. Those expenses relating to commerce, finance, and transportation also represented income for their respective sectors, which, in turn, was converted into the depreciation of fixed capital (railroads, port facilities, commercial buildings, etc.), input costs (fuel, etc.), payrolls, taxes, and profits.

Furthermore, we can assume that taxes would be used to acquire means of production and to meet payrolls, and that profits would be divided between the consumption of luxury goods (capitalists' consumption) and accumulation, and that wages would be devoted entirely to the purchase of food and manufactured consumer goods. It is clear, then, that coffee production simultaneously comprehended a demand for land, labor, and means of production on the side of accumulation, and a demand for foodstuffs, wage goods, and luxury goods on the side of current expenditures.

Both the accumulation of means of production and capitalists' consumption were financed with the importing capacity generated by the coffee export complex itself. However, once Brazil's commercial food production had expanded and an industrial sector was in place, domestic output could attend to the demand for food and manufactured wage goods, at which point the reproduction of labor became internalized.

The movement of coffee capital tended to follow a cyclical pattern, which was accentuated to some degree by the nature of official economic policy. The "natural" cycle of coffee production followed from the fixed character of cultivation, in particular the maturation period of four to five years. Thus the supply of coffee was inelastic in the short run and responded slowly to variations in external demand (which responded to fluctuations within the importing economies).

Expansion began with a rise in external prices prompted either by prosperity abroad (which boosted demand) or by a contraction in supply owing to climatic factors. The rise in external prices would be transferred to domestic prices according to the movement of the exchange rate. Profits would climb and the rate of accumulation would increase or not, depending on profit expectations. On the assumption that new investments would prove lucrative, additional productive capacity would be created. Once the young coffee trees began producing, world and internal prices would fall in relation to, respectively, conditions abroad and the evolution of the rate of exchange. The rate of return would diminish, gradually retarding accumulation, and a period of depression would begin.

When we look more closely at the impact of a decline in external and internal prices on the coffee export complex, we must necessarily distinguish among (1) productive capacity in use, (2) productive capacity under construction, and (3) the projected increase in productive capacity.

The first obviously consists of the coffee trees actually producing. Some planters in the productive nucleus barely managed to cover their monetary costs and became marginalized because their plantations were located on low-yield lands and their trees, on the average, had passed the optimum age for maximum productivity. When depreciation is taken into account, these enterprises showed negative rates of return. In contrast, the intramarginal producers enjoyed positive profit rates that, nonetheless varied according to soil fertility, the average age of their coffee trees, and freight charges, which reflected proximity to the ports of embarcation.

Productive capacity under construction includes the young coffee trees planted but not yet producing. At this stage, money costs consisted entirely of wages and the servicing of the bank loans inevitably contracted at some point to meet payrolls and/or to purchase land.

Finally, the desired rate of increase in productive capacity refers to the number of new seedlings the planters hoped to cultivate. This was largely determined by profit expectations.

The initial result of a decline in external and internal prices would be a reduction in the profit margins of working enterprises, part of which would immediately be absorbed by a fall in money wages. Marginal producers, together with the least productive intramarginal planters, would be ruined and a portion of the coffee sector's productive capacity would be wiped out. The proprietors of new trees that became productive during the depression would find themselves near insolvency, unable to meet their bank debts; the planting of new seedlings would cease altogether.

The crisis originating in the productive nucleus would soon spread to the urban branch of the export complex. It would not only engulf the commercial-financial and transportation sectors but would affect industry and commercial food and raw material production as well (once these were established). The fall in income would curtail the demand for imports and lower government revenues, which were based on tariffs, and this would provoke a new cut in demand, assuming policymakers sought to balance the budget.

In the worst of hypotheses the crisis would have run its course when the coffee export complex reached its lowest point—when intramarginal producers could cover only their monetary costs and capitalists' consumption. Then, under the combined stimulation of a diminished productive capacity on the one hand, and the reactivation of external demand (reflecting conditions within the importing countries) on the other, recuperation would begin.

In sum, the development of the capitalist coffee export economy not only responded to cyclical movements within the importer nations but was also governed by factors operating on the side of supply, in particular the four- to five-year delay between planting and the first harvest.

Moreover, while the *duration* of expansion and depression was clearly tied to fluctuations within the importing economies, it further depended on the economic policies of the government. This is not to say that policy was formulated in a vacuum, but that, given the structural exigencies imposed by the pattern of accumulation, official policy could strengthen expansion or deepen depression.

The First Coffee Cycle (1886–1918)

During the years 1886 through 1897 the coffee economy enjoyed a period of remarkable growth. Average production climbed from 5.2 million bags* between 1886–1887 and 1890–1891 to 6.5 million bags between 1891–1892 and 1895–1896. Then, in the years 1896–1897 to 1902–1903, when the coffee trees planted from 1891 to 1897 became fully productive, average output reached 11.4 million bags.[8] For the most part, expansion took place in the state of São Paulo. That region's installed productive capacity— that is, its stock of coffee trees—trebled from 220 to 665 million plants between 1890 and 1902, while its share of Brazil's total yield increased from 40 percent in 1885 to 60 percent at the turn of the century.[9]

At the time conditions were extremely favorable for accumulation. The extension of the railroad system opened new lands for coffee cultivation, while mass immigration generated a supply of labor that was more

---

*One bag equals 60 kilos.

than sufficient to satisfy the urban and rural requirements of the coffee export complex. Between 1888 and 1900 nearly 1 million immigrants arrived in Brazil, 890,000 of whom settled in São Paulo.[10] Economic changes in Europe in the last two decades of the nineteenth century had led to the formation of an international labor market composed of large contingents of unemployed workers disposed to emigrate. It is well known that during the 1880s central-north and western Europe were the principal points of origin, while during the 1890s the source shifted to southern Europe, to Italy in particular. Ninety percent of all newcomers to Brazil in this period came from southern Europe and the Italians alone represented 60 percent of the total.

Considering the North American and Argentine competition for manpower, the existence of a large pool of free laborers in the international market does not by itself explain the strong current of migration to Brazil. As it happened, however, the diversionary effect of competition faltered during the 1890s as the North American economy entered a period of crisis (1893–1897) and the Argentine economy stagnated. Douglas Graham explains:

> In sum, the indicators strongly suggest that around 1885–1906 the cyclical prosperity of the Brazilian economy became less dependent on the cyclical movements of the American, Argentine, and Italian economies. This fact played an important part in permitting Brazil to import so large a number of immigrants (principally Italians) during the 1890s. It would in fact have been difficult, if not impossible, for Brazil to attract so many immigrants if the Argentine, and particularly the North American, economies had been expanding, and if the Italian economy had been prospering as well.[11]

Thus special conditions at work in the international labor market explain both the abundant supply of labor on hand for the coffee export complex and the prevailing levels of wages (see Table 1).

Wage scales such as those registered during the 1890s were possible only because the coffee complex was able to minimize the effects of the poor development of domestic commercial food production and manufacturing on the physical reproduction of the labor force and on its cost by importing necessary wage goods. The importation of wage goods was substantial in this period, and this importation was, in turn, made possible by an increase in the average value of exports.[12] (see Table 2). At the same time, export receipts facilitated the purchase abroad of means of production both for the urban and rural components of the coffee export complex and for the installation of a domestic wage goods industry.

The enlargement of Brazil's importing capacity reflected favorable marketing conditions abroad. Although exchange appreciation absorbed a good share of the increment, international coffee prices climbed from 10.7

U.S. cents per pound in 1886 to 20.0 cents per pound in 1891. Together the growth of world markets—particularly that of the United States—and the poor harvests of 1887–1888 and 1889–1890 stimulated this upswing.[13] When coffee groves planted under the influence of this price trend began producing in 1891, North American prosperity (which, unlike that of Europe, lasted until 1893) helped prevent a dramatic fall in international prices. More important, when the demand for coffee began to falter, the rate of exchange plummeted, which had the effect of elevating internal prices between 1891 and 1894 and cushioning their fall between 1895 and 1898 (see Table 3).

The result of all this was a sustained rise in profit margins between 1886 and 1894. In the first part of this period (1886–1890) profits expanded in response to the upward movement of all prices and the marked contraction in money wages; and from 1890 to 1894 profits continued to grow— despite the decline in international prices—because the increase in internal prices was proportionally greater than the rise in money wages. Even when the subsequent stability of money wages that was accompanied by a decline in internal prices cut profit margins between 1895 and 1898, the reduction was less than it would have been had the fall in world prices been transferred whole to domestic prices. Thus exchange depreciation was intimately linked to the prolonging and acceleration of expansion between 1891 and 1894, and to the defense of profit margins between 1895 and 1897.

The coffee crisis broke in 1898 and continued until 1906, since the government had little alternative but to give free rein to market forces. External coffee prices fluctuated between 7 and 8 cents per pound from 1897 to 1906, but internal prices fell after 1900 because of exchange appreciation (see Table 4).

The severity of depression depended, above all, on the flexibility of money wages and, as the figures in Table 5 indicate, wages did decline substantially. Thus, grave though it was, the crisis affecting the coffee export complex was more restricted than it would appear at first glance. Further proof of this assessment is the fact that the volume of coffee production and of exports grew appreciably in these years, while the value of exports recuperated to the level registered in 1894.[14]

With the boom in rubber exports, Brazil's import capacity was greatly enlarged and, given the decline in imports and the Funding Loan of 1898, ultimately generated a pronounced appreciation in the rate of exchange (see Table 6). Nevertheless the movement in the exchange rate had a dual effect on the coffee economy: it lowered domestic coffee prices, as we have noted, but it also reduced the cost of imported commodities purchased by wage earners, thereby contributing to a reduction in wages themselves.

Money wages declined not only because of the impact of the coffee crisis on the demand for and cost of labor but also because of the depressed state of the industrial sector. Industrial problems derived in the first instance from conditions within the coffee complex, but they were aggravated by a cut in government spending and by a contractionist monetary policy. Given this set of circumstances, the available evidence indicates that internal prices fell approximately 30 percent between 1899 and 1901, so that while money wages deteriorated, there was no appreciable reduction in real wages.[15]

In sum, because the profit margins of intramarginal producers most certainly had been very high in the previous period, and because money wages proved flexible, most of the installed productive capacity within the coffee sector was preserved at the cost of a pronounced urban crisis. Furthermore, the incomes of enterprises within the productive nucleus remained at elevated levels.[16]

Nevertheless, precisely because most productive capacity was left intact, the gathering of large harvests continued to exert pressure on the coffee market. At the same time, the exchange rate appreciated further, stimulated by the level of receipts from coffee and rubber exports and by the inflow of foreign capital after 1903. This was the state of affairs in 1906, when predictions of an unprecedented harvest threatened to intensify the existing crisis.

As is well known, relief came in the form of the coffee valorization policy embodied in the Taubaté Agreement of 1906. In terms of its objectives, this price-support scheme was unquestionably successful: internal and external prices were held steady until 1909 and climbed between 1910 and 1912, while the exchange rate remained constant (see Table 7).

In addition, productive capacity was stabilized until 1910; only 38 million new trees were cultivated in the state of São Paulo between 1907 and 1910, in contrast to the 460 million planted between 1886 and 1897. Not surprisingly, a new expansive phase began to take shape in the years 1911–1913, when approximately 99 million seedlings were planted in São Paulo. However, this new phase, prompted by rising international and internal prices, was cut short by World War I.[17]

Between 1912 and 1913 world coffee prices declined from 13.8 to 10.1 U.S. cents per pound. However, with the wartime collapse of the exchange situation, a depreciation of about 30 percent bolstered internal prices. Devaluation, together with a slight decline in money wages, eased the coffee crisis, but in view of the volume of existing coffee stocks the outlook for 1917 was not particularly encouraging:

In 1917, with the harvest complete and no way to export it (given the resumption of submarine warfare), coffee stocks accumulated in national ports reached alarming proportions. Reserves in the port of Santos passed from less than a million bags in July of 1916, to nearly six million in July of 1917. In such circumstances the price of coffee in national currency would surely plunge to an extremely low level, probably inferior to the average cost of production. . . .[18]

Furthermore, a bumper crop was predicted for 1917–1918. In response to this forecast and to the growing reserves of coffee, the São Paulo government secured a loan from the União to implement a second valorization program, which withdrew 3.1 million bags of coffee from the market at a cost of 4.9 mil réis per 10 kilos. This second valorization scheme was crucial in sustaining prices and in preventing a worsening of the coffee crisis, especially when one considers that in 1917 the rate of exchange appreciated. Quite apart from the valorization program, as early as 1918 international prices advanced significantly when a frost damaged Brazil's coffee trees and reduced the size of the harvest. Favored by a nearly stable rate of exchange, internal prices rose by nearly 15 percent.

The Expansive Phase of the Second Coffee Cycle, 1919–1929

The coffee export complex enjoyed a period of renewed and remarkable expansion during the 1920s. Production that had averaged about 14.1 million bags between 1914–1915 and 1918–1919, as well as between 1919–1920 and 1923–1924, increased to an average of 18.2 million bags in the years 1924–1925 to 1928–1929. Then, from 1929–1930 to 1933–1934, when the trees planted in the second half of the 1920s became fully productive, average output reached 24.2 million bags.[19]

Once again circumstances favored accumulation. Fertile lands suitable for coffee growing were readily available and the manpower supply was elastic. The coffee economy had at its disposal a good part of the natural increment in the economically active populations of the coffee states of São Paulo, Minas Gerais, and Espírito Santo. And coffee entrepreneurs also drew on a growing current of internal migration and on renewed foreign immigration—of which the Japanese constituted an ever-greater share.[20]

The other branches of the Brazilian economy exhibited scant growth in this period and thus offered little competition for the expanding supply of labor. To illustrate the relatively poor performance of the non-coffee export sectors in these years, suffice it to say that coffee's share of Brazil's total exports passed from 56 percent in 1919 to an average of more than 70 percent in the second half of the 1920s. The evidence further indicates that both industrial and commercial agricultural output registered comparatively low rates of growth in this period.[21]

Apart from the abundance of land and labor, both international and internal price movements (see Table 8) greatly encouraged coffee expansion during the 1920s. This came about not only because the prosperity of the industrialized nations spurred the growth of markets but also because it was possible to have constant recourse to coffee-support programs.

Taking the 1920s *as a whole,* the very auspicious conditions of accumulation and realization explain the fact that within the Brazilian economy almost the only dynamic sector was the coffee sector. However, this generalization must be qualified by pointing out that the decade actually bracketed two subperiods, 1919–1923 and 1924–1929, each of which exhibited its own characteristics of growth.

The increase in production registered between 1924–1925 and 1928–1929 attests to the marked acceleration in accumulation that occurred in the coffee sector between 1919 and 1923. Looking first at commercialization, we see that in 1919 and 1920 the international price of coffee attained the high level of 19.5 U.S. cents per pound—nearly the same price prevailing in 1890. This trend can be explained by two factors: frost damage in 1918 reduced the harvests of 1918–1919 and 1919–1920, while in 1918–1919 speculators undertook to rebuild their depleted inventories in the aftermath of war. Internal prices did not gain so much at this time because of exchange depreciation.

A sudden downturn in the North American economy, together with predictions of yet another large harvest, diminished coffee prospects in 1921. However, the implementation of a third valorization program in 1921, followed by the unremarkable yields of 1921–1922 and 1922–1923 and the recovery of the U.S. economy in 1922, checked the sharp decline in external prices and even promoted their slight recuperation in 1922 and 1923. Meanwhile, internal prices increased substantially between 1921 and 1923 owing to a profound exchange depreciation.

In the first period we are examining, then, internal prices advanced at an accelerating pace, moving from 47.4 to 146.9 mil réis per bag of coffee between 1918 and 1923. The rural wages paid by coffee producers also rose at this time, but not so much as prices, and, accordingly, profit margins in the coffee business expanded considerably.[22] It should be underscored that coffee accumulation in these years was not self-sustaining and could proceed only insofar as expanding domestic industrial and commercial food production contributed to the reproduction of the labor force. That is to say, in 1920 and 1921 the buying power of exports diminished substantially and recuperation in 1922 and 1923 was not sufficient to mitigate the exchange crisis. Since the coffee sector could not generate enough foreign exchange to import the required volume of wage goods, it necessarily relied on the growth of internal production to take up the slack.

In sum, the years 1919 to 1923 were characterized by the combined expansion of the coffee export complex, of primary commodity production, and of industry. The accelerated pace of global accumulation permitted an improvement in rural and urban money wages that culminated in the high level of 1923—a year of extensive coffee planting and notable industrial growth.[23]

The pattern of expansion in the period 1924–1929 offers a striking contrast. International prices climbed to 17.5 U.S. cents per pound in 1924 and thereafter stabilized at around 20–21 cents. Until 1926 internal price behavior followed a somewhat less spectacular course, owing to the exchange appreciation resulting from increased exportation and a greater influx of foreign capital. To break this pattern the government created a Stabilization Fund (Caixa de Estabilização), which was designed to operate in much the same way as the earlier Conversion Fund. The currency was devalued by 20 percent and held at about 40 mil réis to the pound sterling until the crisis of 1929.

The very positive price trends in these years can be explained by the evolution of external demand and, above all, by the operation of the Permanent Defense Policy initiated in 1924. Unlike earlier programs, the objective of the Permanent Defense was not to prevent a fall in prices, but rather to maintain coffee prices at high levels.

Rural money wages deteriorated between 1924 and 1927, but recovered in 1928 and 1929 in response to the quickening rhythm of coffee accumulation and a certain degree of industrial growth. In consequence, profit margins widened in 1924 and must have held fairly constant thereafter.[24]

In contrast to the previous period, however, coffee was solely responsible for economic expansion between 1924 and 1929. The value of exports averaged 93.5 million pounds sterling per year in comparison to 74.6 million pounds sterling per year between 1919 and 1923. The terms of trade improved significantly and the inflow of foreign capital grew markedly.[25] Accumulation within the coffee sector no longer depended upon the enlargement of domestic industrial, food, and raw material production; in fact, these sectors were not subjected to intense external and internal competition. The autonomy of the coffee complex discouraged increases in the prices of wage goods, which would have pushed wages up and reduced profits.

For all this, the prosperous years 1924 to 1929 harbored the makings of a general crisis in the export complex that would break abruptly in 1929–1930. The internal symptoms were discernible from 1926 on, and the serious implications of the ceaseless overproduction promoted by the Permanent Defense Policy were brought home by the record harvest of 27 million bags of coffee in 1927–1928. Thus, as we will see at the end of the next part of this essay, the calamitous economic situation abroad did not create the Brazilian crisis in 1929; it only exacerbated an already critical state of affairs.

II. COFFEE ACCUMULATION AND ECONOMIC POLICY

The Economic Policy of the First Republic: An Overview

There are two prevailing views of the economic policies of the First Republic. One holds that the vagaries of fiscal, monetary, and exchange policy resulted from the constant shifting between austere and permissive, or between liberal and protectionist, governments.[26] The second characterizes policy history as a series of expedients designed to serve the short-term interests of "the coffee oligarchy and its foreign ally— international finance capital." From this second perspective, the narrow range of internal and external policy is attributed to the dependent position of the Brazilian economy in the world market.[27]

It is our contention that neither of these interpretations fully appreciates the contradictory nature of economic policy between 1889 and 1930. The belief that everything can be ascribed to the whims of those who govern, or worse, to their ignorance of the sacred principles of Economic Theory, merits little comment since it disregards what is elemental: that any economic program is elaborated by a given state and is implemented to serve the concrete demands of classes and interest groups. The second and quite different interpretation can also be dismissed because it fails to take into account either the relationship between decision making and the cylical dynamics of the coffee economy, or the precarious economic and political foundations of the Brazilian state.

We can begin by approaching the question of economic policy in general terms. Public finances were largely determined by the fluctuations of external trade, and it fell to the central government to levy import duties, while the state governments were empowered to tax exports. The financial frailty of the Brazilian state was therefore twofold: Because the coffee sector represented the government's principal source of receipts, federal revenues were dependent on the cyclical behavior of the coffee economy. On the other hand, state incomes, which were similarly tied to foreign commerce, were unequally distributed; in reality, only the coffee states possessed a stable tax base. Yet a government that functioned without benefit of an integrated national market, and was unified by the preeminent interests of only a minority of truly national classes, nevertheless was a national body; and as such, it was compelled to consider the needs and demands of other classes and interest groups in formulating spending policy. In those years when exports were expanding, the pressures on federal spending were intense, both for attending to export requirements, however indirect (for example, those related to the urbanization of Rio de Janeiro), and for meeting the more urgent regional needs that tended to accumulate and fester during times of depression.

Fiscal deficits inevitably developed despite the efforts of the government to augment taxes. The impossibility of permanently carrying and financing such deficits by expanding the means of payment led to a persistent increase in external indebtedness—precisely because the growth of exports facilitated the negotiation of foreign loans. It became ever more difficult to cover the public debt, and even before they reached a critical state, public finances showed signs of deterioration, evident in the evolution of the exchange rate or in budgetary overruns. When the crisis arrived, falling revenues threatened the state with internal and external bankruptcy. Whether because of this calamitous financial situation or because of the near collapse of the balance of payments, further enlargement of the external debt was out of the question and renegotiation became the order of the day.

Thus, to guarantee its own survival, the government found it necessary to cut short expansion and to anticipate and even deepen the crisis by curtailing spending, elevating tariffs, and attempting to broaden its fiscal base. To be sure, all these measures were undertaken with the understanding and encouragement of the international bankers, who always recommended sound fiscal measures in such circumstances in order to ensure that commitments would be honored.

The question naturally arises as to why, given increased urbanization and a rapidly expanding internal capitalist market, the federal government did not raise its revenues through internal taxation in the interest of greater financial autonomy. The contention that the coffee oligarchy and foreign bankers were responsible for the failure of the excise or income tax as an alternative source of revenue is far too simplistic. The agro-export oligarchy would have been affected far more by a tax on its patrimonial base or by the removal of the export tax—measures obviously never contemplated by the administrations of the First Republic. But from the beginning, both the sales and the income tax were considered. Why, then, did the state fail to implement these measures, which would have strengthened it financially?

As it happened, in Brazil, as in the rest of Latin America, internal taxes proved workable only when the economic base of the urban masses had expanded sufficiently to support the cost of taxation. The elite groups and the petty rural and urban bourgeoisie never bore the brunt of, or submitted gracefully to an increase in, the internal tax burden. Without a decisive advance in industrial accumulation to promote the formation of a large urban proletariat, a tertiary sector based on salaried labor, and a growing bureaucracy of petty functionaries, the objective conditions for creating an adequate urban fiscal base and for freeing the government from its financial dependency on external trade did not exist.

The increments in internal taxes actually registered were effected erratically and were essentially emergency expedients (such as raising rates or diversifying rate schedules) designed to counter the worsening of deficits. Only with the coming of the Vargas regime (and particularly the Estado Novo) and the emergence of a new phase of capitalist development did the state begin to augment internal tax revenues. It was only after 1937 that the contribution of import duties to total revenue diminished, and income and excise taxes (besides the stamp tax) gradually assumed a preponderant position in public finances.[28]

Having explained the inevitable shifts in fiscal policy, it is appropriate to add a few comments on monetary and exchange management. At the start of an expansive phase the enhanced buying power of exports—in all likelihood reinforced by new infusions of foreign loan and venture capital—brought pressures to revalue the currency. To avoid exchange appreciation, which would imply a reduction in the profits of exporters, the government was prevailed upon to establish support mechanisms. Thereafter, the increase in the rate of accumulation—which was necessarily sanctioned by monetary policy—inasmuch as it found no support in the growth of importing capacity, inevitably led to deepening exchange difficulties. Devaluation emerged then as the only admissible course of action, becoming at times an instrument of anticyclical policy. In times of crisis—which devaluation could not prevent—the state had little recourse but to apply orthodox fiscal and monetary measures in order to restore fiscal and external equilibrium; such measures not only accepted, but actually accentuated, a fall in employment and income. When export receipts were growing, in response to a greater volume of exports and perhaps to a slight rise in world prices, the exchange situation eased and the exchange rate tended to appreciate, especially if the foreign debt had been renegotiated.

Thus at times the state found itself in the position of utilizing devaluation even when the income from exports was still rising, and with it coffee profits, the *ad valorem* tariff, and protection to industry. On the other hand, under the accumulated pressure of external commitments and the need to refinance the public debt, the government was obliged at times to revalue the currency in spite of a decline in international coffee prices, and, in doing so, to cast aside both the precarious profitability of the coffee sector and industrial protectionism.

Similarly, we can see that the coffee bourgeoisie promoted an official economic policy that repeatedly ran counter to its own immediate interests in order to serve the larger interest of preserving the existing machinery of government and the balance of political power.

We can further note the relative ease with which the coffee bourgeoisie periodically secured and extended foreign loans, even without the backing of the federal government. This was possible in the first place because of the autonomy of state governments and the particular influence wielded by coffee interests. Their semimonopolistic position as exporters with diverse markets that were not controlled by a monopoly of buyers, greatly expedited negotiations with a variety of commercial and financial groups within international capital. In addition, the change in the relative importance of North American versus British finance capital (beginning with World War I) provided some leeway to those Latin American nations not strictly dependent on Britain.

Having offered these general comments, we can now reconstruct Brazilian's economic policy from the beginning of the First Republic to the crisis of 1929.

The Period 1886–1898

During the years 1886 to 1898 important political, economic, and institutional changes took place that were connected to two decisive historical events: the abolition of slavery in 1888 and the proclamation of the Republic in 1889. Policymaking in the first years of the Republic addressed several serious problems of internal and external financing built into the cyclical character of the coffee economy and aggravated by the particularly unfavorable financial conjuncture inherited from the Empire. Scarce liquidity (which had become more acute in the last decade of the Empire), an enormous public debt, and the financial turmoil that followed abolition in all agricultural regions except São Paulo all prompted the first administration to undertake fundamental banking and tax reforms that, nonetheless, succumbed to the financial crisis of 1891 known as the *Encilhamento:*

> The emphasis placed in our literature on the "monetary chaos" and the "avalanche of paper" that characterized the *Encilhamento,* with its enormous monetary expansion and exchange depreciation, obscured for a long time the true significance of effective accumulation in the period. Arguments that seek to demonstrate that any potentially positive effects obtained from expanding banking operations and the means of payment would have been nullified or offset by exchange depreciation and by the rise in internal prices—both of which would augment the costs of internal investment and production—or others that view the *Encilhamento* as a period of "internal paper speculation and ghost enterprises," contribute little to our understanding of the era.[29]

The significance of reforms implemented under the early Republic and the general lines of economic policy up to the crisis of 1899 appear to be the following: The banking reform that empowered private banks to issue paper money was largely an effort to expand the sources of liquidity and internal financing and to separate them from the fluctuations in the public debt and in external trade that severely hamstrung federal monetary and financial policymaking. The law further permitted banks to engage directly or indirectly in extrabanking activities through the creation of corporations, thereby transforming financiers of current activities into active agents of capital accumulation.

The race between monetary expansion, progressive exchange depreciation, and rising prices was translated, however, into an open and unrestrained inflationary process. If inflation favored the accumulation of urban capital in this period, it also created internal financial disorder, which, together with the requirements of renegotiating the external debt, led to the adoption of a series of exchange stabilization measures. The first of these, in 1896, provided for the suspension of decentralized emissions and the replacement of bank notes by treasury notes. Reform continued with the negotiation of foreign credit to establish an exchange stabilization fund, and culminated with the drastic stabilization and exchange revaluation plan (1899) designed by Joaquim Murtinho, Minister of Finance in the Campos Salles government.[30]

The central problem of tax reform at this time was the same: that of maintaining fiscal revenues in real terms and avoiding repeated and sizable losses due to exchange fluctuations. For this purpose a gold quota was established in 1890; however, it was soon abolished (1891) with the argument that the depreciation of the exchange rate and the resulting rise in wage costs made it extremely difficult for buyers to pay customs duties in gold. Thereafter tariffs were levied *ad valorem* according to the official schedule set in 1890. Since exchange depreciation persisted until 1899, customs receipts did not hold their own in real terms as a proportion of imports. This obliged the central government to resort to successive elevations in customs duties, including a general tariff revision in 1896. Yet once again effective tariff reform was blocked because of the adverse impact it had on the cost of living. In spite of a declining importing capacity and the corrosive effect of exchange depreciation on fiscal receipts, the government in 1897 decreed a new tariff schedule that was 25 percent lower than that of the previous year.[31]

Given the uncertain progress of tariff reform and its own inability to broaden its tax base, the federal government was forced drastically to curtail expenditures related to consumption and, particularly, to investment. Even so, it could not prevent the growing accumulation of budget deficits after 1892.[32]

The public debt was financed in part by paper issues but primarily by the expansion of the external debt, which grew by approximately 30 percent between 1890 and 1897. This, in turn, fed internal inflation. Because the external debt had to be amortized in hard currency, debt servicing absorbed an ever-greater proportion of fiscal receipts. Moreover, since both exports and imports began to decline after 1896, the rapidly failing ability of Brazil to meet and extend its foreign commitments produced the near-insolvency that necessitated the funding loan that was part of Murtinho's broad stabilization program.

Before we examine the crisis of 1899 and the serious stabilization policy pursued by the Campos Salles/Murtinho administration, we will digress for a moment to clarify the problem of exchange depreciation and its contradictory character vis-à-vis the cyclical movement of coffee accumulation.

The Contradictory Character of Exchange Depreciation

The essential point to be made here is that exchange depreciation derived, above all, from the cyclical dynamics of the accumulation of coffee capital. To the degree that the rate of accumulation quickened in response to the internal and external prices that prevailed in the previous stage of the economic cycle, it placed additional pressure on Brazil's importing capacity—at precisely the time when the purchasing power of exports was declining in response to "new" and lower international prices. At this point any attempt to restore equilibrium through the rules of the gold standard would have a drastic effect on current profit rates within the coffee economy. It was in this context that devaluation emerged as the one course of action that would simultaneously curtail the excessive demand for imports and preserve, for better or for worse, profit margins and capital accumulation in the coffee sector.

Depending on whether public spending was expansionist or contractionist, official policymaking obviously furthered or arrested depreciation; furthermore, the steps taken to finance the public debt either stimulated or retarded accumulation in the coffee complex, particularly in its urban division. Nevertheless, we must not lose sight of the fact that persistent exchange depreciation originated in the global process of accumulation in the coffee complex; it did not derive—as has been claimed by those who favor "structuralist" explanations—from the special interests of the export entrepreneurs. The view of Furtado in this respect has gained wide acceptance:

> In the ultimate analysis, the process of correcting external disequilibrium implied an income transfer from those who paid for imports to those who sold exports. Since imports were paid for by the community as a whole, the

exporters were actually promoting the socialization of the losses which economic mechanisms tended to concentrate on their profits.[33]

Yet the problem is considerably more complex once we abandon the exporter-importer dichotomy, which Furtado uses as a point of departure, and incorporate the concept of coffee capital into our explanation. From this perspective, a substantial proportion of coffee accumulation consisted of urban accumulation, which necessitated the importation of means of production and absorbed a significant part of the immigrant labor force. Inasmuch as the reproduction of labor in the productive nucleus and in the urban sector also required the overseas purchase of food and manufactured wage goods, this process further strained Brazil's import capacity. We have noted elsewhere that the percentage of wages used to buy imported commodities was particularly high during the first short cycle of coffee expansion. Thereafter this share diminished, as coffee prosperity itself stimulated domestic food production and engendered the large-scale production of consumer wage goods, both of which began satisfying a growing part of internal demand.

While exchange depreciation did have the effect of elevating the costs of both the means of production and the reproduction of the labor force, it does not necessarily follow that the favorable impact of devaluation on coffee accumulation was therefore neutralized, or that the increments in internal costs were "socialized" or paid by "the community as a whole."

In fact, the critical determinant of profit margins within the coffee complex was not the escalation in the cost of imported means of production provoked by exchange depreciation, since this was proportional to the rise in internal coffee prices and did not, on the average, modify the price-cost relationship of constant capital. Rather, the decisive factor had to do with *variable* capital, that is, with the determination of the cost of wages.

Because wages increased less rapidly than prices, the profit margins of *all* entrepreneurs, not just exporters, rose throughout the period of devaluation; at the same time, internal prices climbed and real wages fell concurrently, approaching intolerable levels for the subsistence of the urban labor force. In other words, in the last stage of coffee's expansive cycle, the "socialization of losses" was accomplished above all at the expense of wage earners.

At a certain minimum level of subsistence, however, money wages tended to become rigid and so could no longer offset the fall in the domestic price of coffee. At this point, devaluation was demonstrably incapable of cushioning the fall in international prices. Certain latent tendencies in the economy became apparent with a corresponding narrowing of profit margins in the coffee sector that could not be counterbalanced by intensifying the rate of labor exploitation.

If the more moderate but persistent exchange depreciation registered between 1895 and 1898 was not sufficient to maintain current profit margins in the coffee sector, it nevertheless prevented a sharp decline in returns, and continued to produce a growing disparity between domestic and external prices. This spurred further accumulation (in spite of the pronounced decrease in coffee prices), which later aggravated the general crisis of overproduction, a crisis from which producers would only extricate themselves with the first valorization plan of 1906.

On the other hand, devaluation continued to favor the industrial sector until the general crisis of 1899 and the implementation of Murtinho's stabilization and exchange revaluation policies. Infant industry had already benefited from tariff and exchange protection, as well as from the period of easy credit (1890–1894) promoted in the first years of the Republic to stimulate investment.[34] By utilizing the productive capacity installed earlier to strongly expand both current output and profit taking, the industrial sector managed to live with a restricted importing capacity—made worse by the fall in exports. In other words, infant industry was self-financing in the years 1895 to 1899 in spite of the monetary and credit restraints exercised by the federal government to combat inflation.

Thus a policy of devaluation originally conceived as a means of supporting the coffee export complex, in practice, encouraged capital accumulation in the industrial sector and actually intensified the cyclical movement of the coffee economy, thereby precipitating a profound crisis that affected not only coffee but the financial foundations of the central government as well.

The serious contradictions of devaluation were particularly evident in its impact on public finance. Although they were genuinely alarmed by real losses in revenues from import duties, policymakers nevertheless faced a dilemma: Not raising tariffs meant that public receipts would lose even more ground, which was tantamount to accepting the financial ruin of the state. On the other hand, an upward revision of the tariff schedule to offset real losses in income would escalate the cost of living and, therefore, of wages, and would reduce the already fragile profit margins of the export sector.

The reactions of the coffee bourgeoisie were equally contradictory. As long as profit margins were expanding, the coffee economy could tolerate some fiscal pressure to prevent too great an erosion of government revenues; however, when profit margins narrowed, coffee interests demanded a reduction in tariffs and in the level of protection afforded to industry.

The decision to limit the tax burden and maintain expenditures at a minimum signified still greater reliance on external indebtednesses as a means of financing the federal deficit. However, declining fiscal receipts sharply diminished the government's ability to meet its foreign obligations. Eventually the impossibility of amortizing accumulated debts necessitated a comprehensive renegotiation with creditors abroad.

The Crisis of 1899 and Economic Recovery up to 1913

The crisis that had been averted between 1891 and 1894, and relatively contained between 1895 and 1896, began emerging in 1897–1898 and broke near the end of 1898, when the Campos Salles administration took office. The new government simultaneously confronted two grave problems: falling internal and external coffee prices and the financial bankruptcy of the state.

There were clamors for official intervention to solve the coffee problem; the government was to withdraw surplus production from the market with the objective of "valorizing" the product by boosting, or at least preventing a fall in, international prices. This course of action was hardly feasible, however, because the government lacked the means to finance it except through currency issues, a move that would generate inflation, depreciation, and a general worsening of the already critical state of public finances. Neither could the Brazilian government resort to further borrowing abroad at this time, since it was already incapable of meeting its commitments and was seeking a funding loan from its international creditors. The only solution that remained was to live with the coffee crisis. Minister of Finance Murtinho observed:

> In relation to present consumption, the cultivation of coffee can be considered to be composed of two elements: one established in fertile soils, favored by climate, and undertaken by intelligent agriculturists in good economic circumstances; the other established in inferior lands and climates by routine-bound growers in poor economic conditions.[35]

He concluded:

> Convinced that official intervention would only increase our difficulties, the government permitted coffee production to decline through natural selection. Those unequipped for survival were eliminated, leaving production in the hands of the most hardy and best prepared for the struggle.[36]

It was decided, then, to allow the coffee crisis to run its course through the free operation of market forces. As a result, the "coffee problem" drew out until 1906, when intense and mounting pressure for a price-support policy led to the signing of the Taubaté Agreement and intervention by Campos Salles's successors.

In order to deal with the desperate state of public finances, the Murtinho ministry adopted a series of austerity measures that deepened the rural and urban crisis. To begin with, the government responded to the exchange emergency by establishing a gold tariff requiring that 10 percent of the value of import duties be paid in specie, to which another 5 percent would be stabilized. The accomplishment of this objective beginning in 1902 was due in large part to the impact of the funding loan of 1898, which consolidated external debts—whose servicing had come to greatly exceed the capacity to pay afforded by the balance of trade—and suspended amortization payments for thirteen years.[37] Furthermore, by 1902 a new foreign loan secured in 1901 had steadied the exchange market and the exchange rate appreciated until the end of 1906, when the valorization scheme went into effect.

A second set of expedients addressed the problem of budgetary equilibrium and provided for higher internal taxes and the retiring of excess paper currency in circulation. These measures can be classified as "internal" even though they were the terms imposed by overseas creditors in exchange for refinancing the foreign debt. This illustrates, once again, the degree to which "internal" and "external" policy measures were intertwined even while the general economic policy of which they were part was essentially contradictory in nature.

As a result of the stabilization program, internal prices declined by 30 percent between 1900 and 1902. Deflation was severely felt in all economic activities and even provoked a bank panic.[38]

Having attained the desired budgetary equilibrium, a new government began to pursue a vigorous investment program in 1903, preserving, nonetheless, the essential lines of existing monetary and fiscal policy. Aimed primarily at the transportation infrastructure (railways and ports) and at urban improvements, investments were intended to remedy deficiencies accumulated during nearly a decade of paralysis of capital outlays in the federal public sector.

This investment effort was consciously undertaken as a "program of economic reconstruction" that would later be substantially expanded and would generate new and large budget deficits. This time, however, deficits emerged within the context of steadily growing federal receipts, provided by recuperation itself beginning in 1903. The program proved viable in part because the ever-higher level of exports and of foreign borrowing (particularly in the form of loans for public works) facilitated the importation of needed capital goods.[39]

Urban improvements and general economic recovery offered a striking contrast to conditions within the coffee sector, where the structural crisis continued unabated. The considerable inflow of foreign capital and the boom in rubber exports had improved the balance of payments, but the ensuring appreciation in the rate of exchange in no way benefited coffee producers who, given the relentless gathering of large harvests, remained engulfed in a crisis of overproduction.

When a record harvest was predicted for 1906, pressures for official intervention could no longer be ignored and the Agreement of Taubaté was formalized with the following objectives: (1) to maintain coffee prices at between 55 and 65 mil réis a bag; (2) to negotiate an external loan of 15 million pounds sterling to finance intervention in the market; (3) to tax the planting of new coffee trees; (4) to create a conversion fund designed to stabilize the exchange and prevent appreciation; and (5) to prohibit the exportation of low-quality coffee.[40] In sum, the coffee bourgeoisie that controlled 75 percent of the world's production resolved to utilize its monopoly power as a class to manipulate international prices.

The chief obstacle at this point was the difficulty of securing the foreign funds necessary to finance the withdrawal of coffee "surpluses" from the market. When skeptical European and North American bankers declined to offer their backing, the government of São Paulo turned to private European commercial groups, who agreed to supply 80 percent of the amount required to purchase 2 million bags of coffee at 7 U.S. cents per pound. In 1907, following its initial success, the program won the support of international finance capital, which then undertook to furnish the São Paulo government with the massive funding necessary to continue the program.

For its part, the federal government also consented to back the price-boosting scheme—to which only the states of São Paulo, Minas Gerais, and Espírito Santo had originally subscribed. The central government further agreed to create a Conversion Fund (Caixa de Conversão) that would attract foreign exchange by maintaining an exchange rate superior to that prevailing on the open market, but not so high as to encourage international arbitrage dealings.[41] By issuing stabilization notes for the purchase of foreign exchange, the Conversion Fund expanded the money supply. In this way, monetary policy simultaneously sanctioned an increase in public spending and budget deficits, and a rise in total economic activity and in the rate of accumulation in the coffee sector.[42] In the meantime, the rate of exchange stabilized, owing to a favorable level of exports and the substantial infusion of foreign capital.[43]

The War Years

The threat of war provoked both a run on imports and a fall in the world price of coffee that created an unprecedented commercial deficit. Additionally, capital flight also occasioned by the impending conflict, made the gravity of Brazil's exchange and monetary situation apparent. The intensified demand for foreign exchange on the one hand, and the contraction in the money supply due to Conversion Fund operations on the other, created an extraordinary scarcity of liquidity:

> To convey some idea of this movement it is enough to remember that the issues of the conversion fund fell from 410,000 contos de réis in 1912 to something under 300,000 contos in 1913, to less than 160,000 contos in 1914. This reduction in monetary circulation had a shock effect on internal commercial relations that was further exacerbated by the outbreak of war.[44]

Moreover, given its lack of reserves, the Brazilian government could not meet its foreign commitments, which were now higher than ever. The debt progressed from 40 million pounds sterling to 162 million pounds sterling between 1897 and 1914. The negotiation of a new funding loan substantially alleviated this difficulty.[45] In the meantime, given the fall in international coffee prices and the persistent overflow of capital, the rate of exchange depreciated around 30 percent between 1913 and 1916; hence internal coffee prices could be defended in a relative sense.

As we observed in Part I, business prospects in 1917 were not encouraging, and the extensive wartime amassing of coffee stocks,[46] together with the promise of yet another large harvest in 1917–1918, prompted the government of São Paulo to withdraw another 3.1 million bags of coffee from the market at a cost of 4.9 mil réis per 10 kilos. This second valorization program sustained internal prices and (given the exchange depreciation of 1917) averted a severe depression in the coffee sector.[47] Then, as early as 1918, world coffee prices increased significantly, mostly because frost damage had reduced the harvest. The exchange rate held steady and internal prices rose by nearly 15 percent.[48]

Federal receipts plummeted in response to a fall in imports and, in spite of a cutback in total spending, the deficit expanded dramatically in 1913. The government was once again obliged to adopt the emergency expedient of taxing consumption—by raising rates in 1914 and 1917 and by widening the tax base to cover new products. By the end of World War I these measures had somewhat mitigated the budgetary imbalance.[49]

The Period 1919–1929

The fundamental lines of economic policy during the years 1919 to 1929 were determined, once again, by the difficulties confronting the coffee export complex. During the initial expansion of coffee production in the 1920s the purchasing power of exports fluctuated sharply in response to changing international coffee prices, which rose in 1919 and 1920 and then plunged until 1923. Moreover, the strong demand for foreign exchange both for private remittances and for the payment of the accumulated external debt put pressure on the exchange situation:

The decline of export receipts led to the disappearance of the balance of trade surplus in 1920/22 and generated a deficit in 1920/21 which brought in consequence (given the requirements of capital remittances) a serious disequilibrium in the balance of payments. . . . Thus the balance of trade surplus in 1923 was, in reality, much less, falling from £.22.571.000 to £.10.571.000. The external debt alone absorbed £.14 million in 1923 and private remittances totalled £.12 million. This conveys some notion of the size of the balance of payments deficit in that year, which exceeded £.15 million and which occasioned a dramatic depreciation in the exchange rate.[50]

Thus the rate of exchange, which had stayed level at 16.5 mil réis to the pound sterling in 1919 and 1920, depreciated significantly, reaching 28.7 mil réis in 1921, 33.2 in 1922, and 44.3 in 1923. In response to this movement internal coffee prices remained relatively stable until 1921 and registered a marked upturn in 1922 and 1923.[51]

Nevertheless, devaluation was not the only factor favoring accumulation in the coffee export complex. In view of harvest predictions and a crisis in the North American economy, a third valorization program was implemented in 1921 to withdraw 4.5 million bags of coffee from the market.[52] The newly created rediscounting department of the Bank of Brazil furnished necessary funding, which, together with other smaller loans, was later consolidated through the Coffee Guarantee Loan granted by the Rothschild, Schroeder, and Baring Brothers in 1922. This aid, together with resources obtained to finance both railway expansion and public works projects in the Northeast in 1921, represented an aggregate of 38 million pounds sterling, and increased by 25 percent the accumulated external debt registered in 1920.[53]

The fluctuations in foreign trade naturally had an adverse effect on the level of federal revenues. Nevertheless, the central government continued to pursue a vigorous program of public investment, which produced large deficits between 1919 and 1922.[54] This program, combined with the coffee support scheme of 1921 and the expansion of credit through the creation of the rediscount department of the Bank of Brazil, laid the basis for increased liquidity and clearly delineated an expansionist monetary policy.[55]

It is therefore evident that there was a very close relationship between the vicissitudes of the coffee complex and the economic policies of the state. Put more forcefully, economic policy sanctioned and stimulated coffee expansion even while spending decisions were of necessity at least minimally responsive to the demands of the non-coffee bourgeoisie and the concerns of other regional oligarchies.

It must be emphasized, further, that the positive impact of monetary, exchange, and spending policies on industry and on the commercial production of primary commodities supported—rather than undermined—the process of accumulation in the coffee sector; it did this by helping to assure the reproduction of variable coffee capital without adversely affecting profit margins in the process.

Circumstances were substantially different beginning in 1924, when the Permanent Defense Policy began operating.[56] The undeniable success of the valorization programs nurtured the idea of a Permanent Defense Policy. According to this approach, official intervention was designed to maintain coffee prices at high levels rather than to prevent prices from falling below a certain point in times of crisis. The one effective measure adopted while the Permanent Defense was executed by the federal government provided for the construction of regulatory warehouses whose storage facilities were intended to avoid a glut on the market that would depress prices. The elevation of world coffee prices in 1924 attests to the success of this undertaking. Nevertheless:

> The growers soon realized that the entire weight of defense rested on their shoulders because the receipts issued by the regulatory warehouses were not easily negotiable, since the dispatch orders for the port had a delay of more than 90 or 120 days, the minimum term the banks allowed for commercial transactions.[57]

Demands that the Permanent Defense be administered by the state of São Paulo became effective in November 1924 with the creation of the São Paulo Coffee Institute. This agency established the following policy guidelines: (1) coffee entering the port of Santos would be controlled through warehouse stockpiling and transportation restrictions; (2) low-interest loans would be granted on the coffee deposited in the regulatory warehouses; (3) coffee would be purchased when deemed necessary to limit supply; and (4) the program would be financed by a permanent defense fund based on foreign loans guaranteed by a duty levied on coffee transported in the state of São Paulo.

With respect to the harvests of 1925–1926 and 1926–1927, the intervention of the Coffee Institute was limited to the division of production into monthly quotas through warehouse stockpiling; the Banco do Estado de São Paulo provided the necessary funding in this instance. However, when a record yield was forecast for 1927–1928—a development bound to disturb the relative equilibrium of the coffee market—the institute resolved to effect what became known as the "valorization of Rolim Telles." A 1926 loan obtained from the Lazard Brothers enabled the institute to advance 60 mil réis per bag of coffee to growers, a sum that covered nearly half the costs of production in the newer coffee zone and nearly a third in the traditional coffee-growing region. The Rolim Telles program, with the aid of a comparative reduction in output in 1928–1929, sustained external prices in 1928 and 1929.

Because the Permanent Defense Policy was adopted at a time when the industrial nations were enjoying a period of prosperity, world coffee prices were held at extremely elevated levels and the annual value of exports averaged 93.5 million pounds sterling.

From the point of view of policymaking, coffee expansion after 1924 presented two types of problems. In the first place, it became necessary to block, at all costs, an appreciation in the exchange rate that would compress profits in the coffee sector. Accordingly, in 1926 the government created a Stabilization Fund, much like the earlier Conversion Fund. In effect, the currency was devalued by 20 percent and held at about 40 mil réis to the pound sterling until the crisis of 1929.[58]

It was equally essential to prevent a rise in money wages, which, like appreciation, would have the effect of narrowing profit margins in the coffee complex. The required action in this case involved subjecting the industrial sector to intense competition—a course of action made possible by Brazil's enlarged importing capacity.[59] The government did not revise the tariff schedule in these years, and consequently the degree of protective duties afforded industry diminished significantly.

In executing the federal budget, officials followed "orthodox" monetary and fiscal guidelines. A sizable cut was made in capital expenditures and public spending grew slowly; deficits contracted and there were even surpluses in 1928 and 1929. Monetary expansion was relatively modest and the means of payment expanded only in 1927 and 1928.[60]

The Crisis of 1929 and the Mechanisms of Recuperation

The critical state of affairs confronting the coffee export complex beginning in October 1929 has not always been clearly understood. The Brazilian crisis was not merely an economic transfer or reflex of the Great Depression that engulfed the world's leading economies. Rather, the vicissitudes of the coffee complex can be explained, above all, by the contradictions that inevitably accompanied the accumulation of coffee capital—contradictions that were at once tempered and deepened by official economic policy, particularly from 1924 on.

In maintaining the rate of profits in coffee agriculture at extraordinarily high levels for several years, the Permanent Defense Policy encouraged a great increase in productive capacity. To convey the magnitude of this change, suffice it to say that between 1928–1929 and 1933–1934 no fewer than three harvests yielded in excess of 28 million bags of coffee each.

At the same time, the elevation of international prices promoted a considerable broadening of *external* productive capacity that intensified foreign competition and gradually eroded the near-monopoly position enjoyed by Brazilian coffee interests in the world market. In his classic work Delfim Netto clarifies the issue:

> The central rationale of the defense consisted in artificially adjusting the relationship between supply and the world demand for coffee in order to support prices. As we see in a report of the President of the Republic, probable world consumption was calculated and the exportable output of our competitors was subtracted. The difference was to be supplied by Brazil. Thus, in order to keep prices high Brazil voluntarily assumed the position of residual supplier. The apologists for the defense never understood that price supports presented our competitors with an enormous incentive and a completely open market.[61]

Thus the fundamental explanation of the coffee crisis is to be found in the great excess productive capacity *concentrated in Brazil*. It is true that in terms of its impact on external demand and its contribution to the dislocation of Brazilian produce from the market, the Great Depression probably anticipated and certainly deepened the crisis that was, in any case, inevitable. The Crash of '29 administered the coup de grâce to the international monetary system based on the gold standard, a structure that had already been shaken in the years following World War I. Subsequently, the foreign trade policies of most nations came to be based on a bilateral system of payments or on equilibrium within a block. Furthermore, the metropolitan countries promoted the substitute cultivation of primary products previously imported from other areas within their own colonies. Accordingly, throughout the 1930s African production expanded in the shelter of high preferential tariffs.[62]

Having clarified this central point, we can turn to the crisis itself and to the mechanisms of recuperation. Beginning in October 1929 the defense system elaborated by the Coffee Institute began to fall apart, not only because demand faltered but also because the federal government elected to leave the coffee sector to its own devices. Preoccupied with salvaging the Stabilization Fund, President Washington Luiz, once an ardent defender of institute policies, became a confirmed advocate of nonintervention in the market.

It is instructive to speculate on how severe and protracted the Brazilian depression would have been *if* the government had abstained from *any* form of intervention in the coffee economy and if it had implemented an orthodox fiscal policy in order to balance the budget.

In this hypothetical set of circumstances the balance between supply and external demand would be restored by adjusting capital stocks, that is, by destroying excess productive capacity. The fall in world prices would eventually be transferred to internal prices, and devaluation would lose its effectiveness as a defense mechanism. In this respect Furtado rightly observes:

> The depreciation of the currency, although cushioning the impact of the fall in international prices on the Brazilian entrepreneur, induced him to continue harvesting and maintaining pressure on the market. This situation led to a new price decline and renewed depreciation of the currency, contributing to further intensification of the crisis. As the degree of depreciation of the currency was much smaller than the fall in prices—inasmuch as the former was influenced by other factors—a point would clearly be reached where the loss to the growers would be large enough to induce them to abandon their plantations. Only then would a balance be reached between supply and demand.[63]

Both those planters who increasingly produced at variable monetary costs superior to prices and those who had secured bank loans during expansion and were now insolvent would necessarily be eliminated. Moreover, as profit expectations vanished, at a certain point the installation of new productive capacity would cease altogether. The low point of the crisis would be reached when external and domestic prices only barely covered the variable monetary costs and capitalists' consumption of all working enterprises. And there can be no doubt concerning the severity of the crisis, since we know for a fact that international prices plunged nearly 60 percent between 1929 and 1933 in spite of the withdrawal of millions of bags of coffee from the market. Thus the adjustment of coffee agriculture could only have been achieved at the cost of destroying a large part of the installed productive capacity, of imposing a very high level of unemployment, and of tolerating a substantial fall in money wages.

The crisis would spread from coffee agriculture to the rest of the economy. Without detailing the mechanisms of transfer, we may note that in view of the reduced demand for commercial, financial, and transportation services, as well as the insolvency of coffee businesses, the depression would almost at once extend to the urban sector of the coffee complex. The cut in consumption would have an immediate impact on the wage goods industry and on commercial agriculture that would produce new adverse repercussions throughout the economy. The fall in imports and in the general level of domestic economic activity would undermine public finances, and the government (according to our hypothesis) would assume a passive role, maintaining expenditures at the level of receipts.

The low point of Depression does merit close attention. We have observed that for coffee producers this stage obtained when prices scarcely covered the variable monetary costs and capitalists' consumption of working units. Given the profound nature of its problems, coffee agriculture would transmit its low point to the other sectors of the economy. The collapse of demand would compress profits in the urban coffee sector and in industry to the level of capitalists' consumption alone. The same would hold for internal market agriculture organized along capitalist lines. Agricultural food and raw material production undertaken on small private holdings and within the great domains would regress to a subsistence level.

Finally, we may comment on the possible operation of automatic recovery mechanisms. In view of the state of the world market for agricultural commodities, the outlook for a rapid recovery based on export agriculture would not be bright. Nor would the prospects for recuperation through industrial growth be encouraging—in the first place because the replacement of industrial investments would have only a limited dynamic impact since their effects would largely be channeled to the exterior, and in the second, because it is extremely difficult to imagine a block of innovations capable of reviving the prostrate economy.

It seems logical to conclude, therefore, that had the government abstained from any form of intervention in the coffee market, and had it pursued an orthodox fiscal policy, not only would the Depression have reached extraordinary depths but it would also have been difficult for Brazil to achieve complete recovery by the end of World War II.

As it happened, the Depression did not assume catastrophic proportions in Brazil, although it was indeed serious, considering that the gross domestic product (GDP) fell around 4 percent between 1928 and 1931 (its lowest point). Furthermore, in comparison to other countries, recovery in Brazil was relatively swift, and as early as 1932 the GDP surpassed the level registered in 1928.[64] The simultaneous operation of several mechanisms both prevented catastrophe and promoted recovery. Unquestionably the principal of these was the coffee defense policy, insofar as it maintained internal prices sufficiently high to at least cover the variable monetary and capitalists' consumption costs of most intramarginal producers, and in doing so, [permitted] relatively sustained operations and [stabilized] income levels within the urban division of the export complex.

Since the defense policy has generated considerable controversy, it is best to analyze its operation with care. Once the financing capacity of the Banco do Estado de São Paulo had been exhausted and President Washington Luiz assumed his noninterventionist stance, the impotence of the Coffee Institute became apparent. Accordingly, the state government sought and obtained a loan of 20 million pounds sterling (720,000 contos) from four international bankers. A portion of this sum funded the purchase of 3.1 million bags of coffee at a rate of 100 mil réis each, while the balance refinanced another 13.5 million bags.

Following the cautious approach of Withaker's policy, the provisional government resolved to create the National Coffee Council, which, through the buying and destroying of coffee stocks took charge of the price support policy. The council purchased coffee valued at nearly 30 percent of export receipts in 1931 and 1932 and destroyed 14.4 million bags between May 1931 and February 1933. Sixty-five percent of the cost of this project was financed by taxes and the rest through the Bank of Brazil and the national treasury.

It was precisely these massive purchases that formed the basis of all subsidization of the coffee export complex. In significantly diminishing the pressure exerted by supply, they helped to establish higher international prices. Furthermore, it became possible for currency devaluation to function once again as a defense mechanism, cushioning the fall in internal prices. Had the market been allowed to operate freely, this mechanism (through which extenal prices declined considerably more than internal prices) would have lost all effectiveness. Even if purchases had been financed entirely through taxation, the withdrawal of surplus output would have been a decisive policy. Moreover, as Fishlow reminds us, given the inelasticity of the demand for coffee, the burden of the export tax necessarily fell in part on the consumer.[65]

The expansionist impact of purchases financed by treasury and Bank of Brazil notes—no small matter—should not be viewed solely as a corollary effect. Rather, it must be borne in mind that the defense policy was a broadly conceived program based on the combined operation of external price supports, exchange depreciation, and the antidepressive repercussions of funding purchases by issuing notes.[66]

Granting the critical weight of the coffee defense policy, we should nonetheless acknowledge the positive intervention of yet another factor—the budget deficit. First, however, we should explain why it is not the balance-of-trade surplus—functioning as a defense mechanism for domestic income—that we consider to be important. The favorable balance of trade reflected the failure of internal demand, which was translated into a decrease in the importation of consumer goods, particularly capital goods, and did not derive from a specific economic policy designed to remedy the crisis. That is, the positive balance of trade was primarily a *result* of the Depression rather than a measure adopted *ex ante* to combat it. To the contrary, what concerns us are the budget deficits accumulated between 1930 and 1932, which originated in expenditures related to the Revolution of 1930, the Paulista Rebellion of 1932, and aid extended to the northeastern states devastated by the great drought of 1930–1933. In 1930 the deficit put the brakes on the fall in income, and in 1932 it was the driving force for recuperation. By itself, the finding that the state did not attempt to balance the budget means very little. The important point is that although their objectives were quite different, the policies implemented by the government in 1930 and 1932 "in practice" followed Keynesian lines.[67]

III. THE RELATIONSHIP BETWEEN COFFEE CAPITAL AND INDUSTRIAL CAPITAL: THE EMERGENCE AND CONSOLIDATION OF INDUSTRY

There can be little doubt that the intense development of coffee capital between 1886 and 1929 stimulated the formation and consolidation of industrial capital in Brazil. To examine this relationship, we can begin by tracing the emergence of large-scale industry during the expansive phase of the first long coffee cycle, that is, between 1886 and 1894.

The Formation of Industrial Capital

Before 1887 Brazil's industrial capital was only marginally significant. A few industrial establishments existed, but even at the regional level they never constituted an industrial sector of any magnitude. For example, the state of São Paulo contained only seven textile plants and twenty-one other industries specializing in foodstuffs, hats, beverages, and footwear. The declared value of these installations represented only 17.6 percent of the total industrial capital registered in the 1907 state census.[68]

Nevertheless, between 1886 and 1894 investments in industry grew considerably, according to the findings of Fishlow and of Wilson Cano. Cano's figures show that about 40 percent of São Paulo's industrial capital in 1907 had been installed between 1887 and 1894. Fishlow's research indicates, moreover, that the importation of capital goods in this period was not surpassed [until much later].[69] Thus the timing of industrial birth coincided with the "momentum" of expansion of the coffee export complex, while industrial development took place increasingly in the coffee zone itself. By 1907 approximately 60 percent of the nation's industrial output originated in the states of Rio de Janeiro, São Paulo, and Minas Gerais.

Industrialization and the evolution of the coffee sector were, in fact, profoundly related. It was the coffee economy, in which production was based on a series of capitalist relationships, that created the social and economic prerequisites for the formation of industrial capital. Fernando Henrique Cardoso has placed the issue in its proper perspective:

> The process of industrialization in any region assumes the existence of a certain degree of capitalist development and, specifically, the presence of a mercantile economy; it further implies a relatively developed social division of labor. The latter, insofar as division proceeds within a capitalist

framework, results in the formation of a labor market. . . . Nevertheless, these prerequisites are created by the capitalist organization that predates industrial production properly speaking. Before the emergence of the industrial entrepreneur the Brazilian capitalist already existed, as merchant, planter, or financier, and as such he laid the groundwork for the elaboration of a capitalist regime of industrial production.[70]

The capitalist coffee sector, then, provided patterns and conditions basic to the emergence of industrial capital and large-scale industry. To explore the specific problem of industrial capital formation in Brazil, we can focus on three issues: how a given social class operating within a given context accumulated resources capable of being transformed into industrial capital; why this class chose to invest in industry, thereby breaking with traditional investment patterns; and finally, how these resources were used to acquire the labor force and the means of production necessary for large-scale industry.

First, it is evident that the coffee capitalists—that is, the coffee bourgeoisie—formed the social matrix of the industrial bourgeoisie. In other words, industrial capital was generated by investments made in the coffee export complex, both in its productive nucleus and in its related urban activities, in particular the import trade.

The involvement of coffee planters (i.e., the agrarian element within the coffee bourgeoisie) in industrial undertakings was impressive. According to the figures compiled by Bandeira, Jr., in 1901, about 50 percent of all workers in São Paulo were employed in businesses owned by coffee *fazendeiros*.[71] Moreover, the import sector contributed decisively to the formation of industrial capital. The large import houses not only purchased foreign merchandise but took charge of its distribution and ultimately assumed control of much of the nation's internal commerce as well. As a rule, the import merchants were immigrants—precisely the persons best able to establish contacts in their countries of origin and obtain credit from banks abroad. Accordingly, a sizable share of the Paulista industrial bourgeoisie had immigrated to Brazil and begun their careers as importers. Matarazzo, for example, was initially an importer of edible oil, flour, and rice; the Jafet brothers, Crespi, Diedrichsen, and many others first established import houses.[72]

We may ask what prompted agrarian and commercial coffee interests to invest in industry. As we know, industrial capitalism did not emerge when the coffee export complex was in the midst of crisis, but rather during an export boom, when returns most certainly attained very high levels. It happened, however, that the profits realized between 1889 and 1894 could not be fully absorbed by the coffee economy itself. Earnings could not be reinvested in the productive nucleus in part because the rhythm of incorporating new lands was subject to a series of natural factors, such as the timing of clearing, planting, and so forth; moreover, once the coffee trees were in place, productive accumulation became essentially a "natural" process; and finally, between planting time and the first harvest labor costs were almost completely reduced to remuneration for weeding. Nor could importers readily channel their profits into increased buying abroad because Brazil's import capacity expanded less rapidly than profit margins. Consequently, domestic industry became the only profitable application for surplus commercial profits.

Stated another way, there was a siphoning of capital funds from the coffee export complex because the amassing of money capital outstripped the possibilities for productive accumulation. Industrial projects had only to promise the overall reproduction of profits in order to attract investors. It is also true that the transfer of capital from coffee to industry was greatly aided by the easy credit facilities afforded by early Republican reforms and the expansionist monetary policy pursued until 1894.

The conversion of surplus money capital into industrial capital was accomplished in the following manner: In the first place, industrial capital benefited from the ample supply of free labor. Not only did coffee capital stimulate the formation of a labor market; more important, the volume of immigration exceeded the demands of the coffee export complex. Immigration permitted the reproduction of rural and urban capital and still "deposited" a "surplus" of labor in the cities.

Nevertheless, as we have pointed out in another connection, a ready supply of workers did not by itself assure the reproduction of the labor force, since this process also demanded adequate provisions of foodstuffs and manufactured wage goods. Insofar as internal production was initially restricted, the cost of reproduction depended on the ability of the export complex itself to generate the necessary importing capacity. Similarly, given the absence of a domestic capital goods industry, the transformation of money capital into productive capital hinged on the ability of the coffee economy to supply foreign exchange for the importation of essential machinery and equipment.

Of course the coffee complex absorbed a portion of the economy's import capacity to supply its own demand for means of production, foodstuffs, and manufactured consumer goods, while the state required foreign exchange for its own consumption and investment costs. On the other hand, rubber, sugar, and cacao exports augmented the importing capacity generated by coffee sales, while the inflow of liquid capital from the exterior further enhanced Brazil's ability to buy abroad.[73]

It is difficult to draw conclusions about the period 1890–1894, apart from the fact that imports grew appreciably in response to the expansion of coffee receipts and, to a lesser extent, to receipts of rubber and cacao. Moreover, on balance, these years experienced a net inflow of capital from abroad. Even so, the pressures placed on the economy's capacity to import were considerable. And in contributing to the strain, the construction of new industrial plants helped provoke an internal adjustment of prices that in advancing the cost of wage goods and reducing real wages, fostered a realignment (inevitably altered later on) between the demand for imports and importing capacity. Similarly—although to a lesser degree—the erosive effect of exchange depreciations on government revenues necessarily held down public spending and constricted the demand for imports generated by this source.

In sum, the coffee export complex itself both furnished the means and created the conditions for the conversion of money capital into industrial capital; it provided labor power and generated the foreign exchange used to purchase capital goods as well as the foodstuffs and manufactured commodities that were indispensable to the reproduction of an industrial labor force.

Investments in industry brought at least minimally positive returns for several reasons. Apart from the "natural" advantage of relatively lower transportation charges, infant industries could count on a high degree of tariff protection. At this level of discussion it hardly matters whether tariff policy embodied explicitly protectionist objectives; rather, the important point is that import duties represented the only revenue instrument at the disposal of the federal government that would prevent the burden of taxation from falling directly on the export bourgeoisie. Protection was relatively high until the introduction of the gold tariff in 1891, and thereafter fell off—although only slightly—until 1894. New manufacturers were further sheltered to a substantial extent by currency devaluation, which altered the rate of exchange approximately 300 percent between 1889 and 1894.

The profitability of industrial capital in this period was therefore amply favored by a fall in wages and a high degree of protection. It also benefited from tax exemptions extended to the importation of machinery and equipment.

The question arises as to why industrial growth in this era was specialized and, for the most part, consisted of the production of consumer wage goods, textiles in particular. Certainly the reason is not the absence of a market, since, as we have emphasized, the coffee export complex created a market not only for consumer commodities but also for means of production. At first glance, yet another type of explanation is appealing: Because heavy industry required a relatively higher ratio of capital to labor and relied to a greater extent on imports in the formation of constant capital, the profound exchange depreciation and the evolution of wages in this period would have a greater adverse effect on its profitability in comparison to that of the consumer goods industry. Nevertheless, there are indications that in spite of these and other obstacles (e.g., the steel industry's difficulties in gaining access to raw materials), decisions were made to invest in heavy industry.

Obviously we must look elsewhere for an explanation of investment preferences. It should be noted that in the last two decades of the last century, during the "second industrial revolution," the capital goods industry underwent a profound technological transformation that led to the creation of immense economies of scale that required both higher initial investments and a larger minimum scale of operation for profitable production. For Brazil, this change introduced almost insoluble problems related to the concentration and centralization of capital, while investment risks assumed formidable proportions. Finally, and equally important, the technology of heavy industry was simply not available on the international market.

In contrast, light industry, and the textile industry in particular, relied on a comparatively simple technology that was more or less stable, easily mastered, and entirely contained in equipment accessible on the world market. In addition, both initial investments and the scale of production could be managed by the Brazilian economy of the time. These factors, rather than the problem of preexisting demand or relative factor costs, appear to be at the root of the preference shown by investors for the consumer goods industry.

Judging from the statistics on capital formation in São Paulo, the years 1895 to 1898 saw a pronounced advance in industrial production.[74] Although the investment rate of earlier years was apparently not sustained, general economic conditions were such as to permit the firm establishment of infant industry. Although public spending stagnated in real terms (even falling somewhat), the movement of the exchange rate preserved profit margins, relatively, within the coffee export complex. As accumulation proceeded, albeit at a slower pace, not only was a cut in demand for manufactured goods prevented, but demand actually grew. Furthermore, exchange depreciation improved competitive conditions, while the degree of protection afforded by the tariff schedule increased in 1896 and diminished in 1897 and 1898.

The industrial sector was in a position to take advantage of the stimulating conditions operating on the side of demand because it possessed a reserve of underutilized productive capacity accumulated during the favorable investment climate of the years 1890–1894. Without this excess capacity it would have been difficult to expand output so much at a time when new accumulation was hampered by the curtailment of importing capacity occasioned by the fall in exports from 1896 on.[75] Industry also benefited from an elastic manpower supply created by continued mass immigration; this situation, coupled with inflation, most likely reduced real wages substantially. Finally, the imported components of constant capital were less costly between 1895 and 1898, since the elevation in internal prices was more than proportional to the fall in the rate of exchange.[76] Therefore profit margins in the industrial sector must have widened considerably.

At the same time, in view of the excess capacity inherited from earlier years, the rate of accumulation of productive capital obviously declined.[77] Accordingly, much of the increment in earnings would have been applied to current operations, at a time when monetary policy was being tightened in order to hold down internal prices and support coffee profits.

It is not necessary to dwell on the difficulties industry faced from 1899 to 1902, which stemmed as much from the coffee crisis as from the cut in public spending and the sizable increase in excise taxes that had to be absorbed in a clearly deflationary context. What does merit close attention is the fact that despite all those difficulties nascent industry did in fact survive. It did so, first, because the fall in earnings was offset by the flexibility of money wages permitted by unemployment (linked to the depression) and by the cheapening of variable and constant capital imports owing to the valorization of the exchange rate.[78]

Second, given the recuperation of exports after 1900, the reduction in protectionism afforded by the exchange rate (because of appreciation) would have been fatal had it not been counterbalanced by the added customs protection provided by the gold tariff that same year. In sum, several defense mechanisms—the fall in money wages, the declining costs of imported primary materials, and tariff reform—enabled industry to weather the storm.

The available figures on capital goods imports attest to the recovery of the industrial sector after 1905, a process undoubtedly promoted by increased public spending beginning in 1903.[79] (see Table 9). The same data suggest that growth accelerated continually through 1912.

The circumstances favoring industrial development between 1905 and 1912 included, first, the enlargement of Brazil's import capacity after 1905 (and especially after 1909), which reflected both the growth in coffee and rubber exports and an improvement in the terms of trade.[80] Besides this, the significant infusion of foreign capital—for public and private investments and for the coffee valorization program—greatly augmented Brazil's foreign exchange reserves. If we further consider that the export complex generated no demand for foreign exchange in this period, we can see why industry was able to rely on either exchange appreciation or the economy's capacity to import capital goods to support its rate of accumulation.

The supply of labor power also contributed to industrial expansion:

manufacturers could tap both the natural increment in the urban population and a renewed current of immigration. As one might expect, immigration had fallen off between 1898 and 1905, not only because the depressed economy offered little attraction to newcomers, but also because the recuperation and expansion of the Italian, Argentine, and North American economies had weakened the push factors and strengthened the diversionary forces that conditioned migration to Brazil. After 1905, however, immigration revived and an aggregate of 995,000 newcomers arrived between 1905 and 1913—680,000 (69 percent) of whom came between 1909 and 1913. This dramatic change reflected the extraordinary increase in supply on the international labor market, although it is no less true that in various years (1908, 1909, 1911, and 1912) Brazil benefited from the decline in migration to the United States.[81]

It should not be assumed, however, that additions to the labor supply through immigration were entirely at the disposal of industrial capital. The growth in public investments, as well as the notable expansion of commercial food production, generated a demand for labor.[82] Elsewhere we have emphasized that coffee prosperity during the 1890s depended on the massive importation of foodstuffs. However, once in crisis, the coffee complex maintained a level of accumulation that, although not insignificant, was much lower than in the previous period. Accordingly, it became possible to diversify production and seriously engage in the production of food items, particularly in São Paulo; so significant was this trend that by the end of World War I a small volume of commodities was actually marketed abroad.[83]

In summary, owing to the natural growth of the economically active population and to mass immigration, labor power was sufficiently abundant to support the combined expansion of industry, public investments, and commercial food agriculture.

For its part, the balanced growth of agriculture, together with that of industry, permitted the reproduction of the labor force without exerting pressure on real wages. Money wages even tended to rise, as prices stayed level between 1903 and 1905, moved upward only in 1906, and stabilized thereafter.[87]

This said, the conditions of industrial realization can be duly noted. Industry and agriculture were mutually supportive, since they provided markets for each other and both benefited from increased public spending, which they in turn supported by making available edible and manufactured consumer goods. Finally, industry was equipped to meet foreign competition, not only because it enjoyed a measure of tariff protection, but also because it modernized, acquiring from abroad equipment whose efficiency equaled or nearly matched that of foreign rivals.[85]

Expansion was cut short in 1913, and the ensuing crisis deepened in

1914. Industry's problems originated, in the first instance, in the financial turmoil created by the contraction in the money supply that was brought about by a run on foreign exchange held by the Conversion Fund. On the other hand, as the figures on capital goods imports indicate, the growth of productive capacity had greatly accelerated after 1910, creating an excess that would be utilized during the war years.

The War of 1914–1918

The debate over whether World War I had a beneficial or harmful impact on Brazilian industrial development—to which the work of Warren Dean on the industrialization of São Paulo furnished additional arguments in support of an "obstructed growth" thesis—has been clarified by a series of recent works beginning with that of Fishlow in 1972. Cano's doctoral thesis on the roots of industrial concentration in São Paulo provides what we feel to be a definitive treatment of the problem, based as it is on an investigation of the available empirical data and a careful interpretation of the relevant facts. To summarize, Fishlow and Cano demonstrate that Paulista industry grew not only by exporting to other regions and to the exterior (Dean's thesis) but also because the internal market itself expanded under the stimulus of recovery from the crisis of 1913–1914.[86]

In order to counter the adverse effect of the crisis of 1913 and the progressive contraction in spending and in the national debt, the government embarked upon a program of "assistance to national production" that consisted of a contractual authorization of credit expansion through the Bank of Brazil; this institution began operating as a commercial bank at the same time it financed the treasury deficit. Thus the monetary restraint exercised from 1899 to the crisis of 1913–1914 was finally relaxed.[87]

This policy particularly benefited manufacturers, who could now finance new production, utilizing the excess capacity accumulated primarily in 1912 and 1913. For this reason, the decline in capital goods imports during the war can scarcely be viewed as an obstacle to industrial growth.[88] In reality, despite their reduced volume, such imports were adequate to create favorable conditions for the expansion of industrial demand and to enlarge industry's productive capacity. The aggregate data compiled by Cano on the capacity of the Paulista textile industry and on the number of new plants established during World War I clearly demonstrate that once industry recuperated from the slump of 1913–1914, further growth was not simply a function of an increase in the number of shifts worked by laborers, nor was further development obstructed by a lack of machinery—a thesis favored by Dean. Instead, Cano finds that "The total capital employed by industries established in years 1915 to 1919 amounted to 24 percent of all industrial capital registered in 1919, representing 5936 new plants created in that four-year period."[89]

Moreover, the movement of the exchange rate clearly enhanced the advantageous condition of demand at this time. After the exchange crisis of 1914, the mechanism of devaluation—despite a slight appreciation in 1916–1917—produced an alignment of internal and external prices that increasingly favored industry.

It was not only the industrial sector that profited from the inflationary boom of World War I. High rates of inflation in the context of stable nominal wages (and even declining wages in some categories) boosted earnings in nearly all rural and urban activities.[90]

The marked advance after 1905 in the agricultural production of food and raw materials that accompanied coffee expansion does not appear to have been additionally stimulated by wartime restrictions on Brazil's importing capacity. In other words, it was not import substitution that encouraged agricultural growth, but rather the combined influence of easy credit, the opening of new areas for cultivation in the years before the crisis, and finally, the emerging possibility of exporting internal surpluses of industrial raw materials such as cotton—a relatively scarce commodity on the international market.

The current emphasis on the wartime import substitution of foodstuffs, evident, for example, in the works of Dean, and Villela and Suzigan, finds little support in the empirical data Villela himself presents. The decline in food imports paralleled the expansion of Paulista agriculture after 1905, and thus began well before World War I. In the years 1915 to 1918, in the midst of conflict, exports were already growing at an accelerating pace (see Table 10).

The 65,000-ton reduction in food imports between 1909–1913 and 1914–1916 noted by Dean in fact reflected restrictions imposed on the purchase of nonessential items. Significantly, European wine *alone* accounted for nearly 85 percent of the decline registered.[91]

In summary, World War I, which has provoked much debate concerning its positive or adverse impact on industrialization, appears to have brought no dramatic change to either the conditions of production or the pattern of accumulation within the Brazilian economy. The internal market expanded primarily in São Paulo, through industrial and agricultural (food and raw materials) growth, and this process only confirmed the dominance of the Paulista economy, a phenomenon clearly visible from the end of the nineteenth century. In addition, the elevation of world food and raw material prices (other than coffee prices) gave some relief to the other regional export economies, some of which (like the old sugar complex of the Northeast) were clearly decadent, and provided the Amazon rubber economy with its last burst of activity.

Everything indicates, then, that the war merely represented a test of affirmation of the internal conditions of accumulation of an embryonic capitalism whose urban-industrial and agricultural diversification had become increasingly pronounced since the end of the last century.

The 1920s

Brazilian industry had already undergone considerable development by the early 1920s owing to the expanded production of wage goods. The census of 1919 reveals the near-domination of the sector by the food- and beverage-processing industries, which represented nearly 40 percent of the value of production, and by the textile and apparel industries, which accounted for 32 percent of the value of output. The figures in Fishlow's paper indicate that industrial growth afforded Brazil a high degree of self-sufficiency in terms of consumer goods.[92]

The 1919 census further demonstrates that the industrial preeminence of São Paulo was well established by that date.[93] Although space limitations prohibit a detailed examination of the issue of regional concentration, we may note that São Paulo's industrial superiority was established early (between 1905 and 1907), gained impetus from 1907 to 1913, and became consolidated during World War I. The origins of this position are to be found in the unparalleled, dynamism of the coffee economy, the growth of a vigorous branch of commercial food agriculture, and the existence of a sizable labor market. In sum, São Paulo's success can be attributed to the greater development of capitalist social relations of production.

It has been emphasized that the 1920s were characterized by low rates of industrial growth. Moreover, the available fiures indicate that production advanced between 1919 and 1922, stagnated from 1923 to 1926, and expanded again only in 1927 and 1928.[94]

Nevertheless, we believe that it is necessary to go a step further and acknowledge two other fundamental traits of industrial evolution between 1919 and 1929: the modernization of the wage goods industry, and differentiation within the industrial structure. The data on machine and accessory imports for the textile industry clearly indicate that the wage goods sector underwent an intense modernization process.[95]

Unquestionably this transformation proved possible only because of the enlargement of Brazil's importing capacity, which resulted as much from the enhanced purchasing power of exports as from the infusion of foreign capital, particularly for the coffee valorization policy. On the other hand, as Brazil's exchange situation eased, the rate of exchange appreciated in 1919–1920, 1925, and 1926, and relatively cheapened the cost of imported machinery and equipment.

If the widening of Brazil's importing capacity was a *sine qua non* for modernization, given the erosion of tariff protection, it nevertheless implied an intensification of external competition, at least between 1924 and 1926. It is this line of reasoning that underlies the current belief that industrial development during the 1920s was weak.[96]

However, the intensification of intercapitalist rivalry during the 1920s should not be interpreted solely as an extension of heightened external competition: it should also be viewed in terms of the tendency toward overaccumulation at work in a relatively concentrated market structure. The means employed was continued modernization, and the result was a greater concentration and centralization of capital, with a marked regional bias. Specifically, it was the São Paulo industrial sector that emerged as the driving force and chief beneficiary of the expansion of the period 1919–1923.

Brazil passed through an extremely volatile stage of development between 1924 and 1926. Whether because of the corrosive effect of prolonged inflation on tariffs, or because of exchange appreciation, the degree of industrial protection diminished considerably.[97] The expansion of demand tapered off (even allowing for that generated by the coffee sector) at a time when the potential for accumulation was very great. In consequence, intercapitalist competition intensified and assumed the form of an interregional contest in which São Paulo industry held a considerable advantage—a situation that provoked a severe industrial crisis in 1926.[98] In 1927 and 1928, in all likelihood because of the reactivation of the demand for coffee and the rise in the degree of protection, production increased and intercapitalist competition subsided.

Cotton textiles, of course, were only one part of industry. Several other branches exhibited somewhat more favorable patterns of development. Moreover, the consumer wage goods industry underwent a degree of diversification: industries specializing in the production of woolen, natural silk, rayon, and knitted goods were installed; the manufacture of such items as stoves, electrical lamps, and enameled goods was introduced; and food processing branched out to include the extraction and refining of vegetable oils, the production of canned animal and vegetable goods, and so forth.[99]

Similarly, the mediocre level of national growth was not representative of all sectors. Either because it penetrated and gained control of other markets or because it diversified to a greater extent, the Paulista consumer wage goods industry augmented production at the significant rate of approximately 6 percent per annum.

In sum, the consumer wage goods industry modernized to an important extent during the 1920s, and the industrial sector of São Paulo assumed a highly advantageous position at the expense of its counterparts in other states.

A second distinguishing feature of industrial evolution during the

1920s was the greater diversification achieved with the embryonic development of a capital goods sector. Not surprisingly, a few such industries already existed, particularly those installed during World War I. However, these consisted of small factories devoted to repairs and assembling or to the manufacture of simple machines and parts, or else they were installations of minor import, such as brickyards. Even a handful of ironworks had been present since the turn of the century, but they used the most primitive of processing techniques.[100]

Accordingly, there was little continuity between Brazil's early capital goods industries and those that came into being during the 1920s, i.e., small-scale steel production, the cement industry, and the manufacture of electric motors, machines for the sugar and textile industries, etc. Furthermore, limited as it was, the development of the capital goods sector was vital for the future because it laid the groundwork for the eventual reproduction of industrial capital relatively independent of mercantile-export capital.

TABLE 1
MONEY WAGES, 1884–1898
(MIL REIS)

Year	Weeding*	Harvesting[†]
1884	50	500
1886	80	400
1888	50	300
1890	60	300
1895	90	600
1898	90	680

SOURCE: Michael Hall, "The Origins of Mass Immigration in Brazil 1871–1914" (Ph. D. diss. Columbia University, 1969), p. 186.
*Wages for weeding are annual, mil reis per 1,000 trees.
[†] Wages for harvesting are annual, mil reis per 50 litres.

TABLE 2
EXPORT RECEIPTS, 1889–1898

Year	Value (£ thousands)
1889	28,552
1890	26,382
1891	27,136
1892	30,854
1893	32,007
1894	30,491
1895	32,586
1896	28,333
1897	25,883
1898	25,019

SOURCE: Annibal Villela and Wilson Suzigan, *Política do governo e crescimento da economia brasileira 1889–1945* (Rio de Janeiro: IPEA/INPES, 1973), p. 439.

TABLE 3
EXTERNAL AND INTERNAL COFFEE PRICES, 1889–1898

Year	External Prices (1889 = 100)	Internal Prices (1889 = 100)
1889	100	100
1890	113	120
1891	90	171
1892	87	201
1893	103	276
1894	92	290
1895	91	262
1896	69	252
1897	47	180
1898	41	163

SOURCE: A. Delfim Netto, *O problema do café no Brasil,* (2nd. ed. (São Paulo: Faculdade de Ciências Econômicas e Administrativas, Universidade de São Paulo, 1966), p. 29.

TABLE 4
EXTERNAL AND INTERNAL COFFEE PRICES, 1897–1906

Year	External Prices (U.S. cents per pound)	Internal Prices (mil réis per 60-kilo bag)
1897	7.5	55.6
1898	6.5	50.3
1899	6.7	48.2
1900	7.4	52.9
1901	6.4	34.5
1902	6.6	31.2
1903	7.0	29.7
1904	8.1	39.1
1905	8.6	30.0
1906	7.9	29.9

SOURCE: C. M. Pelaez, "Analise econômica do programa de sustentação do café," *Revista brasileira de economia,* 25, no. 4 (December 1971), p. 205.

TABLE 5
MONEY WAGES, 1898–1904
(MIL REIS)

Year	Weeding*	Harvesting[†]
1898	90	680
1899	85	650
1901	65	500
1904	60	450

SOURCE: Hall, "The Origins of Mass Immigration in Brazil, 1871–1914," p. 186.
*Wages for weeding are annual, mil reis per 1,000 trees.
[†]Wages for harvesting are annual, mil reis per 50 litres.

TABLE 6
IMPORTING CAPACITY AND EXCHANGE RATES, 1901–1906

Year	Quantum Index of Importing Capacity* (1928 = 100)	Exchange Rate (mil réis per pound sterling)
1901	53.1	21.1
1902	44.9	20.1
1903	44.9	20.0
1904	45.3	19.0
1905	53.1	15.1
1906	58.9	14.8

SOURCE: Pelaez, "Análise econômica do programa de sustentacão do café," p. 205. Villela and Suzigan, *Política do governo e crescimento da economia brasileira 1889–1945,* p. 441.
*The index of importing capacity is given by a value index of total exports divided by a price index of imports.

TABLE 7
INTERNATIONAL AND INTERNAL COFFEE PRICES AND EXCHANGE RATES, 1906–1913

Year	Internal Prices (mil réis per 60-kg bag)	External Prices (U.S. cents per pound)	Exchange Rates (mil réis per pound sterling)
1906	29.9	7.9	14.8
1907	28.9	7.6	15.8
1908	29.1	7.5	15.8
1909	31.6	7.9	15.8
1910	39.6	10.3	14.8
1911	53.9	13.3	14.9
1912	57.8	13.8	14.9
1913	46.1	11.1	14.9

SOURCE: Pelaez, "Análise econômica do programa de sustentação do café," pp. 205–206.

TABLE 8
INTERNATIONAL AND INTERNAL COFFEE PRICES AND
EXCHANGE RATES, 1919–1929

Year	External Prices (U.S. cents per pound)	Internal Prices (mil réis per 60-kg bag)	Exchange Rates (mil réis per pound sterling)
1919	19.5	94.6	16.5
1920	19.5	74.7	16.5
1921	10.7	82.4	28.7
1922	12.9	118.7	33.2
1923	13.5	146.9	44.3
1924	17.5	205.9	40.0
1925	22.3	215.1	38.9
1926	21.6	170.7	33.3
1927	18.5	170.4	40.6
1928	21.3	204.6	40.3
1929	20.4	191.9	40.6

SOURCE: Pelaez, "Análise econômica do programa de sustentação do café," pp. 205–206.

TABLE 9
IMPORTATION OF CAPITAL GOODS, 1900–1913
(1900 = 100)

Year	Quantum Index 1900 = 100
1900	100.0
1901	56.8
1902	31.7
1903	38.0
1904	41.3
1905	62.3
1906	66.1
1907	93.0
1908	96.4
1909	102.9
1910	118.7
1911	153.6
1912	205.3
1913	152.6

SOURCE: Villela and Suzigan, *Política do governo e crescimento da economia brasileira 1889–1945*, p. 347.

TABLE 10
FOREIGN TRADE IN FOODSTUFFS, 1911–1918
(EXPORTS MINUS IMPORTS, IN TONS)

Year	Rice	Beans	Potatoes	Corn
1911	− 16,480	− 8,058	− 17,846	− 3,798
1912	− 10,189	− 9,388	− 28,971	− 6,262
1913	− 7,728	− 8,540	− 29,800	− 8,892
1914	− 6,532	− 5,310	− 18,970	− 1,119
1915	− 6,945	1,042	− 8,757	− 2,066
1916	410	44,599	4,526	3,551
1917	44,603	93,402	4,401	23,867
1918	27,914	70,883	4,766	12,976

SOURCE: Villela and Suzigan, *Política do governo e crescimento da economia brasileira, 1889–1945*, p. 145.

TABLE 11
GROWTH OF SÃO PAULO CONSUMER GOODS INDUSTRY, 1918–1928

Year	Quantum Index A (1920 = 100)	Quantum Index B (1920 = 100)
1918	78.7	78.6
1919	93.0	92.3
1920	100.0	100.0
1921	102.5	99.9
1922	114.7	113.5
1923	188.1*	136.4
1924	131.6	137.1
1925	118.1	123.5
1926	130.2	131.8
1927	144.1	168.6
1928	169.1	215.7

SOURCE: Cano, *Raízes da concentração industrial em São Paulo*, p. 185.
NOTE: Index A is a composite of ten products, including four types of cloth, footwear, hats, beer, alcohol and cane brandy, sugar, and chilled meat. Index B includes all the products of Index A except cotton cloth.
*The large volume of cotton cloth accounts for this high figure.

NOTES

1. J. M. Cardoso de Mello, *O Capitalismo tardio* (São Paulo: Brasiliense, 1982).

2. On this point see E. Williams, *Capitalism and Slavery*, 2nd ed. (New York: Russell and Russell, 1961); F. Novais, *A crise do antigo sistema colonial* (São Paulo: Cadernos do CEBRAP, No. 17, 1974).

3. On the change in the pattern of accumulation in Britain, see, for example, David S. Landes, *The Unbound Prometheus: Technological Change and Industrial Development in Western Europe from 1750 to the Present* (Cambridge, Eng.: Cambridge University Press, 1969), pp. 41ff.; J. A. Schumpeter, *Business Cycles: A Theoretical, Historical and Statistical Analysis of Capitalist Process*, abridged ed. (New York: McGraw Hill, 1964), pp. 201ff.; E. Hobsbawm, *Industry and Empire* (Harmondsworth, Penguin Books, 1969), pp. 109ff.

4. K. Marx, "Futuros resultados de la dominación británica en la India," in K. Marx and F. Engels, *Sobre el colonialismo* (Cordoba: Siglo XXI, 1973).

5. On the exportation of British capital to Latin America, see J. F. Rippy, *British Investments in Latin America (1822–1849)* (Minneapolis: University of Minnesota Press, 1959), pp. 17–35; I. Stone, "La distribuzione geografica degli investimenti inglesi nell'America Latina (1825–1931)," *Storia Contemporanea*, 2 (1971): 495–518.

6. On the transformations that occurred between 1873 and 1896, the period of the "Great Depression," see especially Landes, *The Unbound Prometheus*, Ch. V.

7. The expression is Paulo Santi's. See his "El debate sobre el imperialismo en los clásicos del marxismo" in *Teoría marxista del imperialismo* (Cordoba: Ediciones Pasado y Presente, 1975).

8. C. M. Pelaez, "Análise econômica do programa de sustentação do café," *Revista brasileira de economia*, (December 1971), p. 209.

9. W. Cano, *Raízes da concentração industrial em São Paulo* (São Paulo: DIFEL, 1977), pp. 41 ff.

10. D. Graham, "Migração estrangeira e a questão da oferta de mão-de-obra no crescimento econômico brasileiro," *Estudos economicos* 3 (São Paulo: IPE-USP, 1971): 11 and 13. See also Cano, *Raízes da concentração industrial em São Paulo*, pp. 47 ff.

11. D. Graham, "Migração estrangeira e a questão da oferta," p. 30.

12. On this point see the conclusive evidence in Villela and Suzigan, *Política do governo e crescimento da economia brasileira, 1889–1945*, (Rio de Janeiro: IPEA, 1973), pp. 112–119. See also Cano, *Raízes da concentração industrial em São Paulo*, p. 58. Note that import values were generally quoted in pounds sterling but import prices were quoted in U.S. cents per pound.

13. For Brazilian and world coffee production, 1850–1944, see Pelaez, "Análise econômica do programa de sustentação do café," pp. 208–211. For U.S. import and Brazilian export prices for coffee over the same period, see ibid., pp. 204–7.

14. Pelaez, "Análise econômica do programa de sustentação do café," p. 205.

15. On public spending, monetary policy, and price trends, see Villela and

132   *Cardoso de Mello and Tavares*

Suzigan, *Política do governo e crescimento da economia brasileira 1889–1945*, pp. 105 ff.

16. Michael Hall, "The Origins of Mass Immigration in Brazil, 1871–1914" (Ph.D. diss., Columbia University, 1969), p. 157.

17. Cano, *Raízes da concentração industrial em São Paulo*, p. 41.

18. A. Delfím Netto, *O Problema do café no brasil*, 2nd Ed. (São Paulo: Faculdade de Ciências Econômicas e Administrativas, Universidade de São Paulo, 1966), pp. 95, 96.

19. Pelaez, "Análise econômica do programa de sustentação do café," p. 210.

20. Cano, *Raízes da concentração industrial em São Paulo*, p. 308.

21. A. Fishlow, "Origens e consequências da substituição de importações no Brasil," *Estudos econômicos* 2 no. 6 (1972), p. 64. On production, see also Villella and Suzigan, *Política do governo e crescimento da economia brasileira 1889–1945*, Appendix A and *passim*.

22. The evidence on prices and salaries is presented in Cano, *Raízes da concentração industrial em São Paulo*, p. 282.

23. For trends in wages and industrial production during this period, see ibid., pp. 279, 282, 291–293.

24. Ibid., p. 282. See also Villela and Suzigan, *Política do governo e crescimento da economia brasileira, 1889–1945*, p. 431.

25. For series on the terms of trade and foreign capital flows, see Villela and Suzigan, *Política do governo e crescimento da economia brasileira, 1889–1945*, pp. 441, 451, 452.

26. Pelaez writes, for example: "Industrial development was retarded in large part by the inadequacy of their monetary, banking, exchange, and fiscal policies. This inadequacy, in turn, derived from the slavish adherence to one school of thought, here defined as the school of 'monetary orthodoxy.' " C. M. Pelaez, "Las consequências econômicas da ortodoxia monetária, cambial e fiscal no Brasil entre 1889 e 1945," *Revista brasileira de economia* 25 no. 3 (July–Sept. 1971), p. 8. Villela and Suzigan share the same view: "The evolution of Brazilian economic policy, expressed in monetary, exchange, and fiscal measures, was characterized by sudden and frequent changes in orientation. . . . The lack of administrative continuity was itself a powerful element of confusion in the directing of economic policy. In the first eight years alone the new Republic had twelve finance ministers. And each one formulated his own policies, in most cases according to a strictly personal point of view." And later: "It is evident that any critique of the orientation of government policy (monetary, exchange, fiscal, and tariff) should take into account the economic doctrines in vogue in that particular era." Villela and Suzigan, *Política do governo e crescimento da economia brasileira 1889–1945*, pp. 31 and 233.

27. For example, see Caio Prado Júnior, *História economica do Brasil*, 12th ed. (São Paulo: Brasiliense, 1970), Ch. XXII.

28. See Villela and Suzigan, *Política do governo e crescimento da economia brasileira 1889–1945*, pp. 420–423.

29. Cano, *Raízes da concentração industrial em São Paulo*, p. 145.

30. J. Murtinho, *Relatório do ministro da fazenda* (Rio de Janeiro: Imprensa Nacional, 1899).

31. For more details concerning Murtinho's fiscal reforms, see Villela and Suzigan, *Política do governo e crescimento da economia brasileira 1889–1945*, pp. 105 ff.

32. On the evolution of public spending and the fiscal deficit, see Villela and Suzigan, *Política do governo e crescimento da economia brasileira, 1889–1945*, pp. 140, 156, 185, 414–415.

33. Celso Furtado, *Formação econômica do Brasil*, 4th ed., (Rio de Janeiro, Ed. Fundo de Cultura, 1961), p. 168. Translated as *The Economic Growth of Brazil* (Berkeley and Los Angeles: University of California Press, 1965), p. 182. The translation is that of Ricardo W. de Aguiar and Eric Charles Drysdale.

34. On industrial investment in the period, see Fishlow, "Origens e consequências da substituição de importações no Brasil," p. 13.

35. Murtinho, *Relatório do ministro da fazenda*, p. xv.

36. Ibid., pp. 3–4.

37. On the exchange crisis and the consolidation of the external public debt in this period, see Villela and Suzigan, *Política do governo e crescimento da economia brasileira 1889–1945*, pp. 334 ff.

38. For price data, see Villela and Suzigan, *Política do governo e crescimento da economia brasileira, 1889–1945*, p. 425.

39. The details of the "Programa de Regulamento Economico" are described in Villela and Suzigan, *Política do governo e crescimento da economia brasileira, 1889–1945*, p. 100.

40. For an appraisal of the Agreement of Taubaté, see Delfim Netto, *O Problema do café no Brasil*, pp. 63ff.

41. On the Conversion Fund, see Villela and Suzigan, *Política do governo e crescimento da economia brasileira, 1899–1945*, p. 314.

42. On the money supply during this period, see Villela and Suzigan, *Política do governo e crescimento da economia brasileira, 1899–1945*, pp. 412–413.

43. For data on exchange rates, capital flows, and exports, see Villela and Suzigan, *Política do governo e crescimento da economia brasileira, 1899–1945*, pp. 424–425, 439–454; Cano, *Raízes da concentração industrial em São Paulo*, pp. 263–278.

44. Delfim Netto, *O Problema do café no Brasil*, p. 93. One conto de réis equals 1,000 mil réis.

45. On the Funding Loan, see Villela and Suzigan, *Política do governo e crescimento da economia brasileira, 1889–1945*, pp. 138ff., 337, 338.

46. Delfim Netto, *O Problema do café no Brasil*, pp. 95–96.

47. Ibid., pp. 92ff. (on the second valorization scheme).

48. For coffee prices in 1918, see Pelaez, "Análise econômica do programa de sustentação do café," *Revista brasileira da economia* (December 1971), p. 206.

49. On federal finances between 1913 and 1918, see Villela and Suzigan, *Política do governo e crescimento da economia brasileira, 1889–1945*, pp. 140, 414–423.

50. Villela and Suzigan, *Política do governo e crescimento da economia brasileira, 1889–1945*, pp. 318–319.

51. On coffee prices and exchange rates between 1919 and 1923, see Pelaez, "Análise econômica do programa de sustentação do cafe," *Revista brasileira de*

economia (December 1971), p. 206, and Villela and Suzigan, *Política do governo e crescimento da economia brasileira, 1889–1945*, p. 424.

52. For a description of the third valorization program, see Delfim Netto, *O Problema do café no Brasil*, p. 92ff.

53. Villela and Suzigan, *Política do governo e crescimento da economia brasileira, 1889–1945*, p. 338.

54. On fiscal trends, see Villela and Suzigan, *Política do governo e crescimento da economia brasileira, 1889–1945*, p. 140, 156, 185, 414–423.

55. On monetary evolution, see Villela and Suzigan, *Política do governo e crescimento da economia brasileira, 1889–1945*, p. 412–413.

56. On the Permanent Defense Policy, see Delfim Netto, *O Problema do café no Brasil*, pp. 115ff.

57. Ibid., p. 121.

58. Villela and Suzigan, *Política do governo e crescimento da economia brasileira, 1889–1945*, pp. 157–159.

59. On the development of Brazil's importing capacity, 1901–1945, see Villela and Suzigan, *Política do governo e crescimento da economia brasileira, 1889–1945*, p. 441.

60. Villela and Suzigan, *Política do governo e crescimento da economia brasileira, 1889–1945*, p. 156, 413.

61. Delfim Netto, *O Problema do café no Brasil*, p. 170.

62. Ibid., pp. 139ff.

63. Furtado, *Formaçao econômica do Brasil*, p. 188. (*The Economic Growth of Brazil*, pp. 205–206.)

64. See the appraisals of Villela and Suzigan, *Política do governo e crescimento da economia brasileira, 1889–1945*, and Fishlow, "Origens e consequências da substituição de importações no Brasil."

65. Fishlow, "Origens e consequências da substituição de importações no Brasil," p. 28.

66. In contrast to this view, see the works of C. M. Pelaez on the question.

67. The role of the public deficit has been appropriately underlined in the works of C. M. Pelaez. However, Pelaez unaccountably insists that it was not "intentionally" generated and concludes, curiously enough, that "effective" policy was not Keynesian. Pelaez also misinterprets the balance-of-trade "deficit." For a good indication of the debate see Fishlow, "Origens e consequências da substituição de importações no Brasil," p. 29.

68. Cano, *Raízes da concentração industrial em São Paulo*, p. 142.

69. Fishlow, "Origens e consequências da substituição de importações no Brasil"; Cano, *Raízes da concentração industrial em São Paulo*, p. 142.

70. F. H. Cardoso, "Condições sociais da industrialização: o caso de São Paulo," in *Mudanças sociais na América Latina* (São Paulo: DIFEL, 1969), pp. 188–189.

71. A. F. Bandeira, Jr., *A indústria no estado de São Paulo*, 2nd ed. (São Paulo, 1908).

72. José de Souza Martins, *Empresário e empresa na biografia do Conde Matarazzo*, (Rio de Janeiro: Instituto de Ciências Sociais, 1967). Warren Dean, *A industrialização de São Paulo*, (São Paulo: DIFEL, 1971).

73. For foreign loans of the government, see Villela and Suzigan, *Política do governo e crescimento da economia brasileira, 1889–1945*, pp. 451–452.

74. Cano, *Raízes da concentração industrial em São Paulo*, p. 142.

75. Villela and Suzigan, *Política do governo e crescimento da economia brasileira, 1889–1945*, pp. 439–440.

76. Ibid, pp. 424–425.

77. Compare the figures for capital formation in the Paulista industrial sector between 1895 and 1897 with those for the period 1890–1894. See Cano, *Raízes da concentração industrial em São Paulo*, p. 142.

78. Villela and Suzigan, *Política do governo e crescimento da economia brasileira, 1889–1945*, pp. 424–425.

79. See Villela and Suzigan, *Política do governo e crescimento da economia brasileira, 1889–1945*, pp. 414–415.

80. For the evolution of coffee and rubber exports, see Cano, *Raízes da concentração industrial em São Paulo*, p. 270. For the terms of trade, see Villela and Suzigan, *Política do governo e crescimento da economia brasileira, 1889–1945*, p. 441.

81. On immigration, see D. Graham, "Migração estrangeira e a questão da oferta," p. 18.

82. On the development of commercial food agriculture, see Cano, *Raízes da concentração industrial em São Paulo*, pp. 57ff.

83. See Table 10.

84. For the evolution of prices, see Villela and Suzigan, *Política do governo e crescimento da economia brasileira, 1889–1945*, pp. 424–425.

85. Fishlow, "Origens e consequências da substituição de importações no Brasil," p. 17.

86. The three works referred to in this paragraph are: Dean, *A industrialização de São Paulo;* Fishlow, "Origens e consequências da substituição de importações no Brasil"; and Cano, *Raízes da concentração industrial em São Paulo.*

87. On the policy of "assistance to national production," see Villela and Suzigan, *Política do governo e crescimento da economia brasileira, 1889–1945*, p. 142.

88. On the wartime importation of capital goods, see Villela and Suzigan, *Política do governo e crescimento da economia brasileira, 1889–1945*, p. 437.

89. Cano, *Raízes da concentração industrial em São Paulo*, p. 168.

90. On wage trends during World War I, see Cano, *Raízes da concentração industrial em São Paulo*, p. 282.

91. Cano, *Raízes da concentração industrial em São Paulo*, p. 169.

92. See Fishlow, "Origens e consequências da substituição de importações no Brasil," pp. 21–22.

93. See Cano, *Raízes da concentração industrial em São Paulo*, p. 241.

94. See Fishlow, "Origens e consequências da substituição de importações no Brasil," p. 64.

95. See Cano, *Raízes da concentração industrial em São Paulo*, p. 278.

96. See Fishlow, "Origens e consequências da substituição de importações no Brasil," pp. 26–27.

97. On tariffs, see, for example, Nicia Villela Luz, *A Luta pela indus-*

trialização no Brasil [São Paulo: DIFEL, 1961], pp. 193 Nicia ff; Villela and Suzigan, *Política do governo e crescimento da economia brasileira, 1889–1945,* pp. 346ff.

98. The intensification of interregional competition was first noted by S. Stein, *The Brazilian Cotton Manufacturers: Textile Enterprise in an Underdeveloped Area, 1850–1950* (Cambridge, Mass.: Harvard University Press, 1957), pp. 114, 144–145.

99. On diversification within the consumer goods industry, see W. Dean, "A industrialização durante a República Velha," in *O Brasil republicano* (São Paulo: DIFEL, 1975), p. 264.

100. W. Baer, *Siderurgia e desenvolvimento brasileiro* (Rio de Janeiro: Zahar Editores, 1970), pp. 80–81.

4
The Growth of the Nitrate Industry and Socioeconomic Change in
CHILE
1880–1930

Carmen Cariola and Osvaldo Sunkel*

THE GROWTH OF THE NITRATE INDUSTRY AND SOCIOECONOMIC CHANGE: THE INTERPRETATIVE HYPOTHESIS

The great influence of the nitrate industry in Chilean economic and social life at the end of the nineteenth and beginning of the twentieth century is well known in general terms.[1] Equally well known is the importance that the new copper industry began to achieve in the decade of the 1920s, at the very time when nitrate production was at its maximum, before it entered on a stage of decline that ended in stagnation.[2]

In the literature on recent Chilean development it has been noted that the world economic crisis of 1930 and World War II both emphasized and extended the process of industrialization.[3] Attention has also been given to the key and increasing role foreign enterprise has played in this process

*We wish to thank the Institut für IberoAmerica Kunde and the Fundación Volkswagen for their support toward the completion of this project. We also wish to express our appreciation to Luz María Méndez, Eduardo Astroza, Cristian Donoso, Amelia Palomino, Jorge Bravo, and Stephany Griffith-Jones, who collaborated, successively, in the preparation and presentation of the statistical data.

since World War II.[4] These writings develop a framework of interpretation that delineates the extraordinary importance to national development of the manner in which the Chilean economy has been linked to the international economy.[5]

This factor is, of course, neither new nor limited to the period of the rise of the nitrate industry. It is part of a pattern of historical development that began when the first Spaniards arrived in America, and was henceforth *one* of the basic and permanent formative elements of Latin American economies and societies. The *other*, often neglected element, to which we wish to give in this study the importance it merits, is the combination of local preexisting characteristics and conditions that interacted dialectically with the new external factors and forces and gave rise to complex, historically specific processes and reactions.

The search for precious minerals, especially gold, and for other products highly valued on the European market and in the Viceroyalty of Peru was one of the fundamental motives for the Spanish conquest and settlement of Chile in the second half of the sixteenth century. This process changed the social relations of production of native agriculture as it became necessary to supply foodstuffs to the conquistadores in their new urban centers and to the Indians withdrawn from agriculture to exploit deposits of precious metals, and to engage in other activities connected with foreign trade.

When precious metals were found to be scarce in Chile, in contrast to the spectacular production of silver in the Viceroyalty of Peru, there was a great expansion of livestock herds in the seventeenth century to supply the strong demand for leather and for fats for making candles and soap. This increase in cattle production in what came to be called *el siglo del sebo* gave rise to new changes in the structure and extent of agricultural landholding, and in the utilization of native labor, changes that brought forth new social groups and, correspondingly, new political interest and pressures.

The eighteenth century saw the transformation of the pastoral economy developed in the previous century into an agricultural economy. The basis of this transformation was the capture of the Peruvian market for wheat at the end of that century and the expansion of that market in the following years. This process began with independence from Sapin, and continued through the course of conflicts and contradictions among colonies, between colonial towns and countrysides, between colonies and the colonizing country, and among empires. Once again, the social and productive structure of Chile underwent important changes as a result of these alterations in the forms of external economic and political relationships, and their interaction with the preexisting situation.[6]

The nineteenth century, in large measure as a result of the termination of the colonial situation and the integration of the Chilean economy into an expanding world capitalist market, was a period in which mining became fundamentally important, especially after the 1860s. As we have noted in another study, the period from 1830 to 1930 is clearly divided into two major cycles of expansion and crisis.[7] The first, whose growth was primarily based on the export of gold and, especially, silver and copper, to which was added in the 1850s and 1860s a significant outflow of grain, began to decline about 1875. It finally ended with the start of the War of the Pacific in 1879.

After the war, with the incorporation of the provinces of Tarapacá and Antofagasta into Chilean territory, the second main cycle of expansion of the Chilean economy began. During this cycle, which reached its height about 1920 and ended with the Great Depression of 1930, the enormous expansion of nitrate production in the provinces of Norte Grande not only relegated grain and flour exports to a secondary place but also surpassed the exports of copper, silver, and gold from the Norte Chico. The grain exports originated in the Núcleo Central and in Concepción and La Frontera, and had been very important in the previous export cycle.

In the earlier phases of the growth in foreign demand for agricultural products, as in the search for precious minerals during the era of conquest and colonization, the interaction between the expansion of production for the external market and the economic, social, institutional, technological, and political transformations in the preexisting situation were readily seen and appreciated. However, when the export operations were in mining, as in the case of nitrates in Chile, they were developed with strong and increasing foreign participation, and in a region that was distant, arid, and isolated from the rest of the country, especially from its agricultural base. For these reasons, some important aspects of the interaction were either not observed or were neglected.

Because of the geographical conditions, the growing influence of foreign interests, particularly British, and the ascendancy after the Civil War of 1891 of social groups of liberal persuasion, a dominant current of opinion became established in Chile that viewed the growth of the nitrate industry as having a series of disastrous consequences for national development—without, in our opinion, sufficiently appreciating the profound transformations in social, economic, political, and institutional life that were stimulated by the industry.

According to this point of view the nitrate industry was basically an alien enclave largely isolated from the remainder of Chilean social and economic life. In this view, the high foreign participation in nitrate production signified that the principal portion of the profits generated by the industry was kept abroad, and did not benefit the national economy. The scanty portion that remained in the country was controlled directly, or indirectly through the Chilean government, by a small clique that misspent the funds on extravagant national and imported consumer goods and on unnecessary expansion of the bureaucracy. The emigration to the north of workers who were attracted by jobs in the nitrate industry was said to have ruined agriculture in the Valle Central, causing a labor shortage and a rise in wages there. Something similar had occurred with certain manufactures that had flourished temporarily after 1850 but then declined, owing to the competition of imported goods purchased with the proceeds of the nitrate industry and the failure of the reigning liberal ideology to follow a policy of protection and development. In addition, it was alleged that the internal and international financial bonanza derived from the nitrate boom had led to a weakening of entrepreneurial energy and even of the spirit of Chilean nationalism.

This is a brief and simplified summary of the interpretation found in the influential writings of Encina and other contemporary authors, and recently developed by Pinto Santa Cruz, Ramírez Necochea, Jobet, and others.[8]

In this essay we wish to present an interpretative hypothesis that differs substantially from that sketched above, especially in the extreme version set forth by A. Gunder Frank. Our argument, which we shall try to demonstrate empirically, is along the following lines: During the period 1880–1930, and even much earlier, the Chilean economy underwent a notable increase in its export sector, principally on the basis of nitrates. Given the size and growth of world demand, the high rates of profits on investments, the geological characteristics of the nitrate deposits, and the technical aspects of their exploitation, the development of nitrate resources required a substantial labor force both for the mining activities and for transportation and shipping facilities in a broad territorial domain.

This necessitated a large capital investment; the displacement of a considerable number of people to the Norte Grande; the building of a broad infrastructure of railroads, telegraph services, and urban and port facilities; the building or expansion of housing in the nitrate areas and on the coast; the organization of production and export of great amounts of material; the securing of capital equipment and current supplies and of the necessary capital to finance them; the supply of consumer goods for the population of Norte Grande, a desert region in which agricultural production was almost nonexistent; and the organization of the corresponding public, commercial, financial, and other services.

It seems reasonable to assume that the great economic expansion in Norte Grande gave rise to a significant movement of human resources, partly, at least, of rural origin; the creation of a market for capital equipment and current supplies and of capital for mining operations and consumer goods for the people in the north; and the generation of a surplus of financial resources. Under certain sociopolitical conditions, an important part of the surplus might have accrued to the government, which could have expanded at least some of it for investment in infrastructure and development of agricultural and industrial activities. If this in fact happened, and we will endeavor to show that it did, the stimulus to migratory, commercial, and financial movements between the central and northern zones of the country may well have contributed to the founding and growth of an infrastructure of transport, communications, and institutions between these regions, promoting both industry and urbanization, and, in addition, fostering in the southern part of the country the effective incorporation of the agricultural regions beyond Concepción into the national economy.

In this manner, it is reasonable to assume that the interaction among the mining regions of the north, the urban zones in the center, and the agricultural sections of the center and south would have brought about significant transformations in the raising of crops and cattle. The growth of demand for these products in the cities and towns of the center and north would have contributed, in the first place, to the extension of the agricultural frontier to the south of Concepción, either by bringing under cultivation new lands or by taking over those still occupied by the indigenous population. In the second place, this process would have stimulated the reorganization of agricultural production in the traditional areas of the Central Valley, especially in view of the emigration of a part of the rural labor force. Out of this combination of dynamic factors, set in motion by the expansion of the nitrate industry, and governmental services that took place broadly through the center and south of Chile, one may observe distinct types of regional and urban-rural migratory flows; changes in landholding; novel developments in rural social relationships; modifications in land use; technical innovations; development of an infrastructure of transport and communications; and development of corresponding networks in the commercial and financial realm, accompanied by the broadening of services and institutions furnished by the state.

It may be maintained, therefore, that this enlargement of the territorial bases of the Chilean economy through the incorporation of the mineral resources of Norte Grande and the agricultural resources of the zone of Concepción and La Frontera to the south would have been accompanied by a transformation of the traditional agriculture of the central provinces and by a notable process of urbanization and expansion of governmental activities, particularly around the major cities of Santiago, Valparaíso, and Concepción. These urban centers would in this way have become important administrative, commercial, and financial complexes, providing an opportunity for the development of manufacturing activities of some importance, as well as for a considerable transformation of the social and political structure of Chile.

Hence, as we shall try to demonstrate, the expansion of nitrate exports, even though controlled in large measure by foreign capital, far from constituting an isolated enclave that inhibited the development of capitalism in Chile, was instead a fundamental factor contributing to its healthy growth. The state, labor, consumer and capital equipment and current supplies markets in the north were probably the principal mediatory mechanisms through which significant social, economic, and political changes of a capitalist type were stimulated in other sectors of Chilean society, especially the industrial and agricultural sectors. Why this capitalist development did not replicate that of the mature industrial countries, but adopted the form (though not the stage) of underdeveloped, structurally heterogeneous, and dependent capitalism, is a question so broad and complex that we cannot consider it here.[9]

In the analysis that follows, which is no more than a first step in the analysis of this vast topic, we shall endeavor to formulate in a more detailed fashion the interpretative line that we have sketched and to set forth the empirical evidence and theoretical assumptions on which it is based. Obviously in a study of the present scope it is impossible to "prove" our hypothesis in an exhaustive fashion. Our aim is a restricted one: to construct a case sufficiently solid and empirically buttressed to justify our disagreement with the conventional interpretation, especially in the extreme form set forth by Frank, and to stimulate further research.[10]

II. BACKGROUND OF THE NITRATE CYCLE

The complex interaction of a dialectical character that occurred in the period 1880–1930 between the strong expansive force of the nitrate industry and the remainder of Chilean economic and social activity cannot be understood adequately without appreciating the most important elements of the preceding socioeconomic situation, a major part of which was generated in the long cycle of earlier growth from 1830 to 1880.

During this earlier period there was intense mining activity in the provinces of Norte Chico that was concentrated in the exploitation and exportation of gold, silver, and copper. These activities were carried out by a group of Chilean entrepreneurs, among them Diego de Almeyda, José Antonio Moreno, José Santos Ossa, and Tomás Urmeneta. This group of individual pioneers, along with many others, explored Norte Chico and prospected in the desert to discover its wealth. Together with European entrepreneurs and technicians such as Meiggs and Wheelwright, they began the building of railroads and smelters. English financiers and businessmen, and others of British origin like Agustín Edwards, provided links with foreign markets and their sources of financing. Valparaíso, an essential stage in the voyage to Europe by way of the Straits of Magellan or Cape Horn, and also the main port for Chilean coastal traffic, became the great commercial and financial center of Norte Chico.[11]

The growth of mining in Norte Chico caused a substantial increase in the urban population of the region.[12] The number of communities with more than 2,000 inhabitants grew from nine to fifteen according to the censuses of 1865 and 1875 (Table 1), and the population of these places increased from 56,000 to 68,000 due in part to the arrival of migrants from the rural zones of Norte Chico. The population of these rural zones declined from 183,000 to 176,000 inhabitants in the same period (Table 2). In consequence, the expansion of mining in Norte Chico caused an appreciable increase in the labor force.

The expansion of mining activity in Norte Chico thus gave rise to an important entrepreneurial group, to a labor force accustomed to work in the mines, to greater technical knowledge of mining and of mineral deposits, and to an understanding of the necessary commercial and financial links with the center and south of Chile and the world market. Thus was born and nurtured a substantial capitalist sector in Chile, capable of introducing technological innovations, financing the necessary infrastructure, accumulating and reinvesting capital in order to engage in new activities, and selling its products in the world's markets.

On this solid economic base the penetration of the Peruvian nitrate territories of Tarapacá and those of Bolivia in the province of Antofagasta was initiated in the 1860s. The exploitation and exportation of nitrate from these regions was carried out before the War of the Pacific, and it reached an annual average of around 300,000 tons in the period 1875–1878 (Table 3). During the decade of the 1870s the building of various nitrate railways was begun, and in the early years of the decade the silver resources of Caracoles were exploited, which contributed greatly to the flow of capital, businessmen, and workers to Norte Grande. According to Bermúdez,

[B]eginning in the 1850s there were Chilean workers and businessmen in the nitrate fields of Tarapacá, but their numbers increased greatly in the early years of the 1870s. From four to six thousand Chileans are estimated to have worked on the construction of the nitrate railways of Iquique, to La Noria and Pisagua in the interior, with branches to other sectors. When these works were finished, the laborers remained in the province as workers in the nitrate fields and on port facilities.

The Peruvian census of 1876 lists 38,226 inhabitants of the province of Tarapacá. Of this total, there were 17,013 Peruvians, 9,664 Chileans, and the remainder of other nationalities. Of the districts of the province, that of

Iquique contained a majority of Chileans, namely, 6,048, as compared to 4,429 Peruvians. In addition, in this district, there were 1,063 persons of unknown nationality, among whom probably some were Chilean.

The situation was considerably more important for Chile on the Bolivian coast. A census taken in 1875 by the City of Antofagasta gave for this port a population of 5,384 inhabitants, of whom 4,530 were Chileans and only 419 were Bolivians. We do not have corresponding data for Cobija, Calama and agricultural communities of the interior, in all of which Bolivians were the predominant element. Chileans formed the great majority in mining activity in Caracoles, in the nitrate zone, and in the city of Antofagasta.

In November 1878, three months before the occupation of the coastal area, the city of Antofagasta carried out a census of the district of Antofagasta, a district that included the communities of Antofagasta, Salar del Carmen, Mantos Blancos, Punta Negra, Carmen Alto, and Salinas. These latter two places, and also Salar del Carmen, were inhabited exclusively by workers and employees of the Compañía de Salitres y Ferrocarril. According to the census, the total population of the district was 8,507, of which 6,554 were Chileans, 1,226 Bolivians, 226 Argentines, 121 Peruvians, 102 English, and 276 of other nationalities. The Chilean population, advancing by way of the Atacama Desert, and along the seacoast, had, in effect, invaded the Bolivian coastal plain and had installed industrial centers in it, thus initiating an era of progress in a region that had formerly been neither developed nor populated.[13]

These figures demonstrate the significant penetration of the provinces of Tarapacá and Antofagasta by Chileans, but the Chilean contribution to the growth of the nitrate industry was not limited to the provision of a labor supply. As noted earlier, the growth of mining in Norte Chico, and of commerce and banking in Valparaíso, resulted in Chile's becoming the most readily available source for capital, machinery, and general merchandise on the Pacific coast. For equipment and merchandise, contemporary reports confirm that Chile was an important supplier for Tarapacá and Antofagasta.[14] The volume of coastal traffic from the ports of the central region to those of Norte Grande after the War of the Pacific (which we shall later examine in detail) demonstrates that this commerce had begun before the war. In addition, we may mention the specific example of the establishment by José Santos Ossa in the central agricultural area of Chile of a wholesale agency for Chilean fruits in Chillán and Tomé. Santos Ossa also leased the property known as "San Vicente" for a similar purpose.[15]

Concerning capital investment in the nitrate industry in Tarapacá, Hernández states:

From 1870 on, the development of industrial credit in Valparaíso for the nitrate industry of Tarapacá commenced a period of more rapid growth than in earlier years. The Compañía Chilena de Consignaciones invested some two million pesos in equipment for nitrate exploitation. The Banco de Edwards . . . and four or five firms in Valparaíso invested a similar amount. . . . These corporations invested in the nitrate industry not only their own capital, but also substantial sums borrowed from banks in Valparaíso.[16]

Thus by the end of 1878 the distribution of production of nitrates, by the nationality of enterprises, was as follows: Peruvian 58.5 percent, Chilean 19.0 percent, British 13.5 percent, German 8.0 percent, and Italian 1.0 percent.[17]

In summary, the first cycle of expansion of the Chilean economy laid the foundation for a deep penetration in the nitrate industry of Antofagasta and Tarapacá in the decade preceding the War of the Pacific. Consequently, conditions favorable to a rapid growth of Chilean control after the war were created, since these territories then became a part of the domain of Chile.

The considerable expansion of agriculture in the central region of Chile, especially from 1850 to 1879, constituted a second element in the foundation for the boom in the nitrate industry. The clearest evidence for this development is visible in the notable rise in the production and exportation of wheat and flour.[18] In the mid-1840s wheat exports were of the order of 50,000 metric quintals (Table 4). In the second half of the 1850s, as a result of the temporary demands of the Australian and Californian markets—whose importance has been greatly exaggerated by historians—annual figures for wheat exports reached about 140,000 quintals in several years, with the exceptional maximum of 189,000 in 1855. In the following decade the British market grew more and more important, and in the 1870s total wheat exports from Chile exceeded 1 million quintals in some years. The maximum was reached in 1874, with more than 1.5 million quintals. So wheat exports rose more than twenty fold in less than twenty-five years, a truly exceptional rate of increase. The same may be said of flour exports, which showed an annual average of about 50,000 quintals in the mid-1840s, surpassed 200,000 quintals in some years of the 1850s, and reached more than 500,000 quintals by 1865—a tenfold growth in twenty years.

Together with the phenomenal increase in these exports, there occurred a comparable increase in the growing and milling of wheat, in the means of transport to the seaports, and in the corresponding financial and commercial networks. In other words, in this prewar period the lands of the central valley, from the province of Aconcagua to that of Bío–Bío, were incorporated into the system of commercial agriculture. Previously the major part of these lands—except those near Santiago, Valparaíso, and Concepción—had been only sparsely cultivated, mainly on a subsistence basis. Hence the 1850s, 1860s, and 1870s were decades in which a flourishing and significant commercial agricultural economy, fully integrated into the world market, was established in the central region. Whereas in the 1840s 90 percent of Chilean wheat exports were destined for the markets of Bolivia and, especially, Peru, this proportion fell rapidly as the importance of the British market increased; in the period 1870–1875 it amounted to only 32 percent, and in 1885–1890 to only 15 percent. According to Sepúlveda, the distribution of exports of wheat in 1874 was as follows: Great Britain 63.5 percent, other European countries 2.9 percent, the Atlantic coast of South America 9.2 percent, Peru 19.2 percent, Bolivia 2.6 percent, and elsewhere in the Pacific 1.3 percent.[19]

The transformation in the economy of the central region is reflected in the extension of the railway system. In the decade of Montt, the 1850s, work was started on the line that was opened to traffic between Santiago and Valparaíso in 1863. In the same period construction began on the longitudinal line to the south, which was completed in stages: 1859, to Rancagua, 82 kilometers; 1862, to San Fernando, 139 kilometers; 1868, to Curicó, about 200 kilometers; and 1877, to Concepción, about 570 kilometers. As a result of this railway policy (including other feeder lines), the integration of the transport system of the central region, and its communications with the main ports for exports and coastal trade, were completed.[20]

In the 1850s the first banks, both private and public, were established. These financial institutions expanded greatly in the following years, not only in the principal cities but also in minor towns in the interior, with the opening of branch offices by the larger banks (Table 5).[21]

To summarize, during the period of our concern an important expansion and transformation of capitalist agriculture occurred in the central region. From a relatively restricted and isolated activity, agriculture became one that covered the whole central section of Chile. Close commercial relationships also developed, not only with internal markets, but also with distant world markets such as California, Australia, and Great Britain, as well as with others nearer at hand, including Peru and Bolivia.

Although wheat and flour are the most spectacular indicators of the growth and transformation of Chilean agriculture, other agricultural products show marked increases in production, which are recorded in reports of exports of cattle, lumber, and various agricultural products including hay, potatoes, nuts, honey, dried meats, fruit, eggs, and cheese. In 1872 this group of exports attained a value of 3 million pesos, or 8 percent of total exports and approximately 16 percent of agricultural exports, which in those years represented about half of exports of all kinds.[22] According to the same source, these products were exported to Peru and Bolivia, another indication of the importance that the provinces of Tarapacá and Antofagasta were acquiring as markets for the Chilean agricultural sector.

The remarkable capitalist development of agriculture in the central region during this period was thus the second main foundation for the cycle of nitrate expansion, for it meant the creation of an important farming sector that was capable not only of reacting positively to demands of foreign and domestic markets but also of forming strong institutional ties with them.

The third principal foundation for the cycle of growth between the War of the Pacific and the Great Depression was the firmness, scope, and energy demonstrated by the apparatus of the Chilean state in the preceding era. This phenomenon originates in the nature of the struggle for independence in Chile, which permitted the consolidation of the Creole landowning oligarchy as the dominant element of the postcolonial social structure.[23] In addition, this group contributed significantly to the remarkable growth of mining and agricultural activities already noted, and especially to the corresponding growth in exports, which made possible an expansion of imports. Consequently, the increase in external and domestic commerce created an important and constantly growing tax base that allowed the state to greatly augment its income and expenditures. This specific development, combined with burgeoning foreign commerce and the formation of links with business and financial institutions abroad, opened new sources of international credits and loans.[24]

The statistical series are eloquent with respect to the trends that have been delineated (Table 6). At the beginning of the period in question, early in the decade of the 1830s, the total revenues of the state were of the order of 1.2 million dollars (at current exchange rates), half of which was derived from customs duties. These grew rapidly, doubling by the end of the decade, so that their proportion of total revenues reached nearly two-thirds, since total revenues doubled only in the first years of the 1840s, as compared to their beginning level. Customs revenues continued to increase rapidly, as did those from internal taxes and the income from public services, demonstrating the greater effectiveness of governmental administration. This development facilitated the securing of loans, which later fostered the receipt of significant additional income. In consequence, total revenues attained the level of more than 4 million dollars by about 1850, doubled again by the end of that decade, arrived at 20 million dollars by 1865, and then leveled off. The annual rate of growth from 1830 to about 1865 was 6.3 percent for ordinary revenues, and 8.8 percent for total revenues. These rates were augmented in the later years as a result of the great increase in additional revenues due to the loans secured to finance the costs of the war with Spain.

This remarkable surge in the resources of the government of Chile not only promoted the consolidation of the administrative structure of the state but also allowed the government to engage in various important developmental projects. One of the most significant of these, to which we have already referred, was the railway policy, which led to the integration of the central region of Chile by means of a unified transportation system.

A second policy, begun at mid-century and culminating during the cycle of the expansion of the nitrate industry, was the effective incorporation of the lands south of Concepción into the national territory and economy. This policy had four main objectives: (1) the pacification of the Araucanian Indians, which would open access to the south, unify the national territory, and incorporate the area into Chilean agriculture as a whole;[25] (2) the colonization of the provinces of Valdivia and Llanquihue by immigrants from Europe, and the integration of the provinces into the agricultural economy; (3) the linking of the region of Chiloé and its important production of potatoes to the Chilean economic system; and (4) the securing of control over Magallanes, the most southerly region of the country, and its incorporation into the national territory and economy.

In the decades 1850–1870 the foundations were laid for achieving these aims, and substantial progress was made, so that, as we will show, the nitrate expansion of Norte Grande following the War of the Pacific was accompanied by a no less significant expansion in agriculture and cattle raising in the lands south of Concepción.[26]

This thesis, so far presented, may be summarized in the following manner. During the first great cycle of expansion of the Chilean economy from 1830 until 1880, the resources of Norte Chico and the central valley were developed, and the administrative and communications infrastructure was created, including financial and commercial networks. These laid the basis for the building of a relatively integrated national economy, both in terms of its activities and geographical units and of its strong connections to the capitalist world economy. However, this economy operated only in the territory between the provinces of Coquimbo and Bío–Bío (Norte Chico and Núcleo Central), which constituted only 28.8 percent of the present territory of Chile.

During the last decades of the period with which we are concerned, the expansionist energy of the Chilean state and economy created the basis for a northerly extension toward Bolivian and Peruvian territory, and toward Chilean territory south of the Núcleo Central. As noted, in this fashion the conditions were created for incorporating into the country the region of Norte Grande, a large area containing mineral riches that formed almost a fourth of the national territory; the regions of Concepción and La Frontera and Los Lagos, which together constituted 13.8 percent of the country and had lands of great potential for agriculture, ranching, and lumbering; and the vast territory of Los Canales, constituting not less than a third of the national patrimony, with a considerable potential for cattle raising (Table 7). The cycle of nitrate expansion, as we will outline below, represented essentially the incorporation of these new regions in the north and south into the national economy, along with a profound transformation of the traditional economy in Norte Chico and the Núcleo Central.

III. GROWTH OF THE NITRATE INDUSTRY

In contrast to the generally accepted view, nitrate of soda *(salitre)* is not found exclusively in the Chilean deserts; it exists in numerous other countries. However, elsewhere it is found in small and isolated deposits of low quality and therefore is of no economic importance. Chile became the sole world producer of natural nitrate because of the richness of its deposits, their great size, the high quality and thickness of the strata, and the relatively easy access to the deposits.

Deposits of nitrate are composed of various horizontal beds, or strata. The first layer is the surface, formed of earth, dust, and rocks, from 20 to 40 cm. in thickness, and is called *chuca.* The second is hardpan, and is made up of clay, stones, and sand held together by salts; it is the *costra,* which varies in depth from one-half to several meters and contains a measurable amount of nitrate. Below this is found the *caliche,* the layer containing the major proportion of nitrate, along with other materials. The *caliche* may be fairly soft, or so hard that its extraction requires the use of explosives.

In the northern desert the nitrate deposits lie approximately between the nineteenth and twenty-sixth parallels of south latitude—that is, between the ports of Pisagua and Chañaral, including the provinces of Tarapacá and Antofagasta and the northern part of Atacama. The area contains a discontinuous set of deposits, over a distance of some 750 km., which vary from 0.5 to 10 km. in width, and are found inland at from 40 to 80 km. from the sea, and at altitudes that fluctuate between 650 to 2,300 m.

From this combination of physical characteristics it can be seen that nitrate mining differs appreciably from the unified, centralized, regular character of other types of mining. The chief difference is that nitrate exploitation is carried out within a long and wide area of a considerable territory; thus it involves what we may call an "extensive" style of mining. This is a very important point, for it determined the formation of many agglomerations of population in the nitrate fields as well as along the coasts, together with an extensive network of communications, not only to facilitate the exportation of nitrate, but also to provide the nitrate installations with supplies and equipment, and the miners and their families with consumer goods.[27]

In the years 1870–1872 eighteen nitrate mines (óficinas) were established, and by 1878 an additional fifty-five had begun to operate.[28] In the 1890s the number of active nitrate mines fluctuated around fifty, increasing in 1910 to one hundred and two, and by the eve of World War I reaching about one hundred and thirty, where it stayed in the best succeeding years (Table 8). Concerning the distribution of mines by size, we find that in 1907 only 2 mines exceeded the figure of 1 million Spanish quintals of exports (46,000 metric tons) and only 17 exported more than 500,000 Spanish quintals (23,000 metric tons), while 103 exported more than 100,000 Spanish quintals (4,600 metric tons) and seventeen exported less than this figure (Table 9). The twelve largest mines produced only 27 percent of total exports, resulting in a relatively wide and equal distribution rather than a great concentration among the nitrate mines along with a comparable number of population centers spread across the nitrate fields. The census of 1907, for example, provides population figures for one hundred and forty towns, villages, and hamlets, and nitrate mines in the province of Tarapacá alone.[29]

This large number of mines distributed widely in the nitrate area, was linked to ports on the coast by privately owned nitrate railways. These began to be built in the 1870s, and in 1881 their length was 339 km.; in 1887 it was 861 km.; in 1894, 1006 km.; and in 1905, 1787 km.—a substantial expansion of lines and of rolling stock (Table 10).

On the coast there were nine main ports in the nitrate region: Iquique, Caleta Buena, Junín, and Pisagua in the province of Tarapacá; and Tocopilla, Mejillones, Antofagasta, Caleta Coloso, and Taltal in the province of Antofagasta (Table 11). In addition, there was a fair number of minor ports, such as Cobija and Paposo.

Population growth in the ports and interior communities was very rapid. Between 1885 and 1895 the population grew from 88,000 to 141,000 people, an increase of 60 percent. Between 1895 and 1907 the population of Norte Grande reached 234,000 inhabitants, an increase of 66 percent. This represented an accumulated annual rate of 4.8 percent for the first period and 4.3 percent for the second. After 1907 the growth rate diminished greatly: in 1920 the figure of 288,000 was attained, representing an increase of 23 percent but by 1930 only 4,000 individuals had been added to this figure (Table 2). It is of interest to note in passing that in 1940, despite the great development of copper mining in Chuquicamata, the population had declined in absolute terms to no more than 249,000. The new copper mining was highly concentrated geographically and was capital intensive, while the declining nitrate industry was labor intensive and extended over a broad territory. The consequences for regional and national development were, therefore, very different when combined with other factors.

The spectacular growth of population in Norte Grande is especially noteworthy with reference to urban inhabitants—that is, those residing in centers having more than 2,000 people. There was only one such community in 1875, but ten years later there were six, in 1895 the number had grown to twelve, and by 1930 there were twenty-six. This figure however, does not signal economic expansion but, in effect, represents economic decline. The people living near the works in the interior in groups of less than 2,000 had been classified as the rural population, although in Norte Grande there was almost no rural population, properly speaking. With the coming of the nitrate crisis, many of the works were closed, and unemployed persons emigrated to larger localities. The result was that many of these localities surpassed the statistical limit of 2,000 required for the urban classification (Table 1).

The marked increase in the population of Norte Grande offers an interesting contrast to the very slow population growth of Norte Chico, which between 1865 and 1885 increased only from 239,000 to 252,000, and remained near the latter figure until about 1930. As a result of these contrasting trends—which are explained by the decline in the mining of gold, silver, and copper in Norte Chico, the expansion of nitrate mining in Norte Grande, and the consequent flow of migrants toward the latter from the former—the total population of Norte Grande almost equaled that of Norte Chico in 1907 (234,000 and 255,000 inhabitants, respectively) and by 1920 it well surpassed it (288,000 and 224,000 persons, respectively) (Table 2).

Finally, it is interesting to note the relative magnitude of the population of the nitrate region. In 1885 the population of Norte Grande represented only 3.5 percent of total Chilean population, but in 1920 it reached 7.7 percent, declining thereafter to 6.8 percent in 1930 and to 5.6 percent in 1940 (Table 12).

If, however, one desired to gauge the order of magnitude that this population represented as a market, the above figures would be deceptively low. Since Norte Grande possessed practically no agricultural resources, and nearly all the inhabitants lived in villages or smaller localities with no possibilities for producing their own food, the whole population depended almost entirely on supplies from outside. In contrast, in the remainder of the country the market for agricultural products was almost exclusively urban dwellers. For these reasons, it is necessary to compare the total population of Norte Grande with the total *urban* population of the country (excluding the urban population of Norte Grande). Then one realizes that that proportion grew from 13 percent in 1885 to a maximum of 21.1 percent in 1907, after which it diminished. If one compares the population of Norte Grande with that of Santiago, the proportion (47 percent in 1885) rose rapidly until it was 70 percent of that of Santiago in

1907, after which it declined. Even though the average income level prevailing in Norte Grande was certainly below that of the rest of the urban population, especially in Santiago, these percentages suggest that the relative size of the Norte Grande market was not insignificant, and that it experienced a rapid rate of expansion over more than three decades.

The magnitude and energy of the nitrate industry may be appreciated also in an examination of available information on the number of mines, employment, and production and exports by weight and by value (Tables 3 and 8). The War of the Pacific did not have a very great effect on the industry in terms of levels of production. It is true that exports were substantially reduced in 1879 and 1880, but in 1881, when a figure of 358,000 tons was attained, the level of exports surpassed that of the best prewar years. Between 1882 and 1886 exports were of the order of 500,000 tons, and in the following years exports increased until, in 1890, they surpassed 1.8 million tons. There followed a reduction in exports, caused no doubt by the effects of the Civil War of 1891, but beginning in 1894 exports never fell below the 1890 figure. Toward the end of the century exports were about 1.4 million tons, and thereafter the amount of 1.5 million tons was regularly exceeded in an expansionist phase that culminated in the maximum of 2.7 million tons in 1913, on the eve of World War I. After 1913 the growth trend was interrupted, although the figure for that year was reached and even slightly exceeded immediately after the war and at the end of the 1920s, and there were violent fluctuations in exports at a much lower level between 1921 and 1927. After the high rate of exports in 1928 and 1929, the figures were drastically reduced in the Great Depression, and the precrisis levels have never since been attained.

Although the production figures differ from year to year from those for exports owing to variations in stocks of nitrate, especially in the periods when policies called "combinations" were followed in the attempt to limit sales, the long-term trends of both series are very similar.[30]

A similar trend is observable in the case of employment, since there were no basic changes in mining technology until the end of the 1920s. On the contrary, because of the falling off of quality of the deposits, the quantities of nitrate produced per worker tended to diminish, with the result that employment tended to grow somewhat more than production itself. Employment figures at the commencement of the period varied between 4,500 and 7,000; between 1889 and 1892 they varied between 11,500 and 13,500; in the years 1894, 1895, and 1896 the average per year was more than 20,000; then there is a great reduction in the succeeding years of crisis. The highest earlier levels for jobs in the industry were again attained about 1900, when a strong and uninterrupted expansion began until some 53,000 persons were employed in 1913. Later, in 1917 and 1918, there were more than 56,000 employees; in 1925 the maximum,

60,000, was reached. There had been a deep recession in 1922 when only 25,000 jobs were open, and in the years of the Great Depression employment was offered only to 8,000 persons. Following this exceptionally unfavorable period, when the industry entered on its definitively decadent stage, employment rarely surpassed 23,000 workers.

To appreciate the importance of the nitrate industry in terms of employment, the maximum of about 60,000 persons that it engaged in certain years of the 1920s may be compared to the total employment in large and middle-scale manufacturing enterprise, which at the same time fluctuated around the figure of 80,000. But in 1930 the estimates of Hurtado give the distribution of the working population by activities as 84,000 in mining, 63,000 in construction, and 232,000 in manufacturing, including small industries and artisans.[31] These figures confirm the importance of employment in nitrate activities and show why a crisis resulted from its collapse at the end of the 1920s, when employment in nitrate production was drastically curtailed.

Another way in which the considerable importance the nitrate industry gained in a short period of time may be appreciated is by examining the industry in terms of its influence in the international sphere.

Toward the middle of the nineteenth century scientific studies in Germany (Justo Liebig, 1840) and in England demonstrated the effects of nitrate of soda and other mineral nutrients on agricultural production. In the succeeding decades the cultivation of cereals was displaced from European countries to the great semivirgin lands of the United States, Argentina, Russia, and elsewhere. European agriculture was profoundly transformed by the intensive cultivation of new crops and the adoption of inorganic fertilizers. These changes brought about a broad and dynamic market for nitrate, the only one of the nitrogenous nutrients that was found in a natural form. Thus, from the beginning, nitrate held a privileged status among fertilizers on the world market.[32] Before World War I Chilean nitrate represented more than half of world production of nitrogenous fertilizers, but with the development of artificial fertilizers in Germany during the war, the proportion of Chilean nitrate production was greatly reduced (Table 13).

The international network of nitrate markets was considerable, since it included nearly all the European countries, as well as the United States and many others (Table 14). So the introduction of artificial nitrate during World War I had an enormous impact, particularly in the major markets of Germany and Great Britain. However, the disappearance of the German market, which was second in importance at the start of the war, and the severe contraction of the British market after the termination of the war, did not adversely affect total world demand for Chilean nitrate. On the contrary, that demand expanded owing to the extraordinary and temporary upsurge of the North American market in the years 1917–1919. This factor explains the augmentation of production and export of Chilean nitrate in those years, as well as the new sales of nitrate fields by the Chilean government (Table 15). These events indicate that the industry was in expansion, despite its having been in a technological crisis over a period of several years.

The increasing international interest in the nitrate industry, which was the logical consequence of the breadth, diversity, and growth of its markets and the resulting opportunities for profits, gave rise to substantial foreign capital investments right from the start of large-scale exploitation of the resource.[33] In 1878, the year before the outbreak of the War of the Pacific, more than half the nitrate enterprises were Peruvian owned, while Chileans owned about a fifth of the total, but British (13.5 percent) and German (8 percent) interests were already significantly engaged. (Tables 16 and 17).

The war with Peru radically changed this state of affairs. Peruvian ownership disappeared completely, and the holdings were at first distributed in approximately equal proportions among British, German, and Chilean firms. It is particularly interesting that the share of Chilean properties rose from 19 to 36 percent of the total. This indicates that even though the well-known and notorious Mr. North and his British associates did well for themselves at the expense of the Chilean government,[34] which had won the war and managed to annex the Bolivian and Peruvian nitrate regions, their success did not prevent *private* Chilean capitalists from extending their participation in the industry at the cost of the former Peruvian capitalists.

In the ensuing decade British interests grew rapidly and eventually succeeded in controlling 60 percent of nitrate production, at the expense of a reduction in the share held by Chilean companies. Since, however, this severe reduction in Chilean participation took place at a time(1884–1895) when both production and exports were doubling, the loss in absolute terms was far less.

Subsequently, in the period of highest production of the nitrate industry from 1900 to 1914, the British share was significantly reduced. In view of the expansion of the industry as a whole in those years, this reduction presumably meant that the British firms remained relatively stationary, and that the expansion was principally due to Chilean capitalists, whose share in production grew from 14 to 37 percent between 1901 and 1912. This proportion increased even more in the following decade, reaching 68 percent in 1925, while British production fell to 23 percent of the total.[35] The Chilean growth took place during a time of expansion of both production and exports; the latter rose from about 2.6 million tons in 1912–1913 to more than 2.8 million tons in 1916–1918. As noted earlier, the European markets were in a crisis in those years, so European investments in the nitrate industry were necessarily lowered. However, as also noted, there was a remarkable expansion of the North American market, and this phenomenon seems to have prevented Chilean capitalists from realizing that a crisis was at hand. In fact, they continued to believe that the nitrate industry would enjoy a promising future in the postwar period. Hence the sale of nitrate fields in 1917 and 1918 was unusually large: it constituted almost a third of the fields sold by the state in the whole period 1882–1925 (Table 15).

In summary, the great expansion of the nitrate industry in Norte Grande after the War of the Pacific without doubt signified an extraordinary growth of productive activities in this desert region, a remarkable increase in employment and population as a whole, the building of an urban and transportation infrastructure, and the creation of a highly important volume of income, both public and private, for Chileans and foreigners.

IV. ROLE OF THE STATE

The Chilean state played a crucial role in the development of the nitrate industry before, during, and after the War of the Pacific. In fact, nitrate policy became, in the period 1880–1930, one of the central and enduring issues of governmental policy. It is not possible in this study to survey the many facets of Chilean policy having to do with the nitrate industry, but it is useful to emphasize at this stage that the state played an important role, first as collector of a large part of the wealth generated by the nitrate industry, and then as the allocator of those resources. The most direct and significant sources of income from nitrates were the export taxes on nitrates and iodine. In 1880 these taxes represented only 8.5 percent of the total exports of these products. This percentage was increased to the considerable proportion of more than 43 percent about 1890, and despite the Civil War of 1891, it was kept at this level until 1900. From then until 1914 it was reduced to about 30 percent, and in 1920 it was lowered to 20 percent in consequence of the crisis in the nitrate industry (Table 18).

For the whole of the period 1880–1924 the average of export taxes on the total value of exports of nitrates and iodine was about 33 percent, and it has been estimated that the remaining two thirds of the value was divided equally between net profits of the entrepreneurs and the costs of production. In other words, *the Chilean government was able to appropriate for itself approximately half of the gross profits engendered by the nitrate industry.*[36] According to the same source, most of the other half of the profits garnered by the entrepreneurs was sent abroad. This was largely due to the high share of foreign capital in the industry (about two thirds at the end of the century), the higher rate of profit enjoyed by foreign concerns as compared to those managed by Chileans, and the fact that the nitrate railways and other enterprises that provided goods and services to the nitrate works were also predominantly under foreign control. It is especially noteworthy, therefore, that the Chilean government succeeded in securing through export duties a high proportion of the profits arising from nitrate exports.

This fact is of the greatest importance, and not only from the economic point of view. Viewed from a political angle, it meant that the government exercised enough power to impose strict obligations on foreign and national capitalists in the nitrate industry, and was therefore able to capture a substantial portion of profits that would otherwise have gone abroad. From the social point of view, the exercise of this power by the government signified that the administrations of the period relied for their support on a complex coalition of groups, and possibly social classes, whose interests did not necessarily coincide with those of the nitrate industry. Hence they adopted policies that allowed them to appropriate a large share of the profits of the industry and redirect them in accordance with their own interests. This is even more significant when it is realized that the government's power did not diminish with the political changes resulting from the defeat of President Balmaceda and the Civil War of 1891. It is appropriate here to recall the first section of this study, concerning the antecedents of the nitrate cycle. There, we endeavored to show that in the first major cycle of expansion in the Chilean economy, from 1830 to 1870, there was a notable development of mining in Norte Chico and of agriculture in the central valley, together with an incipient industrial growth—all of which provided a solid social base for the state. It was also indicated that the state had created a strong and highly centralized bureaucracy. The victory in the War of the Pacific doubtless reenforced these trends. The government, along with the civil and military bureaucracy of the central region, was in this fashion converted into the instrument of the entrepreneurial and landholding groups in order to secure one half of the profits generated by the capitalist expansion of Norte Grande.

The very high tax on nitrate exports generated a large governmental income. In 1880 the taxes paid by the nitrate industry provided only 5 percent of the ordinary revenues of the government. This share increased rapidly to around 50 percent ten years later, and it fluctuated around that level until 1918, after which it declined greatly (Table 19). In terms of current U.S. dollars, the revenues of the Chilean government from nitrate exports grew from less than 1 million dollars in 1880 to more than 12 million dollars in 1890. In 1905 this revenue had reached a figure of more than 20 million dollars, and in 1910 it was almost 30 million dollars. In the most productive years of 1917 and 1918, which were those preceding the final crisis, annual revenues from nitrate exports were in the order of 40 million dollars, but they varied greatly below this level in the following years. In the fifty-one years from 1880 to 1930 the total accumulation of taxes from exports of nitrates and iodine was almost 1 billion dollars (Table 20).

It is also interesting to compare the total income from customs duties, including those on imports as well as those on exports, with the total ordinary income of the government. It is, of course, evident that the great surge of nitrate exports very quickly gave rise to a substantial growth of imports, thus indirectly augmenting state revenues through the collection of import duties. The significance of this factor may be appreciated by noting that the value of exports of nitrate and iodine came to constitute about 80 percent of the total value of exports between 1905 and 1915 (Table 21).

As a whole, customs duties constituted approximately 60 percent of ordinary governmental revenues between 1835 and 1860 (Table 22). In the following two decades, this proportion was reduced to 38 percent in 1880 because of rises in internal taxes. With the nitrate boom, the burden of internal taxes was reduced in absolute terms, and the proportion of governmental income from customs revenue rapidly increased; it rose to 80 percent of the total income in 1895, and then stabilized at around 75 percent until 1910, after which it went down to about 40 percent in 1920 and 1930.

Import duties amounted to 80 percent of total customs revenue before 1880. With the subsequent great rise in revenue from export duties, the share of import duties declined to a third of the total realized from all customs revenue, although the absolute value of import duties rose substantially and thus contributed to the rise in the total ordinary income of the state. In absolute terms, expressed in current U.S. dollars, these revenues were 17 million dollars in 1880. Subsequently they rose steeply until they attained a total of 63.1 million dollars in 1910, after which the income from nitrates and from foreign commerce began to lose importance relative to other forms of taxation.

These developments took on great importance not only for the tax structure as a whole but also for the budgetary process and the political process in general. In the years of burgeoning governmental revenues a series of internal taxes was eliminated. The sales tax was terminated in 1884, and in 1888 *los derechos de imposición* were lifted. In addition, as a result of the Civil War of 1891 and the impetus it gave to administrative decentralization in the country, the collection of taxes on household goods, inheritances and gifts, commercial and professional licenses, and the agricultural tax devolved upon the municipal authorities. The fact that certain taxes were terminated and others transferred to local authorities, at the same time that the taxes on the nitrate industry were greatly increased, is a clear indication that there were domestic groups capable of exercising enough political power to bring about this reorganization of the tax burden from themselves to exporters, who, in large measure, passed it on to importers of nitrate on the world market. It is also evident that the growing profits from nitrates exports were used to some extent to lighten the burden on domestic taxpayers. However, the revenue losses caused by reduced internal taxation could be offset by only a fraction on the new revenue from foreign commerce.

Interestingly, beginning in the first decade of the twentieth century the tendency just described was reversed. As the *relative* contribution of the nitrate sector to foreign trade and governmental income reached a stable level and then, in the 1920s, declined, some of the taxes that had been eliminated reappeared in the tax system, and a whole new series of imposts was instituted. This process culminated in 1924 with the passage of the law creating the income tax. Toward the end of this period, revenues derived from this tax became the second main source of governmental financing, customs duties remaining the first. As is well known, this whole process was part of the profound and turbulent social and political changes in which Chile was involved in this epoch.[37]

Reference will be made at a later point in this chapter to industrial and agricultural policies of the Chilean government. As regards state expenditures, they experienced a rise similar to that for revenues in the nitrate industry's years of affluence. An analysis of the size of the public sector in terms of the number of officials in government service demonstrates that, in 1880, the number of persons employed in public administration was small—a mere 3,000. By 1900 there were more than 13,000, and in 1919 over 27,000, which indicates a qualitative change that doubtless gave rise to denunciations of waste and of a bloated bureaucracy (Table 23). Of greater interest for our purposes, however, is an examination of trends in the categories of public expenditure. This will reveal the directions taken by Chilean political leaders in allocating unprecedented profits from the nitrate industry. For this purpose we shall utilize the estimates developed by Humud, who has elaborated a classification of public expenditures according to various functions of the public sector: administration, defense, development, social services, and finance.[38] (Table 24)

The share of expenditures on administration grew from about 20 percent at the end of the War of the Pacific to around 30 percent at the turn of the century, when it began a long decline. This increase was principally due to the expansion of the Ministry of the Interior. This included the creation of a uniformed police corps, and the establishment and/or expansion of various public services: postal and telegraph, drinking water, sewage systems, street lighting, paving programs, and the customs service. These developments illustrate the extension of the state's administrative control throughout the country, especially the improvement of the urban infrastructure. The Ministry of Foreign Affairs, though it continued as a fairly modest establishment, underwent a notable expansion compared to its very small size in 1880. This expansion is assuredly associated, at least in part, with the growing complexity of the network of international economic relations resulting from the nitrate trade.

The defense sector increased its share of public expenditures during the 1880s until it reached 24 percent in 1890, but later this proportion was reduced, and remained stable at about 20 percent.

The developmental functions of the government included the activities of the Ministry of Industry, Public Works, and Railways, and, after the administrative reforms of 1925, the ministries of Agriculture and Industry, of Public Lands and Colonization, of Public Works, of Commerce and Communications, and of Development. This area of services was allocated 28 percent of the budget between 1888 and 1905, and 30 percent after 1910. In the first phase, which lasted until about 1914, the main portion of these funds was expended on railway construction. The state railway system amounted to 1,100 km. in 1890, and was extended to 5,000 km. by 1913, and was maintained at this level (Table 25). In this same period the construction of highways and bridges received more funding, along with the construction of public buildings, especially port facilities. Another activity of lesser budgetary importance was ensuring a potable water supply.

Social services were provided by the ministries of Justice, Education, and, in the later years of the period, Public Health and Social Security (which was created in 1925 and replaced in 1929 by the Ministry of Social Welfare). Of this group, the Ministry of Education received the major portion of funds—less than 60 percent in 1880, but more than 70 percent in 1930. This increase corresponded to a considerable rise in the number of schools and students, and in the administrative and teaching staffs in the field of public education. The latter category comprised no more than 500 individuals in 1880, but it reached 3,700 in the year 1900, and 12,650 in 1930.[39]

The number of students in public schools grew from about 20,000 in 1869 to more than 152,000 in 1895, almost 300,000 by 1910, and over 500,000 in 1925. Public educational institutions numbered about 500 in 1860, increased to 1,300 by 1895, to more than 2,700 in 1910, and to nearly 3,600 in 1925. In this expansive process public education, which in 1860 had not been much more important than private schooling, achieved a clearly preponderant position, especially with respect to primary education (Tables 26 and 27).[40]

Finally the financial function—which includes the expenditures by the state to pay off the public debt, with interest—required a high proportion of the available funds after the War of the Pacific because of the extraordinary costs of military and naval forces. Subsequently, however, the portion of the budget required for debt amortization did not exceed about 12 percent.

No doubt the preceding data are insufficient to provide a definitive conclusion about the efficiency with which the new resources obtained from the nitrate industry were expended. Further empirical study would be required to discriminate among current expenses, those of investment and transfer, and their distribution by sectors, activities, and regions. Nonetheless, we can safely say that the government directed the resources from the nitrate industry to the expansion of its own national administrative structure; to the carrying out of a substantial amount of public works in urban communities; and to a notable expansion of public education at all levels. It may, of course, be claimed that the productivity of these public investments might have been greater; that there were wasteful expenditures and an unnecessarily large increase in the size of the bureaucracy; and that the public funds should have been directed toward the founding and expansion of productive capacity of industry and agriculture rather than so largely devoted to the social and economic infrastructure. It would be very interesting to have more in-depth research along these lines. However, with the reservations and limitations already expressed, it seems to us entirely reasonable to maintain that the public expenditure, both in expansion and the direction which that expansion took, tended to favor the development of the country. It certainly did not inhibit it.

V. URBANIZATION AND INDUSTRIALIZATION

The extraordinary expansion in governmental activities had important effects on the geographical distribution of the Chilean population.[41] The accelerated growth of the bureaucracy, of educational institutions, and of urban services in general, as well as the accompanying public works, brought about a marked increase in opportunities for employment, both for the middle class and for manual workers. In addition, the stimulus given by the state to the construction of railways and telegraph installations throughout the country created important labor markets in rural areas.

As we have noted, the expansion of the nitrate industry also contributed to an urban expansion in Norte Grande, encouraging a strong migratory movement into the region. This development, as will be shown in the next section of this chapter, created an important new market for the products of the center and south of Chile, since about one third of the value of nitrate exports represented local costs of production, and the greater portion of this third was spent on supplies for the mining operations and consumer goods for the workers. This new market augmented the coastal commerce among the principal ports of Norte Grande and Valparaíso and Talcahuano.

The growth of imports, made possible by nitrate exports, also contributed to the commercial and financial activities of Valparaíso and Santiago, which, in turn, generated new opportunities for employment in the country's principal cities.

In addition to a great expansion of urban life, which made the cities attractive to rural dwellers, a process of change was occurring in the agricultural sector. As we shall see, during the last decades of the nineteenth century agricultural acreage was extended, cattle raising was vastly increased, the landholding structure was modified, and technological innovations were introduced. The combined effect of these changes was to displace large numbers of persons in the countryside, and they streamed toward the cities. This phenomenon was evident especially in the Núcleo Central, since the population of the areas south of Concepción, both rural and urban, was augmented by the incorporation of these territories into the national economy.

The magnitude of the urbanization process that emerged from these several factors is impressive. The rural population of the Núcleo Central remained nearly stationary at about 1 million persons between the censuses of 1875 and 1930, while the urban population of the region rose in the same period from somewhat over 400,000 to 1.33 million, an increase of more than 900,000 (see Table 2). The proportion of rural population to total population in this area fell from 71 percent to 44 percent, and the proportion of the rural population of the Núcleo Central to the total rural population of the country tumbled from 48 to 24 percent. A notable characteristic of this intense process of urbanization was the tendency toward a concentration in the principal cities. In effect, while the rate of demographic growth of the total population averaged around 1.5 percent annually, and that of minor places (from 2,000 to 20,000 inhabitants) fluctuated around 2 percent, the rhythm of increase in population of the major cities—those with more than 20,000 inhabitants—rose above 3 percent at the end of the nineteenth century, and remained at slightly below this figure in the early years of the twentieth century (Tables 28 and 29).

The combination of rapid urbanization concentrated in the principal cities and an equally large expansion of incomes—derived primarily from the local expenditures of the nitrate companies, the income and expenditures of the government, and the multiplying effects of both—created favorable markets and conditions of demand for the development of manufacturing industry in Chile. It is, of course, well known that the establishment of mining and manufacturing enterprises began in the 1850s, and these enterprises were accompanied by the emergence of an entrepreneurial sector of some importance. However, the industrial sector did not succeed in becoming firmly rooted or in achieving a vigorous expansion until after the War of the Pacific.[42]

The wartime requirements of the government, which had to arm, equip, and maintain a large expeditionary force in the north for a period of five years, were of unprecedented proportions. This period (1879–1884), one of exceptional prosperity for manufacturing establishments, saw the beginning of a strong stimulus to industry, which continued after the war due to the direct and indirect effects of the nitrate boom.

The stimulus to industry was enhanced by the devaluation of the peso, which began with the crisis in the mid-1870s and brought about a great rise in the cost of imports. Influential in the same direction was the tariff policy introduced by President Aníbal Pinto at the outbreak of the war to finance the military effort. Many articles that in 1872 were taxed at a 25 percent *ad valorem* rate became taxed at 35 percent, and an additional tariff of 10 percent was imposed on all imports. In 1878 specific duties affecting a series of products, including beer, were increased appreciably.

To summarize, the War of the Pacific, the expansion of the nitrate industry, and the policies of the Chilean government created a combination of conditions enormously favorable to industrial expansion: a growing and relatively protected national economy; an infrastructure of communications and transport; abundant cheap labor in the urban centers. These favorable circumstances permitted the consolidation of manufacturing firms founded by isolated entrepreneurs in previous decades. In addition, the opportunities for industrial profits stimulated investments in other sectors that had been organized and continued to expand, such as mining, trade, banks, importing firms, and agriculture. In all these undertakings foreign capital frequently participated, especially foreign technology, often in the form of immigrant managers, engineers, technicians, and specialized workers. Selective immigration and subsidies for the importation of capital goods intended for manufacturing firms were two important governmental policies intended to develop this element of the economy.

The formation within the national managerial bourgeoisie, and in close association with it, of industrial entrepreneurs acquired an institutional character with the foundation of the Sociedad de Fomento Fabril in the year 1883. This institution quickly gained importance as a pressure group representing the interests of industrialists, particularly in its relationships with the state and public opinion.[43] In 1884 the society counted 305 members, a third of whom formed local councils in the principal provincial towns. Some of the society's main activities were sponsoring industrial expositions in 1885, 1890, 1894, and 1904; setting up an immigration office to foster the entry of managers and specialized workers into Chile; and organizing industrial schools. Such schools were operating in Santiago, Valparaíso, Concepción, La Serena, Talca, Chillán, and Valdivia in 1908, and by 1909 more than 900 students were in attendance, half of them in Santiago.

Although the *Sinópsis estadística* of 1883 recorded for the first time the existence of large-scale industry in the production of flour, sugar, metallurgical products, and textiles, systematic information in the form of statistics on industrial development in Chile is very unreliable until 1914. As Kirsch[44] notes after a detailed analysis, any attempt to construct an overall series of manufacturing production for this period seems destined to fail. However, there is enough quantitative evidence of a partial character which, added to qualitative information, indicates that the period constituted the initial phase of consolidation and expansion of manufacturing, in terms both of the rate of growth and of the process of industrial diversification, the development of intraindustrial relationships, and integration with other elements of the Chilean economy. This conclusion is based on a set of partial but convincing data, of which we present some outstanding examples, although we cannot reproduce in detail the mass of information gathered by Kirsch.

In view of the dependent character of the birth of modern industry in Chile and countries like it, which was based on the importation of supplies, capital goods, and technology, the import figures offer perhaps the most systematic foundation for understanding the development of manufactures. Using these figures to compare the period 1870–1874 with that of 1898–1902, Hurtado[45] found that the importation of consumer goods increased only 0.9 percent annually, while that of machinery and other industrial supplies, and materials for the arts and professions, grew at an annual rate of 3.7 percent, and that of raw materials at an annual rate of 6.7 percent. This estimate agrees with another formulated by Lagos,[46] in which a great change in the structure of imports was demonstrated: there was a fall in the share of consumer goods and an increase in the shares of capital goods and raw materials. The significance of these figures is reinforced by recalling, first, that raw materials made up more than 40 percent of total imports, and that their absolute value tripled between 1880–1884 and 1915–1919; and second, that the capital goods imported specifically for the industrial sector enlarged their proportion of total imports from 2.8

percent in 1880–1884 to around 6 percent in the first years of the new century, and multiplied by almost six times between the beginning of the period and the beginning of World War I (Table 30).

Another important source of quantitative data, at least with respect to the beginning of the period, is the industrial census carried out by the Sociedad de Fomento Fabril in 1895. As may be seen in Table 31, of the establishments enumerated in 1895, 75 percent were founded after 1880 and 42 percent after 1890. This indicates a rate of annual growth of 5.9 percent in the period 1870–1895. This rate is very similar to that which Hurtado estimated for the increase in importation of raw materials. The census figures are also consistent with data relating to the age of industrial establishments that exhibited at the industrial exposition of 1894, although the number of firms is much lower. According to an analyst at the time, of the 256 exhibitors of industrial products, only 18, or 7 percent, were founded before 1875.[47] For its part, the census recorded that only 9.8 percent of the firms it surveyed predated 1870. Both sources, with very different coverage, tend to confirm the marked acceleration of industrial development after the War of the Pacific. Another significant datum, which confirms the preceding conclusion, is that of the 1052 industrial patents registered from 1840 to 1899, more than 43 percent were recorded in the years 1890–1899.

Beginning in 1914 there was a marked improvement in industrial statistics, resulting from the compiling of a new industrial list in the previous year and the use of a new questionnaire to be administered by the officials of the Central Statistical Office rather than by local governments or (as done earlier) the Sociedad de Fomento Fabril. Because of inflation, which influenced the validity of the figures on the value of production, the absolute size, organization by branches, and growth of industry were to be measured by means of employment statistics. As evident in Table 32, the labor force employed in middle- and large-scale industry, which excluded firms employing fewer than 5 persons, amounted to 53,000 individuals in 1915. This figure rose rapidly to over 70,000 in 1918, remained stationary until 1921, and resumed a strong growth to about 85,000 in 1924–1925. The annual accumulated rate was 3.7 percent between the extreme biennia of the period. Assuming that this annual growth in employment was accompanied by a fairly modest increase in productivity, of no more than 1.5 percent, the rise in production may have attained an annual rate of over 5 percent.

To summarize, the favorable conditions for the expansion of the national economy as a whole that were created by the nitrate boom, and transmitted to the rest of the system by the state and the markets in the north of Chile, and by the demographic movements resulting from the expansion, produced a situation highly advantageous for the development of manufactures. Although it is incomplete and partial, the available empirical evidence suggests that this situation created opportunities for industrial development that were seized by a new capitalist entrepreneurial sector. This sector was formed from the pioneering managers of manufacturing firms established before the War of the Pacific, from entrepreneurs with experience in other economic fields (mining, commerce, banking, and agriculture), and from an important group of immigrants.

V. THE MARKET OF NORTE GRANDE

The section on the expansion of the nitrate industry provided an overview of the development of this activity in Norte Grande. We considered, among other matters, the geographic extent of nitrate mining, the numerous settlements that grew up, the amount of nitrate produced, and the value of exports. As we saw, Norte Grande was converted into a dynamic and fairly large market in a relatively short time. It may be recalled, for example, that the population of Norte Grande amounted to 233,900 persons in 1907, that is, 70 percent of the population of Santiago, which in that year counted 333,000 inhabitants (Table 12). Since Norte Grande is a region of deserts in which there is practically no agricultural production, this market had to be supplied almost entirely via maritime transport. Therefore the import figures, and those for coastal trade to the ports of Norte Grande, offer in principle a dependable record of the form in which the market was supplied.

Imported agricultural and animal products from abroad were of very little importance for Norte Grande. For these products as a whole, the proportion imported from other countries (as compared with those imported from the south of Chile) was generally around 15% (Table 33).

Consequently, the sustenance of the population in the nitrate fields was provided basically by coasting vessels. In the statistics "nationalized" products, that is, imported goods that were subsequently re-shipped in coastal trade, were separated from products of purely national origin, so that we are able to conclude that the supplies received by Norte Grande were basically of national origin.

We now turn to an examination of the volume and trends in this northern market. Unfortunately, its statistical measurement offers difficulties because of the marked process of external devaluation of the Chilean peso beginning in 1876 (see Table 34) and the internal inflation. To entirely overcome this problem, it would have been necessary to construct a series of the real value of coastal trade, which would have taken us beyond the scope of this study. We have therefore fallen back on an indirect procedure of estimates whose results seem reasonably worthy of confidence.

In the first place, to understand the volume and actual trends in the Norte Grande economy, we have had recourse to the series on the nitrate exports valued in 6-pence pesos. This was the actual exchange rate with the pound sterling only in the late 1920s. Its use over a longer period is an accounting unit which really measures trends in foreign exchange earnings, the most important world currency being the British pound. In those terms, the value of nitrate exports was about 150 million 6-pence pesos between 1880 and 1887. At the end of the decade they reached 230 million 6-pence pesos, a level maintained until 1900, when the figure was 350 million. This growth was at accumulated annual rate of 5.1 percent in the last decades of the nineteenth century, then increased to 8.2 from 1900 to 1913. At the outbreak of World War I, exports attained the value of 900 million 6-pence pesos. The war caused a severe contraction in exports, since it isolated Chile from its principal markets, but in 1917, 1918, and 1920 the value of exports rose to the extraordinary height of over 1,500 million 6-pence pesos.

Those extraordinary years marked the end of the stage of expansion of the nitrate industry. During the 1920s the value of exports fluctuated greatly between 500 million and 1,000 million 6-pence pesos, with an average above 750 million 6-pence pesos (Table 8).

In the second place, it is assumed that there is a structural relationship between the level of economic activity and the demand for agricultural and animal products. To gauge this relationship, we have used the series on current values of nitrate exports and of the coastal trade of agricultural and animal products to Norte Grande,[48] in order to establish the *ratio* of the latter as compared to the former. In comparing these series, we find that the ratio of coastal trade to nitrate exports varied during the whole period, except for a few unusual years, between 17 and 30 percent.[49] There is an early stage, between 1880 and 1892, in which the percentage tends to be closer to 25 percent; a second phase, from 1893 to 1904, in which the ratio approximates 17 or 18 percent;[50] during the remainder of the period the ratio is close to 20 percent (see Table 35).

The results of these empirical studies seem fairly reasonable, despite the tentative hypotheses that sustain them. First, the relative stability of the ratio derived from statistical series of completely independent origin, confirms the structural relationships between the level of nitrate activity and the demand for agricultural and animal products that was assumed in this study. Second, the average levels of the ratio are consistent with independently made estimates of the relationship between the value of exports and the costs of production. In effect, according to a study already cited,[51] the value of the costs of nitrate production is estimated at about one third of the value of the exports. Taking into account the costs of depreciation of capital, direct imports from the northern ports, and a certain minimum of local production, the ratios of 20–25 percent appear reasonable—in fact, conservative.

The decline of the percentage after the first ten years of expansion could also be anticipated, since during this period the bulk of investments for both capital and the infrastructure was made, so that equipment was required on a larger scale than it would have been for an established operation. This consideration also explains the slight increase in the ratio from about 1900, when there was a new phase of expansion that lasted until 1914.

Clearly the large fluctuations in nitrate exports, caused by changes in production, stocks, and prices, did not proportionately and directly influence, year by year, the market for agricultural and animal products. We are here mainly concerned with the middle- and long-range trends.

With the establishment, in this indirect fashion, of the significant size and great growth of the northern market in its several phases, a study was undertaken to construct statistical series of the coastal trade to Norte Grande for the period 1880–1905, by individual products and groups of products (Table 36).

The great majority of these series show a very rapid rate of expansion in the first part of the period, until 1893–1895. Some of them show a contraction in the second part. Specifically, footwear, wheat and flour, hay *(pasto seco),* and bottled beer underwent a notable increase in both phases of expansion; other commodities, including cattle, dried meat, lumber, potatoes, barley, barreled beer and aguardiente grew in the first part of the period and declined in some measure during the second.

In order to assess the importance of the Norte Grande market for agricultural production, which our original assumption regarded as considerable, we may compare the average annual production of certain products in the biennia 1884–1885 and 1904–1905 with the volume of coastal trade of the same products in those years (Table 37). This table should not be regarded as the final result of our analysis, but rather as the quantitative basis for making approximate estimates of the relative importance of the Norte Grande market. In fact, the direct comparison between production and coastal trade evidently underestimates the relative significance of the latter, and therefore that of the northern market. This is so because a correct comparison would involve discounting the portions of agricultural production that were exported, consumed by the producers, held back for seed, and lost to spoilage—the last a fairly important factor. Thus for example, for wheat, the most important agricultural product, the trade with Norte Grande more than doubled from 160,000 quintals in 1884–1885 to 351,000 quintals in 1904–1905. At the beginning of the period the wheat trade with the northern area absorbed 4 percent of total wheat production, while toward the beginning of the twentieth century its share had risen to 8 percent. These figures seem rather low, but it should be noted that they were later greatly expanded.

To bring out the significance of these figures, it is necessary to take into account the fact that a substantial part of total wheat production was exported. In 1884–1885 an annual average of 1,070,000 metric quintals of wheat (including wheat in the form of flour) was exported and for 1904–1905 the figure was 514,000 (Table 4). Consequently, in 1884–1885 the Norte Grande market accounted for about 5 percent of apparent internal consumption, and in the period 1904–1905 about 10 percent. Assuming that about 30 percent of the wheat produced was not available for internal consumption because of spoilage, retention for seed, and self-consumption (and this is not an exaggerated figure), the real internal consumers' market is reduced to 1,790,000 metric quintals in 1884–1885, and to 2,430,000 metric quintals in 1904–1905. Using these figures, Norte Grande's share of the national market would have been 9 percent (1884–1885) and 14 percent (1904–1905), which are substantial proportions. In addition, when it is recalled that the *increase* in the total internal market would have been about 650,000 metric quintals during this period, while that of Norte Grande was of 191,000 metric quintals, it is seen that the Norte Grande market accounted for some 30% of the expansion of the internal market. It may be noted, further, that the Norte Grande market for wheat came to constitute, toward the end of the period, a figure close to that of total exports, or almost a half million quintals.

A similar development occurred with respect to potatoes. The situation is different for barley and dried meat, which are products intended to be sold; and only small amounts are consumed on the farm. For these products, the Norte Grande market was of major importance from the beginning of the period (35 and 40 percent, respectively), but these proportions were reduced toward the end of the period to 25 and 27 percent, respectively. It is possible that in the case of barley the decline was due to the substitution of mechanical power for animal power, which occurred in the nitrate fields toward the end of the century; the same trend denotes the replacement of dried meat by cattle on the hoof.

We have been able to establish then, that the Norte Grande market was a dynamic one for certain products, including wheat, flour, and potatoes. In other cases, while Norte Grande was not more dynamic than the national market, it still constituted an important part of that market, notably for barley and dried meat. Therefore because of the dynamism of the market for some products and the absolute size of the market for others, we think it is possible to substantiate the hypothesis that the nitrate market of Norte Grande was important to the development of agriculture in the period under consideration, although clearly its importance was secondary to that of the expansion of urban markets in central Chile.

Our analysis comparing the northern market with agricultural and animal production has been limited to the period 1881–1905, for which figures are available for both production and coastal traffic by individual commodities. The compilation of statistics for coastal commerce for the period 1903–1928, however, renders this kind of comparison difficult.

For the latter period we have available only the series of coastal trade to Norte Grande in agricultural and animal products in current values. This series is not of great utility, because between 1903 and 1928 there were periods of high inflation. In addition, the index of the cost of living began to be calculated only after 1913. Nevertheless, in order to provide an approximate measure of the real value of the series for coastal commerce we have formulated an index of monetary devaluation, by extrapolating the cost-of-living index back to 1903 on the basis of the exchange rate between the Chilean peso and the pound sterling. The result is that the "real" value of the trade to Norte Grande more than doubled between the beginning of the period and the start of World War I (Table 38). This tendency coincides perfectly with the estimates of the evolution of the northern market which we indicated earlier on the basis of exports in constant pesos, and on the ratio of the coastal trade to exports in current values. As in the case of these estimates, the 1914–1919 period shows a contraction; the immediate postwar era evidences a sharp recovery; and the decade of the 1920s manifests a trend toward a stationary position, with strong annual fluctuations at an average level rather below that achieved before 1914.

All the foregoing analysis therefore, indicates that in this second period of the first three decades of the twentieth century the Norte Grande market demonstrated two very different types of behavior. In the first decade and a half it grew in sustained and accelerated form; if the estimates in Table 38 are used to indicate the trend, the market more than doubled between 1903 and 1913. Afterward, with the sharpening of the nitrate crisis, the northern market not only ceased to expand but actually came to a standstill at a level somewhat below that of the prewar era, although with considerable annual fluctuations.

In conclusion, although it would be desirable to extend and deepen research into the interrelationships between Norte Grande and the economy of the center and south of the country in the period 1880–1930, all the empirical data presented in this preliminary study, and the diverse alternative methods of indirect estimates, together support our hypothesis that the epoch of nitrate expansion created a market for agricultural and animal products in Norte Grande that was an important factor, at least until 1920, in the agricultural expansion and transformation of Chile.

VII. EXPANSION AND TRANSFORMATION IN AGRICULTURE

In the two previous sections, on the urbanization process and industrial growth, and on the Norte Grande market, data were presented that delineated a vigorous expansion of the demand for agricultural and animal products in the urban centers of the northern and central sections of Chile. According to our hypothesis, this growth in demand—as well as the transfer of capital and the development of the infrastructure of transportation and of commercial and financial networds—gave rise to a great expansion and transformation of Chilean agriculture, and to a notable development of industries engaged in processing the raw materials produced in the countryside.

The conventional interpretation of the economic history of the period that we are studying is that Chilean agriculture entered into a period of crisis and decline following the War of the Pacific.[52] The detailed study of the statistics of agricultural and animal production by products and by provinces that we have carried out suggests a different interpretation, one that is more consistent with the process of the expansion of the Chilean economy as a whole. According to our interpretation, this period saw both a vigorous expansion of Chilean agriculture in general, and in the regions south of Concepción in particular, and a transformation and diversification of agriculture in the Núcleo Central.

The interpretation that there was a crisis and decline of Chilean agriculture in the period in question is mainly based on statistical data that are inappropriate for drawing such a conclusion. The majority of authors who support the crisis-and-decline thesis rely on the trend of exports of wheat and flour. But as we pointed out earlier, those exports underwent a great expansion between 1850 and 1880; they reached an exceptional maximum of over 2 million metric quintals in the year 1874, and were as high as 1.5 million metric quintals in the majority of years in the preceding decade. (Table 4).

It is true that in the subsequent decades the exports of wheat and flour did not reach the level attained in 1874, but it should not be forgotten that until 1896 export levels were generally above 1 million quintals, and often on the order of 1.5 million quintals, rising in 1891 and 1893 to 1.8 million quintals. Consequently, if it is possible to assert that from the decade of the 1870s the expansion of exports of wheat and flour that had begun in the 1850s was not continued, it cannot by any means be maintained that in the two following decades those exports diminished, since in reality they remained approximately at the same high level attained about 1870. It is true that from 1896 onward those exports declined markedly, but occasionally they exceeded 1 million quintals in later years (i.e., 1908, 1909, 1918, 1924, and 1925).

Clearly, the stabilization and later decline of wheat and flour exports cannot be entirely identified with similar tendencies in the internal production of wheat. In fact, the production of wheat in Chile increased between 1877–1878 and 1884–1885 by more than 1.2 million quintals, and was maintained at essentially that level during the following two decades, a trend that coincided with the stabilization of exports to which we have referred (Table 39). However, beginning with the first years of the present century, the production of wheat increased substantially from 4.2 million quintals in 1904–1905 to 6.2 million on the eve of World War I, and to 7.3 million at the end of the period.

With regard to the stagnant period from 1884–1885 to 1904–1905, we have not referred to wheat production during the 1890s. This omission is due to statistical problems that will be explained in detail, and that may have colored the interpretation that there was a decline in wheat production during this period.

In the first place, from 1891 to 1902 no reports of agricultural production were published. Second, the comparable statistics for the decade of the 1880s indicate a drastic decline in production after 1885. In the case of wheat, the figures for total production for the years 1889–1890 are less than half those for 1885 and earlier. These figures have been taken by various historians as pointing to a severe crisis in agriculture beginning in 1885. However, such a precipitous fall in production is difficult to accept, since the exports of wheat and flour remained stable at about 1 million quintals from 1885 until 1888. Although exports declined steeply in 1889 and 1890, they amply surpassed a million quintals from 1981 until 1896, except for 1895, but only in 1895 were they inferior and even then they attained a level of more than 800,000 quintals (Table 4).

This apparent contradiction led us to a more detailed examination of the statistics of agricultural production, which involved securing information on production and cultivated areas of the principal agricultural products, by provinces, from 1881 until 1890, and from 1902 to 1905; and securing data on production and cultivated area for 1877 and 1878, and for the biennia 1884–1885, 1904–1905, 1912–1913, 1917–1918, and 1926–1927.[53]

From the study of these data it is possible to extract three major conclusions. First, there was a marked deterioration in the quality of statistical information, illustrated by the fact that after 1886 there was no information on a growing number of provinces. In 1885 information was lacking for two provinces—Malleco[54] and Cautín—and in 1889 and 1890 there was no information for eleven provinces, among them provinces of major importance for agricultural production (Table 40). On reviewing the statistical yearbooks for these years, we found numerous complaints by the director of statistics about the lack of funds that prevented him from securing reports from those responsible for supplying information from the provinces. Apart from the administrative confusion arising from the Civil War of 1891, this is evidently a principal cause for the failure after that year to publish these figures.

A second conclusion of enormous importance is that in *all* the years of the period 1881–1890 the provinces of Malleco and Cautín provided no information. It is well known and was noted earlier in this chapter that the beginning of the 1880s saw the completion of what has been called the pacification of the lands of the Araucanians. That was the process of incorporation of the territories of La Frontera—specifically the provinces of Malleco and Cautín—into the national agricultural economy and the restriction of the indigenous population to certain "reservations." The decade of the 1870s was therefore a period of colonization and appropriation of new and fertile areas that gradually became productive, as is revealed by the statistics for exports of wheat from the ports of Talcahuano and Tomé. In fact, the exports from these southern ports rapidly replaced those via Valparaíso and Constitución, which were the principal ports for wheat and flour in the era when those exports flourished. (Table 41).

The production of the provinces of Malleco and Cautín appeared when agricultural statistics began to be published again in 1902. The production of wheat in those provinces in that year and in the three succeeding years varied between 500,000 and 1 million metric quintals, which constituted about one fourth of the national production of grain at the time (Table 39). From what has been said, it may be inferred that production from this region, which during the last two decades of the nineteenth century was developed into an agricultural region of enormous significance, was largely unrecorded in the official figures. This is an additional factor tending to invalidate the governmental statistics.

The third major conclusion we may cite on the basis of data we have examined is this: the severe contraction of wheat exports at the ports of Valparaíso and Constitución reveals the existence of a phenomenon of primary importance. Since we have been able to determine that total wheat production in Chile did not diminish between 1885 and 1905, the reduction in exports via Valparaíso and Constitución and their expansion via Talcahuano suggest an incipient regional redistribution of growing areas. In fact, Table 39 demonstrates that the participation of the provinces from Malleco to the south in total wheat production grew to about a third in the first decades of the twentieth century, and to about 40 percent by the end of our period. On the other hand, between 1884–1885 and

1904–1905, there was a marked reduction of wheat production in the provinces of Coquimbo, Aconcagua, Valparaíso, Santiago, O'Higgins, and Colchagua. This group of provinces produced 1,604,000 quintals in 1884–1885, or 40 percent of national production; their production diminished to 846,000 quintals in 1904–1905, or only 20 percent of total national production. The remaining provinces of the Núcleo Central, from Curicó to Bío–Bío, maintained a fairly stable level of absolute production, so their share of national production fell gradually from 55 to 50 percent. Obviously, then, wheat production did not diminish in the whole of the central valley, but only in the province of Colchagua and farther north.

The regional redistribution of wheat growing that we have just noted is related on the one hand to the extension of the agricultural frontier toward the south, and on the other to a redirection of cultivation and agricultural and animal production in the Núcleo Central. The decline of the international price of wheat, combined with the expansion of domestic urban markets, offered new profit opportunities to farmers in the Núcleo Central. A particularly important feature in this connection is the striking increase in cattle raising that has been pointed out by several scholars. According to Sepúlveda, in 1874 cattle numbered about 250,000; this figure soared to 1.6 million by 1910, and to 2.2 million in 1919.[55] This level remained steady in the early 1920s, then rose to 2.4 million by 1930. The increase in the number of cattle was accompanied, at varying rates, by a growth in the populations of sheep, pigs, and goats (Table 42).

Concerning agricultural products, the most remarkable case is offered by the acceleration in wine production. In 1877–1878 only about a half-million hectoliters of wine were made, but at the end of the period under study this figure had risen to more than 2.5 million hectoliters. In the context of our analysis of the transformation of agriculture in the Núcleo Central, the most interesting point is that this expansion in wine production was concentrated primarily in that region, which by 1926–1927 produced nearly 2.1 million hectoliters, or 83 percent of all wine made in Chile (Table 43). Moreover, between 1916 and 1927 the total area under cultivation in the country continued to expand, both in the Núcleo Central and elsewhere (Table 44), thus confirming the trends already noted with regard to certain selected products (Table 45). In addition, the cultivation of new lands expanded at a more rapid pace (6.2 percent annually) than in the traditional area of the Núcleo Central (4.4 percent annually), but nevertheless the rate of growth of the latter region was fairly high. Finally, from the data for the year 1916, the relative importance of the growing of legumes, potatoes, fodder, and fruits, especially grapes, as compared with the more traditional cultivation of cereals, is notable. In order for this group of crops to acquire an importance nearly equal to that of cereal cultivation, a substantial degree of diversification in agricultural land use must have taken place before 1916, both in the Núcleo Central and in the remainder of the country. This diversification was carried forward strongly between 1916 and 1927, a period in which the share of cereals in the total acreage under cultivation was reduced from somewhat more than half to about a third.

These expansionist and diversifying processes in agriculture and cattle raising were accompanied by substantial improvements in productivity and yields. This is demonstrated by our statistics of production and of areas under cultivation for six products: wheat, barley, beans, potatoes, corn, and peas, a group of products that represented a very high proportion of the total land under cultivation (Tables 44 and 45), so that it is eminently representative. In each case large increments in yields per hectare were achieved, especially in the period 1877–1878 to 1912–1913. The yields of wheat and potatoes doubled; those of barley and beans rose by 2.3 times; those of corn quintupled; and those of peas increased almost threefold (Table 45).

To the increases in yield per hectare should be added an increment in the productivity of agricultural workers. As has been amply shown in this section, agriculture and animal husbandry expanded greatly in the period under consideration, both in the Núcleo Central and elsewhere in Chile. Nevertheless the rural population of the Núcleo Central fluctuated between 988,000 in 1875 and 1,047,000 in 1930 (Table 2); in other words, it remained nearly stable at about a million persons. Consequently agricultural productivity per worker must have increased substantially during the period. The introduction of farming machinery, documented for the first time in 1915, provides a partial explanation of this phenomenon (Table 46).

To summarize, the preceding data appear to fully confirm the hypothesis that Chilean agriculture underwent a considerable expansion in the years 1880–1930, both in the traditional region of the central valley and in the new areas south of Concepción. It has also been demonstrated that agriculture in the Núcleo Central experienced important changes, especially with respect to the diversification of products through the introduction of new crops. Further, it is clear that in this process the productivity of farm labor was augmented, and in addition, for all the crops for which we have been able to secure data, a high increase in yield was obtained.

It is evident that such an intense expansion and transformation was part of a larger process of modernization that took place in other sectors as well as in agriculture, and that this process accompanied economic expansion and modernization on a national scale. In fact, various commentators at the end of the last century and in the early 1900s, as well as documents of the National Society of Agriculture and governmental records, make reference to the progress made in agriculture.

In a small and interesting work Silvia Hernández outlined and summarized the qualitative changes occurring in the agricultural and animal husbandry sector in the course of the second half of the nineteenth century, especially in the last quarter.[56]

The developments to which Hernández refers are the following: the building of fences and digging of irrigation ditches, and extension of the area of irrigated land; experiments with varieties of seeds and new crops, and the incorporation of some of them into regular plantings; the gradual introduction of the system of crop rotation to replace the old custom of letting the land lie fallow for long periods; the importation of high-quality cattle for milk and meat; the use of cultivated pastureland; the replacement of traditional rural implements by imported tools and machinery; the diffusion of technical expertise by the National Agricultural Society, through numerous publications and agricultural fairs, through travel and immigrants who entered into farm communities, and through the activity of foreign firms that imported agricultural equipment; changes in the organization of agricultural enterprises; and experiments with different types of wage and salary arrangements. These and other developments were doubtless the consequence of the growth of a modern sector of capitalist entrepreneurs who saw the potential profits in agriculture, as well as from other elements of the economy in a period of thrust and prosperity.

In this chapter we have not attempted to do more than demonstrate the existence of this type of process through the systematic examination of the available quantitative sources. A detailed study of qualitative changes in landholding, in the forms of organization of ranches and farms and other types of agricultural property, in prevailing social relationships on the land, and so forth would require a different type of research based on primary sources of another sort. Our study has tried rather to confirm, through the use of large-scale quantitative data, the hypothesis that the expansion of the nitrate industry influenced and changed the economic and social life of Chile in diverse ways, and that the impact of that expansion was reflected, to a significant degree, in growth and change in agriculture.

TABLE 1
URBAN CENTERS IN VARIOUS REGIONS OF THE COUNTRY

Region	1865	1875	1885	1895	1907	1920	1930	1940
Norte Grande	*	*	6	12	11	11	26	18
pop. 2,000–20,000	*	*	6	11	9	9	24	16
pop. 20,000+	*	*	—	1	2	2	2	2
Norte Chico	9	15	13	11	10	11	11	13
pop. 2,000–20,000	9	15	13	11	10	11	10	12
pop. 20,000+	—	—	—	—	—	—	1	1
Núcleo Central	20	32	39	43	36	52	53	58
pop. 2,000–20,000	18	31	35	40	31	47	47	51
pop. 20,000+ [†]	2	2	4	3	5	5	5	7
Concepción y La Frontera	7	9	17	22	29	32	35	43
pop. 2,000–20,000	7	9	16	21	28	29	31	39
pop. 20,000+	—	—	1	1	1	3	4	4
Los Lagos	1	2	3	4	5	6	8	11
pop. 2,000–20,000	1	2	3	4	5	5	7	8
pop. 20,000+	—	—	—	—	—	1	1	3
Los Canales	1	1	1	2	2	3	4	6
pop. 2,000–20,000	1	1	1	2	2	2	3	5
pop. 20,000+	—	—	—	—	—	1	1	1
Total	38	60	79	94	93	115	136	149
pop. 2,000–20,000	36	58	74	89	85	103	122	131
pop. 20,000+	2	2	5	5	8	12	14	18

SOURCE: C. Hurtado, *Concentración de población y desarrollo económico; el caso chileno* (Santiago, 1966), Table 9.
*These regions were under Peruvian and Bolivian control during these years.
[†] Including Santiago.

TABLE 2
DISTRIBUTION OF THE CHILEAN POPULATION BY REGION
(IN THOUSANDS)

Region*	1865			1875		
	Urban[†]	Rural	Total	Urban[†]	Rural	Total
Norte Grande	—	—	—	—	2	2
Norte Chico	56	183	239	68	176	245
Núcleo Central	300	952	1,252	408	988	1,395
Concepción y La Frontera	33	174	208	54	231	285
Los Lagos	3	57	61	6	77	83
Los Canales	5	54	59	4	61	66
Total	398	1,421	1,819	540	1,536	2,076

TABLE 2 (continued)

Region*	1885			1895		
	Urban[†]	Rural	Total	Urban[†]	Rural	Total
		1885			1895	
Norte Grande	38	50	88	90	52	141
Norte Chico	69	184	252	58	177	235
Núcleo Central	504	1,038	1,542	608	992	1,600
Concepción y						
La Frontera	91	354	445	140	357	497
Los Lagos	12	93	105	19	120	139
Los Canales	4	72	76	6	77	83
Total	717	1,790	2,507	922	1,774	2,696
	1907			1920		
Norte Grande	112	122	234	137	151	288
Norte Chico	66	189	255	72	153	224
Núcleo Central	784	1,018	1,802	1,040	1,008	2,048
Concepción y						
La Frontera	210	438	648	261	513	774
Los Lagos	34	151	186	60	196	226
Los Canales	16	90	106	27	112	139
Total	1,222	2,009	3,231	1,598	2,132	3,730
	1930			1940		
Norte Grande	222	70	292	187	63	249
Norte Chico	90	169	259	117	213	330
Núcleo Central	1,328	1,047	2,375	1,695	1,135	2,830
Concepción y						
La Frontera	307	587	894	390	649	1,039
Los Lagos	86	243	329	108	299	408
Los Canales	35	104	139	52	116	168
Total	2,068	2,219	4,287	2,548	2,475	5,024

SOURCE: Hurtado, *Concentración de población y desarrollo económico*, Table 2.
[†]Urban centers are those with 2,000 or more inhabitants.
*Regional lines are those of 1960.
NOTE: Regional figures may not seem exactly to total because of rounding.

TABLE 3
ANNUAL NITRATE EXPORTS FROM NORTE GRANDE, 1830–1879
(IN THOUSANDS OF METRIC TONS)

Period	Nitrate Exports (annual average)
1830–1834	3.3
1835–1839	7.0
1840–1844	14.6
1845–1849	19.0
1850–1854	30.0
1855–1859	51.9
1860–1864	64.2
1865–1869	97.5

Year	Nitrate Exports
1869	115.3
1870	181.3
1871	165.9
1872	203.3
1873	288.1
1874	256.8
1875	330.7
1876	290.5
1877	229.5
1878	323.0
1879	145.4

SOURCE: Chile. Ministerio de Hacienda, *Memoria de hacienda, año 1902* (Santiago : Imprenta Nacional, 1903), p. 329.

TABLE 4
WHEAT AND FLOUR EXPORTS, 1844–1940
(THOUSANDS OF METRIC QUINTALS)

	Total Exports			Exports to Countries in Region of Pacific Ocean*			
							Percentage Exported Pacific Region
Year	(1) Flour	(2) Wheat	(3) Total	(4) Flour	(5) Wheat	(6) Total	$\frac{(6)}{(3)} \times 100$
1844	55,629	50,106	119,642	50,412	49,281	112,296	93.9
1845	28,148	46,987	85,122	23,703	46,648	76,276	89.6
1846	47,937	63,039	122,960	39,750	56,393	106,080	86.3
1847	69,463	93,412	180,240	46,840	78,975	137,525	76.3
1848	82,312	77,346	180,236	44,710	65,619	121,506	67.4
1849	137,492	131,105	302,970	114,965	83,562	227,268	75.0
1850	296,054	131,576	501,643	287,874	92,646	452,488	90.2
1851	186,760	55,393	288,843	175,848	48,168	267,978	92.8
1852	175,696	116,648	336,268	175,288	106,745	325,855	96.9
1853	210,859	48,606	312,179	193,446	26,501	268,308	85.9
1854	219,719	91,014	365,662	187,998	70,051	305,048	83.4
1855	318,877	188,968	587,564	265,232	163,604	495,144	84.3
1856	156,045	134,018	329,074	138,785	119,538	293,019	89.0
1857	74,546	149,395	242,577	69,499	93,951	180,242	74.3
1858	77,823	112,928	210,206	76,057	112,903	207,974	98.9
1859	108,655	114,495	250,313	104,709	114,222	245,108	97.9
1860	164,630	223,006	428,793	137,703	191,612	363,740	84.8
1861	203,460	409,173	663,498	78,643	253,956	352,259	53.1
1862	96,760	270,567	391,429	78,333	178,295	276,211	70.6
1863	95,987	318,156	438,139	81,089	186,250	287,611	65.6
1864	339,614	294,829	719,346	263,686	149,092	478,699	66.5
1865	554,835	520,060	1,213,603	445,005	466,961	1,023,217	84.3
1866	464,209	864,382	1,444,643	286,065	452,046	809,627	56.0
1867	360,612	1,003,584	1,454,349	56,396	141,898	212,393	14.6
1868	291,295	1,160,844	1,524,962	109,075	191,080	327,423	21.5
1869	331,615	629,087	1,043,605	102,436	249,393	377,438	36.2
1870	230,613	655,635	943,901	93,880	275,153	392,503	41.6
1871	407,818	1,025,131	1,534,903	153,214	276,935	468,452	30.5
1872	247,568	1,097,280	1,406,740	147,076	403,088	586,933	41.7
1873	268,054	1,115,318	1,450,385	117,332	238,455	385,120	26.6
1874	381,355	1,592,589	2,069,282	150,796	289,829	478,324	23.1
1875	265,673	827,070	1,159,161	111,051	302,951	441,764	38.1
1876	145,059	847,143	1,028,460	78,189	330,511	428,247	41.6
1877	109,453	695,153	831,969	62,903	266,875	345,503	41.5
1878	124,529	375,638	531,299	109,526	272,115	409,022	77.0
1879	135,309	1,421,829	1,590,965	78,172	145,663	243,378	15.3
1880	114,189	1,387,776	1,530,512	43,930	69,498	124,410	8.1
1881	189,380	896,688	1,133,413	125,094	79,548	235,828	20.8
1882	156,255	1,290,575	1,485,893	61,017	180,644	256,915	17.3

TABLE 4 *(continued)*

	Total Exports			Exports to Countries in Region of Pacific Ocean*			
Year	*(1)* *Flour*	*(2)* *Wheat*	*(3)* *Total*	*(4)* *Flour*	*(5)* *Wheat*	*(6)* *Total*	*Percentage Exported Pacific Region* $\frac{(6)}{(3)} \times 100$
1883	101,073	1,233,891	1,360,232	63,615	166,828	246,346	18.1
1884	66,321	913,494	996,395	41,645	219,928	271,984	27.3
1885	56,396	1,073,471	1,143,966	38,769	235,887	284,348	24.9
1886	69,216	1,221,028	1,307,548	41,198	228,759	280,256	21.4
1887	30,433	1,245,519	1,283,560	24,882	152,140	183,242	14.3
1888	31,525	928,854	968,260	24,196	199,708	229,953	23.7
1889	31,404	496,959	536,214	19,505	143,956	168,337	31.4
1890	21,648	289,279	316,339	16,230	254,057	274,344	86.7
1891	56,921	1,780,482	1,851,633	27,349	223,036	257,252	13.9
1892	38,872	1,458,016	1,506,606	25,612	355,317	387,332	25.7
1893	21,809	1,859,627	1,886,888	16,679	260,004	280,852	14.9
1894	31,157	1,162,350	1,201,296	21,625	242,692	269,723	22.5
1895	36,558	785,813	831,510	32,957	287,037	328,233	39.5
1896	30,838	1,375,653	1,414,200	25,092	295,407	326,772	23.1
1897	52,393	723,941	789,432	28,629	238,859	274,645	34.8
1898	60,720	769,646	845,546	34,907	173,209	216,842	25.6
1899	66,515	458,126	541,269	64,030	264,893	344,930	63.7
1900	9,149	94,350	105,786	6,857	75,423	83,994	79.4
1901	3,519	15,608	20,006	382	8,305	8,782	43.9
1902	24,739	250,018	280,941	22,719	157,782	186,172	66.3
1903	46,638	538,635	596,932	26,094	243,487	276,104	46.3
1904	91,799	740,514	855,269	76,675	247,032	342,875	40.1
1905	74,388	80,068	173,053	70,970	55,071	143,763	83.0
1906	39,588	2,133	51,618	35,453	973	45,289	87.7
1907	33,541	353,118	395,044	30,882	10,074	48,676	12.3
1908	17,467	1,346,195	1,368,028	14,269	225,630	243,466	17.8
1909	52,272	1,092,561	1,157,901	49,064	131,372	192,702	16.6
1910	98,646	611,395	734,702	95,113	151,150	270,041	36.8
1911	51,500	138,419	202,794	48,302	9,250	69,627	34.3
1912	56,884	655,955	727,060	9,384	158,981	170,711	23.5
1913	56,115	523,726	593,869	51,809	142,901	207,662	35.0
1914	25,369	41,479	73,190	22,640	18,707	47,007	64.2
1915	679	4,907	5,755	—	1,570	1,570	27.3
1916	28,838	105,829	141,876	26,601	42,099	75,350	53.1
1917	112,399	144,023	284,521	100,048	104,129	229,189	80.6
1918	409,517	625,306	1,137,202	209,446	636,683	885,490	77.9
1919	234,522	397,630	690,782	233,239	296,296	687,844	99.6
1920	104,484	228,289	358,894	102,690	124,749	253,161	70.5
1921	123,677	414,816	569,412	120,980	240,161	391,386	68.7
1922	120,897	19,012	170,133	118,657	18,217	166,538	97.9

TABLE 4 (continued)

	Total Exports			Exports to Countries in Region of Pacific Ocean*			
Year	(1) Flour	(2) Wheat	(3) Total	(4) Flour	(5) Wheat	(6) Total	Percentage Exported Pacific Region $\frac{(6)}{(3)} \times 100$
1923	144,376	215,755	396,225	141,866	132,943	310,275	78.3
1924	221,384	1,645,124	1,921,853	218,978	592,253	865,975	45.1
1925	139,074	1,413,710	1,587,552	136,913	184,239	355,380	22.4
1926	105,651	284,458	416,521	104,384	133,855	264,335	63.5
1927	95,892	6,759	126,624	94,537	3,872	122,043	96.4
1928	71,303	117,694	206,822	69,118	89,600	175,997	85.1
1929	75,165	68,121	162,077	73,733	4,483	96,649	59.6
1930	86,246	395,721	503,528	84,700	99,842	205,717	40.9
1931	10,775	14,841	28,309	10,320	13,113	26,013	91.9
1932	10,757	5,834	19,280	7,530	6,018	15,430	80.0
1933	111	2,320	2,459	7	2,320	2,337	94.7
1934	30,819	504,331	542,854	30,607	431,269	469,527	86.5
1935	18,716	187,628	211,023	18,530	38,679	61,841	29.3
1936	18,207	475,941	493,699	18,030	59,162	81,699	16.4
1937	113	6,151	6,292	23	6,150	6,178	98.2
1938	39	8,236	8,284	—	8,236	8,236	99.4
1939	1,161	9,042	10,493	924	7,156	8,399	80.0
1940	1,869	11,691	14,027	1,559	11,171	13,119	93.5

SOURCE: Sepúlveda, S., *El trigo chileno en el mercado mundial; ensayo de geografía histórica,* (Santiago: Editorial Universitaria, 1959), Appendix 1, pp. 127–129.
*Including Peru and Bolivia.
NOTE: Totals of columns (3) and (6) include flour quantities multiplied by 1.25 to obtain weight equivalents in wheat. Wheat and adjusted flour figures in the source did not add exactly to totals for some years. Corrections have been made in ten cases where alternative data were available, but some discrepancy remains.

TABLE 5
THE BANKING SYSTEM IN 1885, 1893, AND 1905
(IN PESOS)

Bancos (Banks)	Location	Paid-in Capital 1885	Paid-in Capital 1893	Paid-in Capital 1905
Nacional de Chile*	Santiago	4,000,000	—	—
de Valparaíso*	Valparaíso	4,125,000	—	—
A. Edwards y Ca.	Valparaíso	1,500,000	3,000,000	3,500,000
D. Matte y Ca.	Santiago	1,000,000	1,000,000	—
Agrícola*	Santiago	1,593,000	—	—
Mobiliario	Santiago	1,125,000	2,000,000	7,000,000
de la Unión	Santiago	227,384	1,024,000	—
de Concepción	Concepción	400,000	400,000	1,025,000
Melipilla	Melipilla	70,000	500,000	500,000
José Bunster	Angol	200,000	200,000	—
Curicó	Curicó	100,000	450,000	650,000
Caupolican	Rengo	66,960	—	—
Santiago	Santiago	647,250	4,000,000	3,200,000
Talca	Talca	275,000	1,750,000	3,000,000
de Chile*	Santiago	—	14,550,000	20,000,000
Internacional	Valparaíso	—	4,000,000	—
Comercial de Chile	Santiago	—	4,000,000	—
Crédito Unido	Santiago	—	1,000,000	—
Ñuble	Chillán	—	250,000	250,000
La Serena	Serena	—	350,000	500,000
Arauco	Arauco	—	38,000	39,300
San Fernando	San Fernando	—	300,000	—
Llanquihue	Puerto Montt	—	92,120	140,344
Popular Hipotecario	Santiago	—	400,000	—
Rere	Yumbel	—	61,260	—
Colchagua	San Fernando	—	42,500	—
Tacna	Tacna	—	280,000	280,000
Mercantil	Tacna	—	—	400,000
Punta Arenas	Punta Arenas	—	—	450,000
Nacional	—	—	—	4,000,000
de la República	—	—	—	2,800,000
Crédito	—	—	—	1,500,000
Industrial	—	—	—	400,000
Unión Comercial	—	—	—	500,000

SOURCE: Chile, Oficina Central de Estadística, *Sinópsis estadística y geográfica de la República de Chile,* issues for 1885, p. 44; 1894, p. 158; 1905, p. 441.
*The Banco de Chile was formed by the merger of the Banco Nacional de Chile, Valparaíso, and Agrícola.

TABLE 6
FISCAL REVENUES, 1830–1930
(IN THOUSANDS OF U.S. DOLLARS)

Year	Customs Revenues	Other Taxes	Public Companies and Services	Other Ordinary Revenue	Total Ordinary Revenue	Extraordinary Revenue	Total Revenue
1830	618.0	—	343.0	272.9	1,233.9	—	1,233.9
1831	643.9	—	291.7	240.7	1,176.3	—	1,176.3
1832	803.1	—	282.2	216.0	1,301.3	—	1,301.3
1833	785.1	—	355.1	221.9	1,362.1	185.5	1,547.6
1834	977.2	—	344.5	192.4	1,514.1	246.4	1,760.5
1835	1,003.2	—	376.4	173.4	1,553.0	249.6	1,802.6
1836	951.5	—	385.7	258.9	1,596.1	80.4	1,676.5
1837	1,131.0	50.8	385.3	396.0	1,963.1	30.7	1,993.8
1838	1,016.6	21.8	372.6	352.8	1,763.8	30.7	1,794.5
1839	1,076.4	33.4	409.4	345.6	1,864.8	31.1	1,895.9
1840	1,415.1	47.4	454.5	366.9	2,283.9	5.7	2,289.6
1841	1,283.3	370.3	505.1	15.9	2,174.6	—	2,174.6
1842	1,536.7	369.2	519.5	14.7	2,440.1	128.1	2,568.5
1843	1,366.4	477.8	551.9	16.1	2,412.2	74.8	2,487.0
1844	1,648.5	630.2	776.6	35.5	3,090.8	154.7	3,245.5
1845	1,367.2	533.5	568.5	29.2	2,498.4	103.3	2,601.7
1846	1,808.3	637.7	667.1	38.1	3,151.2	81.7	3,232.9
1847	1,894.6	693.0	707.4	51.0	3,346.0	1,155.8	4,501.8
1848	1,687.4	669.2	700.0	32.6	3,089.2	331.8	3,421.0
1849	2,093.4	713.3	774.4	54.2	3,635.3	449.7	4,085.0
1850	2,478.7	679.2	882.3	48.7	4,088.9	235.9	4,324.8
1851	2,550.9	690.3	854.9	41.1	4,137.2	302.7	4,439.9
1852	3,238.6	940.5	888.6	54.2	5,121.9	592.5	5,714.4
1853	3,229.3	1,053.3	987.9	68.4	5,338.9	2,145.7	7,484.6
1854	3,375.7	1,049.6	917.0	63.3	5,405.6	238.5	5,644.1
1855	3,453.6	1,237.3	963.2	114.2	5,768.3	362.6	6,130.9
1856	3,848.9	1,091.4	1,037.9	49.4	6,027.6	1,734.8	7,762.4
1857	3,730.8	1,018.4	1,136.3	54.6	5,940.1	473.2	6,413.3
1858	3,196.8	1,043.9	1,023.9	204.9	5,469.5	855.2	6,324.7
1859	3,674.9	1,000.0	1,025.4	116.8	5,817.1	3,249.7	9,066.8
1860	4,190.6	1,037.5	1,130.3	99.1	6,458.0	1,042.7	7,500.7
1861	3,159.6	1,014.9	979.9	69.5	5,223.9	1,220.9	6,444.8
1862	4,043.5	1,245.5	1,280.1	48.9	6,618.0	2,748.2	9,366.2
1863	5,460.9	1,422.6	1,707.0	—	8,590.5	3,121.7	11,712.2
1864	7,359.6	2,040.0	2,554.7	—	11,954.3	8,329.1	20,283.4
1865	5,378.2	1,462.4	3,489.2	100.2	10,430.0	13,293.7	23,723.7
1866	4,017.6	1,380.1	2,705.2	51.1	8,154.0	14,560.3	22,714.3
1867	5,356.8	1,293.3	2,215.6	338.8	9,204.5	9,983.1	19,187.6
1868	5,641.7	1,331.5	2,595.5	426.4	9,995.1	1,943.5	11,938.6
1869	5,949.9	1,638.8	2,850.1	195.2	10,634.0	2,732.2	13,366.2
1870	5,961.2	1,463.7	3,009.4	248.8	10,683.1	7,211.7	17,894.8
1871	5,554.1	1,427.2	3,435.7	475.6	10,892.6	1,825.6	12,718.2
1872	6,891.3	1,689.1	3,660.5	462.2	12,703.1	837.4	13,540.5

TABLE 6 *(continued)*

Year	Customs Revenues	Other Taxes	Public Companies and Services	Other Ordinary Revenue	Total Ordinary Revenue	Extraordinary Revenue	Total Revenue
1873	7,208.2	1,514.7	4,222.2	564.2	13,509.3	9,167.7	22,677.0
1874	6,928.2	1,567.3	5,059.7	319.4	13,874.6	235.0	14,109.6
1875	6,903.9	1,851.2	4,655.0	693.4	14,103.5	4,562.5	18,666.0
1876	6,080.5	1,678.2	4,373.1	458.4	12,590.2	3,067.9	15,658.1
1877	5,404.8	1,706.8	3,975.6	513.5	11,600.7	4,271.4	15,872.1
1878	4,950.6	1,567.3	4,028.3	679.2	11,225.4	3,251.2	14,476.6
1879	4,566.5	1,479.7	3,914.8	303.3	10,264.3	8,466.7	18,731.0
1880	6,701.6	1,891.4	4,553.6	2,862.0	17,646.2	9,937.9	27,584.1
1881	13,928.5	2,128.3	3,638.1	2,909.7	22,988.3	2,125.5	25,113.8
1882	20,771.5	2,699.2	4,026.3	1,792.9	29,289.9	1,199.6	30,489.5
1883	21,491.3	2,930.3	4,301.0	2,659.4	31,382.0	2,526.0	33,908.0
1884	16,828.2	2,322.4	4,245.8	1,230.5	24,626.9	500.8	25,127.7
1885	12,203.0	1,733.8	3,360.8	1,204.1	18,501.7	1,798.3	20,300.0
1886	11,182.2	1,708.4	3,399.8	1,585.6	17,876.0	11,167.6	29,043.6
1887	14,721.1	1,773.0	3,578.0	2,533.2	22,605.3	11,030.0	33,635.3
1888	19,785.1	1,444.1	3,943.6	1,378.4	26,551.2	1,450.7	28,001.9
1889	21,840.1	1,264.5	4,624.1	1,421.9	29,150.6	4,069.2	33,219.8
1890	18,415.2	1,035.5	4,292.6	1,834.8	25,578.1	2,818.4	28,396.5
1891	14,721.4	554.9	3,911.1	1,838.6	21,025.7	18,578.2	39,603.9
1892	17,403.3	653.8	3,835.6	1,504.9	23,397.6	7,258.7	30,656.3
1893	17,788.7	207.3	4,069.5	1,092.2	23,157.7	3,358.7	26,516.4
1894	18,576.4	160.8	3,410.4	1,105.6	23,253.2	2,766.8	26,020.0
1895	22,582.3	171.9	4,712.2	1,157.0	28,623.4	14,672.0	43,295.4
1896	22,212.0	176.6	5,244.4	1,003.8	28,636.8	28,613.6	57,250.4
1897	21,549.5	184.6	5,049.4	1,132.5	27,916.0	2,168.1	30,084.1
1898	20,716.2	142.5	4,541.8	2,421.1	27,821.6	17,565.2	45,386.8
1899	24,831.8	150.9	4,465.1	4,432.1	33,879.9	9,241.7	43,121.6
1900	28,366.4	197.6	5,376.8	3,067.7	37,008.5	11,073.4	48,081.9
1901	26,187.3	189.6	5,637.2	1,652.6	33,666.7	26,227.3	59,894.0
1902	25,972.9	662.4	5,639.0	927.7	33,202.0	26,903.5	60,105.5
1903	28,763.1	636.5	6,913.5	2,651.9	38,965.0	30,601.8	69,566.8
1904	30,118.9	753.9	7,096.1	1,822.0	39,790.9	26,248.6	66,039.5
1905	32,844.0	970.8	7,354.7	2,031.3	43,200.8	37,533.1	80,733.9
1906	46,443.5	1,164.1	7,650.8	1,137.4	56,395.8	50,591.5	106,987.3
1907	38,522.1	1,360.5	9,214.8	2,470.1	51,567.5	41,236.4	92,803.9
1908	33,159.2	999.5	9,304.4	2,616.6	46,079.7	43,022.6	89,102.3
1909	41,403.7	933.4	10,428.9	2,433.9	55,199.9	48,676.9	103,876.8
1910	46,907.7	2,265.9	11,598.7	2,299.9	63,072.2	31,060.3	94,132.5
1911	42,311.0	2,836.4	12,478.9	2,935.0	60,561.3	109,679.3	170,240.6
1912	42,961.5	2,928.7	14,925.8	3.945.9	64,761.9	90,687.4	155,449.3
1913	44,833.4	3,743.1	14,934.2	3,772.6	67,283.3	30,030.9	97,314.2
1914	31,964.4	3,099.1	12,452.0	6,077.0	53,593.0	48,892.0	102,485.0
1915	32,749.2	7,003.3	19,843.1	3,921.2	63,516.8	—	63,516.8
1916	49,855.5	5,649.7	26,047.9	3,580.5	85,133.6	5,622.4	90,756.0
1917	57,148.3	8,439.3	40,460.6	6,503.6	112,551.8	187.2	112,739.0

TABLE 6 *(continued)*

Year	Customs Revenues	Other Taxes	Public Companies and Services	Other Ordinary Revenue	Total Ordinary Revenue	Extraordinary Revenue	Total Revenue
1918	65,545.5	11,468.2	67,832.8	8,870.8	153,717.3	1,319.9	155,037.2
1919	24,453.4	8,567.6	39,215.3	6,441.4	78,677.7	283.7	78,961.4
1920	39,060.7	8,592.9	42,570.8	6,162.8	96,387.2	1,981.5	98,368.7
1921	21,932.9	5,866.8	17,431.5	5,797.7	51,028.9	21,553.9	72,582.8
1922	25,699.5	6,479.8	24,415.3	7,670.7	64,265.3	24,759.1	89,024.4
1923	47,318.2	7,525.3	27,277.7	7,841.8	89,963.0	33,785.4	123,748.4
1924	45,902.5	12,169.4	24,232.0	8,628.0	90,931.9	36,359.1	127,291.0
1925	54,160.6	19,939.9	30,551.8	8,055.8	112,708.1	39,301.4	152,009.5
1926	52,567.7	26,466.3	35,002.6	7,969.6	122,006.2	2,482.8	124,489.0
1927	60,732.4	31,700.4	34,776.6	11,003.3	138,212.7	—	138,212.7
1928	67,956.1	36,277.3	34,684.6	17,585.8	156,503.8	65,535.2	222,039.0
1929	84,460.5	45,902.9	36,350.2	16,498.5	183,212.1	46,193.9	229,406.0
1930	65,157.3	46,912.7	32,409.1	13,099.5	157,578.6	70,423.7	228,002.3

SOURCE: C. Humud, *El sector público chileno entre 1830 y 1930,* (Santiago: Universidad de Chile, Facultad de Ciencias Económicas, Memoria de Licienciado, 1969), Tables A–1, A–2, pp. 223–226.

NOTE: Humud's presentation of fiscal data in U.S. dollars was intended to facilitate comparisons with international trade statistics, in a currency which had maintained parity with gold over the period considered. The figures can be converted back to current pesos through multiplying by the peso–dollar exchange rates presented in Table 34.

TABLE 7
AREA OF CHILE BY REGIONS

Region	Area (millions of hectares)	Percentage
Norte Grande	17.84	24.0
Norte Chico	11.98	16.2
Núcleo Central	9.30	12.6
Concepción y la Frontera	5.44	7.3
Los Lagos	4.84	6.5
Los Canales	24.78	33.4
Total	74.18	100

SOURCE: Corporación de Fomento de la Producción, *Geografía económica de Chile* (Santiago, 1950), Vol. II, p. 371.

TABLE 8
EXPANSION OF NITRATE INDUSTRY, 1880–1930

(1) Year	(2) Number of Active Mines	(3) Persons Employed (Thousands)	(4) Production (Thousands of tons)	(5) Exports (Thousands of tons)	(6) Prices (6–pence pesos per ton)	(7) Exports (Millions of 6–pence pesos)
1880	—	2.8	—	226	—	—
1881	—	4.9	—	358	358.0	128.2
1882	—	7.1	—	489	341.3	166.9
1883	—	7.1	—	585	292.3	171.0
1884	—	5.5	—	560	281.3	157.5
1885	—	4.6	—	430	305.1	131.2
1886	—	4.5	—	453	264.9	120.0
1887	—	7.2	—	713	240.3	171.3
1888	—	9.2	—	784	260.9	204.5
1889	—	11.4	—	921	247.7	228.1
1890	—	13.1	—	1,026	216.3	221.9
1891	—	11.7	—	892	237.5	211.9
1892	—	13.5	—	798	256.5	204.7
1893	—	14.8	969	947	257.2	243.6
1894	51	18.1	1,094	1,081	260.0	281.1
1895	53	22.5	1,308	1,220	234.8	286.5
1896	53	19.3	1,139	1,117	242.8	271.2
1897	42	16.7	1,187	1,048	226.2	237.1
1898	46	16.0	1,314	1,294	202.3	261.8
1899	58	19.9	1,440	1,381	212.0	292.8
1900	51	19.7	1,508	1,466	226.9	332.6
1901	66	20.3	1,329	1,292	272.4	351.9
1902	80	24.5	1,349	1,331	281.9	375.2
1903	72	24.4	1,485	1,443	282.6	407.8
1904	76	—	1,559	1,500	313.4	470.1
1905	90	—	1,755	1,650	329.7	544.0
1906	96	—	1,822	1,728	367.1	634.0
1907	110	39.7	1,846	1,656	375.0	621.0
1908	113	40.8	1,971	2,051	327.4	671.5
1909	102	37.8	2,111	2,135	296.2	632.4
1910	102	43.5	2,465	2,336	298.3	696.8
1911	107	43.9	2,521	2,450	318.3	779.8
1912	118	47.8	2,586	2,493	346.0	862.6
1913	127	53.2	2,772	2,738	340.1	931.2
1914	137	44.0	2,463	1,849	302.5	559.3
1915	116	45.5	1,755	2,023	300.0	606.9
1916	123	53.5	2,913	2,981	332.8	992.1
1917	129	56.4	3,001	2,776	544.6	1,511.8
1918	125	57.0	2,859	2,919	527.2	1,538.9
1919	125	44.5	1,703	804	449.8	361.6
1920	97	—	2,523	2,746	710.9	1,952.1
1921	101	33.9	1,310	1,193	469.9	560.6

TABLE 8 *(continued)*

(1) Year	(2) Number of Active Mines	(3) Persons Employed (Thousands)	(4) Production (Thousands of tons)	(5) Exports Thousands of tons)	(6) Prices (6–pence pesos per ton)	(7) Exports (Millions of 6–pence pesos)
1922	53	25.5	1,071	1,252	397.7	497.9
1923	82	41.1	1,093	2,243	404.0	906.2
1924	94	59.6	2,406	2,333	403.5	941.4
1925	96	60.8	2,524	2,519	390.6	983.9
1926	91	51.6	2,016	1,668	385.8	643.5
1927	67	46.8	1,614	2,271	336.8	764.9
1928	69	60.0	3,280	2,961	333.1	986.3
1929	71	58.4	3,000	2,199	309.8	681.3
1930	33	44.5	1,575	1,682	261.0	439.0

SOURCES: For (2), (3), (4), and (5): 1900–1927, Chile, Oficina Central de Estadística, *Sinopsis estadística de la República de Chile, 1926–1927,* (Santiago: Sociedad Imprenta y Litografía Universo, 1929), p. 72. 1928–1930, *Sinopsis estadística,* 1933, p. 199. 1894–1899, *Sinopsis estadística,* 1924, p. 96.

For (2): 1880–1893, *Sinopsis estadística,* 1900, p. 375.

For (5): 1880–1893, *Sinopsis estadística,* 1905, p. 411.

For (6): Chile, Dirección General de Estadística, *Anuario estadístico de la República de Chile,* 1937, Vol. IV, p. 7.

For (7): Column (5) times column (6).

NOTE: Exact title of *Sinopsis estadística* varies over the years. Other issues of *Sinopsis estadística* (e.g., 1900, pp. 378–379) contain earlier export series not fully in agreement with those shown in this table. The export value series in column (7), being derivative from export quantity and price series, approximates but does not exactly match the published value series (*Sinopsis estadística,* 1926–27, p. 137).

TABLE 9
NITRATE EXPORTS BY MINE AND COMPANY, 1907
(THOUSANDS OF SPANISH QUINTALS*)

Company	Mines	Exports Mines	Exports Companies
Compañía Salitrera			
H.B. Slomann i Ca.	Buena Esperanza	351	
	Empresa	1,000	
	Grutas	479	
	Rica Ventura	825	2,655
Cia. Salitrera Alemana	Alemania	792	
	Atacama	11	
	Chile	983	1,786
Granja i Ca.	Aragón	164	
	Bonasort	—	
	Cataluña	197	
	Cata	633	
	Democracia	156	
	Pepita	181	
	San Francisco	244	1,575
Lautaro Nitrate Co.	Ballena	363	
	Lautaro	322	
	Santa Catalina	—	
	Santa Luisa	863	1,548
Compañía de Salitres i			
F.C. de Agua Santa	Agua Santa	545	
	Primitiva	407	
	Valparaíso	411	1,363
Alianza Co., Ltd.	Alianza	1,311	
	Slavonia	—	1,311
Rosario Nitrate Co.	Arjentina	285	
	Puntilla de Huara	364	
	Rosario de Huara	650	1,300
Compañía Salitrera Progreso			
de Antofagasta	Aconcagua	—	
	Ausonia	657	
	Filomena	445	1,102
Gildemeister i Ca.	La Hansa	194	
	Peña Chica	589	
	San José	306	
	San Pedro	—	1,086

TABLE 9 *(continued)*

Company	Mines	Exports	
		Mines	*Companies*
Pedro Perfetti	California	275	
	Flor de Chile	403	
	Maroussia	66	
	Tres Marías	298	1,043
Colorado Nitrate Co.	Buen Retiro	320	
	Carmen Bajo	598	
	Peruana	—	918
Anglo Chilian Nitrate and Railway Co.	Peregrina	350	
	Santa Isabel	528	878
Lagunas Syndicate	North Lagunas	363	
	South Lagunas	506	869
Tarapacá and Tocopilla Nitrate Co.	Cholita i Yungay Bajo	74	
	Paposo i Limeña	—	
	Santa Ana	—	
	Santa Fé	475	
	Virjinia	288	836
Granja i Astoreca	La Granja	791	791
Compañía de Salitres i F.C. de Junín	Compañía	162	
	Recuerdo	110	
	San Antonio	—	
	Victoria	109	718
Amelia Nitrate Co.	Amelia i Aurora	220	
	Josefina	407	628
Santiago Nitrate Co.	Mapocho	202	
	Santiago	407	609
Compañía Salitrera Pampa Alta	Anita	528	528
Compañía Salitrera Lastenia	Lastenia	522	522
New Tamarugal Nitrate Co.	La Palma	497	
	La Patria	—	497
Solar del Carmen Nitrate Syndicate	Santa Lucia	446	446

TABLE 9 (*continued*)

| Company | Mines | Exports | |
		Mines	*Companies*
Compañía de Salitres de Antofagasta	Carmen	437	
	Carmen Alto	—	437
Liverpool Nitrate Co.	Ramírez	408	408
London Nitrate Co.	Puntunchara	407	407
Pacific Nitrate Co.	Aurelia	293	
	Celia	113	407
Compañía Nacional de Salitres La Unión	Unión i Porvenir	404	404
Moro i Sukinovich	Hervatska	196	
	Napried	138	
	Sioga	55	388
Compañía Salitrera Riviera	Riviera	384	384
Compañía Salitrera María Teresa de Aguas Blancas	María Teresa	305	
	Petronila	79	384
Compañía Salitrera Iberia	Iberia de Sáez	376	
	San Manuel	—	376
Laguna Nitrate Co.	Lagunas	365	365
Compañía Salitrera Castilla de Antofagasta	Castilla	340	340
Sucesión José Devéscovi	Constancia	336	336
Santa Rita Nitrate Co.	Santa Rita i Carolina	333	333
Cia. Salitrera Pampa Rica	Pampa Rica	329	329
Compañía Salitrera Carmen	Carmen	328	328
Anjela Nitrate Co.	Anjela	326	326
Pan de Azúcar Nitrate Co.	Pan de Azúcar	320	320
Compañía de Salitres La Americana	La Americana	196	
	San Gregorio	112	307
Santa Rosa Nitrate Co.	Rosario de Negreiros	156	
	Santa Rosa de Huara	138	294

TABLE 9 *(continued)*

Company	Mines	Exports	
		Mines	*Companies*
Andrés E. Bustos	Esmeralda	126	
	Santa Elena	154	280
Camiña Nitrate Co.	Camiña	275	275
San Donato Nitrate Co.	San Donato	273	273
Santa Catalina Nitrate Co.	Santa Catalina	272	272
New Pacha and Jazpampa Nitrate Co.	Jazpampa	261	
	Pacha	—	261
Jil Galté	Los Pirineos	—	
	Providencia	247	247
Jazpampa Bajo Nitrate Co.	Trinidad	247	247
Reducto Nitrate Co.	Reducto	247	
	Huáscar	—	247
Cia. Salitrera Aurrerá	Aurrerá	241	241
San Lorenzo Nitrate Co.	San Lorenzo	240	240
Barrenechea Nitrate Co.	Cóndor	220	220
Pablo S. Mimbela	Cala Cala	204	204
Cia. Salitrera Oriente	Oriente i Santa Lucia	198	198
San Patricio Nitrate Co.	San Patricio	182	
	Vis	—	182
Tricolor Nitrate Co.	Tricolor	182	182
Zapiga Nitrate Co.	Enriqueta	165	165
Cia. Comercial i Salitrera "La Aguada"	Aguada	163	163
E. Quiroga i Hermano	Progreso	158	158
Harrington, Morrison i Cia.	Keryma	154	154
San Sebastián Nitrate Co.	Sacramento	137	137
Cia. Salitrera Esmeralda	Luisis	135	135
Compañía Salitrera Miraflores de Taltal	Miraflores	133	133

TABLE 9 *(continued)*

| Company | Mines | Exports | |
		Mines	Companies
San Jorge Nitrate Co.	San Jorge	132	132
Jorge Jeffery	San Pablo	132	132
Remijio Gazzari	Tarapacá	125	125
Cia. Salitrera Candelaria	Candelaria	116	116
Hawes i Pirreta	Rosita	114	114
Dueños de Buenaventura	Buenaventura	110	110
Cia. Salitrera Santa Clara	Santa Clara	109	109
Soc. Salitrera La Perla	La Perla	91	91
J. Arturo Hidalgo	Sebastopol	90	90
Juan Pellerano	Palmira	88	88
Compañía Salitrera San Agustin de Tarapacá	San Agustín	82	82
Compañía Salitrera de Aguas Blancas	Eujenia	66	66
Cia. Salitrera Sacramento	San Enrique	59	59
Sucesión Alberto Yames	San Estéban	55	55
Agrupación Carolina de Taltal	Carolina	34	34
Esperanza Nitrate Co.	Esperanza	28	28
Cia. Salitrera Valparaíso	Valparaíso	25	25
Compañía Salitrera Alianza de Taltal	Alianza	16	16
Florencia Nitrate Co.	Florencia	4	4
Total			35,971

SOURCE: Guillermo Yunge, *Estadística minera de Chile en 1906 i 1907* (Santiago: Imprenta, Litografía i Encuadernación Barcelona, 1909), Vol. 3, pp. 280–294. Sponsored by Sociedad Nacional de Minería.

NOTE: Some mines are listed without export data, either for not having made statistical reports or for not having exported. In addition, five companies, not included in this table, were listed in a similar way in the original source. Mine figures do not sum to company totals in some instances because of rounding. In two cases, however (Cia. de Salitres i F.C. de Junín and Gildemeister i Ca.), the discrepancy was in the original source, presumably because of typographical error.

*The Spanish quintal equals 46 Kg.

TABLE 10
PRIVATELY OWNED RAILROAD LINES IN NITRATE FIELDS, 1881, 1887, 1894, 1905
(KILOMETERS)

1881

Mejillones to Cerro Gordo	26
Antofagasta to Salinas de Dorado	128
Taltal to Cachiyuyal	97
Chañaral de las Ánimas to Pueblo Hundido	88
Total	339 Km.

1887

Pisagua to Tres Marías, Agua Santa, and Puntunchara	106
Iquique to Tres Marías, Virginia, and branch lines	194
Patillos to Salitreras del Sur	93
Mejillones del Sur to Cerro Gordo	29
Antofagasta via Salinas de Dorado to Calama and Ascotán	297
Taltal to Cachiyuyal and El Refresco	82
Chañaral to Las Ánimas and Salado	60
Total	861 Km.

1894

Pisagua to Tres Marías, Agua Santa, and Puntunchara	106
Iquique to Tres Marías, Virginia, and branch lines	194
Patillos to Salitreras del Sur	93
Tocopilla to El Toco and Sante Fé	93
Antofagasta to Bolivian frontier	438
Taltal to Cachiyuyal and El Refresco	82
Total	1,006 Km.

1905

Iquique to Pisagua and Lagunas	556
Agua Santa to Caleta Buena and branch lines	174
Branch lines from Junín	100
Tocopilla to El Toco	112
Antofagasta to Ollagüe	490
Coloso to Aguas Blancas	125
Taltal to Cachinal and branch lines	230
Total	1,787 Km.

SOURCE: Oficina Central de Estadística, *Sinopsis estadística,* 1880–81, p. 18; 1887, pp. 61–62; 1894, pp. 193–194; 1905, p. 104.

TABLE 11
NITRATE EXPORTS BY PORT OF EMBARKATION, 1907
(THOUSANDS OF SPANISH QUINTALS)

Port	Quantity Exported
Iquique	11,884.2
Caleta Buena	4,152.2
Junín	2,189.8
Pisagua	2,818.2
Total for Tarapacá Province	21,044.4
Tocopilla	4,383.4
Mejillones	1,526.2
Antofagasta	2,436.7
Caleta Coloso	2,468.1
Taltal	4,128.5
Total for Antofagasta Province	14,942.9
Grand total:	35,987.2

SOURCE: Yunge, *Estadística minera de Chile en 1906 i 1907, p. 279.*

TABLE 12

POPULATION OF NORTE GRANDE IN RELATION TO URBAN AND NATIONAL POPULATION, AT SELECTED DATES

Year	(1) Total Population of Chile (thousands)	(2) Population of Norte Grande (thousands)	(3) $\frac{(2)}{(1)} \times 100$	(4) Urban Population of all Chile, except Norte Grande (thousands)	(5) Population of Santiago (thousands)	(6) $\frac{(2)}{(4)} \times 100$	(7) $\frac{(2)}{(5)} \times 100$
1885	2,507.0	88.0	3.5%	678.4	189	13.0%	46.6%
1895	2,695.6	141.5	5.2	831.8	256	17.0	55.5
1907	3,231.0	233.9	7.2	1,110.6	333	21.1	70.3
1920	3,730.2	288.2	7.7	1,460.6	507	19.7	56.8
1930	4,287.4	292.1	6.8	1,776.1	696	16.4	42.0

SOURCE: For (1), (2) and (3), see Table 2. For population of Santiago, Hurtado, *Concentración de población y desarrollo*, Table 6.

TABLE 13

WORLD PRODUCTION OF NITROGENOUS FERTILIZERS
(REDUCED TO PURE NITROGEN)
(IN THOUSANDS OF METRIC TONS)

Year	World Total	Chilean Nitrate	% of World Production	Ammonium sulphate and other Compounds	% of World Production
1913	823	450	54.7	373	45.3
1914	765	395	51.6	370	48.4
1922	712	170	23.9	542	76.1
1923	947	305	32.2	642	67.8
1924	1,061	366	34.5	695	65.5

SOURCE: Chile, Ministerio de Hacienda, Sección Salitre, *Antecedentes sobre la industria salitrera* (Santiago, 1925), p. 61.

TABLE 14
NITRATE CONSUMPTION BY COUNTRY, 1880–1924
(THOUSANDS OF METRIC QUINTALS)

Year	United Kingdom	France	Germany	Holland	Belgium	Russia	Italy and Spain	Austria–Hungary and Switzerland
1880	567	342	548	184	76	—	10	—
1885	984	757	1,478	235	497	—	24	—
1890	1,188	2,010	3,213	479	930	—	140	49
1895	1,199	1,754	4,328	618	1,181	—	122	41
1900	1,396	2,844	4,821	953	1,712	—	275	67
1905	1,069	2,505	5,546	1,167	1,768	—	404[†]	59
1910	1,269	3,374	7,855	1,399	2,875	—	457[†]	1[‡]
1915	3,689	2,540	—	508	—	341	717[†]	3[‡]
1916	4,146	5,407	—	608	—	331	856[†]	2[‡]
1917	2,471	4,536	—	558	—	2	1,041[†]	5[‡]
1918	5,347	2,565	—	11	—	—	970[†]	10[‡]
1919	248	1,561	—	1,513	792	—	128[†]	
1920	714	2,245	641*	1,060	1,345	—	414[†]	—
1921	419	1,500	802*	1,159	1,029	—	248[†]	—
1922	848	2,758	1,003*	1,366	1,868	—	310[†]	—
1923	848	2,706	1,397*	1,236	1,645	—	501[†]	—
1924	796	2,728	1,239*	1,358	1,682	—	578[†]	—
Totals by country**	60,707	98,996	152,287 / 5,084*	37,793	56,575	1,214	14,184	1,260 / 47[‡]

TABLE 14 (continued)

Year	Egypt	Sweden	Scandinavia	Spain	Denmark	U.S.A.	Other Countries	Chile	Annual Total
1880	—	—	—	—	—	300	—	—	2,030
1885	—	—	—	—	—	440	—	—	4,418
1890	—	—	—	—	—	1,220	30	1	9,216
1895	—	64	—	—	10	1,195	64	13	10,602
1900	—	11	—	—	—	1,649	180	15	16,903
1905	—	23	—	60	—	3,217	518	12	16,361
1910	70	—	25	109	—	5,241	846	20	23,596
1915	530	—	339	383	420	7,045	879	27	17,426
1916	193	—	427	447	349	12,379	1,284	45	26,482
1917	326	—	172	523	396	15,679	1,685	52	27,448
1918	28	—	67	187	1	16,738	1,444	75	27,443
1919	544	—	232	582	481	3,696	1,169	52	11,014
1920	771	—	683	1,200	—	12,668	2,152	35	23,933
1921	289	—	512	589	—	2,659	807	46	10,065
1922	791	—	403	1,003	—	7,503	1,206	54	19,113
1923	859	—	776	1,035	—	9,470	1,688	81	22,247
1924	1,261	—	925	950	—	10,314	1,365	99	23,300
Totals by country‡	7,086	396	5,063	8,280	2,376	174,212	22,490	919	648,976

SOURCE: Chile, Ministerio de Hacienda, *Antecedentes sobre la industria salitrera*, p. 39–41.
*Germany and Baltic ports.
† Italy only.
**Totals pertain to all years from 1880 to 1924, not just the selected years shown in the Table.
‡ Switzerland only.

TABLE 15
STATE NITRATE HOLDINGS SOLD BY AUCTION

Year	Auction Number	Exploitable Nitrate (millions of metric quintals)	Price (in current pesos)	Total Paid (millions of current pesos)
1882	1	30.1	0.28	8.4
1894	2 and 3	43.6	0.32	13.9
1895	4	5.0	0.27	1.3
1897	5	1.8	0.21	0.3
1901	6	11.1	0.226	2.5
1903	7	12.5	0.33	5.4
1912	8	8.2	0.66	5.4
1917	9	27.6	0.25	6.9
1917	10	30.7	0.44	13.5
1918	11	6.6	0.305	2.0
1924	12	38.0	0.483	18.3
Totals		215.7		69.9

SOURCE: Chile, Ministerio de Hacienda, *Antecedentes sobre la industria salitrera*, p. 53.

TABLE 16
NITRATE PRODUCTION BY NATIONALITY OF CAPITAL INVESTMENT
(PERCENTAGE DISTRIBUTION)

Nationality	1878	1884	1895	1901	1912	1925
Peruvian	58.0	—	—	—	—	—
British	13.5	20	60	55	38.5	23
Anglo-Chilean	—	14%	—	—	—	
Chilean	19.0	36	13	14	37.0	68*
German	8.0	17	8	15	15.0	—
Others	1.5	13	19	16	9.5	9
Total	100%	100%	100%	100%	100%	100%

SOURCE: Werner Haase, *Die chilenische Salpeterindustrie und ihre Zusammenfassung in der Compañía de Salitre de Chile* (Dusseldorf, 1934), p. 10.
*Includes German-owned nitrate mines.

TABLE 17
DISTRIBUTION OF NITRATE COMPANIES BY NATIONALITY, 1925

Nationality of Companies	Number of Mines	Percentage of Sales	
Chilean	26	13.6	25.5
			—
with part British capital	2	1.2	—
with part Peruvian and Yugoslavian capital	4	1.7	—
British	30	28.0	50.5
with part Chilean capital	24	22.5	—
German	11	13.0	13.0
Yugoslavian	11	5.6	5.6
Spanish	3	0.4	0.4
Peruvian	4	0.6	0.6
Other nationalities	—	4.4	4.4
Total for 71 companies	127	100%	100%

SOURCE: Chile, Ministerio de Hacienda, *Antecedentes sobre la industria salitrera*, p. 9.

TABLE 18
RATIO OF TAXES PAID TO VALUE OF NITRATE AND IODINE EXPORTS
(MILLIONS OF 18–PENCE PESOS)

Year	(1) Value of Nitrate and Iodine Exports	(2) Taxes Paid	(3) Taxes as Percentage of Exports
1880	27	2	8.5
1885	39	14	36.8
1890	81	35	43.7
1895	101	44	43.6
1900	113	50	44.4
1905	189	57	30.3
1910	239	80	33.6
1915	244	68	27.9
1920	536	106	19.7

SOURCES: For (1), Charles A. McQueen, *Chilean Public Finance* (Washington, D.C. : Government Printing Office, 1924), pp. 118–119. For (2), Chile, Ministerio de Hacienda, *Antecedentes sobre la industria salitrera,* p. 21.

NOTE: Export and tax figures have been rounded, and do not correspond exactly to percentages of column 3.

TABLE 19
SHARE OF ORDINARY FISCAL REVENUES PROVIDED BY NITRATE TAXES, 1880–1924

Year	Exports Nitrate (millions of metric quintals)	Iodine (thousands of kilograms)	Nitrate and Iodine Taxes (millions of 18–pence peso)	Ordinary Fiscal Revenues (millions of 18–pence pesos)	Percentage from Nitrate Industry
1880	2.3	84	2.3	48.8	4.70
1885	4.3	257	14.4	51.0	28.21
1890	10.2	220	35.0	72.8	48.15
1895	12.4	180	44.0	78.3	56.12
1900	14.5	326	50.1	102.5	48.90
1905	16.5	572	57.3	119.5	47.99
1910	23.3	590	80.4	156.7	51.32
1915	20.2	709	68.2	113.4	60.16
1916	29.8	1,323	102.0	169.5	60.13
1917	27.7	759	107.7	213.5	50.43
1918	29.8	908	111.7	248.8	44.84
1919	9.4	243	30.5	124.7	24.37
1920	27.7	350	105.6	212.7	40.97
1921	11.4	534	42.2	125.9	33.54
1922	13.0	244	39.2	125.8	31.35
1923	22.8	471	76.4	187.2	40.61
1924	24.2	598	79.6	201.0	39.80
Total	661.9	17,850	2,240.5	5,191.9	41.65%

SOURCE: Chile, Ministerio de Hacienda, *Antecedentes sobre la industria salitrera*, p. 21.

TABLE 20
NITRATE INDUSTRY TAXES, 1880–1930
(MILLIONS OF U.S. DOLLARS)

Year	Nitrate and Iodine Taxes
1880	0.8
1885	5.2
1890	12.6
1895	16.1
1900	18.1
1905	20.7
1910	29.3
1915	24.7
1918	40.0
1919	10.0
1920	27.6
1921	11.8
1922	12.9
1923	26.2
1924	27.1
1925	30.5
1926	21.5
1927	28.6
1928	35.3
1929	36.3
1930	21.0

SOURCE: Humud, *El sector público chileno entre 1830 y 1930,* p. 47.

TABLE 21
SHARE OF NITRATES IN TOTAL EXPORTS, 1880–1920
(IN MILLIONS OF 18–PENCE PESOS)

Year	Nitrate Exports	Total Exports	Share of Nitrate Exports
1880	27	105	26%
1885	39	102	38
1890	81	142	57
1895	101	147	69
1900	113	166	68
1905	189	244	78
1910	239	302	79
1915	244	322	76
1920	535	789	68

SOURCE: McQueen, *Chilean Public Finance,* pp. 118–119; Henry W. Kirsch, *The Industrialization of Chile, 1880–1930,* unpublished (Ph.D. dissertation, University of Florida, December 1973), p. 256.

TABLE 22
CUSTOMS REVENUES, 1830–1930
(IN MILLIONS OF U.S. DOLLARS)

Year	Import Taxes	Import Taxes as Share of Customs Revenues	Export Taxes	Export Taxes as Share of Customs Revenues	Total Customs Revenues	Total Ordinary Revenues	Customs Revenues as Share of Total Revenues
1830	—	—	—	—	0.6	1.2	50.0%
1835	—	—	—	—	1.0	1.6	64.6
1840	—	—	—	—	1.4	2.3	61.9
1845	—	—	—	—	1.4	2.5	54.7
1850	—	—	—	—	2.5	4.1	60.6
1855	—	—	—	—	3.5	5.8	59.8
1860	—	—	—	—	4.2	6.5	64.8
1865	4.5	84.5%	0.8	15.5%	5.4	10.4	51.5
1870	5.5	91.6	0.5	8.4	6.0	10.7	55.8
1875	6.7	96.9	0.2	3.1	6.9	14.1	48.9
1880	5.5	82.8	1.1	17.2	6.7	17.6	37.9
1885	7.5	61.5	4.7	38.5	12.2	18.5	65.9
1890	7.3	39.9	11.1	60.1	18.4	25.6	71.9
1895	7.6	33.6	15.0	66.4	22.6	28.6	78.8
1900	10.3	36.3	18.1	63.7	28.4	37.0	76.6
1905	21.1	64.3	11.7	35.7	32.8	43.2	76.0
1910	17.6	37.6	29.3	62.4	46.9	63.1	74.3
1915	7.9	24.1	24.9	75.9	32.7	63.5	51.5
1920	11.4	29.1	27.7	70.9	39.1	96.4	40.5
1925	22.7	42.0	31.4	58.0	54.2	112.7	48.0
1930	44.1	67.7	21.0	32.3	65.2	157.6	41.3

SOURCE: Humud, *El sector público chileno entre 1830 y 1930*, p. 130.

TABLE 23
ESTIMATED NUMBER OF PUBLIC EMPLOYEES, 1845–1930

	1845	1850	1860	1880	1900	1919	1930
Presidencia	5	6	5	6	5	8	37
Congreso*	91	90	117	191	170	259	340
Min. Relaciones Ext.[†]	14	15	17	47	784	813	263
Min. del Interior[‡]	161	208	240	568	1,935	13,828	23,145
Min. Hacienda[§]	436	435	579	729	1,564	2,841	2,806
Min. Justicia Culto e Instr.[‖]	346	519	1,012	867	5,948	4,345	14,348
Min. Guerra y Marina[#]	112	938	555	640	2,471	4,067	4,802
Min. Industria y OO. PP.**	—	—	—	—	242	1,308	—
Min. de Fomento[††]	—	—	—	—	—	—	475
Min. Bienestar Social[‡‡]	—	—	—	—	—	—	977
TOTAL	1,165	2,211	2,525	3,048	13,119	27,469	47,193

SOURCE: Humud, *El sector público chileno entre 1830 y 1930*, Table B–30, pp. 245–255.
*Congreso includes parliamentarians and functionaries in the Congreso Nacional.
[†] Ministerio de Relaciones Exteriores includes embassies, legations, and consulates.
[‡] Ministerio del Interior includes telégrafos, intendencias, gobernaciones, estadística, policía, carabineros, etc.
[§] Ministerio de Hacienda includes Dirección de Contabilidad, Contaduría Mayor, Tesorerías, Aduanas, Factoría General de Estanco, Casa de Moneda, Impuestos Internos, etc.
[‖] Ministerio de Justicia Culto e Instrucción includes Corte Suprema, Cortes de Apelaciones, Juzgados de Letras, Prisiones, Educación Primaria, Secundaria, Profesional y Técnica, Eclesiásticos, etc.
[#] Ministerio de Guerra y Marina includes Estado Mayor del Ejército, administrative personnel of the Dirección General de la Armada, Gobernaciones Marítimas, etc. Does not include troops.
**Ministerio de Industria y Obras Públicas includes personnel in charge of agricultural, industrial, and mining training and development, Dirección de Obras Públicas, Servicio de Minas y Geología, etc.
[††] Ministerio de Fomento includes Departamentos de Agricultura, Industria, Tierras y Colonizaciones, Dirección de Obras Públicas, etc.
[‡‡] Ministerio de Bienestar Social includes Dirección General de Sanidad, Inspección General del Trabajo, Dirección de Alcantarillado y Pavimentación, etc.

TABLE 24
FISCAL EXPENDITURES BY FUNCTION, 1835–1930
(IN MILLIONS OF US DOLLARS)

Year	Administration	Percentage of total expenditure	Defense	Percentage of total expenditure	Development	Percentage of total expenditure	Social	Percentage of total expenditure	Finance	Percentage of total expenditure	Total expenditures
1835	1.1	62.5%	0.7	37.5%	—	—	—	—	—	—	1.8
1845	1.1	43.0	0.8	32.0	—	—	0.3	10.0%	0.4	15.0%	2.6
1855	3.1	54.0	1.4	26.0	—	—	0.6	10.0	0.6	10.0	5.7
1865	5.1	33.0	4.0	26.0	—	—	1.4	9.0	4.9	32.0	15.3
1875	10.5	54.0	3.2	16.0	—	—	1.5	8.0	4.3	22.0	19.5
1885	4.7	22.0	4.3	21.0	—	—	1.9	9.0	10.0	48.0	21.0
1889	7.1	22.0	7.6	24.0	8.3	26.0%	4.9	16.0	3.7	12.0	31.6
1900	10.7	28.0	7.0	18.0	9.7	26.0	4.4	12.0	6.1	16.0	37.9
1905	11.8	27.0	7.9	18.0	12.5	28.0	6.0	14.0	5.8	13.0	44.0
1910	16.7	23.0	13.8	19.0	24.1	33.0	8.4	12.0	9.4	13.0	72.3
1915	13.9	22.0	11.9	19.0	19.8	31.0	7.2	11.0	11.1	17.0	63.8
1920	17.8	15.0	23.5	19.0	56.0	47.0	10.0	8.0	12.8	11.0	120.2
1925	20.3	16.0	25.2	20.0	40.2	32.0	18.4	14.0	23.6	18.0	127.8
1930	65.5	40.0	25.3	15.0	33.7	21.0	26.9	16.0	12.5	8.0	163.9

SOURCE: Humud, *El sector público chileno entre 1830 y 1930*, Table A–7, pp. 236–238.

TABLE 25
RAILWAY SYSTEM, 1890–1925
(KILOMETERS)

Year	State-owned railways	Private railways	Total
1890	1,106	1,641	2,747
1900	2,125	2,229	4,354
1905	2,329	2,449	4,778
1910	2,830	3,114	5,944
1913	5,009	3,061	8,070
1915	5,122	3,094	8,216
1920	4,579	3,632	8,211
1925	5,459	3,182	8,641

SOURCE: Oficina Central de Estadística, *Sinopsis estadística,* 1926–27, p. 104.

TABLE 26
NUMBER OF EDUCATIONAL INSTITUTIONS, 1855–1928

Year	Primary Education			Secondary and Special Education			Higher Education			Total		
	Public	Private	Total	Public	Private	Total	Public	Private	Total	Public	Private	Total
1855	303	—	303	—	—	—	1	—	1	303	—	303
1858	450	244	694	16	21	37	1	—	1	467	265	732
1860	512	369	881	18	—	18	1	—	1	531	369	900
1895	1,253	411	1,664	52	6	58	8	2	10	1,313	419	1,732
1900	1,553	568	2,121	63	20	83	10	3	13	1,626	591	2,217
1905	2,109	521	2,630	119	48	167	10	6	16	2,238	575	2,813
1910	2,581	408	2,989	142	106	248	10	6	16	2,733	520	3,253
1915	2,936	445	3,381	151	175	326	12	7	19	3,099	627	3,726
1920	3,214	429	3,643	153	139	292	12	7	19	3,379	575	3,954
1925	3,409	495	3,904	165	148	313	13	12	25	3,587	655	4,242
1928	3,265	495	3,760	168	112	280	15	13	28	3,448	620	4,068

SOURCE: Humud, *El sector público chileno entre 1830 y 1930*, Table B-39, p. 200.

TABLE 27
STUDENTS IN PUBLIC EDUCATIONAL INSTITUTIONS, 1855–1928

Year	Primary Education	Secondary and Special Education	Higher Education	Total
1855	14,854	—	—	14,854
1858	21,349	1,895	—	23,444
1860	18,262	2,223	—	20,485
1895	139,991	11,524	1,190	152,705
1900	157,330	12,624	1,228	171,182
1905	159,379	21,497	1,549	182,425
1910	258,875	30,731	1,824	291,430
1915	322,434	41,739	3,646	367,819
1920	346,386	49,123	4,502	400,011
1925	439,937	56,648	4,475	501,060
1928	519,100	50,523	2,700	572,323

SOURCE: Humud, *El sector público chileno entre 1830 y 1930*, Table B–40, p. 201.

TABLE 28
POPULATION DISTRIBUTION BY SIZE OF CITY
(THOUSANDS OF INHABITANTS)

Year	Rural Population	Cities, 2,000–20,000	Cities, over 20,000, excluding Santiago	Santiago	Total Population
1865	1,421	212	70	115	1,819
1875	1,536	291	97	150	2,075
1885	1,790	354	173	189	2,507
1895	1,774	436	228	256	2,695
1907	2,008	505	383	332	3,231
1920	2,132	554	535	507	3,730
1930	2,219	679	692	696	4,287
1940	2,474	723	873	952	5,023
1952	2,496	901	1,184	1,350	5,932
1960	2,650	953	1,863	1,907	7,374

SOURCE: Hurtado, *Concentración de población y desarrollo económico*, Table 5.

TABLE 29
POPULATION GROWTH RATES BY SIZE OF CITY
(AVERAGE ANNUAL PERCENTAGES)

Year	Rural Population	Cities, 2,000 to 20,000 inhabitants	Cities, over 20,000 inhabitants, excluding Santiago	Santiago	Total Population
1865–1875	0.8%	3.2%	3.3%	2.7%	1.4%
1875–1885	1.5	2.0	5.9	2.3	1.9
1885–1895	0.0	2.1	2.8	3.1	0.7
1895–1907	1.1	1.2	4.4	2.2	1.5
1907–1920	0.5	0.7	2.6	3.3	1.1
1920–1930	0.4	2.1	2.6	3.2	1.4
1930–1940	1.1	0.6	2.4	3.2	1.6
1940–1952	0.0	1.8	2.6	2.9	1.4
1952–1960	0.8	0.7	5.8	4.4	2.8

SOURCE: Hurtado, *Concentración de población y desarrollo económico*, Table 6.

TABLE 30
VALUE OF IMPORTS OF RAW MATERIALS AND
INDUSTRIAL CAPITAL GOODS, 1880–1919
(THOUSANDS OF 18–PENCE PESOS)

Period	Raw Materials			Industrial Capital Goods		
	Value	1910–1914 = 100	Percentage of total imports	Value	1910–1914 = 100	Percentage of total imports
1880–1884	46,927	37	48.5	2,668	17	2.8
1885–1889	49,831	40	47.0	4,209	26	3.9
1890–1894	64,061	51	45.8	6,906	43	4.9
1895–1899	58,265	46	45.9	3,708	23	2.9
1900–1904	67,964	54	48.2	6,527	41	4.7
1905–1909	102,946	82	42.9	15,313	95	6.4
1910–1914	126,220	100	41.9	16,064	100	5.4
1915–1919	142,709	113	46.6	10,761	67	3.6

SOURCE: Kirsch, *The Industrialization of Chile*. Calculated on the basis of data in: Oficina Central de Estadística, *Estadística comercial de la República de Chile, 1880–1920*. (Note: Before 1910 the author is Superintendencia de Aduanos).

TABLE 31

DATE OF ESTABLISHMENT OF FACTORIES IN 1895 INDUSTRIAL CENSUS*

	Chile		Santiago and Valparaíso	
	Number	*Percentage*	*Number*	*Percentage*
Before 1870	241	9.8	136	9.3
1870–1879	336	13.7	188	12.8
1880–1889	846	34.6	546	37.2
1890–1895	1,026	41.9	596	40.7
Total	2,449	100	1,466	100

SOURCE: Kirsch, *The Industrialization of Chile,* Table 8.

*Includes small industry but not handicraft shops such as shoe repair and carpentry workshops. Seven gas and electricity companies included in the census are excluded here. The geographic coverage of the census was from Petorca to Ancud.

TABLE 32
EMPLOYMENT IN LARGE AND MEDIUM SIZED CHILEAN MANUFACTURING INDUSTRY, 1915–1926
(THOUSANDS OF PERSONS)

Industry	1915	1918	1920	1922	1924	1926	Annual Growth Rate, 1915/16–1925/26
Beverage	2.8	3.4	3.5	3.9	4.1	2.8	1.1
Ceramic and Glassware	0.7	2.0	2.4	1.6	2.1	2.0	7.0
Food	11.1	12.8	14.7	14.9	15.8	16.2	3.4
Energy and Fuel	2.5	2.9	2.9	4.0	4.8	4.4	5.9
Shipyards	0.7	1.1	1.0	0.6	0.8	0.8	0.4
Clothing	6.2	10.7	8.3	8.7	10.6	9.1	3.0
Wood and wood products	3.3	3.6	4.4	4.3	5.3	4.3	4.3
Construction materials	1.3	1.7	1.9	1.7	2.0	1.5	1.5
Textile	2.3	2.8	3.1	3.6	4.5	4.7	6.8
Metal and metal products	3.4	4.7	5.5	5.7	7.5	6.7	6.5
Furniture	1.0	1.3	1.6	1.5	1.7	1.3	4.5
Paper and printing	3.8	7.3	5.0	5.5	6.5	6.1	4.8
Leather goods	7.6	8.3	9.5	9.4	10.3	9.2	2.2
Chemical and pharmaceutical goods	2.7	3.4	3.4	3.9	3.5	4.2	4.6
Tobacco	2.0	2.1	2.3	3.0	2.2	1.9	0.2
Auto and transport materials	0.4	0.4	0.5	0.6	0.7	0.7	7.5
Other industries	1.1	1.3	2.7	3.2	2.5	2.5	7.2
Total in manufacturing industry	52.9	70.9	72.7	76.0	85.1	78.5	3.7
Number of establishments (thousands)	2.4	2.8	3.0	3.0	3.3	3.1	2.5

SOURCE: Hurtado, *Concentración de población y desarrollo económico*, Table 25.

TABLE 33
DOMESTIC COASTAL TRADE AND IMPORTS OF AGRICULTURAL PRODUCTS, NORTE GRANDE, 1884–1929*
(THOUSANDS OF CURRENT PESOS)

Year	Animal Products Coastal Trade	Imports	Import Share	Vegetable Products Coastal Trade	Imports	Import Share	Beverages & Liquors Coastal Trade	Imports	Import Share	Total for Three Groups Coastal Trade	Imports	Import Share
1884	3,675	29	1%	7,033	186	3%	3,294	799	24%	14,002	1,014	7%
1894	9,534	2,684	28	14,430	745	5	5,053	971	19	29,017	4,400	15
1900	8,374	1,293	15	14,409	237	2	7,109	288	4	29,892	1,818	6
1905	11,871	1,332	11	19,159	4,093	21	11,283	962	9	42,313	6,387	15
1910	24,324	3,117	13	49,292	7,615	15	17,413	2,458	14	91,029	13,190	14
1920	89,441	12,268	14	59,718	6,792	11	28,352	1,891	7	177,511	20,951	12
1925	123,863	14,626	12	79,739	19,114	24	37,664	900	2	241,266	34,640	14
1929	111,255	11,451	10	67,321	17,814	26	38,996	658	2	217,542	29,923	14

SOURCE: Coastal trade from Appendix A. Imports from Oficina Central de Estadística, *Estadística comercial de la República de Chile*, various years.

*The value ratio of the selected commodities enumerated in Table 49, Appendix A, to the total value of coastal trade for the corresponding commodity group was calculated for 1905 and applied to coastal trade and import data for 1884, 1894, and 1900, in order to put all figures in the table on a common scale. In addition, import figures were converted to current pesos from their published values in 38–pence pesos (1884–1894), 18–pence pesos (1900–1925) and 6–pence pesos (1929), using exchange rates of Table 34.

TABLE 34
EXCHANGE RATES, 1830–1930

Year	Chilean pesos per U.S. dollar	Dollars per pound sterling	Pence per Chilean peso	Year	Chilean pesos per U.S. dollar	Dollars per pound sterling	Pence per Chilean peso
1830	1.31	4.15	44.0	1901	3.13	4.84	15.9
1840	1.29	4.09	45.3	1902	3.27	4.83	15.2
1850	1.06	4.90	46.2	1903	3.00	4.81	16.6
1860	1.14	4.82	43.8	1904	3.02	4.85	16.4
1870	1.08	4.85	45.6	1905	3.19	4.82	15.6
1875	1.13	4.85	43.8	1906	3.50	4.78	14.4
1880	1.61	4.83	30.9	1907	3.92	4.80	12.8
1881	1.61	4.81	30.9	1908	5.14	4.85	9.6
1882	1.40	4.84	35.4	1909	4.59	4.85	10.8
1883	1.41	4.82	35.3	1910	4.62	4.82	10.8
1884	1.56	4.83	31.8	1911	4.68	4.83	10.6
1885	1.95	4.84	25.4	1912	4.93	4.81	10.1
1886	2.09	4.80	23.9	1913	5.12	4.81	9.8
1887	2.03	4.83	24.5	1914	5.74	4.93	9.0
1888	1.89	4.84	26.3	1915	6.07	4.76	8.3
1889	1.88	4.81	26.6	1916	5.37	4.77	9.5
1890	2.08	4.79	24.1	1917	4.07	4.76	12.7
1891	2.65	4.82	18.8	1918	3.47	4.77	14.6
1892	2.63	4.85	18.8	1919	5.21	4.43	10.6
1893	3.31	4.84	15.0	1920	5.73	3.66	12.1
1894	3.92	4.88	12.6	1921	8.84	3.85	7.3
1895	2.93	4.88	16.8	1922	8.41	4.43	6.6
1896	2.84	4.84	17.4	1923	8.21	4.57	6.5
1897	2.84	4.82	17.6	1924	9.29	4.42	5.8
1898	3.18	4.82	15.7	1925	8.55	4.83	5.9
1899	3.44	4.81	14.5	1926	8.15	4.86	6.1
1900	2.97	4.81	16.8	1927	8.27	4.86	6.1
				1928	8.22	4.87	6.1
				1929	8.25	4.86	6.1
				1930	8.26	4.86	6.0

SOURCE: Horacio d'Ottone and Hernán Cortés, "Tasas cambiarias de Chile en relación al dólar y libra esterlina (1830–1964)," (Banco Central de Chile, *Boletín mensual,* 450, Santiago: Imprenta Gutemberg, 1965), pp. 1103–1104.

TABLE 35
NITRATE EXPORTS AND COASTAL TRADE IN SELECTED COMMODITIES
(MILLIONS OF CURRENT PESOS)

| Year | Nitrate Exports | Coastal Trade to Norte Grande | | $\frac{(2)}{(1)} \times 100$ | $\frac{(3)}{(1)} \times 100$ |
		13 Selected Products	3 Commodity Groups		
1881	24.9	6.0	—	24%	—
1882	29.7	7.5	—	25	—
1883	35.6	7.8	—	22	—
1884	37.9	8.4	—	22	—
1885	27.7	7.3	—	26	—
1886	31.0	9.1	—	29	—
1887	47.6	10.3	—	22	—
1888	48.8	10.2	—	21	—
1889	49.5	12.9	—	26	—
1890	60.3	11.2	—	19	—
1891	67.1	4.5	—	7	—
1892	60.0	15.9	—	27	—
1893	98.5	17.6	—	18	—
1894	134.3	17.6	—	13	—
1895	108.3	17.7	—	16	—
1896	95.0	17.2	—	18	—
1897	83.9	14.7	—	18	—
1898	100.1	17.3	—	17	—
1899	118.3	16.3	—	14	—
1900	116.3	18.1	—	16	—
1901	123.5	17.3	—	14	—
1902	148.4	15.2	—	10	—
1903	151.8	—	40.5	—	27%
1904	177.8	21.0	30.0	12	17
1905	210.4	25.7	42.3	12	20
1906	264.8	—	79.3	—	30
1907	291.4	—	78.2	—	27
1908	419.6	—	78.6	—	19
1909	353.0	—	106.8	—	30
1910	387.3	—	91.0	—	23
1911	444.9	—	125.4	—	28
1912	511.0	—	134.7	—	26
1913	578.4	—	145.8	—	25
1914	424.8	—	101.9	—	24
1915	504.7	—	84.0	—	17
1916	641.4	—	127.7	—	20
1917	669.1	—	145.7	—	22
1918	629.9	—	120.7	—	19

TABLE 35 *(continued)*

| Year | Nitrate Exports | Coastal Trade to Norte Grande | | $\dfrac{(2)}{(1)} \times 100$ | $\dfrac{(3)}{(1)} \times 100$ |
		13 Selected Products	3 Commodity Groups		
1919	198.7	—	134.7	—	68
1920	784.7	—	177.5	—	23
1921	676.8	—	131.8	—	19
1922	467.5	—	128.1	—	27
1923	857.9	—	142.0	—	17
1924	1,000.6	—	213.9	—	21
1925	1,049.2	—	241.3	—	23
1926	698.7	—	—	—	—
1927	846.1	—	169.9	—	20
1928	—	—	218.7	—	—
1929	—	—	217.5	—	—

SOURCES: Nitrate exports from Oficina Central de Estadística, *Sinopsis estadística,* 1925, p. 149, and 1926–1927, p. 137, converted from pesos of 18 and 6–pence to current pesos by exchange rates of Table 34. Coastal trade, 1881–1905, from Table 49, Appendix A. Coastal trade, 1903–1929, from Table 47, Appendix A.

TABLE 36
COASTAL TRADE TO NORTE GRANDE IN SELECTED COMMODITIES

Three-year periods	Men's Shoes (thousands of dozens)	Cattle (thousands of head)	Dried Meat (tons)	Wheat and flour† (thousands of tons)	Lumber (millions of pieces)	Potatoes (thousands of tons)	Hay (thousands of tons)	Barley (thousands of tons)	Red Wine (millions of liters)	Beer (bottles) (thousands of dozens)	Beer (millions of liters)	Aguardiente (liters)
1881–1883	16.0	14.0	226	13.1	1.3	12.0	13.0	21.0	2.5	35.3	1.9	794
1893–1895	34.7	34.3	509	29.8	3.7	21.3	24.7	30.0	8.1	152.3	2.8	1,514
1902, 1904, 1905	43.0	27.0	279	32.4	1.3	20.0	44.7	26.3	7.0	632.3	0.1	230
Indexes												
1881–1883	100	100	100	100	100	100	100	100	100	100	100	100
1893–1895	217	245	225	227	275	178	190	143	328	431	148	191
1902, 1904, 1905	269	193	124	247	100	167	344	125	285	1,790	6	29

SOURCE: Appendix A.
†Flour quantity has been multiplied by 1.25 for conversion to its weight equivalent in wheat.

TABLE 37
NATIONAL PRODUCTION AND COASTAL TRADE TO
NORTE GRANDE OF SELECTED COMMODITIES

Product	National Production (1)	Coastal Trade to Norte Grande (2)	$\frac{(2)}{(1)} \times 100$
Wheat (metric quintals)			
1884–1885	4,085,000	160,000*	4%
1904–1905	4,202,000	351,250*	8%
Potatoes (metric quintals)			
1884–1885	1,321,000	70,000	5%
1904–1905	1,713,000	205,000	12%
Beans (metric quintals)			
1884–1885	199,000	10,000	5%
1904–1905	317,000	10,000	3%
Barley (metric quintals)			
1884–1885	528,000	185,000	35%
1904–1905	1,218,000	300,000	25%
Dried Meat (charqui) (kilograms)			
1884–1885	868,000	343,500	40%
1904–1905	952,600	260,000	27%

SOURCES: National production of wheat, potatoes, beans, and barley, Appendix B. Dried meat production estimated from Oficina Central de Estadística, *Sinopsis estadística* and *Anuario estadístico de la República de Chile*, various issues. Coastal trade to Norte Grande, Appendix A.

*Includes wheat flour, whose quantity has been multiplied by 1.25 for conversion to its weight equivalent in wheat.

TABLE 38
COASTAL TRADE IN AGRICULTURAL PRODUCTS TO NORTE GRANDE, 1903–1925

Year	Coastal Trade in Agricultural Products to Norte Grande (Millions of current pesos)	Price Index* (1913 = 100)	Coastal Trade in Agricultural Products to Norte Grande (Millions of 1913 pesos)
1903	40.5	59	68.6
1904	30.0	60	50.0
1905	42.3	63	67.1
1906	79.3	68	116.6
1907	78.2	77	101.6
1908	78.6	102	77.1
1909	106.8	91	117.4
1910	91.0	91	100.0
1911	125.4	92	136.3
1912	134.7	97	138.9
1913	145.8	100	145.8
1914	101.9	108	94.4
1915	84.0	120	70.0
1916	127.7	117	109.1
1917	145.7	118	123.5
1918	120.7	121	99.8
1919	134.7	143	94.2
1920	177.5	168	105.7
1921	131.8	169	78.0
1922	128.1	173	74.0
1923	142.0	176	80.7
1924	213.9	186	115.0
1925	241.3	202	119.5

SOURCES: Coastal trade from Table 47, Appendix A. Exchange rate index from Table 34. Cost of living index from Oficina Central de Estadística, *Sinopsis estadística,* 1923, p. 117; 1924, p. 117.
*1903–1913: Exchange rate index relating peso to pound sterling, inverse of series in Table 34. 1913–1925: Cost of living index.

TABLE 39
AVERAGE ANNUAL WHEAT PRODUCTION BY PROVINCE
FOR SELECTED BIENNIA
(THOUSANDS OF METRIC QUINTALS)

Province	1877–1878	1884–1885	1904–1905	1912–1913	1917–1918	1926–1927
Tacna	—	—	—	—	—	—
Tarapacá	—	—	—	—	—	—
Antofagasta	—	—	—	—	—	—
Atacama	10	10	6	7	7	1
Coquimbo	102	130	108	56	62	23
Aconcagua	149	187	104	102	138	31
Valparaíso	77	92	45	100	87	64
Santiago	598	395	170	324	266	210
O'Higgins	—	398	155	324	345	307
Colchagua	297	402	264	467	450	464
Curicó	240	233	242	351	365	357
Talca	194	265	336	407	445	376
Linares	172	208	156	319	362	326
Maule	204	230	239	226	244	211
Ñuble	181	315	374	480	487	467
Concepción	199	192	136	271	202	188
Arauco	57	110	101	127	134	166
Bío–Bío	242	310	321	629	494	585
Malleco	—	320	456	1,027	889	889
Cautín	—	—	462	395	444	679
Valdivia	39	89	137	234	313	517
Llanquihue	54	96	244	343	399	666
Chiloé	61	103	146	81	74	50
Magallanes	—	—	—	—	—	—
Total	2,876	4,085	4,202	6,270	6,207	6,577
Subtotal, Malleco to Magallanes	154	608	1,445	2,080	2,119	2,801
Subtotal as percent of total	5.4%	14.9%	34.4%	33.2%	34.1%	42.6%

SOURCE: Table 56, Appendix B.

TABLE 40
AVAILABILITY OF AGRICULTURAL STATISTICS BY PROVINCE, 1882–1890 and 1902–1905

Province	1882	1883	1884	1885	1886	1887	1888	1889	1890	1902	1903	1904	1905
Tacna	o	o	o	o	o	o	o	o	o	†	*	*	†
Atacama	*	*	*	*	*	*	*	*	*	*	*	*	*
Coquimbo	*	*	*	*	*	*	†	†	†	*	*	*	*
Aconcagua	*	*	*	*	*	*	*	*	†	*	*	*	*
Valparaíso	*	*	*	*	†	†	†	*	†	*	*	*	*
Santiago	o	o	*	*	*	†	†	†	†	*	*	*	*
O'Higgins	*	o	*	*	*	*	†	†	†	*	*	*	*
Colchagua	*	*	*	*	*	*	*	*	*	*	*	*	*
Curicó	*	*	*	*	*	*	*	*	*	*	*	*	*
Talca	*	*	*	*	*	*	*	*	*	*	*	*	*
Linares	*	*	*	*	*	*	*	*	*	*	*	*	*
Maule	*	*	*	*	*	*	*	†	†	*	*	*	*
Ñuble	*	*	*	*	*	*	†	†	†	*	*	*	*
Concepción	*	*	*	*	*	†	†	†	*	*	*	*	*
Bío–Bío	*	*	*	*	†	*	†	†	*	†	†	*	*
Colonia de Angol	*	*	*	*	†	|	|	|	|	|	|	|	|
Arauco	*	*	*	*	*	*	*	†	†	*	*	*	*
Malleco	o	o	o	o	o	o	†	†	†	*	*	*	*
Cautín	o	o	o	o	o	o	†	†	†	*	*	*	*
Valdivia	*	*	*	*	*	*	*	*	*	*	*	*	*
Llanquihue	*	*	*	*	*	*	*	†	†	*	*	*	*
Chiloé	*	*	*	*	*	*	*	*	*	*	*	*	*

SOURCES: Oficina Central de Estadística, *Anuario estadístico de la República de Chile*, and *Sinopsis estadística*, various issues.
*Statistics published.
†Data not received.
oNot considered.
—Angol was incorporated into Malleco when the latter province was created in 1887.

220

TABLE 41
WHEAT EXPORTS, BY PORT, 1864–1925
(THOUSANDS OF METRIC QUINTALS)

Year	Valparaíso	Constitución	Talcahuano	Tomé	Penco	Valdivia
1864	—	29	69	227	—	—
1871	—	143	27	370	—	—
1874	917	220	183	590	—	—
1875	312	164	172	298	—	—
1876	—	122	63	192	—	—
1877	—	106	194	67	—	—
1883	423	82	673	—	—	—
1885	197	—	711	—	—	—
1895	—	—	726	—	—	—
1896	119	—	1,250	—	—	—
1899	135	—	—	—	—	—
1904	—	17	391	—	—	—
1908	—	3	817	—	—	—
1910	6	—	466	—	92	4
1920	24	—	592	10	—	—
1925	7	—	600	89	131	430

SOURCE: Sepúlveda, *El trigo chileno en el mercado mundial*, pp. 99–100.

TABLE 42
LIVESTOCK IN CHILE, 1910–1930
(THOUSANDS OF HEAD)

Year	Cattle	Sheep	Pigs	Goats
1910	1,635	1,636	178	205
1911	1,640	3,538	160	210
1912	1,760	4,168	166	273
1913	2,084	4,567	184	288
1914	1,969	4,602	221	299
1915	1,944	4,545	229	394
1916	1,869	4,569	260	386
1917	2,030	4,183	301	376
1918	2,225	4,434	326	452
1919	2,163	3,910	292	460
1922	1,996	4,999	263	525
1925	1,918	4,094	247	357
1930	2,388	6,263	331	789

SOURCE: Ballesteros, M., "Desarrollo agícola chileno, 1910–1955," *Cuadernos de economía*, (January–April 1965), Appendix 2, Table 2–1.

TABLE 43
AVERAGE ANNUAL WINE PRODUCTION FOR SELECTED BIENNIA
(THOUSANDS OF HECTOLITERS)

Regions	1877–1878	1884–1885	1904–1905	1912–1913	1917–1918	1926–1927
Norte Grande and Norte Chico	7	13	25	10	15	30
Núcleo Central	312	419	1,000	1,413	1,316	2,107
Concepción to the South	134	125	259	397	367	388
Total	453	557	1,283	1,820	1,698	2,525

SOURCE: Table 55, Appendix B.

TABLE 44

**AREA UNDER CULTIVATION, CHILE AND NÚCLEO CENTRAL, 1916–1927
(IN THOUSANDS OF HECTORES)**

Crop	1916		1927	
	Núcleo Central	*Chile*	*Núcleo Central*	*Chile*
Food Crops				
Grain	268.6	597.5	333.3	745.6
Legumes	42.8	58.9	47.3	70.6
Potatoes	14.0	31.9	12.2	30.6
Other	0.8	1.0	213.7	539.6
Total	326.0	689.2	606.5	1,386.4
Forage Crops				
Alfalfa	59.5	90.2	80.6	117.2
Clover	108.7	135.9	117.0	185.7
Other grasses	10.5*	122.6*	10.6	350.2
Total	178.8	348.7	208.1	653.0
Tree Crops				
Vineyards	36.8	56.2	53.3	81.0
Orchards	11.9	22.4	15.0	30.0
Planted Forests	2.1	8.2	6.1[†]	21.3[†]
Total	50.8	86.7	74.4	132.1
Total Area	555.6	1,124.6	889.1	2,171.5
Average annual growth rate of total cultivated area, 1916–1927.			4.4%	6.2%

SOURCE: Oficina Central de Estadística, *Sinopsis estadística,* 1916, 1917, 1923, and 1926–1927.

*Figures are for 1917, since in that year the scope of "other grasses" was changed.

[†] Figures are for 1923, because the 1927 figures are so large that they evidently encompass all forest area in the country.

TABLE 45
**PRODUCTION, CULTIVATED AREA, AND YIELDS, SELECTED CROPS,
1877–1878 to 1926–1927
(PRODUCTION IN THOUSANDS OF METRIC QUINTALS. AREA IN
THOUSANDS OF HECTARES. YIELDS IN QUINTALS PER HECTARE)**

Crop	1877–1878	1884–1885	1904–1905	1912–1913	1917–1918	1926–1927
Wheat						
Production	2,876	4,085	4,202	6,270	6,207	6,577
Area cultivated	426	465	409	446	521	575
Yield	6.8	8.8	10.3	14.1	11.9	11.4
Barley						
Production	345	528	1,218	857	895	1,247
Area cultivated	44	47	89	47	47	71
Yield	7.8	11.2	13.7	18.2	19.0	17.6
Beans						
Production	199	199	317	442	589	477
Area cultivated	38	41	28	36	44	47
Yield	5.2	4.9	11.3	12.3	13.4	10.1
Potatoes						
Production	895	1,321	1,713	2,508	2,557	2,891
Area cultivated	21	23	37	29	31	28
Yield	42.6	57.4	46.3	86.5	82.5	103.3
Corn						
Production	178	224	350	412	355	380
Area cultivated	54	69	31	25	23	24
Yield	3.3	3.2	11.3	16.5	15.4	15.8
Peas						
Production	51	102	153	123	144	97
Area cultivated	12	18	16	10	16	10
Yield	4.3	5.7	9.6	12.3	9.0	9.7

SOURCE: Appendix B.

TABLE 46
UTILIZATION OF AGRICULTURAL MACHINERY, 1915–1930
(UNITS)

Year	Plows	Seeding Machines	Baling Machines	Threshing Machines	Harrows	Harvesters	Tractors
1915	145,529	2,138	1,453	3,739	—	—	—
1920	160,989	2,950	1,535	3,666	—	—	—
1925	98,448	1,941	2,248	3,551	25,187	—	—
1930	121,415	3,204	3,360	4,542	31,541	239	660

SOURCE: Ballesteros, M., "Desarrollo agrícola chileno," Appendix 4, Table 4.

225

Appendix A
Coastal Trade from Central
Chile to the Norte Grande,
1881–1905

METHODOLOGY

The statistical data published by the Dirección General de Estadística are not homogeneous for the whole period 1880–1930. From 1881 until 1905 (excepting 1903, for which no data were published) there are official figures for coastal commerce on the value and amount of each individual product, by port of origin and destination, and even on whether the merchandise was national and "nationalized"—that is, of foreign origin. Unfortunately after 1903 this information is not provided in this primary form, but is classified by group, and therefore only by value. To complicate the situation further, there was a change in classification in 1915, so that one classification system was used between 1903 and 1914 and another between 1915 and 1929. After 1929 the presentation of coastal trade data became excessively summary, and therefore no longer useful for our purposes.

The problem of the change in classification in 1915 was fairly easy to overcome: a detailed comparison of the two classifications allowed us to identify the principal categories that had been recategorized, so it was possible to reclassify them in order to construct a series that was practically homogeneous, for the purposes of this chapter, for 1903–1929. We made use of the classification applied from 1903 to 1914, since it was more appropriate to our purposes and relatively more comparable than the other with the series of 1881–1905.

For the period 1881–1905, it was not possible to reconstruct a series that would project that of 1903–1929 backward in time. The possibility existed statistically, of course, since the basic data are available, but it would have been necessary to classify for over twenty years all the products in coastal commerce by all ports of origin and destination. Faced with the impossibility of carrying out this enormous mass of basic statistical work, we selected a group of important products and limited ourselves to securing the necessary information on them.

The determination of the most significant products for inclusion in the list was made in two ways. On the one hand, we examined the literature on technological features of mining, processing, and transport of nitrate, in order to identify the main kinds of supplies and equipment used by the nitrate industry. This facilitated appreciation of the great importance of animal transport or pulling power provided mainly by mules in the nitrate fields. In fact, the number of horses and mules reached a figure of more than 15,000 in 1907. Although the mules were obtained almost exclusively from Argentina, and their journey north was by way of the Andean passes in the province of Coquimbo, their food supply (hay and barley) was brought from the center and south of Chile. The study of this literature also highlighted the importance of coal as a fuel for the nitrate railways and for stages in the processing of the nitrate. The importance of lumber likewise emerged from this research.

On the other hand, research into the statistics of the coastal trade itself made it possible to identify the most important products brought by coastal shipping to the ports of Norte Grande. In this way we selected fourteen products, for which series of volume and value were constructed for all the ports from Valparaíso south, and all those from Taltal north, the latter being the receiving ports in the Norte Grande.

The list of selected products is the following: shoes (men's, women's, and children's); cattle and dried beef, which we grouped under the rubric of "animal products"; beans, wheat, flour, lumber for construction, potatoes, hay, and barley, which we grouped as "vegetable products"; and red wine, beer, and spirits, which we classified as beverages. This classification was solely for the purpose of providing a measure of comparability with the series of coastal commerce to Norte Grande from 1903 to 1929, which used the same classification. The earlier list included thirteen products, for coal, as a mineral product, was not included. We have, therefore, excluded the data on this product, although it constitutes an interesting case of an element of production absolutely essential to the nitrate industry, the demand for which contributed in some measure to the coal-mining industry in the region near Concepción. This contribution, however, was not so great as it might have been since coal began to be imported in growing amounts because of its low freight rates (coal was used as ballast in nitrate vessels on their return voyages).

In the list of thirteen products are some that are manufactured: shoes, flour, wine, beer, and spirits. However, all of these were fabricated directly from agricultural or animal materials, which is doubly interesting because it shows the effects of the trade on both the development of certain manufacturing lines and the growth of the corresponding products of agriculture and animal husbandry.

TABLE 47
COASTAL TRADE QUANTITIES, SELECTED PRODUCTS, 1903–1929
(IN THOUSANDS OF CURRENT PESOS)

Year	Animal Products* National Total	Animal Products* Norte Grande Total	Share of Norte Grande	Vegetable Products† National Total	Vegetable Products† Norte Grande Total	Share of Norte Grande	Beverages and Liquors‡ National Total	Beverages and Liquors‡ Norte Grande Total	Share of Norte Grande	Total for Three Groups National Total	Total for Three Groups Norte Grande Total	Share of Norte Grande
1903	49,252	13,762	28%	38,010	20,661	54%	11,135	6,070	55%	98,397	40,493	41%
1904	15,405	9,445	36	26,298	14,061	54	12,856	6,502	50	54,559	30,009	55
1905	21,204	11,871	56	34,716	19,159	55	17,221	11,283	66	73,141	42,313	58
1906	26,686	18,191	68	72,081	45,753	64	24,300	15,338	63	123,067	79,282	64
1907	29,362	18,684	64	64,950	41,939	65	25,587	17,626	69	119,899	78,249	65
1908	32,680	19,101	58	80,812	41,840	52	26,060	17,651	68	139,552	78,593	56
1909	50,929	28,792	57	91,143	54,628	60	30,941	23,336	75	173,013	106,756	62
1910	45,225	24,324	54	85,217	49,292	58	24,996	17,413	70	155,438	91,029	59
1911	47,879	36,737	77	104,092	67,242	65	30,025	21,401	71	181,996	125,380	69
1912	48,443	36,700	76	114,898	74,132	65	34,029	23,910	71	197,370	134,742	68
1913	56,114	43,324	77	110,370	73,283	66	38,863	29,201	75	205,347	145,809	71
1914	54,121	41,986	78	81,799	41,142	50	26,707	18,759	70	162,627	101,888	63
1915	64,328	31,027	48	50,716	39,627	78	21,115	13,301	63	136,159	83,955	62
1916	91,524	61,777	67	57,200	43,702	76	29,714	22,190	75	178,438	127,670	72
1917	94,645	68,736	73	54,577	51,309	94	32,930	25,703	78	182,152	145,748	80
1918	90,526	54,809	61	57,783	42,732	74	31,600	23,196	73	179,909	120,737	67

Year												
1919	110,547	76,168	69	58,317	39,980	69	27,642	18,602	67	196,506	134,749	69
1920	134,160	89,441	67	82,044	59,718	73	37,851	28,352	75	254,055	177,511	70
1921	117,997	76,370	65	60,792	39,157	64	26,291	16,238	62	205,080	131,765	64
1922	119,842	79,601	66	53,083	33,436	63	25,907	15,084	58	198,832	128,120	64
1923	123,335	78,082	63	71,422	44,351	62	28,544	19,563	69	223,301	141,997	64
1924	170,233	105,530	62	99,683	72,811	73	39,822	35,555	89	309,738	213,896	70
1925	191,351	123,863	65	113,357	79,739	70	47,931	37,664	79	352,639	241,266	68
1926	—			—			—			—		
1927	183,596	93,531	51	79,748	50,153	63	39,726	26,193	66	303,070	169,877	56
1928	232,234	124,457	54	93,913	61,640	66	45,562	32,565	72	371,709	218,662	59
1929	217,713	111,255	51	113,078	67,321	60	52,512	38,966	74	383,303	217,542	57

SOURCES: Oficina Central de Estadística, *Estadística comercial de la República de Chile*, 1903–1914; *Anuario estadístico de la República de Chile*, Vol. XI, *Comercio exterior*, 1915–1929.

NOTE: In addition to the three product groups shown, total coastal trade included eight other products (e.g., textiles, industrial oils and fuels, mineral products, machinery) by the classification system then in use. The three product groups represented 78% of total coastal trade in 1912, 75% in 1914.

*Animal Products includes Live animals; Food: Dried and salted meat (carne salada, cecinas, charqui); Industrial; antlers, horns, hides, glue, guano, soap, firewood, wool, furs, grease, sole leather, animal hoofs; Manufactures: leather riding gear, footwear, straps, matresses, saddles, brushes.

†Vegetable Products includes fruits, grains, legumes, herbs, fodder, sugar, canned goods, chocolate, dried potatoes, corn meal, noodles, sweets, flours, starch, soapbark, quillay, totora reeds, baskets, brooms, wicker chairs, lumber, chests, railroad ties, construction lumber, furniture, etc., cigarettes, cigars, tobacco.

‡Beverages and Liquors includes beer, wine, chicha, aguardiente, sodas, syrups, and juices.

NOTE: The above products were aggregated to form the totals shown for 1905–1914. Product classification was slightly different for 1915–1929, but was adjusted to a comparable basis.

229

TABLE 48
COASTAL TRADE, SELECTED PRODUCTS, 1881–1905

Year	Beer (thousands of liters)		Beer bottles (thousands of dozens)		Flour (thousands of tons)		Aguardiente (thousands of liters)	
	National Total	Norte Grande Total	National Total	Norte Grande Total	National Total	Norte Grande Total	National Total	Norte Grande Total
1881	4,956	1,736	39	19	37	11	2,371	927
1882	6,022	2,469	71	50	35	9	2,543	815
1883	5,590	1,515	60	37	38	9	2,266	640
1884	6,504	2,342	55	27	37	14	3,002	1,222
1885	6,958	1,981	33	19	32	10	3,058	760
1886	7,419	1,677	30	11	29	11	3,727	1,118
1887	8,562	2,465	63	39	34	12	3,526	1,001
1888	8,957	2,117	66	37	40	13	4,167	1,061
1889	9,550	4,390	105	79	38	13	4,699	1,669
1890	9,341	3,417	89	61	34	16	—	—
1891	5,679	1,213	51	39	24	5	—	—
1892	7,348	2,478	101	60	44	18	2,654	1,033
1893	7,281	3,198	133	89	34	21	2,378	1,495
1894	7,564	3,507	203	138	48	26	2,653	1,356
1895	5,612	1,769	280	230	43	22	2,637	1,690
1896	6,928	3,216	309	251	46	23	2,811	1,915
1897	6,658	1,751	317	253	36	16	3,083	1,465
1898	5,557	1,426	263	182	45	30	2,524	1,343
1899	4,508	1,100	464	331	37	18	3,283	2,058
1900	7,526	779	561	401	45	23	936	650
1901	4,731	282	517	383	29	10	919	508
1902	3,631	146	502	376	39	20	517	257
1903	—	—	—	—	—	—	—	—
1904	5,557	89	660	560	45	26	441	196
1905	5,533	105	1,229	961	51	27	712	238

TABLE 48 Continued

Year	Red Wine (thousands of liters)		Potatoes (thousands of tons)		Barley (thousands of tons)		Wheat (thousands of tons)	
	National Total	Norte Grande Total	National Total	Norte Grande Total	National Total	Norte Grande Total	National Total	Norte Grande Total
1881	5,588	1,778	9	5	26	15	13	
1882	12,219	2,906	31	25	29	23	14	1
1883	4,832	2,688	11	6	39	25	11	1
1884	5,767	3,297	10	7	28	20	3	1
1885	5,500	2,506	9	7	24	17	9	1
1886	5,558	3,350	10	8	28	20	7	1
1887	6,177	3,225	12	10	34	25	3	1
1888	7,794	4,678	13	10	30	22	10	1
1889	10,263	6,453	20	16	35	26	14	2
1890	10,924	6,720	19	18	29	22	7	2
1891	6,254	3,416	8	5	14	10	8	1
1892	10,556	7,587	19	17	32	26	5	2
1893	10,485	8,242	20	18	32	27	11	1
1894	12,066	6,567	26	23	40	34	8	1
1895	12,696	9,404	27	23	34	29	6	1
1896	12,180	8,537	26	21	38	29	10	1
1897	11,941	9,228	31	27	29	21	13	2
1898	11,312	8,569	41	34	30	20	11	3
1899	10,752	7,831	29	25	25	20	7	3
1900	20,388	17,437	17	14	32	27	5	1
1901	14,224	11,268	21	18	33	28	6	2
1902	8,696	5,549	22	19	24	19	9	2
1903	—	—	—	—	—	—	—	—
1904	14,057	7,227	20	18	38	32	17	2
1905	16,436	8,230	27	23	36	28	22	2

TABLE 48 Continued

Year	Beans (tons)		Dried Meat (tons)		Cattle (thousands of head)		Lumber (thousands of pieces)	
	National Total	Norte Grande Total	National Total	Norte Grande Total	National Total	Norte Grande Total	National Total	Norte Grande Total
1881	4	1	805	214	14	11	3	1
1882	3	1	748	279	19	14	4	2
1883	3	1	535	184	22	17	4	1
1884	3	1	664	383	17	13	4	1
1885	4	1	635	304	17	13	3	1
1886	3	1	738	339	16	13	5	2
1887	3	1	765	331	20	18	3	2
1888	3	1	500	161	22	19	4	2
1889	3	1	714	470	30	14	5	3
1890	3	1	724	465	30	19	4	3
1891	3	1	382	163	19	11	2	1
1892	3	1	1,480	1,129	35	34	4	4
1893	3	1	916	593	37	35	9	6
1894	5	1	1,205	697	38	35	5	3
1895	3	1	663	236	37	33	4	2
1896	3	1	746	315	26	24	3	2
1897	4	1	747	259	22	20	4	2
1898	4	1	919	258	27	21	3	2
1899	4	1	1,171	478	37	33	2	1
1900	3	1	741	301	36	29	4	2
1901	3	1	723	350	32	26	3	2
1902	3	1	741	318	29	25	3	1
1903	—	—	—	—	—	—	—	—
1904	3	1	759	248	23	18	3	1
1905	4	1	574	272	42	38	3	2

TABLE 48 Continued

Year	Hay (thousands of tons)		Men's Shoes (thousands of dozens)		Women's Shoes (thousands of dozens)		Children's Shoes (thousands of dozens)	
	National Total	Norte Grande Total	National Total	Norte Grande Total	National Total	Norte Grande Total	National Total	Norte Grande Total
1881	16	13	22	13	13	4	6	1
1882	15	13	25	14	12	4	9	4
1883	14	13	33	21	8	2	5	1
1884	14	12	34	22	8	2	5	1
1885	14	13	34	22	8	4	3	1
1886	20	18	40	24	6	2	4	1
1887	25	22	40	25	13	8	7	4
1888	18	15	33	21	10	4	8	3
1889	27	26	44	30	15	9	15	11
1890	26	24	30	19	14	9	15	9
1891	10	9	19	11	6	4	7	3
1892	24	23	37	25	14	11	11	9
1893	24	22	41	30	13	11	11	9
1894	25	23	48	35	14	11	14	12
1895	33	29	48	39	7	5	7	4
1896	41	35	44	35	9	6	11	5
1897	37	31	39	29	11	8	9	7
1898	35	26	24	17	8	6	9	8
1899	36	33	37	26	18	13	14	10
1900	55	52	45	34	9	3	6	3
1901	45	43	39	30	8	3	6	3
1902	43	39	36	28	10	6	6	4
1903	—	—	—	—	—	—	—	—
1904	53	50	70	55	—	—	—	—
1905	49	45	60	46	—	—	—	—

SOURCE: Superintendencia de Aduanas, *Estadística comercial de la República de Chile*, 1881–1905.

TABLE 49
COASTAL TRADE VALUES, SELECTED PRODUCTS, 1881–1905
(IN THOUSANDS OF CURRENT PESOS)

Year	Shoes		Dried Meat		Cattle	
	National Total	Norte Grande Total	National Total	Norte Grande Total	National Total	Norte Grande Total
1881	1,222	460	378	115	1,080	994
1882	1,522	744	429	165	1,707	1,348
1883	1,457	732	354	127	1,940	1,782
1884	1,650	837	427	239	1,498	1,339
1885	1,662	968	420	196	1,356	1,253
1886	1,957	1,075	485	257	1,475	1,321
1887	2,261	1,539	562	254	1,926	1,778
1888	1,851	1,077	430	150	2,052	1,844
1889	2,113	1,366	514	339	1,505	910
1890	2,135	1,301	597	397	1,378	840
1891	1,196	642	310	131	823	462
1892	3,843	1,591	1,135	865	3,497	3,410
1893	2,329	1,721	828	539	3,692	3,541
1894	2,886	2,030	919	545	3,927	3,690
1895	2,438	1,804	560	224	4,226	3,795
1896	2,452	1,816	681	307	2,955	2,739
1897	2,055	1,358	662	266	2,507	2,208
1898	1,557	1,092	887	256	3,212	2,516
1899	—	—	1,141	478	4,364	3,983
1900	2,652	1,736	685	290	4,092	3,477
1901	2,315	1,784	723	350	3,190	2,589
1902	2,128	1,610	741	318	2,880	2,522
1903	—	—	—	—	—	—
1904	3,494	2,763	759	149	3,375	2,704
1905	3,829	2,979	574	289	5,081	4,533

TABLE 49 Continued

Year	Lumber National Total	Lumber Norte Grande Total	Hay National Total	Hay Norte Grande Total	Barley National Total	Barley Norte Grande Total
1881	1,951	572	730	586	1,288	678
1882	1,502	713	543	475	1,509	1,135
1883	1,674	659	645	597	1,947	1,250
1884	1,827	703	675	583	1,369	1,001
1885	1,465	614	621	548	1,347	980
1886	2,538	1,024	983	941	1,503	1,082
1887	1,512	763	1,163	1,048	1,913	1,508
1888	1,866	924	897	731	1,737	1,290
1889	2,270	1,211	1,249	1,199	1,838	1,372
1890	2,445	1,659	1,188	830	1,510	1,128
1891	890	291	430	397	698	517
1892	2,126	1,804	1,169	1,107	1,676	1,388
1893	9,288	3,053	1,050	960	1,756	1,107
1894	2,425	1,534	1,091	983	2,187	1,801
1895	1,704	1,142	1,391	1,215	1,997	1,647
1896	1,678	1,093	1,696	1,511	2,133	1,657
1897	1,778	1,081	1,445	1,252	1,739	1,239
1898	1,784	1,147	1,562	1,368	2,377	1,810
1899	852	377	1,639	759	2,023	1,660
1900	2,144	916	2,285	2,154	2,253	1,836
1901	1,887	785	1,997	1,897	2,771	2,327
1902	1,339	516	2,038	1,935	2,361	1,927
1903	—	—	—	—	—	—
1904	1,291	581	2,671	2,509	3,063	2,565
1905	1,856	1,181	2,257	1,663	3,820	2,853

TABLE 49 Continued

Year	Beans		Wheat		Flour		Potatoes	
	National Total	Norte Grande Total	National Total	Norte Grande Total	National Total	Norte Grande Total	National Total	Norte Grande Total
1881	275	93	665	28	3,322	1,010	353	171
1882	197	63	729	47	3,090	855	867	523
1883	283	67	545	73	3,395	916	403	304
1884	258	89	169	60	3,553	1,343	391	287
1885	385	98	512	41	2,836	936	388	299
1886	248	85	403	62	2,867	1,129	484	390
1887	258	75	231	63	3,248	1,203	593	496
1888	250	68	627	62	3,813	1,388	616	495
1889	328	131	872	119	3,791	1,393	973	864
1890	331	108	559	155	3,503	1,588	987	918
1891	306	89	614	77	2,495	509	373	294
1892	284	96	347	138	4,534	1,930	992	896
1893	308	111	748	102	3,642	2,135	1,058	943
1894	486	113	522	89	5,003	2,583	1,535	1,239
1895	275	117	484	90	3,574	2,255	1,615	1,291
1896	329	149	880	101	4,664	2,415	1,384	1,150
1897	523	202	942	198	3,644	1,652	1,648	1,495
1898	402	156	1,035	227	5,008	3,073	1,906	1,826
1899	346	140	705	260	5,529	2,732	1,573	1,455
1900	305	132	397	112	4,925	2,374	1,048	806
1901	359	165	623	164	3,180	1,128	1,161	1,039
1902	354	155	851	153	4,874	2,242	1,216	1,083
1903	—	—	—	—	—	—	—	—
1904	294	140	1,459	234	6,719	3,926	993	906
1905	559	247	2,333	209	6,884	3,449	1,776	1,474

TABLE 49 Continued

Year	Red Wine		Beer		Aguardiente	
	National Total	Norte Grande Total	National Total	Norte Grande Total	National Total	Norte Grande Total
1881	1,194	544	769	353	666	375
1882	2,776	679	1,074	459	742	259
1883	1,132	715	821	316	641	235
1884	1,270	857	1,071	548	961	578
1885	1,251	732	985	415	910	250
1886	1,326	851	1,025	403	1,213	457
1887	1,305	757	1,123	518	1,042	297
1888	1,936	1,288	1,293	489	1,282	377
1889	2,779	1,984	1,535	952	1,479	1,039
1890	2,617	1,589	1,419	713	—	—
1891	1,103	781	882	324	—	—
1892	3,508	1,751	1,145	537	888	395
1893	2,585	2,118	1,388	797	807	476
1894	2,679	1,556	1,727	1,042	933	444
1895	2,855	2,201	1,824	1,154	1,041	793
1896	2,963	2,126	2,142	1,271	1,173	896
1897	2,461	1,910	2,067	1,157	1,347	701
1898	3,021	2,346	1,929	1,004	1,091	562
1899	2,728	2,154	2,541	1,476	1,315	860
1900	4,089	2,530	3,335	1,470	375	280
1901	3,620	2,959	2,032	1,842	460	254
1902	2,120	1,380	2,352	1,243	248	113
1903	—	—	—	—	—	—
1904	4,217	2,168	3,750	2,258	221	98
1905	4,999	2,557	6,118	4,117	356	119

SOURCE: Superintendencia de Aduanas, *Estadística comercial de la República de Chile*, 1881–1905.

237

Appendix B
Agricultural Production and Cultivated Area by Province for Selected Biennia Between 1877–1878 and 1926–1927

TABLE 50
AVERAGE ANNUAL BARLEY PRODUCTION FOR SELECTED BIENNIA,
1877–1878 to 1926–1927
(THOUSANDS OF METRIC QUINTALS)

Province	1877–1878	1884–1885	1904–1905	1912–1913	1917–1918	1926–1927
Tacna	—	—	3	—	—	—
Tarapacá	—	—	—	—	1	—
Antofagasta	—	—	—	—	—	—
Atacama	12	16	10	15	17	25
Coquimbo	13	24	71	40	41	59
Aconcagua	64	88	125	78	85	98
Valparaíso	48	99	76	90	66	143
Santiago	126	129	305	220	220	420
O'Higgins	—	41	131	135	149	167
Colchagua	13	22	70	86	163	143
Curicó	15	22	88	34	41	38
Talca	15	13	37	27	28	28
Linares	4	8	4	3	2	4
Maule	5	8	26	7	3	2
Ñuble	3	2	12	12	3	3
Concepción	6	10	7	7	25	4
Arauco	6	13	17	5	5	7
Bío-Bío	3	4	52	12	4	8
Malleco	—	13	70	18	9	29
Cautín	—	—	37	44	17	42
Valdivia	3	7	26	8	6	14
Llanquihue	7	7	28	14	9	13
Chiloé	2	2	23	—	1	—
Magallanes	—	—	—	2	—	—
Total	345	528	1,218	857	895	1,247

SOURCE: Oficina Central de Estadística, *Sinopsis Estadística* and *Anuario estadístico de la República de Chile,* various issues.
NOTE: Data attributed to Malleco for 1877–1878 was reported for "Colonia de Angol," which became part of Malleco when the province was created subsequently.

TABLE 51
AVERAGE ANNUAL CORN PRODUCTION FOR SELECTED BIENNIA, 1877–1878 to 1926–1927
(THOUSANDS OF METRIC QUINTALS)

Province	1877–1878	1884–1885	1904–1905	1912–1913	1917–1918	1926–1927
Tacna	—	—	4	6	7	1
Tarapacá	—	—	—	1	2	2
Antofagasta	—	—	—	—	—	—
Atacama	1	1	3	3	5	9
Coquimbo	5	8	19	16	14	31
Aconcagua	8	8	9	9	8	16
Valparaíso	3	4	1	5	3	7
Santiago	52	23	95	70	67	64
O'Higgins	—	29	19	55	38	52
Colchagua	42	57	41	98	58	76
Curicó	20	19	25	37	25	33
Talca	22	21	27	26	29	18
Linares	11	15	22	28	26	24
Maule	8	13	12	20	17	12
Ñuble	3	15	2	25	25	18
Concepción	2	4	1	4	5	3
Arauco	—	1	6	—	—	—
Bío-Bío	1	3	1	5	15	8
Malleco	—	2	1	3	8	4
Cautín	—	—	8	1	1	1
Valdivia	—	1	1	—	1	1
Llanquihue	—	—	—	—	—	—
Chiloé	—	—	53	—	1	—
Magallanes	—	—	—	—	—	—
Total	178	224	350	412	355	380

SOURCE: Same as Table 50.

TABLE 52
AVERAGE ANNUAL BEAN PRODUCTION FOR SELECTED BIENNIA, 1877–1878 to 1926–1927
(THOUSANDS OF METRIC QUINTALS)

Province	1877–1878	1884–1885	1904–1905	1912–1913	1917–1918	1926–1927
Tacna	—	—	—	—	—	—
Tarapacá	—	—	—	—	—	—
Antofagasta	—	—	—	—	—	—
Atacama	—	—	1	—	—	1
Coquimbo	11	11	31	5	6	21
Aconcagua	10	11	10	9	18	18
Valparaíso	8	8	1	7	12	11
Santiago	35	9	24	13	34	25
O'Higgins	—	25	53	66	78	55
Colchagua	29	33	35	84	98	84
Curicó	22	17	56	69	97	58
Talca	22	21	43	47	81	46
Linares	36	22	—	39	48	45
Maule	3	6	13	9	8	8
Ñuble	6	17	18	29	43	37
Concepción	8	7	10	30	21	16
Arauco	3	3	6	7	7	4
Bío-Bío	6	6	9	10	18	30
Malleco	—	3	2	16	16	13
Cautín	—	—	4	2	3	4
Valdivia	—	—	1	—	1	1
Llanquihue	—	—	—	—	—	—
Chiloé	—	—	—	—	—	—
Magallanes	—	—	—	—	—	—
Total	199	199	317	442	589	477

Source: Same as Table 50.

TABLE 53

AVERAGE ANNUAL POTATO PRODUCTION FOR SELECTED BIENNIA,
1877–1878 to 1926–1927
(THOUSANDS OF METRIC QUINTALS)

Province	1877–1878	1884–1885	1904–1905	1912–1913	1917–1918	1926–1927
Tacna	—	—	4	4	5	1
Tarapacá	—	—	—	—	—	—
Antofagasta	—	—	—	—	—	—
Atacama	1	5	3	3	4	9
Coquimbo	14	26	31	47	79	154
Aconcagua	87	61	30	84	89	75
Valparaíso	58	68	18	157	140	150
Santiago	136	33	61	135	176	332
O'Higgins	—	81	292	133	215	238
Colchagua	70	218	60	301	308	290
Curicó	33	45	42	111	111	80
Talca	31	29	122	69	75	64
Linares	23	21	—	33	34	44
Maule	18	34	128	89	53	30
Ñuble	23	32	32	108	81	64
Concepción	38	47	14	46	23	23
Arauco	38	74	86	65	50	50
Bío-Bío	12	9	9	13	14	10
Malleco	—	4	10	18	17	29
Cautín	—	—	92	80	80	131
Valdivia	22	53	57	134	153	185
Llanquihue	71	136	134	404	407	514
Chiloé	220	345	488	474	443	416
Magallanes	—	—	—	—	—	2
Total	895	1,321	1,713	2,508	2,557	2,891

SOURCE: Same as Table 50.

241

TABLE 54
AVERAGE ANNUAL PEA PRODUCTION FOR SELECTED BIENNIA,
1877–1878 to 1926–1927
(THOUSANDS OF METRIC QUINTALS)

Province	1877–1878	1884–1885	1904–1905	1912–1913	1917–1918	1926–1927
Tacna	—	—	1	—	—	—
Tarapacá	—	—	—	—	—	—
Antofagasta	—	—	—	—	—	—
Atacama	—	—	—	—	—	—
Coquimbo	—	—	—	—	—	—
Aconcagua	—	—	—	—	—	1
Valparaíso	1	1	1	2	2	—
Santiago	—	—	—	—	2	—
O'Higgins	—	—	—	2	—	—
Colchagua	—	—	2	—	—	—
Curicó	—	1	11	3	7	1
Talca	2	2	11	3	4	1
Linares	5	16	—	13	8	4
Maule	7	13	16	8	7	4
Ñuble	12	17	14	7	9	3
Concepción	10	16	10	5	6	3
Arauco	6	12	23	19	25	19
Bío-Bío	6	11	11	3	6	5
Malleco	—	4	2	11	14	10
Cautín	—	—	39	33	32	35
Valdivia	1	7	9	12	19	10
Llanquihue	1	2	1	2	3	1
Chiloé	—	—	2	—	—	—
Magallanes	—	—	—	—	—	—
Total	51	102	153	123	144	97

SOURCE: Same as Table 50.

TABLE 55
AVERAGE ANNUAL WINE PRODUCTION FOR SELECTED BIENNIA,
1877–1878 to 1926–1927
(THOUSANDS OF HECTOLITERS)

Province	1877–1878	1884–1885	1904–1905	1912–1913	1917–1918	1926–1927[†]
Tacna	—	—	—	1	1	4
Tarapacá	—	—	—	—	—	—
Antofagasta	—	—	—	—	—	—
Atacama	2	5	16	5	6	14
Coquimbo	5	8	9	4	8	12
Aconcagua	52	56	62	50	39	60
Valparaíso	11	4	21	18	22	31
Santiago	58	103	58	132	144	196
O'Higgins	—	38	2	136	125	189
Colchagua	66	76	85	147	124	224
Curicó	18	11	95	107	94	138
Talca	15	18	114	280	241	510
Linares	22	36	—	236	224	372
Maule	29	45	366	163	152	214
Ñuble	41	32	197	144	151	173
Concepción	92	78	177	314	251	263
Arauco	—	—	—	—	—	—
Bío-Bío	42	47	80	79	100	115
Malleco	—	—	1	4	15	9
Cautín	—	—	1	—	1	1
Valdivia	—	—	—	—	—	—
Llanquihue	—	—	—	—	—	—
Chiloé	—	—	—	—	—	—
Magallanes	—	—	—	—	—	—
Total	453	557	1,284	1,820	1,698	2,525

SOURCE: Same as Table 50.
[†] In 1926 and 1927 the figures include chicha. For all years the figures also include chacolí (a special local wine).

TABLE 56
AVERAGE ANNUAL WHEAT PRODUCTION FOR SELECTED BIENNIA,
1877–1878 to 1926–1927
(THOUSANDS OF METRIC QUINTALS)

Province	1877–1878	1884–1885	1904–1905	1912–1913	1917–1918	1926–1927
Tacna	—	—	—	—	—	—
Tarapacá	—	—	—	—	—	—
Antofagasta	—	—	—	—	—	—
Atacama	10	10	6	7	7	1
Coquimbo	102	130	108	56	62	23
Aconcagua	149	187	104	102	138	31
Valparaíso	77	92	45	100	87	64
Santiago	598	395	170	324	266	210
O'Higgins	—	398	155	324	345	307
Colchagua	297	402	264	467	450	464
Curicó	240	233	242	351	365	357
Talca	194	265	336	407	445	376
Linares	172	208	156	319	362	326
Maule	204	230	239	226	244	211
Ñuble	181	315	374	480	487	467
Concepción	199	192	136	271	202	188
Arauco	57	110	101	127	134	166
Bío-Bío	242	310	321	629	494	585
Malleco	—	320	456	1,027	889	889
Cautín	—	—	462	395	444	679
Valdivia	39	89	137	234	313	517
Llanquihue	54	96	244	343	399	666
Chiloé	61	103	146	81	74	50
Magallanes	—	—	—	—	—	—
Total	2,876	4,085	4,202	6,270	6,207	6,577

Source: Same as Table 50.
*The figure for Malleco for 1884–1885 refers to Angol, Tierra de Colonización.

244

TABLE 57
AVERAGE AREA CULTIVATED IN BARLEY FOR SELECTED BIENNIA,
1877–1878 to 1926–1927
(HECTARES)

Province	1877–1878	1884–1885	1904–1905	1912–1913	1917–1918	1926–1927
Tacna	—	—	598	—	1	—
Tarapacá	—	—	—	—	2	2
Antofagasta	—	—	—	—	—	7
Atacama	690	1,000	515	748	1,101	1,527
Coquimbo	1,005	1,505	7,027	2,252	2,643	4,028
Aconcagua	5,135	5,880	12,381	4,708	6,107	6,740
Valparaíso	10,785	10,425	8,241	6,013	4,858	9,040
Santiago	13,635	10,600	12,558	10,216	10,722	21,409
O'Higgins	—	3,060	5,933	7,141	5,810	8,419
Colchagua	1,675	2,070	4,869	4,738	5,750	7,502
Curicó	1,530	2,285	4,964	1,668	3,075	1,904
Talca	2,390	1,865	3,806	1,362	1,419	1,516
Linares	555	965	706	168	238	198
Maule	1,025	1,095	2,971	552	146	243
Ñuble	445	180	1,099	858	203	290
Concepción	1,170	1,455	610	462	885	400
Arauco	1,425	939	1,487	357	445	550
Bío-Bío	700	515	5,865	704	295	684
Malleco	—	810	4,363	1,208	638	2,292
Cautín	—	—	6,755	3,089	1,479	2,505
Valdivia	565	885	752	439	370	1,064
Llanquihue	890	730	2,471	716	465	748
Chiloé	155	300	646	12	23	28
Magallanes	—	—	—	32	13	30
Total	43,775	46,564	88,617	47,443	46,688	71,126

SOURCE: Same as Table 50.

TABLE 58
AVERAGE AREA CULTIVATED IN CORN FOR SELECTED BIENNIA,
1877–1878 to 1926–1927
(HECTARES)

Province	1877–1878	1884–1885	1904–1905	1912–1913	1917–1918	1926–1927
Tacna	—	—	465	666	582	55
Tarapacá	—	—	—	81	124	120
Antofagasta	—	—	—	19	42	46
Atacama	240	280	379	295	499	592
Coquimbo	2,610	3,295	1,663	1,040	1,017	1,754
Aconcagua	2,340	2,690	449	517	548	926
Valparaíso	850	1,755	99	284	236	387
Santiago	11,580	3,895	4,545	2,439	2,900	3,245
O'Higgins	—	6,005	1,457	2,731	1,286	2,087
Colchagua	8,530	8,530	3,320	3,730	3,256	3,863
Curicó	3,535	7,095	1,859	2,235	1,706	2,267
Talca	5,595	6,785	3,232	1,673	1,530	1,110
Linares	7,870	8,983	—	2,050	1,780	1,723
Maule	3,680	3,650	5,027	2,013	1,767	1,597
Ñuble	3,065	8,030	1,928	2,947	2,772	1,929
Concepción	2,085	3,300	279	434	431	267
Arauco	210	480	359	35	51	17
Bío-Bío	1,215	2,325	1,031	668	1,480	868
Malleco	—	680	62	521	739	334
Cautín	—	—	876	91	160	148
Valdivia	200	720	143	53	150	180
Llanquihue	30	30	—	43	4	1
Chiloé	—	—	3,526	—	44	—
Magallanes	—	—	—	3	—	—
Total	53,635	68,528	30,699	24,568	23,104	23,516

SOURCE: Same as Table 50.

TABLE 59
AVERAGE AREA CULTIVATED IN BEANS FOR SELECTED BIENNIA,
1877–1878 to 1926–1927
(HECTARES)

Province	1877–1878	1884–1885	1904–1905	1912–1913	1917–1918	1926–1927
Tacna	—	—	—	1	—	—
Tarapacá	—	—	—	—	—	—
Antofagasta	—	—	—	—	—	—
Atacama	70	105	89	18	23	115
Coquimbo	1,170	1,150	2,843	437	504	1,996
Aconcagua	1,270	1,345	910	818	1,218	1,632
Valparaíso	1,690	900	143	463	886	839
Santiago	5,505	2,690	1,700	889	2,201	2,098
O'Higgins	—	4,820	3,070	3,859	4,672	3,805
Colchagua	6,660	6,255	4,437	6,276	6,184	6,949
Curicó	4,910	3,785	4,128	4,367	5,726	5,248
Talca	5,015	4,365	2,989	4,264	5,846	4,386
Linares	3,825	2,865	—	3,528	4,187	4,639
Maule	805	1,095	1,624	1,181	824	1,097
Ñuble	1,305	4,140	1,881	3,308	4,819	5,359
Concepción	3,055	3,085	1,039	3,157	2,199	2,371
Arauco	990	1,015	872	535	602	427
Bío-Bío	1,725	2,215	1,129	1,446	2,179	3,650
Malleco	—	1,350	281	1,317	1,490	1,555
Cautín	—	—	710	143	220	372
Valdivia	1	160	105	52	86	90
Llanquihue	2	25	—	6	5	2
Chiloé	—	—	—	—	—	—
Magallanes	—	—	—	—	—	—
Total	37,998	41,365	27,950	36,065	43,871	46,630

SOURCE: Same as Table 50.

TABLE 60
AVERAGE AREA CULTIVATED IN WHEAT FOR SELECTED BIENNIA,
1877–1878 to 1926–1927
(HECTARES)

Province	1877–1878	1884–1885	1904–1905	1912–1913	1917–1918	1926–1927
Tacna	—	—	—	5	4	—
Tarapacá	—	—	—	1	20	11
Antofagasta	—	—	—	—	30	24
Atacama	1,030	1,085	427	509	511	135
Coquimbo	9,010	9,570	17,313	5,205	6,757	2,831
Aconcagua	15,540	13,005	7,764	6,277	7,776	2,434
Valparaíso	10,690	7,440	5,697	7,813	8,436	6,215
Santiago	77,270	36,300	13,103	21,230	19,691	17,096
O'Higgins	—	32,990	10,795	18,774	16,685	17,277
Colchagua	39,850	36,575	18,745	34,121	26,488	33,560
Curicó	25,450	22,510	16,266	21,767	22,569	26,508
Talca	45,650	40,185	31,747	22,372	30,492	27,513
Linares	29,150	31,550	14,204	21,124	28,754	30,467
Maule	33,660	37,140	27,804	25,339	28,599	30,255
Ñuble	50,750	54,460	35,436	39,886	48,110	51,845
Concepción	33,430	29,820	19,670	22,894	22,530	23,401
Arauco	10,090	12,010	12,075	9,797	13,727	14,780
Bío-Bío	25,500	43,285	32,932	44,916	51,815	62,615
Malleco	—	22,205	47,882	71,223	84,913	85,234
Cautín	—	—	49,368	28,753	42,880	56,358
Valdivia	5,950	8,760	14,094	17,241	28,414	41,848
Llanquihue	6,270	9,680	21,943	20,769	26,593	40,125
Chiloé	6,680	16,690	11,257	5,769	5,176	3,989
Magallanes	—	—	—	—	—	—
Total	425,970	465,260	408,522	445,785	520,970	574,521

SOURCE: Same as Table 50.

TABLE 61
AVERAGE AREA CULTIVATED IN PEAS FOR SELECTED BIENNIA,
1877–1878 to 1926–1927
(HECTARES)

Province	1877–1878	1884–1885	1904–1905	1912–1913	1917–1918	1926–1927
Tacna	—	—	147	1	10	2
Tarapacá	—	—	—	—	—	—
Antofagasta	—	—	—	—	—	—
Atacama	—	—	—	1	1	2
Coquimbo	10	7	10	6	5	1
Aconcagua	10	170	4	13	53	76
Valparaíso	135	90	147	380	343	86
Santiago	150	110	90	23	166	20
O'Higgins	—	5	—	3	40	49
Colchagua	40	60	247	32	52	21
Curicó	310	60	578	201	591	183
Talca	355	275	1,322	202	449	129
Linares	1,490	1,970	—	989	831	505
Maule	1,870	2,685	1,386	620	710	569
Ñuble	2,700	2,540	743	658	1,022	337
Concepción	1,195	3,095	1,076	509	538	353
Arauco	1,580	2,810	2,209	1,508	2,341	1,708
Bío-Bío	1,945	2,920	1,102	333	600	567
Malleco	—	320	235	1,006	1,565	939
Cautín	—	—	5,385	1,875	3,569	3,323
Valdivia	210	580	668	1,799	2,468	1,307
Llanquihue	220	340	55	256	249	81
Chiloé	50	40	316	7	2	—
Magallanes	—	—	—	—	1	—
Total	12,270	18,077	15,720	10,422	15,606	10,258

SOURCE: Same as Table 50.

TABLE 62
AVERAGE AREA CULTIVATED IN POTATOES FOR SELECTED BIENNIA, 1877–1878 to 1926–1927
(HECTARES)

Province	1877–1878	1884–1885	1904–1905	1912–1913	1917–1918	1926–1927
Tacna	—	—	160	288	262	58
Tarapacá	—	—	—	1	10	10
Antofagasta	—	—	—	—	—	—
Atacama	20	40	76	115	73	162
Coquimbo	250	330	1,504	732	1,085	2,034
Aconcagua	1,100	730	608	882	868	700
Valparaíso	1,160	725	611	1,454	1,125	1,001
Santiago	2,690	405	2,181	1,212	1,211	2,036
O'Higgins	—	775	4,233	1,373	1,971	1,691
Colchagua	1,330	1,780	1,871	2,883	2,303	2,248
Curicó	700	755	1,461	1,109	1,044	804
Talca	580	535	2,250	746	812	593
Linares	370	305	—	496	361	382
Maule	1,690	1,340	2,249	1,426	1,262	711
Ñuble	300	410	1,562	1,323	1,469	784
Concepción	890	650	1,542	1,169	519	371
Arauco	1,180	1,530	2,799	1,433	958	914
Bío-Bío	340	225	488	460	268	187
Malleco	—	110	346	513	414	367
Cautín	—	—	4,388	1,890	2,110	1,926
Valdivia	600	895	2,731	2,618	3,294	2,811
Llanquihue	2,170	2,865	2,078	2,927	4,470	4,323
Chiloé	5,840	8,630	3,370	4,084	4,767	3,950
Magallanes	—	—	—	4	10	28
Total	21,210	23,035	36,508	29,138	30,666	28,091

SOURCE: Same as Table 50.

NOTES

1. See, for example, the different interpretations of F. A. Encina, *Nuestra inferioridad económica,* (Santiago: Editorial Universitaria, 1955); H. Ramírez Necochea, *Balmaceda y la contrarevolución de 1891,* (Santiago: Editorial Universitaria, 1958); Harold Blakemore, *British Nitrates and Chilean Politics 1886–1896: Balmaceda and North,* (University of London, Institute of Latin American Studies, Monograph No. 4, The Athlone Press, 1974).

2. An excellent study written in this period is S. Machiavello Varas, *El problema de la industria del cobre en Chile y sus proyecciones económicas y sociales,* (Santiago: Imprenta Fiscal de la Penitenciaría, 1923). For a more recent analysis, see N. Girvan, *Copper in Chile: A Study in Conflict Between Corporate and National Economy,* (Mona, Jamaica: Institute of Social and Economic Research, University of the West Indies, 1972). See also T. H. Moran, *Multinational Corpo-*

rations and the Politics of Dependence: Copper in Chile, (Princeton, N.J.: Princeton University Press, 1974).

3. P. T. Ellsworth, *Chile, An Economy in Transition*, (New York: Macmillan, 1945); Instituto de Economía, Universidad de Chile, *Desarrollo económico de Chile, 1940–1956*, (Santiago: Editorial Universitaria, 1956); United Nations, Economic Commission for Latin America, *Antecedentes sobre el desarrollo de la economía chilena*, (Santiago: Editorial del Pacifico, 1954). R. Atria, "Tensiones politicas y crisis económica: el caso chileno 1920–1938," *Estudios sociales*, I, (Santiago, March 1973), pp. 35–70.

4. O. Caputto and O. Pizarro, "Dependencia e inversión extranjera," in A. Pinto Santa Cruz, et al, eds., *Chile, hoy*, (Mexico D.F.: Siglo XXI Editores, 1970); S. Bitar, "La presencia de la empresa extranjera en la industria chilena," *Desarrollo económico*, (Buenos Aires, July–Sept, 1973).

5. See e.g., the influential book by A. Pinto Santa Cruz, *Chile, un caso de desarrollo frustrado*, (Santiago: Editorial Universitaria, 1959). For a recent overall bibliographical review, see W. F. Sater, "A Survey of Recent Chilean Historiography, 1965–1976," *LARR*, Vol. 14, No. 2, 1979.

6. H. Godoy, *Estructura social de Chile: Estudio, selección de textos y bibliografía*, (Santiago: Editorial Universitaria, 1971). This work is an excellent introduction to this topic. It provides a careful selection of relevant essays, together with a wide-ranging bibliography on the social history of Chile.

7. C. Cariola and O. Sunkel, "Chile," in R. Cortés Conde and S. J. Stein, eds., *Latin America: A Guide to Economic History, 1830–1930*, (Berkeley and Los Angeles: University of California Press, 1977). This section of the volume comprises an interpretative essay on the period and an annotated bibliography of more than six hundred items. We suggest that anyone who wishes to pursue aspects of the present study consult this bibliography.

8. F. A. Encina, *Nuestra inferioridad económica;* Pinto Santa Cruz, *Chile, un caso de desarrollo frustrado;* Ramírez Necochea, *Balmadeda y la contrarevolución de 1891;* J. C. Jobet, *Ensayo critico del desarrollo económico social de Chile*, (Santiago: Editorial Universitaria, 1955). This thesis is summarized, broadened, generalized, and transformed in his theory of the "development of underdevelopment" by A. Gunder Frank in *Capitalism and Underdevelopment in Latin America: Historical Studies of Chile and Brazil*, (New York: Monthly Review Press, 1976).

9. In our view, this distinction between underdevelopment as a *stage* of development and modernization of capitalist countries, and underdevelopment as a *form* that peripheral capitalism takes in the development of world capitalism is the central issue in the debate about the nature of dependency. See A. Valenzuela and J. S. Valenzuela, "Modernization and Dependence: Alternative Perspectives in the Study of Latin American Underdevelopment," in J. J. Villamil, *Transnational Capitalism and National Development: New Perspectives on Dependence*, (Hassocks, U.K.: Harvester Press, 1979).

10. The interpretation of Chilean development in the course of the nitrate cycle as set forth here, and which constitutes the main line of the research that follows, was suggested originally by O. Sunkel and P. Paz, *El subdesarrollo latinoamericano y la teoría del desarrollo*, (Mexico: Siglo XXI Editores, 1970),

pp. 328–333; and later, in more elaborate and detailed form by Cariola and Sunkel, "Chile."

11. Benjamín Vicuña Mackenna, *El libro de la plata,* (Santiago: Cervantes, 1882); B. Vicuña Mackenna, *El libro del cobre y del carbón de piedra,* (Santiago: Cervantes, 1883); L. Castedo, *Resúmen de la historia de Chile de Francisco A. Encina,* Vol. 2, (Santiago: Zig–Zag, 1954), Ch. 17.

12. C. Hurtado, *Concentración de población y desarrollo económico: el caso chileno,* (Ph.D. dissertation, Harvard University and Instituto de Economía de la Universidad de Chile, 1966).

13. O. Bermúdez, *Historia del salitre, desde sus orígenes hasta la Guerra,* (Santiago: Ediciones de la Universidad de Chile, 1963), pp. 369–371.

14. H. Rumbold, *Le Chili,* (Paris: Lahure, 1877).

15. Ibid., p. 184. See also, M. Segall, *Desarrollo del capitalismo en Chile: cinco ensayos dialécticos,* (Santiago: Pacífico, 1963).

16. R. Hernández, *El salitre, resúmen histórico desde su descubrimiento y explotación,* (Valparaíso: Fisher, 1930), p. 75.

17. Chile, Ministerio de Hacienda, Sección Salitre, *Antecedentes sobre la industria salitrera,* (Santiago: Universo, 1925), p. 8.

18. S. Sepúlveda, *El trigo chileno en el mercado mundial,* (Santiago: Editorial Universitaria, 1959). A metric quintal is 100 kilograms.

19. Ibid., App. I and II and Fig. 1.

20. S. Marin Vicuña, *Estudio de los ferrocarriles chilenos,* (Santiago: Cervantes, 1900); E. Vasallo Rojas, and C. Matas Gutiérrez, eds., *Ferrocarriles de Chile: historia y organización,* (Santiago: Rumbo, 1943). The interrelationships between railway construction and agricultural extension and transformation in the Central Valley are examined by R. Oppenheimer, "Chilean Transportation Development: The Railroads and Socioeconomic Change in the Central Valley, 1840–1885," (Ph.D. diss., University of California, Los Angeles, 1976); and John Whaley, "Transportation in Chile's Bío–Bío Region, 1850–1915," (Ph.D. diss., Indiana University, 1974).

21. G. Subercaseaux, *El sistema monetario y la organización bancaria de Chile,* (Santiago: Universo, 1921); R. Santelices, *Los bancos chilenos,* (Santiago: Imprenta Barcelona, 1893); and A. Ross, *Chile 1851–1910, sesenta años de cuestiones monetarias y financieras y de problemas bancarios,* (Santiago: Imprenta Barcelona, 1911).

22. Rumbold, *Le Chili,* pp. 76–81 and 50–57.

23. A. Edwards Vives, *La fonda aristocrática: historia política de Chile,* (Santiago: Pacifico, 1952) 4th ed.

24. C. Humud, *El sector público chileno entre 1830 y 1930,* (Santiago: Universidad de Chile, Facultad de Ciencias Económicas, 1969).

25. Until 1870 the Araucanians remained in control of the extensive territories of La Frontera, which later were to form the important agricultural provinces of Malleco and Cautín. See H. Lara, *Crónica de la Araucanía; descubrimiento y conquista: pacificación definitiva i campaña de Villa Rica (Leyenda de tres siglos),* (Santiago: El Progreso, 1889).

26. V. H. Fuenzalida, "La conquista del territorio y la utilización de la tierra

durante la primera mitad del siglo XX", in *Desarrollo de Chile en la primera mitad del siglo XX,* (Santiago: Editorial Universitaria, 1951).

27. Bermúdez, *Historia del salitre;* Hernández, *El salitre.*

28. Ministerio de Hacienda, Sección Salitre, *Antecedentes sobre la industria salitrera* (Santiago: Universo, 1925), p. 8.

29. E. Reyes, *El desarrollo de la conciencia proletaria en Chile (El ciclo salitrero),* (Santiago: Editorial Orbe, n.d.), p. 111.

30. J. R. Brown, "Nitrate Crisis, Combinations and the Chilean Government in the Nitrate Age," *Hispanic American Historical Review* 43 (May 1963), 230–246.

31. Hurtado, *Concentración de población y desarrollo económico,* Tables 25 and 26.

32. Bermúdez, *Historia del salitre.*

33. G. E. Billinghurst, *Los capitales salitreros de Tarapacá,* (Santiago: El Progreso, 1889).

34. A discussion of the activities of the "King of Nitrates" is not within the scope of this study. The relevant bibliography is listed in Cariola and Sunkel, "Chile." In addition, see Blakemore, *British Nitrates and Chilean Politics;* and Ramírez Necochea, *Balmaceda y la contrarevolución de 1891.* For an interesting recent study on the crucial decisions taken by the Chilean state concerning ownership of the nitrate industry, see Thomas F. O'Brien Jr., "Chilean Elites and Foreign Investors: Chilean Nitrate Policy, 1880–82," *Journal of Latin American Studies,* 2 (1979), pp. 101–121.

35. Comparing the investment share data of Table 16 with sales share data presented in Table 17 suggests that the investment shares of 1925 may be exaggerated. The trend as indicated is however confirmed.

36. M. Mamalakis, "The Role of Government in the Resource Transfer and Resource Allocation Processes: The Chilean Nitrate Sector, 1830–1930," in G. Ranis, ed., *Government and Economic Development,* (New Haven, Conn: Yale University Press, 1971).

37. Humud, *El sector público chileno entre 1830 y 1930,* pp. 147 ff. See also F. Nunn, *Chilean Politics, 1920–1931: The Honorable Mission of the Armed Forces,* (Albuquerque, N.M., 1970); F. B. Pike, *Chile and the U.S., 1880–1962: The Emergence of Chile's Social Crisis and the Challenge to U.S. Diplomacy,* (Notre Dame, Ind.: University of Notre Dame Press, 1963); M. Rivas Vicuña, *Historia política y parlamentaria de Chile,* (Santiago: Ediciones de la Biblioteca Nacional, 3 vols., 1964); A. Valenzuela, *Political Brokers in Chile: Local Government in a Centralized Polity,* (Durham, N.C.: University of North Carolina Press, 1977), Ch. 8.

38. Humud, *El sector público chileno entre 1830 y 1930,* pp. 170 ff.

39. Ibid., Tables A–11 to A–17, pp. 245–255.

40. A. Labarca, *Historia de la enseñanza en Chile,* (Santiago: Imprenta Universitaria, 1939).

41. Hurtado, *Concentración de población y desarrollo económico,* Chapter 4.

42. The remainder of this section on Chilean industrial development is largely based on an excellent historical study recently carried out on Chilean industrialization in the period 1880–1930, the main theme of which is that the industrialization process gained its real, dynamic impulse beginning with the War of the

Pacific, and that the process was considerably broadened and extended before the crisis of 1930. This study is certainly the most complete and exhaustive that has been done on this theme and period. It has made use of numerous primary unpublished sources, and in particular information on forty–two industrial enterprises of importance, obtained principally from the archives of the Chamber of Commerce of Santiago. All the basic information the following pages that is given without indicating its source is taken from Henry W. Kirsch, *The Industrialization of Chile, 1880–1930*, (Ph. D. diss., University of Florida, 1973). In our opinion, this work definitely confirms the results of the studies of Chilean industrial development during this period that were made by Hurtado, *Concentración de población y desarrollo económico*, Chapter 4; R. Lagos, *La industria de Chile: antecedentes estructurales*, (Santiago: Universidad de Chile, Publicación del Instituto de Economía, No. 90, 1966); O. Muñoz, *Crecimiento industrial de Chile, 1914–1965*, (Santiago: Instituto de Economía y Planificación, No. 105, 1968).

43. P. L. González, *La sociedad de fomento fabril: su labor durante 25 años*, (Santiago: Universo, 1980).

44. Kirsch, *The Industrialization of Chile, 1880–1930*.

45. Hurtado, *Concentración de población y desarrollo económico*, pp. 94–95.

46. Lagos, *La industria de Chile*.

47. Gonzalez, *La sociedad de fomento fabril*, p. 14.

48. For the development of the statistics of coastal commerce, see Appendix A.

49. The validity of this ratio rests on the assumption that the devaluation of the peso and the internal inflation had similar trends, an assumption that appears reasonable in an economy as open as that of Chile over the long run. Changes in the price of nitrates were affected similarly.

50. For the period 1880–1903 the real proportion would be 2 or 3 percentage points larger, since the series of coastal trade constructed for this period was based on a selection of important products, and not on the total of products of agriculture and cattle raising that were shipped to Norte Grande (see Appendix A).

51. Mamalakis, "The Role of Government on the Resource Transfer and Resource Allocation Processes."

52. See especially Encina, *Nuestra inferioridad económica*.

53. Appendix B at the end of this chapter provides detailed information in this connection.

54. Data were provided, however, on "Angol, Land for Colonization," which was probably, approximately, what later became the province of Malleco.

55. Sepúlveda, *El trigo chileno en el mercado mundial*.

56. S. Hernández, *Transformaciones tecnológicas en la agricultura de Chile central, siglo XIX*, (Santiago: Universidad de Chile, Cuadernos del Centro de Estudios Socio–Económicos, No. 3, 1966); L. Correa Vergara, *Agricultura chilena*, 2 vols., (Santiago: Nascimiento, 1938); T. Schneider, *La agricultura en Chile en los últimos cincuenta años*, (Santiago: Imprenta Barcelona, 1904). See also the work of A. J. Bauer, *Chilean Rural Society from the Spanish Conquest to 1930*, (Cambridge, Mass.: Harvard University Press, 1975).

5

Growth and Guano in Nineteenth-Century
PERU

*Shane J. Hunt**

I

For Peru, as for most of Latin America, the nineteenth century seems to have been a period of low growth, perhaps even of economic stagnation. Innumerable scholars have sought an explanation for this unfortunate economic experience, since the divisions that have dominated North-South relations in the twentieth century began in the nineteenth. The per capita income gap between developed and underdeveloped countries was present when the nineteenth century began, but when that century ended, it was enormous.[1]

Peru is only a small part of the southern hemisphere, yet its economic experience is important because it was so distinctive, and that distinctiveness has inspired scholars to tackle the question of what went wrong.[2]

It is no problem at all to see what went wrong in the first three decades of the nineteenth century. A colonial period nearly 300 years long was ended only in 1826, when the last Spanish flag was hauled down from the battlements of Real Felipe Fortress. In its twilight years this colonial experience had been one of economic stagnation and political decay. The opportunities for economic growth presented to countries throughout the

*This research was assisted by grants from the Ford Foundation and from the Joint Committee on Latin American Studies of the Social Science Research Council and the American Council of Learned Societies. In addition, I would like to express thanks to José Luis Ramírez, Doris Garvey, and Jiřina Rybáček for research assistance.

world in the nineteenth century could not even begin to be taken advantage of by Peru until the struggles with Spain were ended. The initial chaos of forming a new nation extended the period of enforced stagnation some years beyond 1826, so at least the first third of the nineteenth century was a total loss as far as economic growth was concerned.

Nevertheless, the remaining two thirds held bright promise. Political independence had its economic counterpart in the freeing of foreign trade. Spanish controls and Spanish taxation were both swept away, and the opportunities of economic progress to be gained by joining the burgeoning world economy and accepting its assignment of specialized production were widely appreciated. Moreover, Peru was the lucky possessor of an export product with buoyant world markets. This product was guano, the dried excrement of sea birds; from 1840 till 1879 Peru was virtually a world monopolist in guano, and guano was the only commercial fertilizer available to the world's agriculture. Yet at the end of the frenetic forty-year boom in guano, Peru seemed to have acquired very little economic progress in exchange for the exhaustion of so valuable a natural resource. Reflecting the national disillusionment that followed the Guano Age, Peru's leading historian has called it *La Prosperidad Falaz.*[3]

Peru's experience in the Guano Age has been made known to a wide audience through the careful synthesis by Jonathan Levin. Levin's framework emphasizes the enclave nature of export sectors that exist independent of the domestic economy, providing no domestic stimulus unless governments are careful to forge linkages through taxation and government expenditure, or through other legislation. In the historical development of export economies, Peru in the Guano Age is offered as a classic example of wasted opportunity, an enclave that existed apart from the domestic economy without ever providing a foundation for self-sustaining domestic growth. To be sure, export taxes were collected in abundance, but Levin argues that the government expenditure this abundance made possible consisted largely of transfer payments to a growing mass of well-to-do bondholders, bureaucrats, and pensioners, whose marginal propensity to import was exceedingly high. Thus no stimulus was created for domestic production, and Peru at the end of the Guano Age was about the same as it had been at the beginning.[4] And half a century of growth opportunities had passed.

This chapter assesses the applicability of Levin's enclave model to the Peruvian Guano Age, but its focus is broader than that. The larger problem is to assess whether economic growth did occur during the century, and if not, why not. This involves a search for emerging points of high productivity that were capable of generating and reinvesting an economic surplus in a largely precapitalist economic landscape. The guano industry was the most important generator of surplus, but other sectors such as mining and agriculture must also receive their due.

The chapter begins with a survey of export expansion during the nineteenth century, with special emphasis on mining and agriculture. Then it analyzes the generation and distribution of earnings from guano, testing the relevance of Levin's enclave model. It concludes that this model does not provide a fully satisfactory explanation of Peruvian economic stagnation, and suggests an alternative that gives greater emphasis to supply inelasticities in the domestic sector and unfortunate choices of public investment projects.

II

When the War of Independence had finished, the stagnant Peruvian economy that embarked upon its republican career held no evident internal mainsprings for economic development. Its economic future appeared to hold promise, but promise that would be realized only through the emergence of sectors capable of generating and reinvesting an economic surplus. Such sectors could emerge only after the transformation of both conditions and the behavioral response to those conditions.

This transformation might have taken place slowly in an autarchic Peru, but the rush of economic change in the nineteenth century gave no opportunity for such evolution. Economic and ideological pressures to become integrated with the world economy were irresistible. Accordingly, external influences determined which sectors would receive the opportunity to generate a surplus. Peru's chance for economic transformation would be transmitted through its export sectors.

All this did not stand to Peru's disadvantage, and Peru responded to the opportunities offered by the world economy by entering a fifty-year period of sustained export growth. This response came largely from good fortune—the luck of having natural resources ready for export—but this circumstance should not diminish the significance of the contrast with earlier periods of both domestic and export stagnation. The growth rates of Table 1 outline the pattern of export expansion. They show substantial growth over the century. The tenfold expansion in total exports from 1830 to 1900 represents an average annual growth rate of 3.35 percent. The average growth rate from 1830 to 1878, the last war-free year of the Guano Age, amounted to 5.7 percent per annum.

Table 1 also shows that overall export growth proceeded by spurts and pauses, as different export products acquired or lost overseas market opportunities. Such oscillations about the long-term trend provide a basis for marking off subperiods of nineteenth-century growth.[5]

Post Independence Recovery (ca. 1825–1840). This period was marked by recuperation of silver production to nearly the levels achieved in the last decade of the eighteenth century. Wool exports also developed significantly during the 1830s.

Early Guano Age (1841–1849). Europe received its first shipments of Peruvian guano in 1841, and within a few years the guano boom was on. Only six years later, in 1847, guano had become Peru's most important export, but the revolution wrought by guano on Peruvian public finances did not come until later. Other export industries had meanwhile entered upon a period of complete stagnation that was to endure for twenty years.

Mature Guano Age (1850–1878). The transition point from an earlier to a later Guano Age is somewhat indistinct, and could be placed anywhere between 1848 and 1854. The periods themselves are clearly separable, however. The Mature Guano Age was characterized by a vast increase in the volume of imports, in guano income as a percent of total government revenue, and in guano exports as a percent of total exports. By the last of these criteria, the dividing line seems best placed between 1849 and 1850, as guano exports jumped from 34.3 to 50.2 percent of total exports and thenceforth contributed more than 50 percent of exports for all but a few scattered years during the ensuing two and a half decades.[6]

Guano's percent of total exports hit a peak in 1854, at 73.8 percent and averaged 57.0 percent for 1850–1860. Guano exports continued to grow in the 1860s and early 1870s, but beginning in 1861, other export industries finally bestirred themselves, so the guano share declined slightly in the 1860s and considerably in the 1870s. Exports of guano rose from an annual average of 351,000 tons in 1850–1860 to 450,000 in 1861–1870 and 468,000 in 1871–1878,[7] but the guano export share of these last two periods fell to 55.5 percent and 40.0 percent, respectively. Peru's dependence on guano thus gradually lessened over time. Unfortunately the major thrust of diversification came through the development of nitrate exports, particularly after government nationalization of the industry in 1873. Nitrate exports doubled between 1870 and 1878, when they amounted to 68 percent of guano exports and 26 percent of total exports.[8] This promising beginning was snuffed out by Chilean seizure of the nitrate provinces at the same time that the War of the Pacific dealt a mortal blow to the guano trade.

Among other export industries, the most important expansion occurred in sugar, which started making inroads in European markets around 1866 and mushroomed in the 1870s. Total exports, which first exceeded 10,000 tons in 1869, exceeded 80,000 tons in the peak year of 1879.[9] Cotton exports also expanded during these decades, but never acquired the importance of sugar. Meanwhile, back in the Sierra, stagnation prevailed. Silver production showed no upward trend whatsoever, and the growth of wool exports was at best modest.

Export growth during the Mature Guano Age averaged 4.5 percent per annum. Exports other than guano and nitrates grew at 6.0 percent per annum during 1860–1878.

Invasion and Collapse (1878–1881). The collapse at the end of the Guano Age was complete and shattering. It involved the exhaustion of guano deposits, territorial loss of the nitrate provinces, destruction of much of the sugar industry through a series of punitive raids, and submission to a Chilean army of occupation from 1880 to 1883. One economic manifestation of these disasters was a precipitous decline in exports. Expressed as a percent of the 1878 peak, total exports slumped to 49 percent, in 1879, 24 percent in 1880, and 21 percent in the trough year of 1881. While guano and nitrates were permanently eliminated as major exports, the sugar, silver, cotton, and wool industries all suffered reverses, so that by 1883 they had declined to 41, 74, 59, and 46 percent of their respective 1879 levels.

Slow Recovery (1881–1895). These four surviving export industries experienced very different patterns of postwar recovery. Wool exports went back to normal as soon as hostilities were concluded and trade channels reopened. The incipient cotton industry and the antiquated mining industry needed only a few additional years, and had recovered their prewar export levels by 1890. The sugar industry had suffered substantially more destruction of capital, however, and the road to recovery was painfully slow: prewar export levels were not exceeded until 1897. Recovery was even slower for exports in the aggregate. The levels of the Guano Age were not regained until about 1905, when export composition had changed drastically and the country was immersed in a new and very different era of export-led growth.

Peru approached that new era through a period of slow economic recovery, characterized by important political and diplomatic consolidation. A shattered polity was put back together, settlement was made with foreign bondholders, and military rule was overthrown by the Revolution of 1895. Average export growth during reconstruction was 4.0 percent per annum.

New Export Economy (1895–1929). This period properly belongs to Peru's twentieth-century economic history. It was based on exports of sugar, cotton, copper, and petroleum, and bore witness to the halcyon days of oligarchic control during the Aristocratic Republic; it continued in modified form under the dictator Leguia until the next collapse, in 1929.[10] In the closing years of the nineteenth century, 1895 to 1900, total exports spurted to a growth rate of 13.1 percent per annum.

This chapter analyzes export trends both because the data for them are available and because there is the *presumption* of a relationship between exports and the key variables of national economic growth and structural transformation. What are these key variables? First of all, real output. Although we know virtually nothing of trends in factor productivity and real wages, we presume that factors drawn into export industries were more productive than they had been earlier in domestic activity. Second, real income. This greater productivity should have resulted in a growing import capacity. The trend in import capacity, or income terms of trade, is given by an index of export quantum multiplied by the net barter terms of trade, as shown in Table 2. The data are derived from official British statistics on U.K.–Peruvian trade and start in 1855 because statisticians began reasonably accurate valuations of British exports only in 1854.

The income terms of trade give a substantially different picture of economic progress in the nineteenth century. In terms of import purchasing power, recovery from post-Guano Age collapse proved far more difficult than indicated by quantum statistics because Peru suffered a sharp deterioration in net barter terms of trade during Europe's "Great Depression." Both import and export prices fell during this period, but export prices fell more. By 1900 cotton textile prices (expressed in pounds sterling) had slumped to 64 percent of their 1870 levels, but wool textiles had declined only to 93 percent of 1870 levels and iron prices had actually risen by 33 percent. On the export side, the declines were more precipitous. Guano, sugar, and silver prices of 1900 stood at only 37, 47, and 45 percent, respectively, of their 1870 values. The only export whose price held firm during the Great Depression was nitrates, but this proved of little consolation to Peru after 1880.

Thus by 1900 net barter terms of trade had plunged to 50–60 percent of 1870 levels. The purchasing power of exports stood at only 65–68 percent of the 1855 level, despite the fact that the export quantum was 22 percent higher. The road back from economic disaster was longer and rockier, thanks to the workings of commodity prices during the Great Depression.

An additional reason for examining export performance turns on the presumption that export sectors held the greatest prospects for generating surplus. Being resource based, production in these sectors might be expected to generate the most significant rents and quasi-rents in the economy. Furthermore, we might expect these sectors to be important sources of saving and reinvestment, the harbingers of capitalism, partly because of their capacity for generating surplus and partly because they stood most closely in touch with the capitalist world economy. A survey of prospects for surplus generation must proceed by a case-by-case examination of the more important export sectors.

An obvious first candidate for examination is mining, the mainspring of colonial wealth. Prohibitive internal transport costs caused a continuation of the traditional specialization in silver production, and our best estimates of silver exports (see Table 1) show persistent stagnation through most of the century. The same problems that had beset the industry in the colonial period continued unresolved: technological backwardness, mine flooding, exhaustion of ore bodies, inadequate labor supply. The first three reasons were perhaps most important and were interrelated: ore bodies above the water table were becoming exhausted, and available technology could not handle the flooding problems created by pushing shafts below the water table.[11]

Organizational structures compounded the technical problems. Their interrelations are best illustrated by the experience of Cerro de Pasco, the most important mining center of the country. In the mountainous terrain of Cerro and other major mines, drainage can always be accomplished by punching long tunnels into lower valleys nearby. Cerro stood completely flooded when the first drainage tunnel was completed in 1760. Production was quickly restored, but Cerro was never again free of water problems. Thenceforth mining progressed in erratic cycles, depending on the precarious balance among exhaustion of newly drained deposits, the excruciating decision to go ahead with new drainage tunnels, and the completion of those tunnels. The Quiulacocha tunnel, for example, was begun in 1806, discontinued in 1816 when new pumps were brought in, resumed in 1825 by an English company that went bankrupt fifteen months later, resumed again by the Peruvian government in 1827, and finally finished in 1839. It provided a bonanza until the new workings became exhausted in 1855.[12] At the passing of this bonanza, there were no new workings ready to open and take up the slack. Another tunnel, the Rumiallana, had been started in 1825 by the quixotic Englishmen of the Pasco Peruvian Company, but the century closed before its completion. Meanwhile, steam-driven pumps proved unreliable substitutes. Rivero wrote in 1828 of "the insecurity of a machine which offers no guarantee that it will function," which also "will blow up when one least expects it."[13] In fact, the boiler had blown up a few months earlier. The best of subsequent efforts with pumps and engines provided only limited success. Of three steam engines contracted for in 1848, only two were ever set in working order, and a report of 1859 found them paralyzed after frequent breakdowns.[14] Another effort with steam engines in 1872 failed utterly.[15]

This experience contrasts sharply with the expectation, widely held

262 *Shane J. Hunt*

on the eve of independence, that British mining technology would put new life into the worn-out mines of Spanish America. Acquiring the instruments of technology proved to be no problem. Even before independence, Cerro de Pasco received the personal attention of Richard Trevithick, inventor of the high-pressure steam engine, who installed engines at Cerro as early as 1817, only to see his works smashed by war.[16] What proved substantially more difficult, however, was the successful adaptation of this technology to a vastly different institutional environment.

Three factors seem to have compounded the difficulty. In the first place, even the competent English companies like the early Abadia–Trevithick enterprise found Cerro a tougher prospect than they had anticipated. After contracting with the Gremio de Mineros (Miners' Guild) to raise water from 40 yards below the San Judas drainage tunnel, the company found it beyond its ability to sink pumping shafts even to half that depth.

If the competent had difficulty, however, the incompetent were lost. The Pasco Peruvian Company was born in the flurry of stock flotations in Latin American mining that excited London investors in 1825.[17] Armed with 150,000 pounds of paid-in capital, Pasco Peruvian contracted with the gremio to finish Quiulacocha drainage tunnel, start Rumiallana, and bring in pumps and steam engines. But after spending about 8,000 pounds (40,000 pesos) on tunnels, it was bankrupt. The steam engines remained in Lima, impounded by creditors.[18] The uses found for the major portion of Pasco Peruvian's capital remain unrecorded, but may be guessed from the following remarks:

> The great error committed by all the English companies established in 1825, for working mines in Spanish America, was in saddling themselves with numbers of people, engaged at high salaries, and workmen at extravagant wages: the expenses attending this force swallowed up much of the funds before any work was begun. These included not only inspectors and mining captains, but artisans, all of whom were sent from England. From a total change of life and circumstances, the mining captains and artisans almost invariably turned out in a short time drunkards, and became good for nothing.[19]

Through its various phases from 1806 to 1839, Quiulacocha tunnel cost upward of 750,000 pesos.[20] To the gremio, this was a lot of money, but it represented the Lima sales value of only about five months of Cerro's production.[21] Drainage tunnels undoubtedly produced high returns on investment. The investment decision became so traumatic only because Peruvian miners had such meager access to lines of credit. Nor could they finance major projects out of their own resources except at the excruciatingly slow pace of a project like Quiulacocha. Perpetually living hand to mouth, mine owners lacked credit for working capital as well as for major investments. To conserve on funds, they customarily paid miners in shares of ore, thereby losing any possibility of efficient mining technique because miners robbed pillars and ransacked workings, causing frequent collapses.[22] This chronic capital shortage persisted throughout the century as a major obstacle to technological innovation and output expansion. It was an obstacle that British participation did nothing to overcome.

Capital shortage is closely related to a third reason for continued stagnation. This concerns the institutional deficiency of small-scale mining operations, loosely coordinated through a *gremio,* when confronted with the need to plan and carry out major investments. Herndon, in his visit to Cerro in 1851, described the gremio's confused decision making at the moment stagnation was setting in.[23] Having decided to install pumps that would drain lower levels into the Quiulacocha tunnel, the gremio had contracted the works to yet another English company. When rumor of mercury strikes in California arrived, promising lower refining costs and therefore greater profit in above-water ores, elements of the gremio pressed for cancellation of the pumps contract. Then good ore was uncovered by the pumping operations and the tide shifted the other way. Paralyzed over the choice between pumps and tunnels, and short of funds in any event, in the end the gremio of Cerro de Pasco chose neither on an adequate scale. The sorry result is unfolded in an 1875 survey of the region that counted only eighty-seven mines in operation out of a total of seven hundred. Steam engines stood abandoned, drainage tunnels remained unfinished, work terminated due to "mistrust and dissention."[24]

Fifty years before, Rivero had marked as one of the main obstacles to progress, "the continual disputes and the arbitrary decisions rendered by the judges and justices of the peace." No wonder that in such pleasant anarchy credit was hard to come by, even for simple grubstakes. "Surely the miners' failure to honor contracts, as well as the vices attributed to them, inspire a reluctance to make loans to them."[25] In the fifty years of the Guano Age nothing changed in Cerro de Pasco. A well-planned, capital-intensive, technologically advanced mining system would remain beyond reach so long as the decentralized decision making of the guild system prevailed. Consolidation and rationalization were the necessary preconditions for the rise of a more advanced stage of capitalism. In the case of Cerro de Pasco, the triumphant new institution took the form of a foreign giant assembled on Wall Street in the closing years of the century by J. P. Morgan himself.

Less important mining areas fared no better than Cerro de Pasco. Those mines that were worked in association with haciendas suffered particularly from labor shortages when the pressure of the *contribución de indígenas* (Indian head tax) was removed. The accounts of perceptive

Andean travelers often include a dreary catalogue of flooded and abandoned silver mines.[26]

Attempts to introduce new technologies continued sporadically throughout the century, but generally met with difficulties and limited financial returns.[27] The most persistent were the German Pfluckers, experts in Saxon refining techniques. In some cases they succeeded, but their most ambitious innovations at Morococha did not. As for Peruvian mine owners, many were new to such ownership, having acquired mines taken from Spaniards at independence, and even those with experience generally knew little about the new European technologies. It was said that they were often so ignorant that they were unable to distinguish the able from the incompetent among the foreign mining engineers in their hire.[28] Through most of the century, therefore, the rate of technological diffusion was low. Only in the 1890s do we see evidence of a wider, more vigorous adoption of new technologies, but by that time a whole century of opportunities had been wasted.[29]

Some sense of the financial condition of Peruvian mining may be derived from the following rather erratic data for Cerro de Pasco:[30]

	1828	1851	1875
Mine owners' gross revenue	9%	26½%	30%
Materials for smelting (mercury, salt)	23½	15½	12¼
Smelting and transport value added	45	39½	69½
Taxes for pumps and drainage tunnels	—	4	—
Taxes to government	—	7	—
Profits	22½	7½	−11¾
Value of silver output	100% (8.5 pesos/ mark)	100% (10 pesos/ mark)	100% (10 soles/ mark)

Comparisons among years should be approached with caution, since very possibly the figures were compiled on different assumptions regarding ore quality and refining conditions. Nevertheless, the data give some clear indications about financial conditions. First, they show that the challenge of profit maintenance through cost-reducing technological change lay mainly with refining rather than with mining operations. Second, they demonstrate that throughout the Guano Age there was a steady decline in profits, at least at the refining stages. What was happening at the mining stage is not at all clear from these data. If we estimate the surplus of taxes and profits as a percent of the value of silver delivered to

Lima, including a reasonable allowance for profits of mine owners, this surplus comes out to over 20 percent in 1828, nearly 20 percent in 1851, and negative in 1875.

It is difficult to determine where this surplus went. The entrepreneurs in silver mining were not terribly rich. Cerro de Pasco witnessed no lavish living.[31] Nor is there any record of miners being multisectoral entrepreneurs who shifted mining profits into investments elsewhere. As for the investments in mining itself, pumps and tunnels represented gross investment, but the failure to extend these works fast enough to maintain output meant that works were being depreciated more rapidly than new works were being built, i.e., net disinvestment was the rule. Aside from the meager tax payments, the only portion of surplus transferred out of mining and possibly made available for investment elsewhere consisted of the payments made by mine and smelting operators to the financiers of Lima who had extended them credit. True, these interest rates were exorbitant, but the volume of such credit seems to have been highly restricted. Furthermore, the use creditors made of interest income remains unknown.[32] Although our ignorance of the details is unfortunately profound, it does seem clear that Peruvian mining generated very little by way of investable surplus during the nineteenth century.

Agriculture in the Sierra remained tied to the fortunes of mining. Among its various products, only wool possessed sufficient value per unit weight to overcome the transportation costs of exporting. However, wool exports grew very moderately during the course of the nineteenth century. Isolation restricted the markets for Sierra crops to mining areas; since mining remained in stagnation, so did Sierra agriculture. Commercial production gave way to subsistence activities. Haciendas tended toward dissolution, despite the increased opportunities for land grabbing at the expanse of Indian communities.[33]

In the south, Bolivian mining output had declined sharply during the disruptions of the independence wars. Averaging over 4 million pesos annually during 1800–1805, output sank below 2 million pesos in 1815–1820, and failed to recover during ensuing decades.[34] Potosí, formerly a vibrant royal city that counted as many as 160,000 inhabitants in the seventeenth century, had withered to merely 16,000 in the mid-nineteenth century.[35] For Moquegua *aguardientes* (grape brandy), Arequipa wheat and Cuzco baizes, a major market was gone forever. In the Central Sierra Cerro de Pasco continued as a focal point of trade, attracting the products of Huanuco, Jauja, and Huaraz, but this trade could not grow while Cerro did not grow. During the nineteenth century the Sierra probably stood more isolated from the rest of the world than at any other time in its post-Conquest history.

A crude indicator of this isolation is offered by the following postal statistics, which show the ratio of correspondence received in a given year to total population in 1876:[36]

	1877	1902–1904 average
Lima	7.4	9.9
6 other coastal cities[37]	2.1	7.8
Arequipa	2.2	10.2
Cerro de Pasco	0.9	7.3
5 cities of southern Sierra[38]	0.75	3.4

By no means could the Sierra be described as a beehive of activity in the opening years of the twentieth century. Yet at the height of the Guano Age its condition was even more moribund. Clearly the Sierra could not provide a pole for economic growth and transformation during the nineteenth century.

While the Sierra's connections to the world economy were being severed, coastal agriculture found new prosperity through new export markets. But these new developments came about only in the 1860s, after thirty years of post-independence stagnation.[39]

The main new opportunity lay with sugar exporting, a long-time Peruvian tradition. In late colonial times Peruvian sugar had dominated the Chilean market and secured additional sales in Argentina and Ecuador.[40] By the mid-1830s the export level of four decades earlier was at last reestablished, entirely on the basis of shipments to Chile. But with that level achieved, the sugar export trade developed no further, for lack of markets. Beginning in 1835, Peruvians attempted to penetrate the English market, but by 1839 the effort was abandoned.[41] Apparently they failed not because of high freight costs but rather because their manner of processing yielded a sugar unsuited to English tastes.[42]

Factor supply problems also obstructed expansion. While arable land existed in overabundance throughout the coastal valleys, one bottleneck was referred to again and again in the history of sugar: *falta de brazos* (labor shortage).[43] Slave labor furnished a solution to the problem until emancipation in 1854, but this solution could not accommodate expansion, since slave importing had been prohibited at the creation of the Republic. Only after the jolt of emancipation was a new and expandable labor supply found in Chinese coolies. Between 1849 and 1874 87,000 coolies were imported into Peru; the conditions under which they toiled closely resembled those of the Negro slaves who had preceded them.[44]

The various obstacles to export expansion suddenly evaporated around 1860.[45] World sugar prices were high. Cotton prices rose out of sight with the coming of the U.S. Civil War and the Cotton Famine. Landowners had acquired the means to purchase coolie contracts, partly through payments received for manumission of slaves, partly through finance available from newly created banks and concentrations of private wealth engendered by guano prosperity. This finance did more than merely purchase a labor force: it permitted coastal haciendas a spending spree on borrowed funds. New machinery, new buildings, and new consumption standards arrived along with the new workers and new plantings. Commercial contacts established through the experience of guano gave Peruvian producers vastly improved knowledge of foreign market conditions and quality requirements. Because of lags in supply response, cotton haciendas did not jump into exporting until 1865–1867, after the passing of the famine. Nevertheless they retained and even expanded their markets in the face of renewed competition from the U.S. South. A steady flow of sugar shipments began to the United States in 1862 and to Great Britain in 1868.

By 1879 sugar accounted for 32 percent of total exports, having grown at an average annual rate of 28 percent since 1862.[46] The expansion was accomplished largely along the north coast, in the same Trujillo-Chiclayo region that had seen an earlier sugar industry crumble in the 1790s. By 1877 this region accounted for 58 percent of Peru's sugar exports. A year later its share was up to 68 percent. As for cotton, in 1877, 14 percent of exports were shipped from Piura, 38 percent from the Department of Lima, and 42 percent from Pisco-Ica.[47] Thus the two decades of prosperity that began in 1860 transformed the geographical pattern of crop production to the form that has continued to the present day.[48] These decades also witnessed the introduction of a more scientific agriculture through trade journals, agricultural experimentation, and irrigation works.[49] But the result was an agriculture highly specialized in only a few crops. Rough estimates from the end of the 1870s put the value of coastal production at 32 million pesos (soles), of which 47 percent was represented by sugar, 5½ percent by cotton, 4 percent by rice, 28 percent by wines and other liquors, and 15½ percent by other food crops.[50]

This transformation operated within distinct limitations imposed by the structure of land tenure. Even with the importation of coolies, *falta de brazos* remained a binding production constraint, with captive labor in limited supply. Haciendas had no interest in paying the higher wages of a free labor market, and opposed the formation of a yeoman class on unused land. Under these conditions, coastal Peru continued underpopulated, and haciendas had little motivation for food crop production. When railroad construction brought a surge in demand for food, it was imported from Chile. Evidently Peruvian haciendas paid no attention to a market created under their noses by Henry Meiggs.[51] As for Lima's urban market, its fruits and vegetables were largely supplied by immigrant Italian farmers.[52]

These phenomena lend confirmation to the image of Peruvian *hacen-*

dados as rather unimaginative entrepreneurs who expanded only a few lines through virtually limitless lines of credit. As Klinge has pointed out, family tradition along the Peruvian coast generally assigned management of the family hacienda to the least able son, whose abler brothers went into politics and the liberal professions in Lima.[53] All members of such a family would contribute to the key attribute of the successful hacienda: access to credit. Credit dried up in the financial crisis that gripped Lima in the last half of the 1870s, however, and this financial collapse was followed by the physical destruction wreaked by the War of the Pacific. Writing from a perspective of 1895, Garland reviewed the sugar industry's trajectory in the following words:[54]

> The commercial history of Peru has seen few bankruptcies more disastrous than those deriving from the loans to the sugar industry, loans made with a recklessness which today seems inconceivable. We estimate, taking into consideration the value of money [in that time], that only 33 percent [of these loans] have been saved from that collapse, causing the loss of the twenty million remaining, the bankruptcy of various commercial firms, the ruin of the mortgage banks and commercial banks, and massive losses to individuals.

Garland estimated that in 1875 the sugar industry's indebtedness amounted to 30 million soles, of which 17.5 million soles was owed to the fledgling banking system.[55] If only a third of this was recoverable in liquidation, 20 million soles seems a generous estimate of the industry's total fixed investment during the Guano Age. As will be seen in the next part of this chapter, 20 million soles amounts to only some 5 percent of total guano income received by the Peruvian government. A meager share of the guano riches was sufficient to transform coastal agriculture. The surplus accumulation opportunities of sugar, although substantial, were dwarfed by the opportunities presented by guano itself.

III

The Peruvian export of overwhelming importance during the nineteenth century was the guano deposited on rocky islands off the country's coast. Guano's economic characteristics were distinctive. Once its importance as a fertilizer had been discovered and publicized in Europe around 1840, it became the world's only fertilizer alternative to manure. Although a few guano deposits were discovered on islands elsewhere in the world, Peru remained essentially a world monopolist in this fertilizer supply for the ensuing forty years.

No other export in history presented fewer problems of production. The guano only had to hacked away from the cliffs and dumped on chutes running to the holds of waiting ships. Capital requirements consisted of picks and shovels; labor requirements were not great; technology was primitive yet satisfactory; domestic transportation was nonexistent. Foreign enterprise had no particular advantage because of sophistication of technology or economies of scale. Nevertheless, the issue of foreign control became a heated one, particularly in the closing years of the Guano Age. It existed because the Peruvian government desired to exploit its monopoly not merely through control of production but also through control of the worldwide network of distribution. The operation of this network required enormous amounts of working capital, which gave foreigners, with their superior access to major capital markets, a decided advantage. It should be noted, however, that this advantage existed only because the simplicity of production techniques led the Peruvian government to aspire to the control of distribution. Peru in the Guano Age was in this sense substantially more ambitious than most primary product exporters are today.

For forty years the world gained a new source of fertilizer supply. Because it was a monopolist and attempted to exploit its monopoly position to the utmost, Peru also should have gained greatly from the exploitation of this resource. Nevertheless, the recent fame of this experience lies in the view that the guano export sector provided minimal benefit to the nation.[56] Levin has argued that Peruvian guano was the archetypal export enclave, providing no backward linkages to the domestic economy and no stimulus to the transformation of other sectors. Given the virtual absence of an income-generating production process, all connection with the domestic economy had to come through profits of Peruvian contractors and government expenditure programs made possible by the government's guano income. However, the final twist of the enclave model closes off the domestic economy from these flows as well. It holds that Peru gained little beyond an initial absorption of consumer goods by the well-to-do, since government expenditure increments generally took the form of transfer payments to pensioners and civil servants, most of whom had a high marginal propensity to import. Levin does point out some more enduring benefits received from the guano industry—the creation of a financial superstructure, some reinvestment in the newly developing sugar industry, and, in the final years, a frenetic attempt to use guano revenues for building railroads—but these are considered qualifications rather than a refutation of the main theme.[57]

Levin formulated the propositions about intersectoral resource flows that constitute an enclave model. He also offered an intriguing historical example. However, his study did not get into the messy business of making the statistical estimates required for assessing the applicability of the historical example. Yet these estimates must be made, here and elsewhere, before we can truly be convinced that the enclave concept appropriately describes Peru in the Guano Age.

The beginnings of these estimates are found in Table 3. It shows that after some poor early contracts, better arrangements were instituted, producing an allocation of guano income in which about 30 percent went to costs, something less than 10 percent to contractors' commissions, and something more than 60 percent to government profit. Even if we were to consider as much as half of costs to be excess charges that really hid contractor profits, this allocation would still be equivalent to a 71 percent tax rate on the profits of a company granted exporting rights. Such a rate is approached today only by the most heavily taxed export industries, and only after several recent decades of rising rates.[58] Furthermore, recent figures that may be used for comparison are based on f.o.b. values rather than on final sales values in foreign markets. Today—aside, possibly, from the Organization of Petroleum Exporting Countries—Third World governments receive virtually nothing of the income generated by the international distribution network through which their exports flow.

The potential benefit of an export sector may be assessed more generally not just by taxes collected but by the totality of income flows, including transfers, that run from the export industry to the domestic economy. The size of these income flows relative to total export value has provided the basis for Reynolds' evaluation of the Chilean copper industry, as well as for Levin's evaluation of export sectors in general and Peruvian guano in particular.[59] These flows, labeled returned value by Reynolds, provide only a proxy measure to our real interest, which lies in backward linkages—i.e., the investment and innovational response of the domestic economy to increased demand for its output; for this reason, the benefit measured by income flows is only potential.

Returned value flows are fairly quickly identified in the case of guano. They consist of labor costs on the guano islands, the profits of ships' chandlers who serviced the guano fleet, contractor profits in those cases where the contractors were Peruvian, and the net income of the Peruvian government.

With regard to labor costs, we must first note that the size of the labor force was minuscule. It was observed, for example, that about 1,000 workers were laboring on the Chincha Islands in 1853, each worker being assigned a daily quota of 4 tons.[60] Even if we assume that labor productivity declined to 2 tons per worker by 1869–1870, this permits our labor force estimate to be inflated to only about 1,600, and still we arrive at the conclusion that for that biennium labor costs were probably less than 4 percent of total costs.[61] Considering guano in the way that export industries are viewed today, as domestic industries that produce a product valued f.o.b. ready for export, guano was a costless monopoly, a pungent version of Cournot's mineral spring, with only one person bottling the water.

In the calculation of returned value, therefore, labor costs were too small to be worth considering, given the unavoidable roughness of the estimates. As for ships' chandlers profits, no information is available, but probably they were also of minor import.

Significant variation in returned value share over the course of the Guano Age was therefore produced only by changes in the nationality of contractors, and by changes in the success of government in driving good bargains. By these changes, the Guano Age divides itself into three periods. The first, from 1841 until 1849, was one of generally poor bargains and generally foreign contractors. The returned value share of exports amounted to little more than the 33 percent gained by the government. This share went up to 65 percent with the Gibbs Contract of 1849, however, and it rose further in later years because of a congressional decision that subsequent contract biddings should give preference to Peruvians. For the succeeding twenty years all major contracts went to Peruvians, so returned value amounted to the sum of government profit, contractors' commissions, and markups to costs that really constituted hidden contractor profits. As Table 3 shows, the first two of these items came to about 70 percent of the final sales value, and the three together may therefore be estimated at something around 75 percent of final sales.

The era of the Peruvian contractors ended with a thud in 1869, when the government canceled all contracts then in force and entered into a single arrangement with the French house of Dreyfus.[62] The change produced a political explosion, since the dispossessed contractors were counted among the wealthiest and most influential people in Peru, simply by virtue of having had the contracts. This fundamental opposition was substantially reinforced by nationalist sentiment greatly offended by the delivery of the country's major export into foreign hands. Here, indeed, was classic *entreguismo* (selling out to foreign interests).

Because of the confusion of this swirling controversy even the indefatigable Rodríguez modestly refrained from putting together a final accounting. The present author's glaring immodesty in this regard is fully evident in Table 3. A residual sense of propriety, however, demands that such unusual results be explained, and that is what Table 4 attempts to do.

The results are unusual because they show no margin with which Dreyfus could have covered costs.[63] The figures suggest that Peru squeezed Dreyfus dry. This interpretation lies so far from conventional historical wisdom regarding the Dreyfus contract that it cannot be sustained purely on the basis of the calculations presented here. Despite some attempt to impart downward bias to Peru's share, particularly in the choice of final sales prices, error still could have crept into the calculations in too many places.[64] However, the data do seem sufficient for a more modest conclusion: that the returned value share established by previous contract arrangements was increased under the Dreyfus contract. Beginning with the Gibbs contract of 1849, the Peruvian government did quite well for itself in guano negotiating. The last line of Table 3 might suggest a bad contract at the end of the Guano Age, but in fact only low-quality guano was left by 1877; returns per ton were down with costs unchanged. Total depletion and total collapse were only a few years away.

If we again use the recent prenationalization history of the Chilean copper industry as a standard of comparison, we must conclude that the returned value share of the guano trade was very high. As we have seen, this share remained in excess of 70 percent after 1849; by contrast, the returned value share of Chilean copper rose steadily from 37 percent in 1925–1929 to 60 percent in 1955–1959.[65] Furthermore, it should be remembered that the guano figure is biased low because it is based on final sales value rather than on f.o.b. export value. In fact, since virtually all costs were incurred beyond the point of export and contractors' profits were derived from shipping, storing, and distribution services, it follows that 100 percent of f.o.b. value had to be returned to Peru.

The somewhat surprising conclusion of this statistical exercise is that, far from being an archetypal enclave, the Peruvian guano sector was, as export sectors go, the very antithesis of an enclave. By its very definition, a true enclave allows no opportunity for domestic development because it prevents any resource flows from coming under the control of domestic decision makers. On the contrary, in the case of guano, a fiscal bonanza was presented to those in control of the Peruvian exchequer. If the opportunity was tremendous, what was done with it?

Table 5 shows how completely the guano bonanza transformed the Peruvian fiscal system. The table begins with 1846–1847, the first years for which we have fairly detailed accounts, which are also a useful baseline since guano had not yet had a major impact on public finances. The great jump in guano income came in the mid-1850s; in 1857 the income from guano alone was greater than total government revenues only three years earlier. In the rows for 1861–1866 we see the revenue structure after full development of the consignment system. Total income hovered around 20 million pesos, a fourfold increase over the level of 1846–1847, and guano's share had risen from 5 percent in that earlier biennium to no less than 75 percent in 1861–1866.[66]

Total income peaked in the early 1870s, when Peru was receiving full payments under both the expiring consignment contracts and the Dreyfus contract. Beginning in 1873, Dreyfus became virtually the only source of guano receipts, and those receipts were in decline thenceforth. During the height of the Guano Age, from 1869 to 1875, guano receipts averaged about 30 million pesos and customs another 7 million pesos. Total government revenues were little more than the sum of the two. Thus guano permitted budgetary expansion by a factor of about 8 in a space of twenty-five years, and the exchequer became almost completely dependent on income and taxes from foreign trade.

Dependence on foreign trade was created not just by expansion of the foreign sector but by a cutback in internal taxes as well. Early in the Guano Age, when guano income was rising so rapidly that it seemed certain to cover all future fiscal needs, it was only to be expected that unpopular internal taxes would be cut. Thus the *contribución de indígenas,* a head tax applied only to Indians, was abolished in 1855. With a stroke the progressivity of the tax system became greatly improved and a remnant of colonial exploitation was wiped out, but at the same time the major internal tax disappeared, ensuring that the fiscal crisis accompanying subsequent export collapse would be all the more severe.

The disappearance of the *contribución de indígenas* provides the main reason why "other income" in Table 5 declined so sharply between the 1840s and the 1860s. Since annual collections under this tax held fairly constant at 1.4 million pesos in the years before its abolition,[67] we may assume that tax income foregone from 1855 through 1877, when guano income dried up, would have been twenty-two times this annual figure, i.e., 30.8 million pesos. Since total guano income is variously estimated at from 381 to 432 million pesos, we conclude that the share of guano income devoted to tax relief for the poor was some 7–8 percent.[68]

The presence of guano income probably created additional unmeasurable erosion in other taxes as well, to the extent that pressures to increase rates or broaden bases remained weak while the bonanza lasted. One cannot proceed too far with what-might-have-been speculation, however, so first approximation must also be final conclusion—that about 7½ percent of guano income was used for tax substitution, leaving some 92½ percent for expenditure expansion. The important question is, which types of expenditures were expanded?

Table 6 gives the basic data for an answer. Taking 1846–1847 as the prebonanza norm, the most apparent effect of the guano bonanza is the enormous expansion of government expenditure in the following thirty years. Part of the expansion shown in the totals of Tables 5 and 6 is spurious, however, since the inclusion of loans received and loan repayments involves double counting. Most loans were devices for spending guano income before it was earned. Such income was counted once as a loan received and again as guano income used for the loan's repayment. Double counting would show up in expenditure as well; in fact, this double counting became multiple counting as loans were rolled over through increasingly complex refinancing. If we net out all debt repayments from the totals in Tables 5 and 6, the expansion of expenditure from 1847 to the peak years of 1872–1873 is about eight times, whereas expansion on the side of revenue is about five times.[69]

Not all debt repayment should be eliminated on the idea that it served merely as an instrument for separating moment of expenditure from moment of receipt. It has been argued that many loan repayments in fact consisted of transfers that never would have been made if the guano income had not existed. These transfer payments are a principal element of the view that the Peruvian exchequer dissipated its resources during the Guano Age.[70]

Nearly all such transfers involved the recognition of long-defaulted debts contracted during the wars of independence. Pressure to begin repayments began in the 1840s in England, and was directly triggered by the expanding guano sales that Peru was beginning to enjoy in the British market. When the Peruvian government reached accommodation with its British creditors in 1849, a repayment precedent was established and it was inevitable that old debts to other Latin American countries as well as to Peruvian citizens would also be honored. During the 1850s old debts were recognized and repayments begun with Chile, Ecuador, Colombia, and Venezuela. Furthermore, it was decreed that the various IOUs issued to Peruvian citizens by foraging armies and provisional governments would be validated by special tribunals and converted into a new internal consolidated debt. The casual way in which many such IOUs had been issued nearly always created some question regarding their validity, but it was further decided that validating tribunals should give nearly any claimant the benefit of the doubt.

The Peruvian government was subjected to significant diplomatic pressure in coming to terms with its British creditors.[71] In the case of these other debts, however, it is important to note the expansive manner in which the government agreed to assume substantial indebtedness. This open-handed manner substantiates the argument that debt assumption may be attributed directly to a guano psychology—that the debts would never have been paid off had there been no guano boom. The expansion of the internal consolidated debt was quite evidently based on corruption as well as expansiveness. Fraudulent claims rolled in with the real claims; the internal debt rose from 4,733,200 pesos in July 1850 to 19,154,200 pesos in October 1852.[72] Realizing the questionable nature of much of this newly created debt, the government feared that a future administration might repudiate it. To avoid this, in 1853 it entered into secret contracts with European financial houses whereby some 9 million pesos of the total debt was converted from internal to external debt. Secret contracts cannot be kept secret for long, however, and the ensuing public outrage triggered the Revolution of 1854. The triumphant revolutionary forces in turn established a tribunal of investigation that declared over 12 million pesos of the internal consolidated debt to be based on fraudulent claims.[73] Nevertheless, the debt was not repudiated.

Aside from these payments left over from the wars of independence, there is one other category of transfer for which it can be argued that payments would not have been made had the guano income not existed: the manumission payments to former slaveowners after abolition in 1854.

With the identification of these loans and the data in Table 6, we have on hand all the information necessary for estimating the uses of guano income. This information is put into some order in Table 7, which accounts for some 454 million pesos of guano-induced expenditure and tax remission. This figure exceeds our earlier estimates of guano income, but we must remember that the comparable figure of government income should include indirect as well as direct earnings from guano. That is, customs revenue must also be included, since it represents the principal tax collection derived from a guano-induced export multiplier. Judicious interpolation of the data in Table 5 permits the conclusion that in the Guano Age customs collections produced an additional 67 million pesos by rising above the 1847 level of 2 million pesos annually. This estimate puts total collections from guano, both direct and indirect, at between 448 and 499 million pesos. Our expenditure estimate sits right at the low end of this range, suggesting a possible shortfall of up to 45 million pesos. This discrepancy may be caused in part by loan-financed expenditures that did not make their way into the regular budget. The purchase of warships with part of the proceeds of the 1865 foreign loan is one such example. Nevertheless, we must recognize the roughness of the statistical exercise and conclude that the final correspondence between sources and uses of income is good.

By consolidating the headings of Table 7, we achieve a final summary on the uses of guano income:

For reducing the tax burdens of the poor	7 percent
For expanding the civilian bureaucracy	29 percent
For expanding the military bureaucracy	24.5 percent
For transfer payments to foreigners	8 percent
For transfer payments to Peruvians	11.5 percent
For investing in railroads	20 percent

Who, we may ask, are these people categorized as recipients of guano income? Where did they fit into the income distribution? We have identified the beneficiary of the tax cut to be the Indians, the poorest class in Peru. We do not care who the foreigners were, and as for railroads, we assume that Peru received value, in track laid, for value paid—i.e., that railroad expenditures were not disguised transfers. The Peruvian recipients of transfer payments were a mixed bag: they included former slaveowners paid off at a rate of 300 pesos per slave, but for the most part they were the holders of IOUs duly certified by the validating tribunals. The half of these holders who won their bonds through fraud are alleged to have succeeded by virtue of political connections. The other half, who had truly extended loans to revolutionary armies, may be presumed to have been people of some means in the 1820s and perhaps also in the 1850s. It is by no means certain that all the Peruvian recipients of transfer payments were wealthy in the 1850s, but even if they were, one must also note that they received only an eighth of total guano income. The argument that guano income was dissipated on the well-to-do, whose import propensities were very high, cannot be sustained on the basis of the social and economic characteristics of those who received transfer payments through public debt. After giving appropriate warning about the questionable accuracy of figures expressed to the nearest half percent, we still conclude that their share simply was not great enough. The enclave argument must instead rest either on the extrabudgetary income of Peruvian contractors or on the economic propensities of the civilian and military bureaucracy, for their share of the budget was clearly the most important.

Turning to the bureaucracy, we must ask what types of expenditure are included in the category. Table 8 gives part of the answer, drawing on the more detailed information to be found in budgets as opposed to audited accounts. Although the categories in this table fall far short of being clearly identifiable by income levels, it seems fairly certain that expenditure increments were not concentrated in the hands of the wealthy few. Pension payments jumped substantially, to be sure, but they had begun at so low a share that their increase consumed only a sixth of the total increment. As for salaries, we get the curious suggestion that top salaries were going down! This is seen by the decline of the generals' share, and is corroborated by salary changes among civilians. Here are some representative examples:

	1846–1847	1869–1870
Minister of government	7,000 pesos	5,548 pesos
Senior official in ministry	3,000	3,200
Clerk in ministry	600	560
Prefect of Lima	5,000	4,000
Clerk—post office	400	640
Porter—post office	180	288
Public prosecutor in Cuzco	2,400	2,400
Relator in Cuzco	800	1,200
Porter in Cuzco	180	144

In general, low salaries went up more than high salaries, but none seems to have gone up in real terms. Various inaccuracies are possible here; for example, the twentieth-century expertise at hiding salary increments in budget publications could already have been well developed before 1869. Nevertheless, prima facie evidence points to the conclusion that the civil service did not expand greatly in either numbers or real income, and that the expansion of military wage payments represented an increase in the number of men under arms rather than of the real wages of the officer class.

More than a third of the total increment falls into a residual civilian category that demands further classification. The 1869–1870 total divides up as follows:

Public works	1,345 (thousands of soles)
Education	969
Health *(beneficencias)*	374
Church	75
Other	243
Total	3,006

Here, then, were the first steps toward using the public purse as an instrument for promoting economic development.[74] Our numbers indicate that some 18–19 percent (i.e., 35 percent of 53.5 percent) of total guano income was devoted to public works alone. This share substantially exceeds the amount of transfer payments received by Peruvians through debt consolidation and manumission, yet the smaller flow is notorious while the larger is totally ignored. On such selection of data has been built the "black legend" of the Guano Age.[75]

It is time to sum up on guano. This extraordinary export sector was a nearly costless monopoly, but it was not an enclave. Over its hectic forty-year life, some 11–12 million tons were shipped to foreign farmers, fetching perhaps 750 million pesos in final sales.[76] From this total the Peruvian treasury received 381–432 million pesos in direct income, a share of 57–59 percent. Peruvian contractors may have received as much as 60–80 million pesos while they controlled the guano trade.[77] Therefore, total returned value comes out to be 65–71 percent of final sales value, a high figure that makes the guano export sector the antithesis of what we normally mean by the term enclave.

As we look down the list of uses for guano income, the recipients who might be expected to have a high propensity to import account for less than half the total. Foreign bondholders, Peruvian bondholders, government pensioners, and national contractors received perhaps 37–39 percent of the total guano income received in Peru.[78] Moreover, even if we suppose that all the commodities consumed by these groups were imported, their marginal propensity to import could not have been much above 0.5, since directly consumed services, distributional markups on imports, and housing would have covered the other half of the marginal peso. The conclusion is inevitable: Income generated by guano must have created a substantial demand for goods and services produced by the domestic economy. Aside from the evidence of income flows traced out in this chapter, more direct substantiation for this conclusion comes from the fact that domestic inflation proceeded apace during this period.[79] The lack of demand hypothesized in the enclave model distorts the reality of Peru in the Guano Age.[80]

IV

In setting aside the enclave model, we should not jump to the conclusion that the domestic economy was stimulated to a development that our twentieth-century eyes can view as satisfactory. Quite the contrary: the stereotypical view of low growth and wasteful, extravagant expenditure is probably correct. Data problems make it difficult to infuse any statistical rigor into this general perception. Nevertheless, we cannot leave the subject without attempting some remarks on the dimensions of economic growth during the Guano Age, and also on the contrast between actual and potential growth performance.

Did the Peruvian economy, for all its difficulties, actually grow during the Guano Age? Undoubtedly it did, since it began the period in a condition of such miserable poverty and prostration. "At Lima I was struck with the change that had taken place since my former visit," wrote the American Charles Wilkes on visiting Peru in 1839, eighteen years after an earlier sojourn.

> Every thing now betokens poverty and decay: a sad change from its former splendour and wealth. This appearance was observed not only in the city, but also in the inhabitants. . . . It may with truth be designated a declining city. The neglected walls and ruined tenements, the want of stir and life among the people, are sad evidences of this decay.[81]

Reviewing unpublished tax reports, Kubler wrote:

> The provincial tax collector [of Huamalíes] in 1842 lamented the disintegration of the economic life of the province, the moral decay of the citizenry, and the alarming degeneration of the standard of living since 1800. . . . In Conchucos the collector lamented the devastation of the province by Republican troops, and the decay of domestic markets for provincial produce, owing to the flooding of the economy by foreign imports.[82]

The possibility of economic growth from this backward starting level can be examined through trends in real wage rates, in regional distribution of the labor force, and in occupational structure. Available wage data are, to say the least, spotty. A survey of wages and prices undertaken in 1870 concluded that a free laborer had been paid 3–4 reales daily in 1854, and 6–8 reales in 1869.[83] By 1877, agricultural laborers around Lima were being paid 2 soles per day. The usually reliable Martinet adds that in the Sierra wages had not changed since 1854, but his estmate of 4–8 reales daily exceeds the 1854 levels for Lima.[84]

These wage figures have little meaning without deflation by a cost-of-living index. The best one we can manage builds on the food prices also reported in the 1870 survey. They indicate an overall price increase of less than 75 percent. Domestically produced products, when combined into an index using weights from a recent survey, show an increase of 76 percent over 1855–1869. When we introduce bread into the index and assume that its price held constant, since wheat import prices held constant during the period, then the cost-of-living increase comes out to only 32 percent.[85]

We therefore conclude very tentatively that real wages in Lima rose during this middle period of the Guano Age, and that this increase may have been as much as 50 percent over a fourteen-year span, or 3 percent per year.[86]

If real wages increased substantially, the increases should first have taken place in localities of particular economic expansion, causing laborers to migrate to those localities. Then wage increases would have diffused throughout the economy as internal migration tightened labor markets in more stagnant areas.

In fact, very little migration from low-wage to high-wage areas seems to have taken place during the nineteenth century. We are fortunate to have these areas well defined by special commissions that determined the going wage for common labor in every part of the country in 1866. Their efforts, which formed part of an abortive effort to impose an income tax on common laborers, were dutifully recorded by Rodríguez.[87]

In Table 9 this wage structure of 1866 is used to trace changes in the geographical distribution of the population, and implicitly of the labor force, from 1795 to 1940. The average national wage shown in the last line of the table varies only through shifts in the regional distribution of the labor force. These wage figures demonstrate that during the first half of the nineteenth century the Peruvian economy was going backward: the population increase in the low-wage subsistence economy of the Sierra was greater than in the high-wage coastal areas. Kubler reached the same conclusion through examining demographic change by caste rather than by region: "In general, changes in caste majority between 1826 and 1854 appear to be related to the alarming economic decline of early Republican government." A centuries-long trajectory of declining Indian share in total population was reversed, the Indian percent rising from 57.6 percent in 1795 to 59.3 percent in 1826–1854.[88]

In the period after 1850, however, population grew somewhat more rapidly in the high-wage areas. A part of this population increase resulted merely from the importation of Chinese coolies, but Table 9 indicates that the non-Asiatic population also shifted toward high-wage areas during the Guano Age. This means that the average real wage for the whole economy increased somewhat more than is indicated by wage increases specific to a particular region such as Lima.

However, the average wage increase induced by regional change was minuscule, averaging only about 0.2 percent per year from 1850 to 1862, and about the same from 1862 to 1876. Low as this rate was, it became even lower—about 0.1 percent per year—during 1876–1940. This result differs somewhat from Kubler's figures, which show that the annual rate of decrease in the Indian share of total population was somewhat more rapid in the 1876–1940 period.[89]

The occupational distribution of Lima's labor force is readily available for two years in the Guano Age, 1857 and 1876 (see Table 10). The changes in labor force composition over the intervening period give little indication of economic expansion. While Lima's population increased by 6 percent, the total labor force decreased by fully 17 percent. The decline of employment in industrial activities, from 9,267 to 8,519, is not surprising. Artisans had suffered considerably from import competition before 1857, and they found themselves in continuing competitive difficulty. The tailors and dressmakers of the apparel industry formed the largest occupational group in the industrial sector. The contraction in their numbers shows that while the tariff level given to ready-made clothing was generally the highest in the Peruvian tariff schedule, that level provided little protection to local industry.

The other major areas of employment contraction were commerce and personal services. Since the categories of cook and washerwoman accounted for the entire employment loss in personal services, there arose the suspicion that apparent changes in employment structure were in fact caused by definitional changes regarding part-time female workers. The separate tabulations of Table 10 for the male labor force were prepared to get around this problem. But the conclusion remains the same: Total employment went down while total population was going up.

The Fuentes statistics of 1857 include an estimate of 5,531 as the total number of adult males "without known profession or occupation." Since Fuentes suggests that "this figure can illustrate the state of morality among the people and the great number of individuals who live in idleness (*ociosidad*)," we may take this as an approximation of the total number unemployed. Even allowing for the inappropriate inclusion of some males who, for reasons of disability or *ociosidad*, were not actively seeking work, the resulting estimated unemployment rate of 16.1 percent is nevertheless startlingly high.[90] Since we have no sure idea of the age level used by Fuentes in defining the adult population, we attempt a similar estimate from 1876 data merely by assuming the adult male population to be the same percent of the total male population as it was in 1857. This assumption gives us an estimate of 7,967 adult males without employment *(sin profesión)* in 1876, and suggests that the unemployment rate rose over the period from 16.1 percent to 23.4 percent.[91] This evolution of Lima's labor force structure suggests economic stagnation.

Our three indicators of economic growth have therefore given us distinctly different signals. Changes in the regional composition of the labor force suggest growth rather than retardation, but they certainly indicate nothing better than a low and halting rate of growth. Confronted by two indicators of low growth or stagnation, the shaky estimates of increasing real wages seem very shaky indeed. We conclude tentatively, therefore, that any growth experienced by the Peruvian economy during the Guano Age was slow at best.

When we turn from growth realities to growth potential, our concern fixes on questions of surplus generation. Was the Peruvian economy able to generate a surplus of such size that, had it been invested productively, a substantial growth rate would have resulted? To answer this question we need an estimate of surplus generated as a percent of national product. The surplus estimate presents no difficulty. We are concerned particularly with the surplus represented by guano income, so guano income is our measure. Estimates of national product are come by with rather greater difficulty, however. The author has fearlessly supplied such an estimate, summarized in Table 11. The methodology is recounted in the appendix to this chapter, where it will be seen that the figures are based on current prices in 1877, and it is assumed that prices had doubled between 1866 and 1877. That gives us a quick fix on current price GNP in earlier years as well. Assuming no change in productivity and adjusting the 1877 figure only for changes in prices and size of labor force, the 1866 and 1870 GNP estimates come out to approximately 110 and 159 million soles, respectively.

The final sales value of guano, expressed as a percent of national product, comes to about 21, 19½, and 11½ percent in 1866, 1870, and 1877, respectively.[92] Since we want to examine the relative size of the available surplus, we should recall an earlier estimate that payments to the Peruvian government and private contractors amounted to about two thirds of final sales value, so these percentages should also be reduced by two thirds.

The potential of guano income to transform the domestic economy was progressively eroded by the increasing price of domestic products and factors relative to the price of guano. That is why the surplus/GNP ratio declined over time. Nevertheless the growth opportunities presented by guano income, particularly in the 1850s and 1860s, were quite evidently enormous. A 15 percent savings rate holds the potential for generating a 3–5 percent growth rate of GNP. It seems reasonably clear that Peru did not approach growth rates of this magnitude.

This conventional connection of savings rates to growth rates implies that the problems enbalmed in the concept of absorptive capacity have been resolved. It implies that an economy possesses the entrepreneurial skills, organizational experience, and social structure to use investment funds effectively. But these qualities were sadly lacking in nineteenth-century Peru. In fact, we shall argue in Part V that the guano experience, while it provided a resource surplus adequate for rapid growth, contributed to a long-term destruction of these other social and entrepreneurial qualities that constitute the *sine qua non* of both growth and development.

V

The low growth and wasteful expenditure that characterized Peru in the Guano Age in large part derived directly from the character of the guano sector. In purely economic terms, the trouble with the Peruvian economy was not that guano income bypassed the domestic economy. Rather it lay in what guano income did to the price-cost structure.

Possessing little of value besides its decaying silver mines, Peru lay relatively isolated from the world economy before the Guano Age. Then as guano income spread through the Peruvian economy, it raised domestic costs and prices and pushed consumers increasingly toward the purchase of imports. Imports flooded in as Peru experienced an abrupt and drastic change in comparative advantage.

The composition and magnitude of this flood has been traced out by Bonilla through French and British export data. From these sources, he found that Peruvian imports had expanded in the following trajectory:[93]

	Index of Total Imports (1840—1844 = 100)	French Share (%)	British Share (%)
1830–1834	60.9	26.5	73.5
1835–1839	73.7	10.2	89.8
1840–1844	100.0	14.0	86.0
1845–1849	137.7	24.6	75.4
1850–1854	216.7	37.3	62.7
1855–1859	276.4	48.5	51.5
1860–1864	281.5	47.3	52.7
1865–1869	284.8	41.4	58.6
1870–1874	452.4	37.9	62.1
1875–1878	273.9	38.6	61.4

Imports had expanded briskly through the 1830s and 1840s, averaging an annual increase of 5.6 percent from 1830–1834 to 1845–1849. But the flood really hit in the early 1850s. In the space of only four years, 1847 to 1851, import value nearly doubled; it maintained or exceeded that level for the rest of the Guano Age. More than anything else, the flood was a flood of textiles: British cottons, French silks, and woolens from both countries. These textiles accounted for fully 73 percent of total Anglo-French imports during 1840–1844, and 53 percent in 1850–1854, after the import spurt.

Import composition is elaborated from Peruvian sources in Table 12, which refers mostly to Callao alone.[94] Besides textiles, French wines and dresses figured prominently, particularly in the early years. French export specialties were such that France's share of total Peruvian imports seems a reasonable proxy for the luxury share. This share held fairly steady between 1857 and 1867, oscillating between 36 and 41 percent,[95] but by 1877 it was down to less than 20 percent.

The import bill diversified over the period. Textiles increased slightly in total value but their share declined from 45 percent in 1857–1859 to 30 percent in 1877.[96] The share of Chilean wheat, and European wines and liquors, also declined, from 13 percent and 9 percent respectively, in 1857 to 7 percent and 3 percent in 1877. The most marked expansion took place in the residual category labeled "Manufactures, etc."; its share nearly doubled, from 21 percent to 40 percent, between 1857 and 1877. The most important components in 1877 were coal (30 percent of the 6,430,000 soles of "Manufactures, etc.," imported into Callao), duty-free materials for public works (5.5 percent), pine boards (4.3 percent), candles (3.5 percent), paper (3.4 percent), iron bars and plates (3.4 percent), mercury (3.3 percent), and lubricating oil (2.2 percent).

The list of supplying countries also diversified. Britain, France (including Panama), and Chile furnished 88.6 percent of Callao's imports in 1857. By 1877 their share had receded to 70.5 percent, although Britain's share alone had risen from 29.8 to 43.4 percent. Among the suppliers of increased importance, Germany figured most prominently, its share having risen from an average of 6.0 percent for 1857–1859 to 9.6 percent for 1877. The U.S. share rose from 2.6 percent to 7.5 percent during the same time. Clearly U.S. export trade to Peru failed to reach the potential anticipated by the English consul Ricketts when he lamented the canny Yankee trader's competitive advantages in the 1820s.[97]

This import flood posed a mortal threat to every workshop producer of import substitutes. It precipitated a struggle over tariff policy that had begun in the earliest days of the Republic and resurged periodically throughout the century. The course of the struggle during the Guano Age becomes apparent in the tariff data of Table 13. The initial Reglamento de

Comercio of 1826 minced no words regarding protectionist intent. After setting a general 30 percent tariff level for most products, it stated: "Since the following articles are damaging to the national agriculture or industry, a tax of 80 percent is levied against them."[98] The list that followed consisted of *aguardiente* (grape brandy), soap, hats, wearing apparel, shoes, nitrates, horseshoes, sugar, coarse cotton and woolen cloth *(tocuyos* and *bayetones),* tobacco, cooking oil, candles, hides, and furniture. In short, any importable then produced in Peru.

Two forces combined to undermine the protectionist position. First, the customs authorities proved incapable of controlling smuggling and corruption in an environment that had made such activities extremely lucrative.[99] In 1828 the government shifted from high tariffs to outright prohibitions, the more easily to plug holes in the leaky wall of protection, but it was up against highly inventive smugglers. Yankee traders, for example, were able to add falsified marks of Peruvian manufacture to cotton cloth so that it was quite easily passed off as Peruvian *tocuyos.*[100]

Second, the power of free trade advocates, particularly merchants engaged in importing, proved irresistible. Their power derived partly from the enormous intellectual respectability of the doctrine of laissez-faire, which in the fullness of its influence could persuade a British consul to write: "[Peru] has no manufactures of the slightest consequence; it is not likely to have any conducted by natives for many years from not possessing any one of the essentials for their establishment, nor is it desirable to promote them."[101] The merchants' power also derived from financial strength. When in a moment of fiscal crisis the government turned to the major merchants of Lima, most of whom were British, it secured a measly advance only on condition that the merchants be allowed to draw up a new tariff schedule.[102] Faced with such pressure, the government's retreat from protectionism became a stampede.[103] The new Reglamento of 1833 reduced the list of prohibited articles. A decree of 1834 substituted a 45 percent tariff for the all-important prohibition on *tocuyos.*[104] When a new Reglamento was issued in 1836, the protectionist motivation in tariff setting had disappeared.

As the import flood swelled ever larger during the 1840s, the artisan classes increased pressure against the public authorities. Finally in 1849 Congress responded with a return to protectionism. Criticizing existing legislation as insufficient to keep out those competing imports, the law called for specific duties equivalent to 90 percent of the sale price of local substitutes.[105] This rate applied to all imports previously subject to *ad valorem* duties for which import substitutes were available.

The new protectionist structure lasted less than two years. A new Reglamento in October 1851 swept away tariff protectionism for the second time, and for the second time any protest from artisans, if it took place, has escaped the attention of historians.[106] With the collapse of this second effort at tariff protectionism, the import flood hit with full force. When the artisans did mount a protest worthy of historical notice, they did so in the streets rather than in the legislative chambers, through riots that swept both Lima and Callao in 1858. The carpenters and blacksmiths led the way, but members of the other major *gremios,* particularly the tailors and shoemakers, were also represented.[107]

The artisans could smash windows and frighten public officials, but ultimately they could do nothing to stop Peru's rapid march to a new pattern of comparative advantage based on guano. Through this march Peru became a rentier economy, exporting guano and importing virtually all manufactured products. This indeed was the efficient thing to do, but the adjustment could not be accomplished with the smooth reallocation of productive factors generally presumed in the abstractions of international trade theory. The factors released by the contracting artisan industries could not possibly be absorbed in an expanding guano industry. Any absorption in agriculture or the sectors producing non-traded goods has passed unnoticed. It is likely to have been limited by downward wage rigidity, since the employment alternatives available to artisans would have signified reduced income and social status. The result of such partial adjustment was chronic unemployment. This unfortunate outcome stemmed directly from the prevailing belief in the virtues of free trade.[109]

Some recent critics of free trade have singled out tariff policy as the key failure in nineteenth-century economic history. If tariffs had protected national industries, so the argument goes, then an industrial foundation would have been preserved, upon which subsequent industrial progress and higher living standards could have developed.[110] While it is easy to criticize the advocacy of free trade from more sophisticated twentieth-century perspectives, alternative policies must be specified carefully in light of the relation between tariffs and exchange rates. Tariffs could indeed have saved certain industries, but they also would have caused exchange rate appreciation and consequent erosion of real protection for other lines of production. Since it seems reasonable to suppose that guano production was totally insensitive to exchange rate variation, it follows that a given volume of foreign exchange was bound to be earned and spent during the Guano Age. Tariffs could have affected the composition of imports, but not the overall volume. Furthermore, any influence on composition would have been accomplished at a real welfare cost.

Across-the-board tariffs therefore would have served no purpose. The essence of tariff policy lay in tariff differentials that could have steered import demand toward products that did not compete with already existing national industry, particularly if that industry employed labor that would otherwise have gone unemployed.

Government policy influenced import composition in two ways during the Guano Age. In the first place, the blanket protection granted national industry in the 1820s and 1840s constituted differential protection, since Peru's artisans produced so limited a line of products. After 1851, however, when Peruvian governments apparently no longer felt obliged to give way before the protests of artisans, the tariff was distinguished by its uniformity. Even the riots of 1858 were followed merely by reductions in the new tariff of 1864. The Peruvian tariff, which was both moderate and uniform at the height of the Guano Age, served useful fiscal purposes but had a negligible allocative effect.[111]

The second means by which government altered the import composition was through direct purchase of imports for railroad construction. Indeed, any kind of investment program would have cut down demand for imports that competed with national industries, while at the same time increasing domestic productive capacity. Railroad investment diverted import demand almost completely, since virtually all inputs were imported and the domestic multiplier was negligible.

Only in this rather curious way could the railroad-building program be considered a success, however, for in terms of social return on investment outlay it was surely a disaster. We must make allowances for the spirit of the time. Throughout the world in the nineteenth century the railroad was viewed as the Great Civilizer, the harbinger of industrialization and economic progress. We must also remember Peru's particular difficulty with internal transport: it was a country scattered over the Andes, held together tenuously by the laborious efforts of mule trains. But even considering these factors, one must conclude that railroad expenditure was pursued with an incredible recklessness. Egged on by the pomp and flattery of Henry Meiggs, the Peruvian government resolved to push railroads through canyons and over heights the likes of which no locomotives ever traversed elsewhere, before or since. No matter that the Andean regions thus to be connected to the modern world were thinly populated and unproductive: the railroads would create their own markets. Two huge bond issues were floated in London, in 1870 and 1872. The expenditure thus financed was set forth in Table 6: railroad construction, not even in the government budget in 1867, by 1872 was consuming 57 percent of total expenditure! The debt service obligations were overwhelming. All guano income became earmarked to cover them, which put the government deficit out of control and made default inevitable. Work was suspended on all railroad construction in August 1875, and the foreign debt went into default on January 1, 1876. The Peruvian government had taken a tremendous gamble and lost.

Peru gambled that railroad-induced economic expansion would expand government revenues sufficiently to maintain solvency. But through what mechanisms could revenues thus expand? The tax system was very inelastic, since very little remained in the way of internal taxes; and import duties, although they did expand, simply could not support the fiscal needs of the nation. The revenue had to come from the operation of the railroads themselves.

Yet as early as 1872 there was ample evidence that the railroads would not make money. Operating rights for the Arequipa line, the first finished, were leased to Meiggs himself in 1870 for an annual rental payment only 3.6 percent of construction costs. By 1872 Meiggs was complaining of "enormous losses," which he attributed to the ruinous competition of mule trains! When the government offered him operation of the Ilo-Moquegua line at 3 percent later in the same year, Meiggs respectfully declined.[112]

Meiggs was only the most spectacular in a long line of foreign carpet-baggers who sold pie-in-the-sky to Peru. The unfortunate misdirection and low productivity that resulted from government investment leads us to another story, from which only one point need be made here: Poor selection of investment projects provides a major explanation for poor growth performance during the Guano Age.[113]

Policies working on the side of domestic supply could also have affected the composition of the import flood. Technical improvement would have made domestic industry more competitive and less needful of defense through tariff protection. Such improvement, however is, accomplished slowly at best. Commentators on the artisan riots of 1858 who rejected tariffs and instead urged programs of technical improvement in effect offered nothing to the artisans. This is also what the government offered. Vocational training was to be advanced through a new Escuela de Artes y Oficios, but schools of this sort could have only a minuscule impact on the average artisan's skill level and need for tariff protection.[114] The technological gap between Europe and Peru loomed so enormous that many thoughtful observers concluded that domestic industry was doomed and Peru's future lay with agriculture.

Peru in the Guano Age, then, was not an enclave economy but a rentier economy, as it had been during its colonial experience when the rents were generated from silver instead of guano. The rentier economy is characterized by its ability to earn enormous amounts of foreign exchange through the exploitation of abundant natural resources.[115] The fundamental problem of a rentier economy lies in its tendency toward chronic disequilibrium between the exchange rate and wage rates. Foreign exchange earnings are so abundant that the exchange rate cannot depreciate. At the same time the normal resistance to the lowering of wage rates is made all the stronger by the new consumption standards set by the beneficiaries of the export bonanza. Caught between increased import competition and irreducible costs, import-substituting industries are squeezed, and no other sector can expand employment to take up the slack. High unemployment rates characterize the rentier economy.

These curiously pernicious effects of an export bonanza are particularly manifest in the early stages of natural resource development, during the transition in comparative advantage. Whereas at a later stage abundant foreign exchange earnings may merely inhibit the development of domestic industry, the early transitional phase witnesses the destruction of old lines of domestic production, along with their accumulation of inherited labor skills. Such was the case of Peru in the Guano Age. Foreign influences and foreign entrepreneurs invaded the Peruvian economy at a moment of particular weakness on the part of domestic entrepreneurs. Foreign merchants, exploiting to the full their knowledge of overseas sources of supply, soon came to dominate the import trade. Attempts to defend domestic enterprise from such competition, either in commerce or in the goods imported by that commerce, were undermined by the widespread adoption of laissez-faire ideology.

Perhaps the most pernicious effect of the rentier economy, and also the most difficult to document, is psychological. In the rentier economy wealth is generated merely by ownership, not by effort. Guano merely provided another phase of a centuries-long history during which the upper classes of Peru had lived as rentiers, not as entrepreneurs. An urban society grown accustomed to owning silver mines and owning Indians acquired another asset in the collective ownership of guano. It is hardly surprising that such a society offered little complaint against the incursions of foreign merchants or foreign influence. In the caustic words of Duffield, "Idleness among the upper classes, i.e., the whole white population, . . . is the order of the day, and is punished by no one."[116]

The rentier psychology spawned a wastefulness and extravagance in both private and public expenditure. Lima's rich, who had hardly been in touch with Europe a generation earlier, quickly adopted the finery of London and Paris as the *sine qua non* of proper dress and well-appointed home. The zenith of conspicuous consumption was reached on festive occasions, and historians have preserved the gory details. At one dance in 1873 the ladies' gowns and jewels, all obtained specially in Europe, cost from 10,000 to 50,000 soles.[117] Even more lavish was the inauguration of the Arequipa railway, an eight-day celebration for which four ships were chartered so that eight-hundred of Lima's governmental and social elite might attend.[118]

The negative moral judgment generally placed upon Peru in the Guano Age rests on the contrast between such excesses of consumption and the condition of the impoverished masses, Chinese coolies, and Indian peasants.[119] It also rests on the fact that the Peruvian nation turned out to be disastrously unprepared for the crisis that followed. Smashed by a relentless foe, both its economy and its polity were reduced to a shambles.

We conclude, then, that the growth opportunities of the nineteenth century were lost partly through the destruction of the artisan class, which could have contributed greatly to the supply of entrepreneurs needed for more advanced stages of development; partly through the shift in comparative advantage, which reinforced a rentier psychology; partly through poor choice of projects for available investment funds; and partly through the failure of traditional institutions to provide the organizational structure required for more advanced stages of production, particularly in the case of mining.[120] Many conscientious Peruvian officials grappled with these obstacles, and in many cases they scored minor victories. But in the end no human effort could accomplish the massive transformations required to put Peru on a path of rapid growth. In 1895 Peru entered a new century of opportunity, still profoundly poor and underdeveloped. The nineteenth century was over, and its opportunities were gone.

APPENDIX

Estimation of National Income, 1876–1877

The national income estimate set forth in Table 11 devolved from three basic sources: the census of 1876, which provides an occupational distribution of the labor force; a scattering of data on the daily wage for common labor *(jornales);* and tax reports on business and rental income. The roughness of the estimates will become apparent as the compilation methodology is explained.

Wages of **Jornaleros** *and Others.* In 1877 the going *jornal* around Lima was estimated at 2.00 soles by Martinet. In 1866 it had been 0.80 soles.[121] Mindful of the casual nature of Martinet's comment, I assume that *jornales* merely doubled between 1866 and 1876–1877, not only in Lima but in the whole country. The wage levels used in Table 9 are therefore doubled.

These wage levels are applied not only to *jornaleros* but also to all other occupations assumed to have incomes equal to those of *jornaleros.* Both male and female *agricultores* are included; for other occupations, only males are considered here. The labor force of particular occupations is as follows:

Agricultores (agriculturalists)	513,277
Cascarilleros (quinine bark gatherers)	1,566
Chacareros (tenant farmers)	25
Domésticos (servants)	20,552
Ganaderos (herders)	15,546
Gañanes (field hands)	50
Labradores and *Jornaleros* (laborers)	153,771
Marineros (sailors)	4,557
Mayordomos (estate managers)	309
Mineros (miners)	6,144
Operarios (workers)	2,169
Pastores (shepherds)	20,530
Peones and *Obreros* (laborers)	85
Pescadores (fishermen)	4,276
Tejedores (weavers)	46,862
Yanacones (sharecroppers)	5(!)
Total	789,724

This labor force was allocated to the various regions defined by the wage structure of Table 9, multiplied by the appropriate regional *jornal,* and then multiplied by 260 to arrive at a figure for total annual wage payments (260 equals 5 days per week, 52 weeks per year). The resulting figure, 115,365,120 soles, constitutes about half of national income and includes all agricultural income except rents and a return on capital in the sugar industry.

Wages of Female Workers in Low-Paid Occupations. In recent years the agricultural *jornal* for women has averaged about two-thirds the level for men.[122] The female labor force in the following occupations is assumed to have received a *jornal* two-thirds the level of the male *jornal* for the corresponding region:

Cocineras (cooks)	9,292
Costureras (seamstresses)	44,376
Domésticas (servants)	19,266
Jornaleras and *labradoras* (laborers)	60,329
Lavanderas (washerwomen)	14,796
Pastoras (shepherdesses)	18,726
Total	166,785

Total annual income of this group, again assuming 260 work days per year, comes to 16,204,240 soles.

Hilanderas. The number of *hilanderas* (female spinners) listed in the census is so extraordinarily high—167,778—that one suspects it denotes a largely part-time employment of rural housewives. Accordingly, it is assumed that *hilandera* income was only half the going *jornal,* and that all *hilanderas* were located in the low-wage Sierra. Annual income therefore averaged 59 soles for this group, again on the assumption of 260 work days per year, and total annual income comes to 9,898,902 soles.

Business Income. Under the *contribución de patentes* and *contribución industrial,* business firms were required to pay taxes equaling 4 percent of their estimated annual income. The tax rolls *(matrículas)* recorded total tax liabilities as follows:[123]

	Patentes (in soles)	Contribución Industrial (in soles)
1850	70,663	84,580
1851	67,842	—
1853	63,322	—
1864	96,017	38,157
1871	314,634	45,451
1872	185,900(!)	50,000
1874	432,000	82,623

There *matriculas* should receive several adjustments in order to provide reliable estimates of total business income. First, although there was some updating every year, at any given moment many *matrículas* in force had been drawn up years before at lower price and income levels. Second, the size of the gap between tax assessment and actual income remains a mystery. Third, further write-up to 1877 price levels is required. Only this last adjustment can be accomplished, by using the 1874 figures increased by 30 percent. The final figure, multiplied by 25 to convert tax liability into tax base, comes to 16,725,248 soles.

Income of Poorer Artisans. Most of the apparently erratic changes in *patente* liabilities can be explained. The huge jump between 1864 and 1871 was caused by the inclusion of commercial activities within the tax net as of 1870.[124] The decline in liabilities in the early 1850s was caused by the exemption of artisans with incomes under 200 pesos per year.[125] Rodríguez provides us with a list of fifty-two artisan occupations thus exempted from taxation.[126] Forty-three of these were recorded in the 1876 census, which numbered 5,620 artisans in Lima and 70,757 in the provinces.

I assume that the income of artisans in these exempted trades actually averaged 200 pesos per year. This implies a *jornal* of 0.77 soles, again assuming 260 work days. Basadre reports that in 1854 *jornales* stood at 3 to 4 reales in Lima, or 0.375 soles to 0.50 soles.[127] I assume, then, that income in these trades was twice the *jornal* in 1877 as well. This implies an annual income of 832 soles per artisan in Lima and 4,675,840 soles for the 5,620 artisans as a group.

Table 9 shows the average *jornal* to have been 0.290 soles in 1876. A separate average calculated for Peru without Lima produces a figure of 0.259 soles, which is 32.4 percent of Lima's *jornal* of 0.80 soles. I assume that this provinces/Lima ratio applies to these forty-three artisan groups as well. Total income for those outside Lima therefore comes to 19,025,300 soles.[128]

Income of Other Workers Not Yet Accounted For. Thus far we have accounted for the following elements of the labor force:

Farmers and male laborers	789,724
Female workers in lowly-paid occupations	166,785
Hilanderas (female spinners)	167,778
Business taxpayers	?
Poorer artisans—Lima	5,620
Poorer artisans—provinces	70,757
Total	1,200,664
Total labor force	1,308,495
Government employees	9,729
Private-sector labor force still unaccounted for	98,102

Some of this unaccounted-for labor force is already included in the taxpaying group. A high estimate for the number so included could be derived from assuming that if the average income of poor artisans was twice the *jornal,* then, on average, taxpaying artisans should have earned at least four times the *jornal.* Eighty-four percent of this income was taxed by *patentes,* and 76 percent of *patentes* were collected in Lima.[129]

Therefore we have:

Taxed income earned in Lima	64 percent of total[30]	10,704,159 soles
Taxed income earned in provinces	Remainder	6,021,089
Total		16,725,248

Four times the Lima *jornal* gives 1664 soles per year for 1877. Assume that provincial artisans earned half of what Lima's did, i.e., 832 soles per year. Then the number of such artisans was:

Lima	6,433
Provinces	7,237
Total	13,670

Therefore a low estimate of the private-sector labor force still unaccounted for is given by 98,102 − 13,670, or 84,432. A quick survey disclosed that only perhaps 10 percent of these workers were located in Lima; hardly any were in agriculture. The only place left was provincial towns and cities. The only such town included separately in the 1866 wage data was Cerro de Pasco, with a *jornal* of 0.40 soles. We double this figure to convert into 1877 wage levels, and add 50 percent over this *jornal* level as an estimate of average income for this residual category. Total income for the group is thus set at 26,342,784 soles.[131]

Government Employees. Wage payments were extracted, as best they could be identified, from the 1875–1876 budget, as follows:[132]

Ordinary Budget	7,367,210 soles
Extraordinary Budget	1,916,754
"Ultimas Partidas" (last minute items)	152,133
total	9,436,097 soles

Rental income. Under the *contribuciones de predios rústicos y urbanos* (rural and urban property taxes), landowners were required to pay taxes equaling 4 percent of rental income from both rural and urban property. The *matrículas* recorded tax liabilities as follows:[133]

	Rusticos	Urbanos
1850	106,662 soles	49,464 soles
1864	89,891	71,708
1871	179,728	95,613
1872	126,000 (!)	69,300 (!)
1874	227,000	192,000

The same three corrections required of *patentes* are also required here. This time we can do somewhat better. For example, the 1871 *matrícula* contains provincial totals, with the date of *matrícula* formation given for each province.[134] About 8 percent of total evaluations were established during the 1850s, 34 percent during 1861–1866, and the remainder during 1868–1871. If we assume that prices and wages increased by about 40 percent during 1866–1871 and write up the value of early *matrículas* by that amount, this implies a 17 percent increase in the national total.[135]

With regard to the gap between assessments and market value, many commentators felt that the degree of undervaluation was scandalous.[136] Nevertheless comparison with wage income in certain provinces produces functional income shares that seem at least plausible. For example, 1871 estimates of the rental share produced figures of 23 percent for Chiclayo and 18 percent for Arica-Tacna. By contrast, Garland estimated the nonlabor share of sugar income to be 32 percent in 1895.[137] This figure includes returns on a substantial capital investment.

The *matrículas* for certain provinces *were* scandalous, however. Lambayeque's population was double that of neighboring Chiclayo, for example, yet its total *matrícula* was only 5 percent of Chiclayo's. Ica apparently had no reported assessments at all.[138] A survey of coastal assessments per capital revealed two other provinces with implausibly low *matrícula* totals. Raising these four provinces to plausible levels increased the total coastal assessment by 28 percent. This adjustment was applied to national totals as an allowance for undervaluation.

Finally, regarding price increases to 1877, it will be noted that the presumed 100 percent price and wage increase from 1866 to 1877 implies an annual increase of some 6.5 percent. The national *matrícula* of *predios rústicos* increased by about 8 percent per year during 1871–1874. We project that increase, 26 percent for a three-year period, for 1874–1877 as well.

The adjusted national *matrícula* total for 1877 is therefore 427,320 soles.[139] It implies total rural rents, 25 times greater, i.e., 10,683,000 soles.

As for urban rents, the *matrículas* require all the adjustments just performed for rural rents. In the absence of further information, the same adjustment factors are applied. Therefore the ratio of urban and rural rental income in 1877 is assumed to be the same as the ratio of unadjusted urban and rural *matrícula* totals in 1871. Urban rents are therefore put at 53 percent of rural rents, or 5,661,990 soles.

Income from Capital in Agriculture. Only the sugar industry is considered. Garland estimated total investment to have been 30,000,000 soles in 1875.[140] At a 5 percent return, this gives an annual income of 1,500,000 soles.

TABLE 1
INDEXES OF EXPORT QUANTUM, 1830–1900
(1900 PRICES; 1900 TOTAL EXPORTS = 100)

	1830	1840*	1850*	1860*	1870*	1878	1880	1890*	1900
Sugar	0.4	0.4	0.5	0.2	3.5	17.6	15.6	11.7	30.1
Cotton	0	0.6	0.1	0.3	2.1	2.0	2.4	4.2	7.3
Wool	0	3.7	3.8	5.6	7.0	7.1	2.7	7.3	7.1
Guano	0	0.3	22.3	33.1	69.0	55.8	0	1.9	1.3
Nitrates	0.1	1.4	3.5	9.3	17.4	38.1	0	0	0
Silver	5.4	11.1	10.0	7.6	9.6	8.5	7.1	9.1	25.1
Total	10	24	49	65	115	145	35	48	100
Total less guano and nitrates	10	22	23	22	28	51	35	47	99
Total annual growth rates over preceding period		9.2%	7.4%	2.9%	5.9%	2.9%	−50.9%	3.2%	7.6%
Total less guano and nitrates		8.2%	0.4%	−0.4%	2.4%	7.8%	−30.3%	3.0%	7.7%

SOURCE: Shane Hunt, "Price and Quantum Estimates of Peruvian Exports, 1830–1962," RPED Discussion Paper no. 33, Princeton University, January 1973, Table 24.
*Three-year averages.

TABLE 2
TERMS OF TRADE, 1855–1900
(1900 = 100)

Net Barter Terms of Trade

	1870 Weights	1900 Weights
1855	188.0	180.0
1860	191.5	178.9
1870	197.9	166.3
1880	174.1	160.2
1890	124.0	149.9
1900	100.0	100.0

Income Terms of Trade

	1870 Weights*	1900 Weights*
1855	154.2	147.6
1860	149.4	139.5
1870	255.3	214.5
1880	60.9	56.1
1890	53.3	64.5
1900	100.0	100.0

SOURCE: Unpublished study by Doris Garvey, Princeton University.
*Quantum index contains 1900 weights in both cases.

TABLE 3
DISTRIBUTION OF FACTOR PAYMENTS FROM GUANO SALES, 1840–1877
(THOUSANDS OF PESOS BEFORE 1863,
THOUSANDS OF SOLES AFTER 1863)

Contract	Gross Sales	Government Profit	Total Costs*	Contractors' Commissions[†]
8 contracts 1840–1849	16,781	5,518 (33%)	—	—
Gibbs Contract 1849–1861	89,055	57,703 (65%)	20,665 (23%)	10,687 (12%)
15 contracts 1850–1859	94,230	61,675 (65%)	21,785 (23%)	5,770 (6%)
1869 (A)	32,197	20,157 (63%)	12,040 (37%)	
1869 (B)	36,351	8,105 (22%)	28,246 (78%)	
1870	40,593	24,419 (60%)	16,174 (40%)	
Dreyfus Contract 1869–1878	139,911	143,106 (102%)		
1872 (Consignment contracts)	62.76 per ton	38.78 per ton (62%)		
1877 (Raphael contract)	47.72 per ton	20.32 per ton (43%)		

SOURCES: 1840–1849 government profit and annual prices on sales from J. M. Rodríguez, "Historia de los contratos . . . ," pp. 90–91. Annual tonnage from Hunt, "Price and Quantity Estimates . . . ," Table 21. 1849–1861 figures from Rodríguez, "Historia de los contratos . . . ," pp. 95, 103. 1869 (A) figures from Perú, Ministerio de Hacienda y Comercio Inspección Fiscal del Perú en Europa, *Oficio dirigido al Señor Ministro de Hacienda y Comercio . . . durante el eño 1869* (Lima, 1870). 1869 (B) and 1870 figures from Emilio Dancuart, *Anales de la hacienda pública del Perú*, VIII, 21. Dreyfus Contract figures from Table 4 of this chapter. Gross sales equals the sum of column 2 times column 3; government profit is the sum of column 4. 1872 figures from Perú, Ministerio de Hacienda y Comercio, *Memoria que presenta el Director de Rentas al Señor Ministro de Hacienda y Comercio*, 1872. 1877 figures from Perú, Ministerio de Hacienda y Comercio, *Memoria presentada al Ministro de Hacienda y Comercio por el Director General de Rentas*, 1878.

*Costs include extraction, loading, ocean freight, unloading, storage in foreign deposits, and interest charges on these costs.

†Contractors' commissions include brokerage fees, premiums, and interest on advances.

TABLE 4
DREYFUS CONTRACT, 1870–1878

Year	Tonnage Shipped (1)	Tonnage Sold (2)	Estimated Sale Price (Soles per ton) (3)	Payments from Dreyfus (thousands of soles) (4)	Net End-Year Indebtedness to Dreyfus (thousands of soles) (5)
1870	30,526	6,391	70	18,515*	13,285[†]
1871	221,044	48,031	70	26,882	27,209
1872	399,029[‡]	42,792	70	29,709	19,990
1873	235,985	342,425	70	20,715	24,262
1874	408,830	336,476	70	21,194	14,516
1875	219,810	373,688	52.1 (59.5)	13,853	21,702
1876	521,080	488,285	41.4 (53.2)	9,052	17,597
1877	305,329	336,265	42.0 (53.5)	3,186	12,727
1878 and later	—	362,278	42.0 (53.5)	—	—

SOURCES: *Tonnage:* 1870–1875 from Perú, Ministerio de Hacienda y Comercio, Inspector Fiscal en Europa, *Informe dirijido al Señor Ministro de Hacienda y Comercio del Perú* (Lima, 1876), p. 26. 1876–1877 shipments from E. Dancuart, *Anales de la hacienda pública del Perú,* X, pp. 59–60. 1876–1877 sales from Perú, Ministerio de Hacienda y Comercio, *Memoria presentada al Ministro de Hacienda y Comercio por el Director General de Rentas,* 1878. *Prices:* Miguel Cruchaga, *Salitre y guano* (Madrid, 1929), pp. 220–227, esp. p. 225. 1875–1877 calculated from decline in gross value per ton, in Perú, Ministerio de Hacienda y Comercio, *Memoria que presenta el Director de Rentas al Ministro de Hacienda* (Lima, 1876), and *Memoria presentada al Ministerio de Hacienda y Comercio por el Director General de Rentas* (Lima, 1878). Alternative figures for 1875–1877 calculated from price of approximately 240 francs per ton (c.i.f.?) earned by Lobos-Pabellón guano instead of normal 312.5. See Inspector Fiscal en Europa, *Informe dirijido al Señor Ministro.* Estimates bracket 47.72 soles sale price earned in 1877 under Raphael contract. See Dirección General de Rentas, *Memoria,* 1878. *Payments and Indebtedness:* 1869–1870 from E. Dancuart, *Anales de la hacienda pública del Perú,* VIII, p. 39. The 1871 payments from Perú, Ministerio de Hacienda, *Cuenta de ingresos de la Dirección de Renta correspondientes al servicio de 1871 y 1872* (Lima, 1872). The 1872–1877 payments and 1871–1877 indebtedness from Perú, Ministerio de Hacienda y Comercio, *Memoria presentada al Ministro de Hacienda y Comercio por el Director General de Rentas* (Lima, 1818).
*Covers the period September 1869–August 1870.
[†]September 1, 1870.
[‡]Includes 185,234 tons transferred from deposits of other contractors at the end of 1872.

TABLE 5
GOVERNMENT REVENUES DURING THE GUANO AGE, 1846–1877
(THOUSANDS OF PESOS/SOLES BEFORE 1863)

Year	Customs	Guano	Loans	Other Income	Total
1846	1,608	513	—	3,992	6,113
1847	2,006	—	—	2,999	5,005
1851	2,225	2,194	—	3,218	7,636
1852	3,112	3,295	—	2,292	8,699
1861	3,252	16,922	—	1,072	21,246
1862	3,257	13,985	1,198	1,510	19,949
1863	3,510	11,167	9,830	1,727	26,235
1866	3,904	13,566	—	2,658	20,128
1868	3,525	21,256	5,574	2,015	32,370
1869	4,659	15,288	17,681	4,608*	42,236
1871	6,213	42,716[†]	—	2,252	51,181
1872	7,416	34,566[‡]	21,167	4,839	67,987
1873	8,263	50,026[‡]	6,936	2,485	67,710
1876	5,542	25,364[‡]	8,306	5,034[§]	44,246
1877	6,885	6,545[‡]	1,178	7,892[§]	22,500

SOURCES: The 1846–66 figures from Dancuart, *Anales de la hacienda pública del Perú*, IV, 122–124; VIII, 129, 132–134. The 1868–1869, 1872–1873, and 1876–1877 figures from Perú, Ministerio de Hacienda, *Memoria*, Anexo no. 3, *Memoria de la Dirección de Contabilidad y Crédito* (Lima, 1870, 1874, 1878). 1871 figures from Perú, Ministerio de Hacienda, *Cuenta de ingresos de la Dirección de Rentas correspondientes al servicio de 1871 y 1872* (Lima, 1872).

*Includes 3,227 comprising two ambiguous entries that could be loans.
[†] Includes 15,834 from consignment contracts and 26,882 from Dreyfus.
[‡] Includes advances made on guano as well as current earnings on guano. Advances in 1872 were 12,454 from consignments and 11,509 from Dreyfus; in 1873, 5,126 and 24,326, respectively; in 1876, 7,987 and 858, respectively, plus 2,659 from the Raphael Contract; in 1877, 1,210, 1,292, and 3,500, respectively.
[§] Includes 3,710 from nitrates in 1876, 5,298 in 1877.

TABLE 6
GOVERNMENT EXPENDITURE DURING THE GUANO AGE, 1846–1877
(THOUSANDS OF PESOS/SOLES)

Year	General Government	Foreign Affairs	Justice, Education, Welfare	Armed Forces	Railroads	Financial Administration	Finance		Total
							Internal Debt	External Debt	
1846–1847*	1,111	217	394	2,239	—	568	888	545	5,962
1851†	1,325	119	926	3,113	—	832	537	748	7,599
1852†	1,211	107	746	3,095	—	748	944	1,528	8,378
1861	2,035	429	1,093	10,285	—	622	1,589	3,393	21,446
1862	2,469	316	1,122	10,015	—	1,340	1,065	3,379	19,707
1863	6,083	264	2,067	8,484	—	2,078	1,157	5,530	25,663
1866	4,894	91	975	7,906	—	1,520	794	3,275	19,558
1868	3,203	322	1,437	7,131	5,000	2,144	2,139	286	26,112‡
1869	4,254	362	2,113	6,977	3,003	2,002	11,741	13,036	48,703‡
1872	5,879	284	2,486	5,719	27,805	6,279	14,000§	27,131§	89,997‖
1873	4,504	233	2,339	5,933	16,873	7,727	13,589¶	28,253¶	90,574‖
1876	5,073	390	683	5,613	485	7,967	10,157	17,214	47,582
1877	6,338	268	886	6,240	—	2,438	2,246	2,462	20,878

Sources: For 1846–1866, Dancuart, *Anales de la hacienda pública del Perú*, IV, 60–69; V, 210, 61–65; VIII, 132–34; Perú *Ministerio de Hacienda, Memoria* (Lima, 1867), p. 78; for 1868–1869, 1872–1873, and 1876–1877, Ministerio de Hacienda, *Memoria*, Anexo no. 3, *Memoria de la Dirección de Contabilidad y Crédito* (Lima, 1870, 1874, 1878); for 1871, Ministerio de Hacienda, Dirección de Rentas, *Cuenta de ingresos de la Dirección de Rentas correspondientes al servicio de 1871 y 1872* (Lima, 1872).

*Budgeted figures.
† Nonmilitary salaries distributed by prorating budget totals.
‡ Includes 4,452 in 1868 and 5,215 in 1869, which defied allocation to any category.
§ Internal debt includes 11,332 paid to guano contractors; external debt includes 19,247 paid to Dreyfus.
¶ Internal debt includes 11,820 paid to guano contractors; external debt includes 26,921 paid to Dreyfus.
‖ Includes unallocated contingent expenditure of 414 in 1872 and 11,123 in 1873.

TABLE 7
USES OF GUANO INCOME, 1847–1878
(THOUSANDS OF PESOS/SOLES)

Exhaustive Expenditure	Total Expenditures 1847–1878	Less 1847 Level 1847–1878	Total Incremental Expenditures
General government, foreign affairs, justice	147,500	44,800	93,100
Armed forces	181,700	70,400	111,300
Financial administration	—	—	37,300*
Railroads	91,900†	—	91,900†

Debt	Amortization through 1869	Interest through 1869	Outstanding Balance end of 1869	Total
Anglo-Peruvian	17,429	8,687	1,771	27,887
Other Latin American countries	6,021	1,443	1,400	8,864
Internal consolidated	22,540	7,353	1,527	31,419
External conversion of internal consolidated	7,809	3,819	672	12,300
Manumission	7,320	1,488	342	9,149
Expenditure				423,200
Plus remission of *Contribución de Indígenas*				30,800
Grand total				454,000

SOURCES: For exhaustive expenditure, see Table 6. Figures for debt are the author's compilations, derived from Perú, Ministerio de Hacienda, *Memoria,* various issues between 1855 and 1863, also Perú, Ministerio de Hacienda, *Memoria,* 1870, Anexo No. 3, *Memoria de la Dirección de Contabilidad y Credito,* and Dancuart, *Anales de la hacienda pública del Perú,* V, 43–44; VI, 67; VII, 97–104, 107.
*The figures in Table 6 for 1872–1876 are inflated by inclusion of many expenses of guano contractors; these are disregarded in this calculation.
†The figures for 1870, 1871, 1874 and 1875, not included in Table 6, are 3,600, 17,600, 9,200, and 5,500, respectively. Also included is 2,800 in principal and interest on foreign loan for Arica-Tacna line, built in the 1850s.

TABLE 8
DETAIL OF GOVERNMENT EXPENDITURE,* 1846–1870
(THOUSANDS OF PESOS/SOLES; BUDGETED FIGURES)

	1846–1847 (one year)	1869–1870 (one year)	Increment	Percentage Distribution of Increment
Civilian government				
Salaries	1,506	2,155	649	8
Pensions	97	208	111	1
Materials	331	84	− 247	− 3
Other	354	3,006	2,652	35
Military (including police)				
Generals	134	109	− 25	0
Other salaries	1,581	3,437	1,856	24
Pensions	299	1,454	1,155	15
Materials	151	1,369	1,218	16
Other	75	382	307	4
Total	4,528	12,204	7,676	100

SOURCE: Dancuart, *Anales de la hacienda pública del Perú*, IV, 60–69; VIII, 174–193.
*Not including debt payments or railroads.

TABLE 9
REGIONAL DISTRIBUTION OF POPULATION, 1795–1940

Wage Categories*	1940	1876	1876 (except Asians)	1862	1850	1795
1. 0.80 soles per day						
Total population	645,172	155,486	142,054	121,806	93,468	62,910
percentage share	10.4	5.8	5.4	4.9	4.7	5.3
2. 0.60 soles per day						
Total population	33,955	18,639	14,664	9,670	5,349	3,334
percentage share	0.6	0.7	0.6	0.4	0.3	0.3
3. 0.50 soles per day						
Total population	147,839	58,684	46,352	68,066	38,981	26,561
percentage share	2.4	2.2	1.8	2.8	1.9	2.2
4. 0.40 soles per day						
Total population	599,467	312,736	293,212	232,845	143,644	136,720
percentage share	9.7	11.6	11.1	9.5	7.2	11.5
5. 0.30 soles and soles 0.20 per day†						
Total population	4,781,534	2,153,561	2,151,638	2,029,549	1,719,681	956,067
percentage share	77.0	79.7	81.3	82.4	85.9	80.7
Total population	6,207,967	2,699,106	2,647,920	2,461,936	2,001,123	1,185,592
percentage share	100	100	100	100	100	100
Average wage (soles per day)	0.313	0.290	0.285	0.281	0.274	0.285

SOURCES: For 1795, Manuel Fuentes, ed., *Memorias de los Virreyes que han gobernado el Perú* (Lima, 1859), "Memoria" by Gil de Taboada y Lemos, Appendix, pp. 1–9; for 1850, Kubler, *The Indian Caste of Peru*, p. 34; for 1862, Pedro M. Cabello, *Guia política, eclesiástica, y militar del Perú para el año de 1871*, pp. 78–82; for 1876, Perú, Dirección General de Estadística, *Censo general de la República del Perú formado en 1876*, 7 vols. (Lima, 1878); for 1940, Perú Dirección Nacional de Estadística, *Censo nacional de población y ocupación 1940* (Lima, 1944), Vol. I, Table 1. Wage categories established in 1866 for implementing *contribución personal;* reprinted in J. M. Rodríguez, *Estudios económicos y financieros*, pp. 259–260.
*Provinces included in various categories: 1, Lima and Callao; 2, Santa; 3, Cañete and Chancay; 4, Trujillo, Chiclayo, Pacasmayo, Lambayeque, Huarochirí, Department of Ica, and Department of Moquequa, including Tacna-Arica and Tarapacá. The city of Cerro de Pasco was originally included in fourth group, but is not here for lack of data.
† 1876 weighted average of 0.30 soles and 0.20 soles, 0.228 soles, used for all years.

TABLE 10
OCCUPATIONAL DISTRIBUTION OF LABOR FORCE
IN DISTRICT OF LIMA, 1857–1876

	Male Labor Force[†]		Total Labor Force	
	1857	*1876**	*1857*	*1876**
1. Agriculture and livestock	1,381	1,298	1,476	1,324
Of which peones	(878)	(653)	(949)	(677)
2. Fishing	30	36	40	39
3. Mining	56	32	56	32
4. Industry				
Textiles	74	90	76	99
Leather products	318	180	319	180
Wood products	77	80	77	80
Metal products	689	776	689	776
Ceramics	229	23	233	23
Chemical products	112	52	112	54
Of which peones	(58)	(40)	(58)	(42)
Food products	1,510	1,280	1,564	1,304
Of which peones	(239)	(165)	(239)	(170)
Wearing apparel	3,877	1,978	5,927	3,423
Printing	200	248	200	248
Furniture	67	187	70	187
Other	—	145	—	145
5. Construction	2,259	3,043	2,259	3,052
Of which peones	(337)	(232)	(337)	(241)
6. Transport				
Rail	—	129	—	129
Land	756	823	756	823
Maritime	22	94	22	94
7. Communications	10	30	10	30
8. Commerce	5,341	3,536	6,360	3,809
9. Services				
Personal and financial	2,202	1,988	7,470	4,948
Of which cooks	(957)	(523)	(2,205)	(872)
Laundry workers	(0)	(161)	(3,147)	(1,625)
Legal professions	534	273	534	273
Medical professions	441	252	534	289
Liberal professions	65	138	71	138
Government	3,903	3,753	3,903	3,753
Religion	484	433	1,793	992
Education	419	168	566	262
Domestic servants	3,363	3,739	5,684	6,460

TABLE 10 (continued)

	Male Labor Force[†]		Total Labor Force	
	1857	*1876**	*1857*	*1876**
10. Unallocated white-collar workers	—	1,206	—	1,271
11. Unclassified	447	40	476	43
Total labor force	28,866	26,050	41,277	34,280
Total population	34,670[†]	52,239	94,195	100,156

SOURCES: For 1857, Manuel Fuentes, *Estadística general de Lima (Lima, 1858);* for 1876, Perú Dirección General de Estadística, *Censo general de la República del Perú formado en 1876,* VI, 307–317.
*Day laborers *(peones)* in 1876 allocated to sectors in same proportions as reported in 1857.
†Adult males.

TABLE 11
PERUVIAN NATIONAL INCOME, 1876–1877
(ANNUAL FIGURES IN THOUSANDS OF SOLES AT CURRENT PRICES)

Category	Income	Labor Force
1. Income of laborers		
Farmers (both sexes) and male laborers	115,365	789,724
Low-paid female occupations*	16,204	166,785
Female spinners	9,899	167,778
2. Business and artisan income		
Taxpayers *(patentes)*	16,725	13,670
Poorer artisans exempt from *patentes*		
Lima	4,676	5,620
Provinces	19,025	70,757
3. Government salaries	9,436	9,729
4. Other earned income	26,343	84,432
5. Rural rent	10,683	
6. Urban rent	5,662	
7. Return to agricultural capital	1,500	
Totals	235,518	1,308,495

SOURCE: See appendix to this chapter.
*Day laborers, shepherds, domestic servants, cooks, washerwomen, and dressmakers.

TABLE 12
IMPORTS INTO CALLAO OR ALL PERU, 1857–1877
(THOUSANDS OF PESOS OR SOLES AT CURRENT PRICES)

Year + port of entry	Cottons	Wools	Linens	Silks	Apparel*	Drugs†	Manufactures etc.	Furniture‡	Wines, Liquors	Food	Total
1857—Callao											
England	1,329	448	126	66	61	29	414	53	54	27	2,608
France	105	394	16	296	448	15	551	61	532	52	2,473
Chile	224	79	19	23	18	13	237	14	48	1,149	1,824
Panama	17	26	12	363	124	17	274	1	0	18	851
Others	95	141	2	68	34	8	401	62	123	62	995
Total	1,769	1,088	175	817	686	82	1,877	191	758	1,309	8,752
1859—Callao											
England	1,401	602	166	71	70	28	428	70	106	31	2,974
France	203	555	25	469	548	17	824	61	145	39	2,885
Chile	87	59	15	36	45	15	298	17	28	897	1,499
Panama	29	21	8	271	140	40	337	0	1	19	864
Others	95	131	6	28	43	8	498	62	40	87	998
Total	1,815	1,367	221	875	846	108	2,384	210	320	1,073	9,219
1866—Callao											
England	1,826	734	354	23	98	—	1,813	—	251	33	5,133
France	578	1,375	86	437	1,603	—	1,573	—	302	97	6,051
Chile	0	0	0	0	30	—	42	—	0	1,594	1,666
Others	26	54	8	10	299	—	1,137	—	48	390	1,973
Total	2,430	2,164	448	470	2,029	—	4,566	—	602	2,114	14,823

1867—Callao											
England	1,611	568	316	34	95	—	1,278	—	174	50	4,125
France	633	925	52	285	840	—	869	—	191	68	3,863
Chile	0	0	0	0	30	—	61	—	0	931	1,022
Others	28	38	2	7	164	—	1,034	—	33	304	1,611
Total	2,272	1,531	370	326	1,129	—	3,242	—	398	1,353	10,621
1877—Callao											
England	1,415	848	285	136	714	218	3,186	—	47	121	6,969
France	645	338	64	85	661	91	717	—	199	60	2,860
Chile	2	15	6	1	11	4	281	—	2	1,176	1,497
Others	663	243	76	94	216	208	2,246	—	198	794	4,740
Total	2,726	1,445	431	316	1,602	521	6,430	—	445	2,151	16,067
1877—All Peru											
England	2,640	1,453	345	154	812	230	4,727	—	112	152	10,626
France	853	657	78	131	800	109	965	—	254	103	3,950
Chile	3	15	9	1	14	6	1,231	—	9	1,550	2,837
Others	1,179	667	101	133	301	244	2,993	—	250	898	6,767
Total	4,674	2,792	533	419	1,926	589	9,917	—	625	2,704	24,179

SOURCES: Perú, Ministerio de Hacienda, *Memoria.* 1858, 1860, 1868. Perú, Dirección de Estadística, *Estadística comercial de la República del Perú en 1877*, Vol. I.

*Shoes and hats are included in apparel for all years.
† Drugs are included in manufactures etc. for 1866 and 1867.
‡ Furniture is included in apparel for 1866, 1867, and 1877.

TABLE 13

NOMINAL TARIFF RATES OF SELECTED PRODUCTS, 1826–1872

(AD VALOREM)

	1826	1828	1832	1833	1836	1839	1852	1855	1864	1872
Cotton Textiles										
Tocuyos	80	Prohibited	Prohibited	Prohibited	20	25	15	20	20	25
Tejidos ordinarios y crudos	30	Prohibited	90	45	20	25	15	20	20	25
Tejidos que no sean blancos	30	30	30	25	20	25	15	20	20	25
Wool Textiles										
Telas toscas (bayetones)	80	Prohibited	Prohibited	Prohibited	20	Prohibited	40	30	30	35
Other	30	30	30	45	20	25	25	20	20	25
Silks	30	30	30	15		18	28	20	20	25
Wearing apparel	80	Prohibited	90	50	50	40	30	30	30	35
Shoes	80	Prohibited	90	50	50	40	30	30	30	35
Flour	48	Prohibited	75	67	38	50	30	33	33	27
Wheat	30	30	86	93	57	43		43	43	17
Machinery and tools	Free	Free	Free	28		Free	1	Free	Free	Free
Metal goods	30	30	30	28	10	12	15	25	25	30
Unspecified residual	30	30	30	28		25	25	25	25	30

SOURCES: Dancuart, *Anales de la hacienda pública del Perú*, Vol. II, pp. 79, 93, 106, 140–141, 185, 207; Vol. III, pp. 116–118; Vol. V, pp. 184–185; Vol. VI, pp. 82–84; Vol. IX, pp. 168–169. Rodríguez, *Estudios económicos y financieros*, pp. 382–384, 457–458, 462–463. Ricketts to Canning, in *British Consular Reports*, p. 147.

NOTE: Flour and wheat subject to specific duties, converted to ad valorem by assumed prices of 6 pesos per quintal (12 pesos per barrel) for flour and 3½ pesos per *fanega* of 135 lbs. for wheat. For 1839 duties include *arbitrio* tax. Real level of high tariffs in early years reduced by practice of allowing partial payment in depreciated paper currency, e.g., 90 percent tariff of 1832 could be paid 50 percent in silver, 40 percent in paper.

NOTES

1. Paul Bairoch estimates the ratio of per capita income between presently developed and underdeveloped countries to have been 1.2:1 in 1770, between 3.4:1 and 5:1 in 1870, 6:1 in 1900, and 10–12:1 in 1970. See his "Les écarts des niveaux de développement economique entre pays développés et pays sous-devéloppés de 1770 à 2000," *Tiers monde* (July–September 1971, 503) and *The Economic Development of the Third World Since 1900* (Berkeley: University of California Press, 1975), pp. 191–192.

2. J. M. Rodríguez, *Estudios económicos y financieros* (Lima: Gil, 1895), and "Historia de los contratos del guano y sus efectos en las finanzas del Perú," *El economista peruano* (July 28, 1921), pp. 85–129; Jonathan V. Levin, *The Export Economies: Their Pattern of Development in Historical Perspective,* (Cambridge: Harvard University Press, 1960), Ch. 2; W. M. Mathew, "Anglo–Peruvian Commercial and Financial Relations 1820–65," (Ph.D. diss., University of London, 1964); Juan Maiguashca, "A Reinterpretation of the Guano Age, 1840–1880," (Ph.D. diss., Oxford University, 1967); Jacques Remy–Zephir, "Le guano du Perou. Les grandes compagnies européennes d'exploitation au XIX siècle" (Thèse de doctorat de troisième cycle, University of Paris, 1968); Heraclio Bonilla, "L'histoire économique et sociale du Perou au 19ᵉ siècle, 1821–1879" (Thèse de doctorat de troisième cycle, University of Paris, 1970); Luis Pásara, "El rol del derecho en la época del guano: formas jurídicas de la dominación," *Derecho,* 28, (1970), pp. 11–32; Heraclio Bonilla, *Guano y burguesía en el Perú,* (Lima: Instituto de Estudios Peruanos, 1974).

3. The term is from Jorge Basadre, *Historia de la República del Perú,* 6th ed. (Lima: Editorial Universitaria, 1969), Vols. 3–5. Juan Copello and Luis Petriconi referred to "una prosperidad ficticia." See their *Estudios sobre la independencia económica del Perú* (Lima, 1876), pp. 15–17. Also see Pedro Dávalos y Lisson, *La primera centuria* (Lima, 1926) Vol. IV, especially pp. 67, 119.

4. Levin, *The Export Economies,* especially pp. 4–15, 112–118. A more concise summary is in Roberto Cortés Conde, *The First Stages of Modernization in Spanish America* (New York: Harper and Row, 1974).

5. The periods are picked from annual data used as the source for Table 1. They differ slightly from the periods marked off by Heraclio Bonilla in his "La coyuntura comercial del siglo XIX en el Perú," *Revista del Museo Nacional* 35 (1967–1968), pp. 159–187; reprinted in *Un siglo a la deriva* (Lima: Instituto de Estudios Peruanos, 1980).

6. Note that these figures refer to shares expressed in constant 1900 prices.

7. Hunt, "Price and Quantum Estimates of Peruvian Exports, 1830–1962," RPED Discussion Paper no. 33, Princeton University, January 1973, Table 21.

8. At 1870 prices the corresponding figures are 53 percent and 24 percent.

9. Hunt, "Price and Quantum Estimates of Peruvian Exports, 1830–1926," Table 14.

10. The definitive economic study is Rosemary Thorp and Geoffrey Bertram, *Peru 1890–1977: Growth and Policy in an Open Economy,* (New York: Columbia University Press, 1978). Also Manuel Burga and Alberto Flores Galindo, *Apogeo y crisis de la república aristocrática* (Lima: Ediciones Rikchay Perú, 1979).

11. Pedro Dávalos y Lisson, "La industria minera," *El Ateneo* 4 (1901), pp. 35–117; C. E. Velarde, *La minería en el Perú* (Lima, 1908); Manuel Fuentes, *Estadística minera del Perú* (Lima 1878); Mariano Rivero y Ustariz, "Memoria sobre el rico mineral de Pasco (Año de 1828)," in *Colección de memorias científicas,* Vol. I, pp. 182–227, "Razón anual de los progresos y trabajos del mineral de Yauricocha, presentada al importante gremio de mineros por el Director General de Minería," Vol. 1, pp. 251–265, and "Visita a las minas del departamento de Puno en el año de 1826," Vol. II, pp. 1–36. Among the accounts of travelers, the most useful is William Lewis Herndon and Lardner Gibbon, *Exploration of the Valley of the Amazon*, 2 vols., U.S. House of Representatives, 33rd Congress, 1st Session, Executive Document No. 53 (Washington, D.C., 1854). See also J. J. von Tschudi, *Travels in Peru* (London, 1947).

12. Rivero, *Colección de memorias científicas*, I, 201–202; Dávalos y Lisson, "La industria minera," pp. 49, 65–68.

13. Rivero, *Colección de memorias científicas*, I, 254, 203.

14. Dávalos y Lisson, "La industria minera," pp. 65–66.

15. Perú, Ministerio de Hacienda, *Memoria*, 1860, Anexo, p. 4.

16. H. W. Dickenson and Arthur Titley, *Richard Trevithick: The Engineer and the Man* (Cambridge: Cambridge University Press, 1934), pp. 159–186.

17. J. Fred Rippy, *British Investments in Latin America, 1822–1949* (Minneapolis: University of Minnesota Press, 1959), p. 24.

18. Rivero, *Collección de memorias científicas*, I, 199, 201, 255. Note that the Peruvian currency unit was the peso until 1863, when it was retitled the sol.

19. Great Britain, Board of Trade, *Commercial Tariffs and Regulations of the Several States of Europe and America, Together with the Commercial Treaties Between England and the Foreign Countries,* Parts XVIII, XIX, XX; John McGregor, *Spanish American Republics* (London, 1847), p. 216.

20. Rivero reports 247,000 pesos spent through 1820, another 40,000 by Pasco Peruvian, and 40,000 in the first year of government supervision (1827–1828) *Colección de memorias científicas,* I, 201–202, 255–260. We assume that the annual spending rate of 40,000 pesos continued through the 1839 completion date.

21. Annual *recorded* output at Cerro averaged 226,256 marks during 1830–1839 (Hunt, "Price and Quantum Estimates of Peruvian Exports, 1830–1962," Table 19). At 8.5 pesos per mark, average value comes to 1,923,000 pesos.

22. Rivero, *Colección de memorias científicas*, I, 204–206, 221.

23. Herndon and Gibbon, *Exploration of the Valley of the Amazon*, I, pp. 101–103.

24. Perú, Ministerio de la Hacienda, *Memoria que presenta el Señor Ministro de Hacienda y Comercio al Director de Administración,* "Cuadro estadístico del mineral del Cerro de Pasco que la Diputación de Minería pasa a la Dirección de Administración en el Ministerio de Hacienda," Lima, 1876, especially pp. 102–103.

25. Rivero, *Colección de memorias científicas*, I, 222.

26. For example, see Herndon and Gibbon, *Exploration of the Valley of the Amazon,* II, pp. 18, 23, 33, 36, 88, 96–98.

27. Many technological pioneers are mentioned in W. F. C. Purser, *Metal-Mining in Peru, Past and Present* (New York: Praeger, 1971), pp. 88–91, 96–97.

28. Dávalos y Lisson, "La industria minera," pp. 69, 80. Tschudi, *Travels in Peru*, pp. 283–286.

29. Dávalos y Lisson, "La industria minera," pp. 83–87.

30. Rivero, *Colección de memorias científicas*, I, p. 214; Herndon and Gibbon, *Exploration of the Valley of the Amazon*, I, pp. 99–100; "Cuadro estadístico . . ." p. 129.

31. Some lavish living was generated from Peruvian mining, however. Witness the case of the Pflucker heirs recounted in Gee Langdon, *Don Roberto's Daughter* (London, 1968).

32. Tschudi, *Travels in Peru*, pp. 334–337.

33. Henri Favre, "Evolución y situación de las haciendas en la región de Huancavelica," *Revista del Museo Nacional* 23 (1964), pp. 240–242. Reprinted in Henri Favre et al., *La hacienda en el Perú* (Lima: Instituto de Estudios Peruanos, 1967).

34. Paul Walle, *Bolivia* (New York: Charles Scribner's Sons, 1914), p. 196. Herndon and Gibbon, *Exploration of the Valley of the Amazon*, II, p. 126.

35. Herndon and Gibbon, *Exploration of the Valley of the Amazon*, II, p. 127.

36. Provincial population figures from Dirección General de Estadística, *Censo general de la República formado en 1876*, 7 vols. (Lima, 1878). Postal data from Dirección General de Correos y Telégrafos, *Estadística de correos y telégrafos del Perú en 1877* (Lima, 1878), table following p. 25; *Estadística postal 1901–1902* (Lima, 1903), pp. 123–145; *Estadística postal y telegráfica*, Vol. I, 1903–1904, pp. 269–365.

37. Huacho, Casma, Trujillo, Chiclayo, Piura, Ica.

38. Puno, Cuzco, Huancavelica, Abancay, Ayacucho.

39. This experience is reviewed in Jean Piel, "The Place of the Peasantry in the National Life of Peru in the Nineteenth Century," *Past and Present*, February 1970, pp. 122–127.

40. Lequanda's estimates of 1793 allocated Peru's sugar exports 65 percent to Chile, 27 percent to Argentina, and 8 percent to Ecuador. See Alejandro Garland, *La industria azucarera en el Perú (1550–1895)* (Lima: Imprenta del Estado, 1895), pp. 7–8.

41. Ibid., p. 9.

42. Great Britain, Board of Trade, *Tables of the Revenue, Population, Commerce etc, of the United Kingdom and Its Dependencies* (Porter's Tables), 1836, p. 392.

43. See Garland, *La industria azucarera en el Perú*, p. 11. Celso Furtado sees this same constraint as the key problem of export expansion in nineteenth-century Brazil (*The Economic History of Brazil* [Berkeley: University of California Press, 1968], Chs. 21, 24.)

44. Garland, *La industria azucarera en el Perú*, p. 11; Watt Stewart, *Chinese Bondage in Peru* (Durham, North Carolina: Duke University Press, 1951); Humberto Rodríguez Pastor, *Pativilca 1870: la rebelión de los rostros pintados* (Huancayo: Instituto de Estudios Andinos, 1979).

45. The subsequent expansion is summarized in Ernesto Yepes del Castillo, *Perú 1820–1920: Un siglo de desarrollo capitalista* (Lima: Campodonico, 1972), pp. 71–73. See also Basadre, *Historia de la República del Perú*, IV, pp. 368–370.

The fundamental changes in land tenure are documented in Manuel Burga, *De la encomienda a la hacienda capitalista* (Lima: Instituto de Estudios Peruanos, 1976).

46. The percentage share is the same at 1870 and 1900 prices.

47. Perú, Dirección de Estadística, *Estadística comercial de la República del Perú en 1877* (Lima, 1878), Vol. I.; L. Esteves, *Apuntes para la historia económica del Perú* (Lima, 1882), p. 18.

48. In 1960 the Trujillo–Chicama region accounted for 93 percent of sugar exports; in the case of cotton, 36 percent came from Piura, 29 percent from Lima, and 34 percent from Pisco–Ica.

49. Irrigation works are summarized in P. Emilio Dancuart, *Anales de la hacienda pública del Perú* (Lima, 1907), Vol. IX, pp. 17–18. The outstanding trade journal was perhaps *Revista de agricultura,* 1875–1879, edited by J. B. H. Martinet.

50. Esteves, *Apuntes para la historia económica del Perú,* p. 27.

51. Watt Stewart, *Henry Meiggs, Yankee Pizarro* (Durham, N.C.: Duke University Press, 1946), pp. 119–120.

52. A. J. Duffield, *Peru in the Guano Age: Being a Short Account of a Recent Visit to the Guano Deposits* (London, 1877), pp. 9–10.

53. Gerardo Klinge, *La industria azucarera en el Perú* (Lima, 1924), p. 6.

54. Garland, *La industria azucarera en el Perú,* p. 13.

55. Ibid., p. 12. Approximately the same figures are repeated in José Clavero, *El tesoro del Perú* (Lima, 1896), p. 42, and reprinted in Yepes, *Perú 1820–1920,* p. 112.

56. Levin, *The Export Economies.*

57. Ibid., pp. 99–104, 120–123.

58. In 1960 the total tax burden of the Peruvian mining industry was 39 percent of the sum of taxes plus net profits. The equivalent figure for Chile in 1955, the year of heaviest taxation for its copper industry, was 68 percent. A 50 percent tax rate for petroleum companies was widely established in both the Middle East and Venezuela during the 1950s, but this rate rose to 57 percent in the Middle East and 75 percent in Venezuela during the 1960s. Comparisons with more recent years are more difficult to make since in many instances nationalization has been substituted for profits taxation. See Banco Central de Reserva, *Renta nacional del Perú: 1942–1960,* p. 94; Clark Reynolds, "Development Problems of an Export Economy: The Case of Chile and Copper," in Markos Mamalakis and Clark Reynolds, *Essays on the Chilean Economy* (Homewood, Ill.: Richard Irwin, 1965), p. 386; Edith Penrose with P. R. Odell, *The Large International Firm in Developing Countries: The International Pertroleum Industry* (London: Allen & Unwin, 1968), pp. 201, 215, 294, 296.

59. Reynolds, "Development Problems of an Export Economy," pp. 275–287; Levin, *The Export Economies.*

60. Levin, *The Export Economies,* p. 88.

61. This derives from the report of Alejandro Garland that the annual cost of maintaining a coolie in 1870 was around 210 soles. See his *La industria azucarera en el Perú,* p. 11. If we assume that laborers had only 200 days of work per year, then annual output per worker would have been 400 tons, and the labor force

required to extract the 1,254,000 tons shipped in 1869–1870 would have been 1,568, receiving biennial maintenance payments of 660,000 soles. Total costs for the biennium are variously shown, in Table 3, to be 28,200,000 soles or 44,420,000 soles. By these figures, labor costs come to be 1.5 percent or 2.3 percent of total costs.

62. Earlier minor contracts for supplying the United States, Cuba, and Puerto Rico continued in force.

63. Payments to Peru do include interest charges on advances, however.

64. The tonnage figures are quite reliable; the total in Table 4 is 2,336,631, which agrees closely with Rodríguez' independent estimate of 2,321,228 ("Historia de los contratos . . ." p. 121). The price data deserve further study, however; the sources used were merely scraps of information. Payments received come from reliable sources, yet their total of 143 million pesos is nearly double the 74 million pesos that Rodríguez asserts Peru gained from the Dreyfus Contract. Cf. J. M. Rodríquez, *Estudíos económicos y financieros,* p. 304. He gives no supporting calculation for his figure, however, so these tables are left as is with the challenge, or plea, that a more specialized historian improve them.

65. Reynolds, "Development Problems of an Export Economy," p. 378. It should be noted, however, that three highly atypical years, 1952–1954, showed a share of 93 percent.

66. This is expressed as a percent of total income net of loans. Loans were merely an anticipation of future guano income.

67. Dancuart, *Anales de la hacienda pública del Perú,* V, 51; VI, 70.

68. Sources: for 1840–1867, Dancuart, *Anales de la hacienda pública del Perú,* VIII, 20; for 1868, Mariano Felipe Paz Soldán, *Diccionario geográfico estadístico del Perú* (Lima, 1877), p. 746; for 1869, Dancuart, *Anales de la hacienda pública del Perú,* VIII, 77; consignment contracts for 1870, Perú. Ministerio de Hacienda, *Cuenta de Ingresos . . .* ; Consignments for 1871–1872, Table 5 of this chapter; Dreyfus Contract for high estimate, Table 4 of this chapter; Dreyfus Contract for low estimates, J. M. Rodríguez, *Estudios económicos y financieros,* p. 304.

69. Part of this expansion is monetary rather than real, since during 1855–1869 prices of agricultural home goods rose by some 75 percent. Bread prices derived from imported wheat actually fell, however. The real value of government expenditure therefore probably expanded more than fourfold during the Guano Age. Price data are summarized in Jorge Basadre, *Historia de la República del Perú,* 6th ed. (Lima, 1969), Vol. VI, pp. 162–63, the original source being Lima, Consejo Provincial, *Datos e informes sobre las causas que han producido el alza de precios de los artículos de primera necesidad que se consumen en la capital,* (Lima, 1870).

70. Levin, *The Export Economies,* p. 117; Maiguashca, "A Reinterpretation of the Guano Age," p. 8.

71. W. M. Mathew, "The Imperialism of Free Trade: Peru, 1820–70," *Economic History Review,* December 1968, pp. 562–579.

72. Dancuart, *Anales de la hacienda pública del Perú,* VI, pp. 5–6, 64.

73. Perú, Junta de Examen Fiscal, *Informe de la . . . creada por resolución suprema de febrero de 1855. Para revisar los expedientes relativos al recon-*

ocimiento de la deuda interna consolidada desde 20 de abril de 1851, (Lima, 1857). This experience is well summarized in Alfonso Quiroz Norris, "La consolidación de la deuda interna peruana, 1850–58," Tesis de bachiller, Universidad Católica del Perú, 1980.

74. For further evolution in the twentieth century, see Shane Hunt, "Distribution, Growth, and Government Economic Behavior in Peru," in Gustav Ranis, ed. *Government and Economic Development* (New Haven, Conn., 1971), especially p. 398.

75. Maiguashca, "A Reinterpretation of the Guano Age," p. 3.

76. J. M. Rodríguez estimates 10,804,033 tons sold for 648,241,080 pesos, i.e., 60 pesos per ton (*Estudios económicos y financieros,* pp. 317–18). My own estimates are somewhat higher: 12,669,190 tons with final sales value of 762,900,827 pesos. Tonnage figures from Hunt, "Price and Quantum Estimates . . . ," Table 21. Prices from Cruchaga, *Salitre y guano,* pp. 220–225, summarized as 10 pounds sterling, 1840–1854; 12½ pounds, 1855–1869; 14 pounds, 1870–1874; 10 pounds, 1875–1879.

77. Total guano income through 1872, not counting the Dreyfus Contract, is estimated at 307 million pesos. (For sources, see note 68.) Deducting income from the Gibbs contract and the contracts before 1849 (see Table 3) leaves 244 million pesos as an estimate of government profit from national consignment contracts. Since our estimates of distribution from consignment contracts were 60 percent to government, 30 percent to costs, and 10 percent to contractors, this suggests that total gross income of Peruvian contractors was one sixth of 244 million pesos, or 40 million pesos. However, we must also allow for the likelihood that contractors gave themselves part of the business subsumed in costs, so the 40 million pesos is quite arbitrarily inflated.

78. Table 7 shows the first two groups received some 90 million pesos of guano income. This total is given by the sum of the debt entries (Anglo Peruvian through Manumission) in the right-hand column of the table. Pensioners received 16 percent of 242 million pesos, i.e., 39 million pesos, and the 60–80 million pesos figure for contractors gives a total of 189–209 million pesos. Total uses of guano income equals the 454 million pesos received by government plus the 60–80 million pesos of contractors. 189/514 = 37 percent. 209/534 = 39 percent.

79. See note 69.

80. In fact, Levin also emphasized the wide dissemination of guano income when he wrote: "These then were the people who . . . shared the guano–export proceeds: the foreign contractors, the Peruvian contractors who succeeded many of them, the coolie traders supplying the laborers from China to Callao, the Chinese coolies on the islands . . . the influential Peruvians who benefited from the consolidated debts, the mass of Peruvians relieved of their tax burden, the soldiers, the bureaucrats, and the pensioners." (*The Export Economies,* p. 115). Yet he fits this historical situation into a model that attributes the failures of domestic development to the absence of demand by "luxury importers" who constitute the only national recipients of export earnings (ibid., pp. 6–15). The others are dismissed as nonsavers: "The soldiers, bureaucrats, and pensioners supported by the government's guano proceeds devoted virtually all the their rising income to a

marked increase in their style of living, with little left for savings and investment." (ibid., p. 117). But this won't do. All we need from this group is demand, not savings. If they provided demand, and the domestic economy remained stagnant, then the growth failure lay with the unresponsiveness to domestic entrepreneurs, not with the enclavelike structure of income flows.

81. Charles Wilkes, *Narrative of the United States Exploring Expedition* (Philadelphia, 1845), Vol. I, pp. 236–237.

82. George Kubler, *The Indian Caste of Peru, 1795–1940*, Smithsonian Institution, Institute of Social Anthropology, Publication No. 14, 1952, p. 40.

83. Basadre, *Historia de la República del Perú*, VI, p. 160. A peso was composed of 8 reales.

84. J. B. H. Martinet, *L'agriculture au Perou* (Paris, 1878), pp. 58–59.

85. Basadre, *Historia de la República del Perú*, VI, pp. 162–163. See note 69 for original source. Consumption weights were taken from a 1957 budget survey of Lima-Callao worker families, in Dirección Nacional de Estadística, *Boletín de estadística peruana*, 1962, p. 240. If bread prices actually declined, as Basadre suggests, and if workers, being poorer in the nineteenth century, devoted a larger share of expenditure to bread than did their descendants of 1957, then the cost–of–living increase would have been even less than 32 percent.

86. This assumes an increase in money wages of 100 percent and of cost of living of 32 percent. Further work on wage and price trends is badly needed.

87. J. M. Rodríguez, *Estudios económicos y financieros*, pp. 259–260.

88. Kubler, *The Indian Caste of Peru*, pp. 40, 65.

89. Ibid.

90. That is, $5,531 \div (28,866 + 5,531) = 16$ percent.

91. The steps in this calculation are as follows: Males formed 52 percent of Lima's population of 1876. When applied to Lima's total population of 1857, this percentage produces as estimate of 48,981 for the total male population. $34,670 \div 48,981$ gives 70.8 percent as the adult proportion of the total male population. This proportion applied to the 1876 total male population of 52,239 produces an estimate of 36,985 for the adult male population in 1876. The difference between these two figures, 15,254, is the population of male minors. There are 23,221 males listed as "sin profesión" (not employed) in 1876. If 15,254 are minors, then 7,967 are adults. $7,967 \div (26,050 + 7,967) = 23.4$ percent.

92. For this calculation, sales value of guano was a three–year average expressed in 1870 prices. Since the price of guano did not change greatly over the period considered, these figures are fairly close to a current-price series.

93. Bonilla, "L'histoire economique et sociale du Perou . . . ," pp. 56, 67, 85, 91, 93. Current values converted to common base at exchange rate of 25.25 francs = 1 pound sterling.

94. Callao gives a fair measure of the national trend, even though 1877 data show that it handled only 66 percent of total imports. This figure underestimates Callao's importance in the import trade of the period, since in 1877 practically all the remainder consisted either of general imports into Mollendo and Arica, much of which was undoubtedly transhipped to Bolivia, or of coal imports into the newly thriving nitrate ports of Iquique and Pisagua. Since Table 12 is denominated

in current values of Peruvian currency, interpretations must be drawn from it with care, because Peru suffered some inflation during the period, while European prices were relatively stable.

95. Panamanian transhipments are assigned to France in the 1857–1859 data.

96. Peruvian sources of Table 12 show that the share of British cottons and woolens and French woolens and silks in Anglo–French imports was 48 percent in 1857, 50 percent in 1859, and 34 percent in 1877. These same figures, taken from the Anglo–French data compiled by Bonilla, come out to be 53 percent, 49 percent, and 47 percent, respectively. The source of the discrepancy for 1877 is hard to pin down. Part of it results from a substantially higher c.i.f. valuation that Peruvian sources placed on coal.

97. Ricketts to Canning, Sept. 16, 1826 (No. 19), F.O. 61/8; cited in R. A. Humphreys, ed., *British Consular Reports on the Trade and Politics of Latin America, 1824–1826,* Camden 3rd ser. Vol. LXIII, (London: Royal Historical Society, 1940), pp. 138–141. See also Heraclio Bonilla, "La emergencia del control norteamericano sobre la economía peruana," in *Un siglo a la deriva.*

98. Dancuart, *Anales de la hacienda pública del Perú,* II, 79.

99. Ricketts to Canning, *British Consular Reports,* pp. 144–145. Raul Rivera Serna, "Aspectos de la economía durante el primer gobierno del Mariscal Don Agustín Gamarra," *Revista histórica* (1959), Vol. XXIV, pp. 437–439.

100. Ricketts to Canning, *British Consular Reports,* p. 141.

101. Ibid., p. 145.

102. W. M. Mathew, "The Imperialism of Free Trade: Peru, 1820–1870," *Economic History Review* (December 1968), p. 566.

103. This does not necessarily mean there was strong pressure from British merchants. Historians have given no indication either of government resistance to any such pressure, nor of counterpressure from producing interests. See, for example, Rivera Serna, "Aspectos de la economía durante el primer gobierno . . . ," pp. 431–433; Mathew, "The Imperialism of Free Trade"; Basadre, *Historia de la República del Perú,* II, 346–350.

104. Dancuart, *Anales de la hacienda pública,* II, 207, 217, 219.

105. Ibid., IV, 189.

106. See, for example, Basadre, *Historia de la República del Perú,* IV, pp. 15–17.

107. Ibid., IV, 357–359; José Silva Santisteban, *Breves reflexiones sobre los sucesos ocurridos en Lima y el Callao, con motivo de la importación de artefactos* (Lima, 1859).

108. The unemployment problem is discussed in Maiguashca, "A Reinterpretation of the Guano Age," pp. 24–27.

109. As advocated by contemporaries like José Silva Santisteban in *Breves reflexiones.*

110. Aníbal Pinto, *Chile: Un caso de desarrollo frustrado* (Santiago, 1959), pp. 30–35; Celso Furtado, *The Economic History of Brazil,* Ch. 18.

111. A breakdown of imports for 1877 shows 58 percent of all imports incurred duties of 25–35 percent, while only 5 percent were charged the lower rates of 8–15 percent. One quarter of imports were duty–free, however, while another 12 percent were charged specific duties. Chief among the duty–free imports were coal,

barley, pine boards, and mercury, all items for which one might suppose a low elasticity of substitution relative to the textiles, wearing apparel, and other consumer goods that incurred the higher levies. Since the duty on wearing apparel was 35 percent and that on textiles 25 percent, effective protection for the apparel industry was higher still, so some allocative effect was no doubt present in this particular case.

112. Stewart, *Henry Meiggs,* pp. 230–232.

113. One might note that this episode clashes with the Principle of the Hiding Hand, which involves a fortunate inability to see the future, thus concealing from government decision makers the inevitable problems of project execution until so much has been invested that there is no turning back (Albert Hirschman, *Development Projects Observed* [Washington, D.C.: Brookings Institution, 1967]). The Hiding Hand is judged beneficent because the typical decision maker "has not yet acquired enough confidence in his problem-solving ability to make a more candid appraisal of a project's prospective difficulties and of the risks he is assuming." It serves "to build up the morale of the slightly frightened decision makers" (pp. 24, 26). This brief story of railroad investment demonstrates that timorousness of decision makers presented no problem in Peru. It follows that the anticipation of problems, and more careful evaluation of projects along the conventional lines of cost-benefit analysis, were (and remain) socially desirable.

114. In the late 1870s the budget of the two Escuelas de Artes y Oficios exceeded the combined budget of the country's six universities. See Paz Soldán, *Diccionario geográfico estadístico del Perú,* pp. 757–758.

115. The most obvious examples available for examination today are the petroleum economies. Many of the characteristics attributed here to the rentier economy are discussed in Dudley Seers, "The Mechanism of an Open Petroleum Economy," *Social and Economic Studies,* (March 1964). In the recent literature, the ailments of such an economy have been entitled "The Dutch Disease."

116. Duffield, *Peru in the Guano Age,* p. 11.

117. Basadre, *Historia de la República del Perú,* VII, 53–54. The final sale price of about 1,000 tons of guano was 50,000 soles.

118. Stewart, *Henry Meiggs,* pp. 129–151.

119. See, for example, Juan Bustamante, *Los indios del Perú* (Lima, 1867); Kubler, *The Indian Caste of Peru;* Clorinda Matto de Turner, *Aves sin nidos;* Isaiah Bowman, *The Andes of Southern Peru* (New York: American Geographical Society, 1912), Chs. 5–7.

120. Heraclio Bonilla's summary assessment of the Guano Age, while differing in emphasis, touches on approximately the same set of phenomena. See his *Guano y burguesía en el Perú,* pp. 163–171.

121. Martinet, *L'agriculture au Perou,* p. 59; Rodriguez, *Estudios económicos y financieros,* pp. 259–260.

122. Perú, Ministerio de Agricultura, *Valor de la mano de obra,* 1961.

123. Sources: Dancuart, *Anales de la hacienda pública del Perú,* V, 155, 215; IX, p. 58; Perú, Ministerio de Hacienda, *Memoria,* 1851, 1853, 1864. *Memoria que presenta el Director de Rentas al Señor Ministro de Hacienda y Comercio,* 1872, p. 24.

124. Dancuart, *Anales de la hacienda pública del Perú,* VIII, 229.

125. Ibid., V, 95.

126. Rodríguez, *Estudios económicos y financieros*, p. 203.

127. Basadre, *Historia de la República del Perú*, VI, 160.

128. That is, (70,757) (0.324) (832) = 19,073,823.

129. 432,000 ÷ (432,000 + 82,623) = 84 percent. Lima's share of *patentes* comes from 1864 data in Perú, Ministerio de Hacienda, *Memoria*, 1864.

130. Since 76 percent of 84 percent equals 64 percent.

131. That is, (84,432) (1.20) (260) equals 26, 342, 784.

132. Dancuart, *Anales de la hacienda pública del Perú*, X, 177–204.

133. Sources: Dancuart, *Anales de la hacienda pública del Perú*, V, 105, 215; IX, p. 58; Perú, Ministerio de Hacienda, *Memoria*, 1851, 1853, 1864; *Memoria que presenta el Director de Rentas al Señor Ministro de Hacienda y Comercio*, 1872, p. 24.

134. Perú, Ministerio de Hacienda, *Memoria que presenta el Director de Rentas*, 1872.

135. Because 40 percent of (8 + 34) percent equals 17 percent.

136. See, for example, Fernando Tola, *Los impuestos en el Perú* (Lima, 1914), p. 45. Perú, Ministerio de Hacienda y Comercio, *Memoria que presenta el Ministro de Hacienda y Comercio a la Legislatura Ordinaria de 1870: Documentos.* Anexo No. 2, *Memoria del Director de Rentas*, p. 19.

137. Garland, *La industria azucarera en el Perú* (1550–1895), p. 31.

138. Perú, Ministerio de Hacienda, *Memoria que presenta el Director de Rentas*, 1872.

139. That is, 179,728 soles times (1.17) (1.28) (1.26) (1.26).

140. Garland, *La industria azucarera en el Perú*, p. 12.

6
The
Export Economy of
ARGENTINA
1880–1920*/**

Roberto Cortés Conde

I. *The Río de la Plata*

The Río de la Plata, which had been an impoverished Spanish colony in the remote confines of the South Atlantic, underwent important changes in the last decades of the eighteenth century and the first decades of the nineteenth. From the middle of the eighteenth century, the port of Buenos Aires (capital of the province of the same name, which, together with the provinces of Córdoba, Tucumán, and the Cuyo region, would soon compose what is now Argentina) had grown as the intermediary for trade between the north—where Potosí silver was mined—and the Spanish me-

---

*The author wishes to thank Tulio Halperín Donghi and Richard Mallon for their comments on the early version of this paper; Peter Smith and Tom Skidmore for their hospitality in Madison, Wisconsin, where he was visiting professor at the time the writing of this essay started; Heidi Goldberg, the original translator of the essay; and Elizabeth Hansen for her assistance in the revision of the translation and the editing.
**In the text, unless otherwise stated, the monetary units are indicated as they appear in the respective sources. The relations between them are detailed in Appendix I, but, to make it easier to understand the text, the "gold peso" and the "hard peso" in practice have the same value. In contrast, the "paper peso" ("corriente" or "moneda nacional") was devalued with respect to the "gold peso" or the "hard peso" during the period under consideration (see the same table in Appendix I).

tropolis, as well as other European powers. Moreover, Buenos Aires gradually began to export agricultural products, *los frutos de la tierra.* This was a consequence of the amazing natural increase of cattle herds in enormous fertile and empty spaces where there were no other competitors for pasture. Their exploitation provided a surplus that began to find a commercial outlet. Cattle herding—or the hunting of wild cattle—was undertaken in order to sell the hides on the overseas market. Silver was also produced for export, but with the decline of production in the eighteenth century, and the later separation of Alto Perú (present-day Bolivia), hides became the most important export from the Río de la Plata.[1]

By the middle of the eighteenth century the value of exports from Buenos Aires had reached 1.5 million silver pesos, and hides figured importantly in this total.[2] The rest was accounted for by gold and silver from Chile and Peru.

Between 1750 and 1820 exports from Buenos Aires again began to increase. In spite of the setback of the independence wars, the value of exports rose from 1.5 million silver pesos to an average of about 5 million silver pesos (17 to the ounce, equivalent to .957 gold pesos according to the Currency Act of 1881). Although silver exports did not cease during the independence period, hides became the major export product. In 1825 they accounted for 53.5 percent of total exports, while jerked beef accounted for 9.3 percent and tallow for 32 percent.[3]

After the Revolution of 1810, and because of the separation of Alto Perú, the government of the provinces of the Río de la Plata was deprived of revenues from the Potosí mines, as well as export duties on the silver.[4] From then on, the cash receipts of the Buenos Aires Customs House were the principal source of treasury revenues (by 1882 customs house receipts made up 82 percent of total revenues).[5] Since the loss of revenues from silver was more than compensated for by the great increase in revenues from agrarian exports, fiscal income rose, instead of falling. Still, during the first years of independence there was severe financial penury and between 1773 and 1776 customs house income did not exceed 50,000 silver pesos. After 1776 annual receipts were, with some variation, between 100,000 and 400,000 pesos. Between 1800 and 1810 receipts oscillated around 1 million pesos, and between 1820 and 1830, they were around 2 million pesos.

Not only the society of the Río de la Plata region but the government as well tied its economic fortunes to the growth of agrarian exports. By 1820 these had quadrupled their eighteenth-century values, partly as a result of the increase in livestock prices. Between 1809 and 1819 the price per head of cattle rose from 3.3 pesos to 9.6.[6]

The increase in exports, so noticeable by the late 1840s, was the result of an accumulation of stocks during the period of the blockade, which meant that once the blockade was lifted the volume of exports was much larger than normal (1849–1851). In addition, exports during the 1830s had also been affected by the French blockade of 1838, whose consequences were felt until 1840. This is to say that during the two decades of the Rosas government internal and international wars had a negative effect on foreign trade. This negative effect is reflected in the revenues of the customs house. Between 1822 and 1845 it remained at the same level: 1.9 million pesos in 1822; 1.8 million pesos in 1845.

It should be underscored that although exports between the end of the eighteenth century and 1820 do not appear to have increased much, this was not the case with customs house receipts. Clearly a strong jump in exports took place between 1750 and the end of the century. The data on trade with Great Britain suggest another strong increase during the second decade of the nineteenth century. Great Britain absorbed the bulk of the region's exports, and Halperín's data on British imports from Argentina (for the years when other data are lacking, 1814–1818) seem to show an increase in exports from the Río de la Plata to Britain. In 1814 their value amounted to 476,653 pounds sterling and in 1818 to 730,908 pounds sterling (an increase of 53 percent over four years, or an eleven percent increase per annum).[7] This gives the second decade of the nineteenth century a more favorable appearance, as does the increase in livestock prices to which Burgin refers (from 3 pesos per head in 1803–1808 to 9.6 pesos per head in 1819).[8]

From the 1820s until the 1840s exports seem to have been almost stagnant. There are strong variations in some of these years, but these are due to the interruption of exports during the blockade, and a disproportionate rise, because of stock accumulations, when the port was reopened. Jonathan Brown's data (Table 2) show a significant increase in the export of jerked beef, wool, and tallow from Buenos Aires between 1820 and 1830, and a sharp increase in the export of hides between 1840 and 1850.

However, because of the decline in prices, at least until the 1840s, export values could not have increased significantly. These were not normal years. During the years of the blockade there was practically no activity; in the following years the accumulated backlog of stock moved out rapidly. Brown's own data on activity in the port of Buenos Aires seem to indicate that there was no increase in the number of ships entering the port between the 1820s and the 1830s. But between 1830 and 1840 such an increase did take place; and yet another, more important, one occurred between 1840 and 1850.[9]

Extensive Cattle Raising

At this time the Río de la Plata had plenty of potentially available land, at least relative to its population. Actually land was less abundant than it is now believed to have been since the frontier was very near the coast of the Río de la Plata. Before 1820 the coastal provinces and the Banda Oriental had abundant and safe lands for livestock raising. With the successive expansions of the frontier by Vertíz, Martín Rodríguez, and Rosas between the end of the eighteenth century and 1833, the province of Buenos Aires came to include approximately 10 million hectares, an abundant acreage in view of the scarce population. On the other hand, this *nonmining* colony suffered from an acute shortage of currency and transportation was difficult, costly, and unreliable. Under these circumstances, producers in search of regular sources of income specialized in a type of production that required abundant land but small amounts of capital and labor. Cattle raising for hides, which became the principal product of the traditional export pattern, was thus a response to the initial availability of resources.[10]

At first the animals were found roaming wild, subsisting on natural grassland. They were killed by the gauchos, who ate the meat—virtually the only item in the Río de la Plata diet at that time. Only the hides were sent to market.

Later a certain amount of processing developed; the meat was dried with salt to preserve it for export for consumption by slaves in Brazil, Cuba, and the United States. There was no market for hides within Argentina, since the population was not large enough to create the demand that would have been an incentive for investment in a leather industry. In more advanced countries there was such a demand, and hide production found a market.

The characteristics of the market were different in the older, settled zones of the Northwest, where production during the sixteenth and seventeenth centuries had been oriented to the Alto Peruvian and, to some degree, the Chilean markets. In the Northwest access to overseas markets was virtually impossible because of the long distances to the ports, the cost of transportation, and the physical characteristics of the area, which made it less appropriate for extensive cattle raising. On the other hand, the Northwest had a relatively greater population density, with ancient Indian settlements long dedicated to agricultural cultivation and artisan craftsmanship.[11] The existence of an important source of wealth—the silver of Alto Perú—had for more than two centuries promoted the development of various economic activities along the border of the Alto Peruvian trade route (Jujuy, Salta, Tucumán, Córdoba), and these supplied travelers and traders with livestock and other supplies. Eventually settlements developed around what were first trail markers and rest points along the road. These later became way stations breaking up the long stretches of a journey that covered thousands of kilometers, along which flourished an active interregional trade.

The oldest areas of the Argentine Northwest entered a period of crisis when the war cut off their access to Peruvian markets, and when they found themselves unable to compete with the overseas products entering the country through Buenos Aires. Their decline, however, was less drastic than has been previously thought. Civil wars and isolation permitted northwestern production to maintain some of its local and to some extent, regional markets. These were protected from foreign products by the high cost of transportation and the general insecurity, which lasted for several decades after independence. During those decades old commercial routes and contacts were reestablished, and production reoriented itself toward markets that had been important in earlier periods: toward the Cuyo, for example, with the export of cattle to Chile, and toward a resumption of trade with Bolivia.[12]

Although the development of the Argentine Northwest in the years of independence is beyond the scope of this chapter, we should point out that the limited agricultural production and the very primitive artisan production that existed in the traditional Northwest would have created only a very small economic surplus. It would be inaccurate to describe the region as a subsistence economy, but technological changes or a different allocation of resources would have been necessary to bring about a significant increase of wealth. Artisan and agricultural production in the Argentine Northwest would have required greater inputs of labor or capital, both of which were scarce resources. The hide-based economy of the Littoral, however, was intensive in the use of one abundant resource: land. The possibilities for obtaining and accumulating a surplus was completely different in the two regions. The new uses of space and the preeminence of the Buenos Aires coastal region corresponded, then, to an adjustment of the relation between existing resources and the possibilities for trade. While favoring the coastal region, this adjustment also introduced structural changes into the economic and political life of the nation that made these advantages more lasting.

Therefore what defined the economic beginnings of nineteenth-century Argentina was the increasing importance in the economy of the agrarian exports of the Littoral.

The Territory

The territory of the country effectively occupied after independence consisted of the old Northwest (Salta, Jujuy, Tucumán, Córdoba, La Rioja, and Catamarca), the Mesopotamia, the northern zone, and the provinces of Cuyo and Buenos Aires, including the recently conquered area to the south of the Salado River, Entre Ríos, Sante Fe, and Corrientes.[13] In 1833 Rosas undertook the Campaign of the Desert, which succeeded in extending the frontier to Bahia Blanca and Patagonia.[14] In the Northwest this frontier ended at the Salado River. The climate is tropical in the North and temperate in the Center, which was at that time the most populated zone.[15] The humid pasturage region was basically in the area of Entre Ríos, Santa Fe, and the new lands of the province of Buenos Aires. Cattle raising in Cuyo and the central zone supplied Chile and the regional markets. The old routes linked Buenos Aires, Alto Perú, and Cuyo through the Carlota and the Cuarto River, eventually connecting with Chile. The Uruguay and Paraná rivers were the principal riverways that linked the Mesopotamian littoral to the Río de la Plata. Although ships risked the South Atlantic–European crossing, they did it infrequently; each crossing took five to six weeks.[16]

The Population

In the second half of the seventeenth century the population of the Argentine territory was estimated at 297,792 inhabitants: broken down by region, the Northwest accounted for 99,000 (33 percent) of the total; the Chaco region for 116,000 (39 percent); Mesopotamia for 28,000 (9 percent) and the provinces of Cuyo for 12,000.[17]

In the second half of the eighteenth century the population was 381,908. Buenos Aires and Santa Fe had 50,000 inhabitants (13 percent); the provinces of the Northwest had 99,000 (26 percent); and the provinces of Cuyo had 26,000.[18]

At the beginning of the nineteenth century the population was estimated at 300,000 inhabitants. An estimated 100,000 inhabitants lived in the Northeast; 115,000 in the Chaco; 27,000 in Mesopotamia; 12,000 in Cuyo; and 10,000 in Patagonia.

The principal demographic changes occurring regionally between 1809 and 1869 are summarized in Table 3. We shall describe here only the major changes during the period from independence until the national organization. The importance of the area of original settlement (Northwest-Center), which held more than half the population at the beginning of the century, is noteworthy. At the same time the Buenos Aires littoral, increasing in population only since the end of the eighteenth century, held little more than a third of the population, much less if we exclude the province of Buenos Aires (10.6 percent). The Cuyo provinces, linked by trade with Chile, were also important. In 1869, the changes promoting the Buenos Aires littoral, with 48.7 percent of the population, appear clearly. The decline of the interior, the Northwest-Center, was important but not drastic.

By 1869 population in the Cuyo region had declined as trade with Chile had fallen off. Trade revived soon after the arrival of the railroad, which definitively linked the area with the coastal and central markets, thereby creating a single national market. Population changes were related to the different regional economies. The province of Buenos Aires and the Mesopotamian littoral showed the greatest development, while the areas of older settlement grew at a slower pace. Nevertheless from 1820 until the fall of the Rosas government the Mesopotamian littoral (Entre Ríos and Santa Fe) lagged behind Buenos Aires, although these areas were in a similar position to devote their resources to the export trade. The proportion represented by the population of Sante Fe in the total population of the country fell from 3.2 percent in 1809 to 2.1 percent in 1849. This population decrease did not occur in Corrientes and Entre Ríos, provinces whose populations formed growing percentages of the national total from 1810 onward. Between 1849 and 1859 the most rapid growth took place in the provinces of the riverine littoral (Corrientes, Entre Ríos, and Santa Fe), where a 32 percent increase in population surpassed Buenos Aires' increase of 22 percent.

Raising cattle required little labor and consequently little population; therefore urban centers did not appear in the cattle zones and the Pampa remained almost uninhabited. Human contact was limited, and urban centers were located at the termini of trade routes or along the rivers, where ports were established to ship hides. Extensive cattle raising therefore inhibited the growth of urban life. After independence, in contrast to the colonial period, relatively few villages developed in Buenos Aires province.[19] Although the amount of land and the population increased after independence, there was no parallel growth of urban centers. As a result of the seasonal nature of the work in cattle raising and of an unstable family system, what developed was a sparsely settled, seminomadic society. Because cattle raising required such a small labor force, income distribution was unequal. The local pattern of social stratification was characterized by a small upper group and a small lower group. It was not a prosperous society, and the tastes, customs, and habits of the powerful landowners did not differ greatly from those of the lower classes. It was only in the urban centers that different life-styles developed, but in the Río de la Plata the brilliance of Peruvian urban life was never approached.

The Pattern of Extensive Cattle Raising

Between the second half of the eighteenth century and the first half of the nineteenth important changes took place in the economic life of the Río de la Plata. In earlier periods the economy had been oriented toward silver mining, the supply of mining centers, and the transporting of silver along the long route that led to the ports and on to Spain. Now the production of hides became the main economic activity.

A number of factors lay behind the transition from mining to ranching, the principal of which was the decline in silver production and the separation of Alto Perú from the newly independent provinces. Another factor was the rapid growth of cattle, which could reproduce in practically unlimited numbers on the vast, unpopulated Pampas. Given the existing resources—the abundant lands, the scarce labor and capital,—export-led growth did not result from deliberate neglect of the domestic market but rather from its inability to absorb the surplus. The problem was not one of resource reallocation between domestic and external markets but of a surplus that the internal market could not absorb.[20]

The existing resources of the Argentinian coastal areas determined the technological nature of production (intensive in land, but not in capital or labor), and this had certain economic consequences.[21] The production of a staple like hides had no backward linkages and only a few forward ones. In view of its low labor requirements, the corresponding income generated by export activities was also minimal. With few settled workers there was no demand for services or supplies, and therefore rural villages did not develop. For the same reasons there was no strong demand for food or clothing, and no incentive to invest in industries that might have met such demand.

Similarly, neither the scarce population nor the commerce in hides justified significant investment in roads or transportation. The technology underlying the production of this staple did not promote other activities, so the economic effects of the income generated from its export were small.

Four decades after independence the volume of exports had not varied significantly, except for a few particular years. Apart from the expansion of the frontier in Buenos Aires, no new urban centers or transportation networks had appeared. This relative stagnation was aggravated by internal conflicts and by external blockades. Nor did the order Rosas established succeed in making the panorama of the Argentine economy a more promising one.

II. FROM CONFEDERATION TO NATIONAL ORGANIZATION (1850–1880)

Changes in Production

As a result of important changes in agricultural production, exports increased noticeably between 1850 and 1880. While the value of exports totaled only 11.3 million gold pesos in 1850, by 1875 it had increased to 67 million gold pesos,[22] a 492 percent increase in twenty-five years, or 7.4 percent annually. (Mulhall offers a value of 50.3 million gold pesos for the exports in 1873 and 11.3 million gold pesos in 1850, representing 345 percent or an annual rate of 6.7 percent.[23]) If one begins in 1865 instead of at the low base of the early 1850s,[24] the growth rate was 10.8 percent per year until 1873 (from 22.1 million to 50.3 million gold pesos). This expansion was not merely the result of increased exports of previously produced goods; it was also a response to the appearance of new products, and therefore represented a change in the composition of exports. Hides, which until 1850 represented 60 percent of exports, had fallen by 1877 to 20 percent. Wool production increased, and until the 1840s exports of tallow and fats increased as well. It was also apparent in the different composition of exports (See Table 5).

A relative decline in the export of hides did not imply a fall in total exports. Hide production remained at previous levels, but was offset by a strong expansion in wool. This was also the pattern in the differential growth of cattle and sheep stocks[25] (see Table 4).

A variety of factors shaped the changes in agricultural production and the composition of exports. There was a gradual adjustment to the technical requirements of wool production, which demanded greater care than did hide production. The Creole sheep, which had been used only for their hides, were replaced by a mixture of Rambouillet and Negrotti breeds, which were raised for their wool. At first sheep farming was deprecated. The Creoles did not like the meat, and sheep offered nothing of greater value. They required more labor, but their hides were neither as useful nor as valuable as cattle hides since they were smaller. When there were too many Creole sheep in the coastal areas, they were simply thrown into the sea to avoid the work of slaughtering them. Nonetheless, by the end of the 1840s sheep were being raised for their tallow, though it was not until the 1850s that sheep raising expanded dramatically. The first wool exports began in 1850, probably stimulated by the demand left unfulfilled by the decline in Russian production caused by the Crimean War. Beginning in the 1860s, Argentine wool began to arrive in European markets on a regular and sustained basis. The North American Civil War interrupted the supply of cotton to Europe, and manufacturers clamored for wool, especially for use in a new combination of wool and cotton. Australia became the principal wool supplier for the British market, and after 1869 Argentina became the main supplier to the French market.

Wool production increased, not only in response to rising demand but also because of changes on the supply side. First, juridical and political stability contributed to the development of productive activities that required more capital and labor investments. Second, labor was available. While a cattle *estancia* of 10,000 hectares needed only one majordomo and two peons, a sheep ranch of two square leagues (5,400 hectares) required fifteen shepherds working in teams. Cattle required little attention; sheep, especially when raised for wool, needed much greater care to ensure the uniformity and quality of the wool.

On sheep farms a certain type of sharecropping developed that avoided wage outlays. In general, the person who cared for the flocks received a third of their production as remuneration. This was possible because sheep ranching was relatively more profitable than cattle ranching. With cattle, the hides were used, but the meat was destined for curing and domestic consumption only. With sheep, on the other hand, the wool was exported as well as the hides. Mulhall estimated that in 1877 a properly cared-for flock of sheep could easily provide a return of 80–100 percent a year. He adds, "The increased expenses have brought down the estimation to 60/70%".[26]

The displacement of cattle did not mean a decline in absolute terms. Cattle were moved toward less fertile land, leaving the best grazing areas for the sheep. The expansion of the frontier in the 1870s was the final condition for the successful growth of sheep ranching.

Agricultural commodities also made important advances as exports, although they never equaled hide exports in importance. The quantity of land under cultivation grew from 150,000 hectares in 1850 to 344,000 hectares in 1874 and to 1,730,000 hectares in 1884 (see Table 6).

Exports, Imports, Public Debt, State Expenditures, and the Crisis of 1874

Previous studies, especially by this author, show that exports were significantly undervalued, but official statistics after 1868 reveal increasing balance of trade deficits. The value of imports rose from 23 million gold pesos in 1864 to 49 million gold pesos in 1870 and to 73 million gold pesos in 1873. The value of exports, however, according to official figures, rose from 22.4 million gold pesos in 1864 to only 30 million gold pesos in 1870 and to 47 million gold pesos in 1873.

If the same underevaluation verified for exports existed for imports, the error would not be very important. However, if official values on imports were closer to market prices, the results would be affected and the actual trade deficit would be considerably lower. At present it is not possible to establish the size of this deficit, which nevertheless was very important. Foreign loans permitted the maintenance of high import levels when a sufficient export surplus could not be counted on for the capital needs of the country. For example, in 1870 the credits for public works represented receipts of 6 million pounds sterling or 30 million hard pesos (hard pesos = peso fuerte; see Appendix I for monetary equivalents), a very considerable amount in relation to the volume of exports, which was between 50 and 70 million hard pesos.[27]

When the war with Paraguay ended, the Argentine government undertook the construction of important public works projects, among them the building of railroads at state expense in remote interior areas. But still, the government had to pay the debts contracted to finance the war. In 1870 the Argentine government authorized the negotiation of a loan for 30 million hard pesos. Bonds were offered at 6 percent interest at 88½ in 1871, but they brought in only 2,222,400 pounds sterling (more than 11 million hard pesos). Direct credits for 1 million pounds were given to railroad contractors from this sum. The rest was deposited at interest in official banks for later use by those with no immediate opportunities to invest. This availability of funds resulted in a strong expansion of credit and currency, which, in turn, promoted public and private demand for imports (which rose from 23.1 million gold pesos in 1864 to 73.4 million gold pesos in 1873.) After the European crisis of 1873, the inflow of capital from abroad was interrupted; consequently, imports dropped off and state income fell (from 20.0 million hard pesos in 1873 to 13.6 million hard pesos in 1875), since a large proportion of funds (about 90 percent) came from customs house collections.

Urgently in need of funds, the government withdrew its deposits from the banks, provoking a crisis in the private sector. Total expenses in 1874 amounted to 29.7 million hard pesos with a deficit of 13.8 million hard pesos.[28] However, it was impossible to cut debt-servicing expenses, as was done with other current expenses. It was also difficult to cut military expenses because of the López Jordán uprising in Entre Ríos.

Faced with this grave situation, the Avellaneda government adopted measures of the most severe orthodoxy. Between 1873 and 1876 state expenses were cut from 31 million hard pesos to 22.2 million hard pesos (30 percent in three years) and the salaries of public workers were nominally reduced by 15 percent. Imports fell from 73 million gold pesos in 1873 to 36 million gold pesos in 1876, successfully balancing trade. Import duties were increased from 25 to 30 percent, while the burden of export duties was reduced from 6 to 3 percent. Since exports were undervalued for tax purposes, the effective burden was even less.

Argentina emerged from the civil wars with a confused monetary situation. Besides the pounds sterling used in international trade, silver pesos had been prevalent since colonial times and were quoted at 16 to the gold peso (as specified by the Law of 1881). Their abundance and fluctuation depended on the market situation. The province of Buenos Aires used a paper peso that originally had had parity with the silver peso but had been devalued in time, so that in 1862, 25 paper pesos equaled 1 silver peso.

At the height of the crisis, the government asked for a credit of 10 million silver pesos from the Bank of the Province of Buenos Aires which at that time was authorized to issue currency for the same amount. The withdrawal of the state's deposits from the banks resulted in a strong contraction of credit, and hence of monetary supply. When the government had no more funds it had to turn to the Bank of the Province of Buenos Aires, asking for a loan, thus placing itself in an embarrassing position and making it even more difficult to manage the crisis. A strong protectionist law was passed in 1876 to solve the problem of the external sector and to reduce the pressure on imports. Nevertheless, it did not arrest the pressure on gold. The National Bank demanded government intervention when its own depositors wanted to convert their deposits from paper into gold. The state intervened in 1876, decreeing the inconvertibility of the peso and saving the bank from bankruptcy. This measure prompted the devaluation of the paper peso. Its value fell from 25 pesos to 1 hard peso, to 32.20 pesos to 1 hard peso in 1879 (a decline of 28 percent, which, when revalued in 1881, became 27 percent). The devaluation of the paper peso raised the price of imports and reduced their volume, and after 1876 this led to a certain relief in the trade balance. The value of imports increased until 1873, then fell and stayed more or less stable from 1876 on, although lagging behind exports. Nevertheless, according to both official and corrected values, exports did not show an important increase during this decade. They were valued at 40 or 50 million hard pesos according to official figures; 50 or 60 million hard pesos according to the correct figures. The crisis of the foreign sector was resolved by a strong drop in demand for imports, not by a rapid expansion of exports.[29]

The first crisis of Argentine development (1873–1876) was the result of the following two circumstances: the lag between the level of imports and exports, and the difference between state expenses and state revenues. A balance-of-trade deficit that could not be solved with new credits obliged the state to reduce imports, which meant a reduction in its own income through the fall of import taxes. In view of the fiscal structure of the period, it was mainly the state that bore the brunt of its own orthodox program, since it had no alternative source of income. Even as the state's resources were reduced, it had to continue servicing the debt; these payments could not be decreased in the way that imports could be cut back. Then, the underdevelopment of the banking and monetary systems aggravated the situation. Furthermore, the government had to pay foreign debts in gold, while collecting its own income in paper pesos.

As a result of introducing protectionist tariffs, as well as credit restrictions and budget reductions, imports were cut back. However, exports did not increase substantially. No additional measures were taken after devaluation and increasing tariffs, and exports did not rise and their prices remained low. After 1876 no more wheat was imported; 21 tons were exported in 1876, 26 tons in 1899, and 1,000 tons in 1890.

Transportation Networks: The Railroads and River Navigation

Wool production and the growing agricultural production in Santa Fe and in the northern part of Buenos Aires Province required far more labor than had cattle hide production. At the same time, transportation networks were necessary to make sheep raising and agriculture profitable. Railroad projects were developed as the first immigrants arrived in Argentina. These early railroad projects were not oriented to the port of Buenos Aires, but rather to the interior and to the west of the country.

The first railroad was the Ferrocarril Oeste, which was inaugurated in 1857; it went 160 km. to Chivilcoy. Other railroads included the Ferrocarril Sud, which reached Bahia Blanca in 1865; and the Ferrocarril Central Argentino, which linked Córdoba, Rosario, and Tucumán in 1876. The Pacific region was covered by the Ferrocarril Andino, which connected Cuyo (San Luis, Mendoza, and San Juan) to Central Argentino. This line was inaugurated in 1873 and later merged with Ferrocarril Buenos Aires–Pacífico. The growth of the railroad network, the upsurge in cargo and passenger traffic, and the increase in immigration (which would solve the chronic labor shortage) can be seen in Table 7. However, it is worth emphasizing that even before the development of the railroads, and later in conjunction with it, mail service, stagecoach travel *(mensajerías),* and commerce along the rivers were all undergoing dramatic development. In 1854 the National Stage and Steam Service was created to move mail and passengers to and from the principal cities of the confederation. The stagecoaches noticeably reduced the length of trips. Instead of the two or three months that were needed to cross Argentine territory by wagon train or on horseback, one could now travel from Rosario to Córdoba in three days; from Córdoba to Santiago, and from Tucumán to Salta, in six; and from Rosario to San Juan in twelve. Whereas the railroads linked the cities of Argentina, the stagecoach lines were an essential element in linking the railroad stations with remote villages. By 1895 there were 179 stage lines with 460 coaches and 1,289 employees.[30] In addition to the railroads—which are mentioned by most writers on the period—and the stagecoaches, the most important factor in commercial development was river transportation. The railroads terminated at the river ports, and from there the merchandise was sent overseas.

If we compare the volume of merchandise carried by the railroads with that carried by vessels originating in or sailing to Buenos Aires, a major increase is apparent by 1880 (see Tables 7 and 8). Until 1865 the volume of cargo arriving at Buenos Aires by ship from the interior was greater than that transported by railroad. By 1880 river trade accounted for 26 percent of cargo. Besides carrying wool, cereals, and fodder to urban areas from the new agricultural centers of Santa Fe and Córdoba, the river trade also transported wool from the province of Córdoba. For some time the Río Paraná–Río de la Plata network absorbed a considerable portion of domestic trade. Only later was it displaced by the railroads, which succeeded in linking the ports and not just the cities of the interior, as in the case of Rosario and Buenos Aires. However, the river trade was never as sizable as the export trade. By 1880, 200,000 tons of river cargo passed through the port of Buenos Aires, compared to 700,000 tons of cargo shipped abroad.[31]

The development of the new transportation networks permitted differential regional development. Labor moved toward areas of greater relative development, and to areas where production was more labor intensive. The population growth records of each province suggest their relative development. It should be kept in mind that specialization in agriculture requires large amounts of labor. This does not imply, however, that wealth grew at a slower pace in cattle-raising areas. Population records are simply useful indicators in the absence of other figures on GNP. Other important indicators of growth are the internal and international labor migrations. In 1869 migration had its greatest impact on the province of Buenos Aires. After examining the data on residence compiled for immigrants in the city and province of Buenos Aires in the national census of 1895, we may presume that an important proportion of the arriving immigrants stayed in the port city in 1869. It is a known fact that newly arrived immigrants tended to stay initially in the port of arrival, before moving on to more remote areas. In 1869 this may have been because of Argentina's still limited agricultural development and the short extension of the railroads. In Santa Fe, where immigrants were later to write the history of colonization and be the principal factor behind the fabulous development of grain production, the greatest part of the nonnative population of the province were not foreigners but rather migrants from other provinces, (30 percent of the population of the province were born in other provinces and only 16 percent were foreign-born). In Entre Ríos 12 percent were natives of another province. The province of Jujuy was a very special case; there a very small population appeared in conjunction with the development of sugarcane cultivation.

Besides Buenos Aires, Santa Fe, Entre Ríos, and Mendoza were the provinces that received the highest percentage of foreigners.

The Population in 1869–1895

Changes in the structure of production and differential regional growth translated between 1869 and 1895 into population displacement from areas that "pushed" to areas that "pulled." The greatest number of native-born Argentines were attracted to the recently settled La Pampa. Jujuy followed, then the Federal Capital, Tucumán, Santa Fe, Mendoza, and Salta. Foreign immigrants represented a higher proportion of the population in the Federal Capital, Santa Fe, Buenos Aires, Entre Ríos, and Mendoza.

Political Economy: The Role of the State

The national state was exceedingly weak and chronically short of resources until 1880. Eighty percent of its funds came from customs house collections, which did not become federal funds until 1862; before that year they had belonged solely to the province of Buenos Aires.

Until 1881 there was no single national currency. Even after that date, although the federal government guaranteed its issuance, the National Bank and the Bank of the Province of Buenos Aires were responsible for the emission of currency. After 1885 the so-called guaranteed banks were also authorized to issue currency.

Until 1870 the federal government's average annual expenditure did not exceed 20 million gold pesos. Moreover, the amount collected was less than the amount spent. This gap continued until the end of the century and caused a chronic state of indebtedness. Expenses increased considerably during Sarmiento's presidency; from 16.7 million hard pesos in 1868 they rose to 29 million hard pesos in 1874. Income, on the other hand, rose only from 12.4 million to 16 million hard pesos, the difference being perhaps the principal reason behind the 1874 crisis. Avellaneda, who succeeded Sarmiento, made an enormous effort to contain expenditures and balance the budget. He finished his term with a level of expenditure of 26.9 million hard pesos, less than that at the end of Sarmiento's presidency, and with 19.6 million hard pesos in revenues. Although income was greater than it had been at the end of Sarmiento's term, it still did not meet the level of expenses.

Argentina was caught in a very peculiar situation. The government negotiated loans that provided funds for public works projects that otherwise could not have been built. An important part of this income was spent on imported goods, since the country did not produce capital goods. This meant increased imports that could not immediately be compensated for by a similar rise in exports. After 1874 the state of the world market made Argentina's situation more difficult. Declining international prices meant that increased export volumes were not translated into corresponding increases in value. In order to pay the debts contracted by loans the federal government counted on customs house collections, especially those derived from imports. The balance of payments was negative when financial payments—a combination of interest and amortization on the loans—came due, and when imports were not matched by the value of exports. This negative balance of payments increased the price of gold, and speculation grew with the expectation that gold prices would continue to rise. Now, if in order to pay its debts abroad, the government attempted to buy gold during a period of high speculative demand for it, it would simply increase the pressure of demand on the price of gold. In order to avoid this pressure and maintain the price of gold, the government was forced to sell its reserves. In view of this situation, the pressure to suspend convertibility was very strong. The government faced two contradictory alternatives: buy gold to pay debts, or sell it to maintain the value of the peso.

To continue selling gold when there were limited reserves and a strong expectation of devaluation was practically impossible. The government chose the apparently easier solution of declaring the inconvertibility of the paper currency. When it did so, the price of gold rose and the value of the paper peso fell, which affected the federal government adversely since its revenues were in paper money but it had to pay its debts abroad in gold. Inconvertibility and the concomitant devaluation of paper money made imports more expensive, and thus reduced demand. This, in fact, was one of the goals of the government's policy. But the policy had contradictory results. By pursuing it, the government also reduced its own income, a substantial part of which was derived from import taxes. Thus fiscal revenue dropped as a result of the policy to reduce imports (see Table 9). Consequently the government's policy of restraint condemned it to a reduction of revenue and to the practical impossibility of balancing its budget. The problem of the foreign debt was made even more difficult now that there was less paper income: what was needed was a much greater volume of paper to buy the same amount of gold in order to meet foreign debt payments. In order to escape this vicious cycle of revenue shortages, borrowing abroad, and the inability to face long-term payments, the country needed to increase exports and obtain more foreign exchange in gold. Increased exports would allow the government to buy gold inexpensively and meet its outstanding loan obligations. Nevertheless, for quite logical reasons, exports did not immediately reach a volume sufficient to cover service payments and current import demands.

Argentina was in a situation that repeated itself throughout the century. A period of rapid growth followed one of crisis in the external sector. The crisis of 1874 differed from that of 1890 only in that exports did not immediately react. In the earlier period the crisis ended because of a strong recession. During the crisis of the 1890s the export sector reacted immediately because of the country's higher level of infrastructural development in transportation and population growth. Similar developments also account for the difference in response between the crisis of 1890 and those of more recent periods.

Rural Population: Patterns of Settlement

The greatest population growth took place in regions where production required a great number of laborers. This was more noticeable in Santa Fe than in any other province. Between 1869 and 1895 the population of Santa Fe grew by 34.6 percent, outstripping the rest of the provinces, including Buenos Aires, where the rate of growth was only 25.5 percent. And the population was no longer concentrated only in large urban centers; people went to work in previously unpopulated rural zones, and brought about a fabulous increase in the amount of land under cultivation. In 1874 land under cultivation had amounted to 500,000 hectares; by 1914 it had reached 24 million hectares.

Agriculture required settled families to work the land and demanded a series of goods and services to supply the new rural centers.[32] The colonies of the first Santa Fe experiment were the first such settlements; others appeared in Entre Ríos and Córdoba. When the second national census was taken in 1895, there were seven hundred such settlements.

III. THE FORMATION OF MODERN ARGENTINA, 1880–1910

The 1880s: Investments, Foreign Trade, and Public Debt

Although the 1880s are known as the decade of the great export boom, this was not the period during which exports rose most. Until the last years of the decade there were significant variations in the size of corn and wheat exports, which by that time added up to several hundred thousand tons. The volume of the principal exports, wool and hides, while variable, rose between 30 and 50 percent; this barely compensated for the decline in wool prices, which fell by 21 percent between 1880 and 1889.[33] The price for salted hides fell by 40 percent.[34] The total value of exports held steady with little variation throughout the decade at about 70 million gold pesos.

The relative stagnation of exports during the 1880s reflected two important facts: first, grain was not yet being massively exported (this would not occur until the 1890s); second, international prices for agricultural goods declined. The expansion of the 1880s was not the result of a powerful export boom, as it was thought, but rather of other circumstances.

Public Credit, Import Pressure and Employment. The Avellaneda government balanced trade, stabilized finances, and consolidated the nation, with Buenos Aires as its capital. As a result of these measures, when Argentine bonds reappeared on the international market, they were favorably received.

Between 1880 and 1885 the Argentine foreign debt reached 100 million gold pesos (see Table 10). Between 1886 and 1889 the national debt doubled again. A careful study by Hansen, the Minister of Finance, presented the Argentine public debt in 1891 as shown in Table 11. The funds were spent abroad, for the purchase of machines, railroad material, port construction material, and other machinery and capital goods. Foreign credits translated into increased imports, which explains why, throughout the decade, there was a growing gap between the values of imports and exports. On the other hand, interest and amortization had to be paid on the loans from abroad, and this meant an additional obligation beyond those incurred by imports. Thus during the second half of the nineteenth century the debt service payments represented an alarmingly high proportion of the foreign debt.

Exports. One of the ways in which the increase of imports over exports was reflected was that while per capita exports declined, per capita imports increased (see Tables 12 and 13). The greater increase in imports was a prerequisite for a similar increase in exports.

The changing composition of exports was the most significant fact of the decade. Agricultural exports, which in 1880 had been less than 1 percent of the total, made up 25 percent of the total by the end of 1890. Nevertheless, they were insignificant in the early part of the decade: they surpassed 10 percent for the first time in 1884 (see Table 14).

Imports. Among imports, there was a notably high proportion of railroad material, which by 1890 constituted a quarter of all imports. This resulted in the great expansion of the railroad network and in the development of state-owned railroad lines (for example, Ferrocarriles del Norte) with funds that the state obtained from abroad. There were also direct investments in railroads, whose profits were guaranteed by the state. The investments in railroads, and the loans obtained from abroad during the second half of the century, suggest an improvement in the balance of payments through narrowing the gap in the commercial balance and permitting a continued high volume of imports. In the future, however, the debt service and the profit guarantees would become a heavy burden.

The composition of imports also changed. Sugar, wine, and cotton cloth imports fell. The decrease did not reflect a fall in consumption, but rather increased local production.

Balance of Trade and the Public Debt. Although statistical errors have led to arguments over the size of the gap between imports and exports, it is reasonable to suppose that the existence of the gap itself resulted from a particular developmental sequence. Thus imports preceded an increase in income from exports, because exports depended on the prior expansion of a railroad network built with imported materials.

The gap between imports and exports was covered by foreign credits during the 1880s, as Williams's study suggests. The credits, in turn, increased the pressure for more imports, and added a further burden to the service and amortization of previous debts. Table 15, taken from the book by Williams, shows how the negative trade balance between 1882 and 1884 could have been compensated for with foreign capital, and resulted in a positive balance of payments (except in 1884).

The gap between interest payments on the foreign debt and the value of exports increased between 1880 and 1890, and this portended grave danger. The crisis could only have been avoided if a continuous flow of loans had been assured to cover the gap, since, although exports were growing, they were growing slowly. It was only in a later period that the value of agricultural exports would pay for imports and for servicing the debt.

Loans from abroad managed to cover the trade balance deficit and maintain a positive balance of payments until 1889. In 1890, however, the growing weight of the debt service and the negative balance of trade were reflected in the large negative balance of payments of 56 million pesos (see Table 16).

At this point we should specify that the corrected value of exports was: for 1888, 66.3 million gold pesos; for 1889, 65.4 million gold pesos; and for 1890, 73.6 million gold pesos.[35] Thus the relation of the debt service to exports was much less favorable than Williams believed. In 1888 the debt service represented 75 percent of the value of exports: in 1889, 90.2 percent; in 1890, 82 percent.

The sequence of events that resulted in these gaps appears to have been the following: It became possible to obtain credit on the European money market, especially in London, because of the availability of foreign capital and the high returns in Argentina, especially in view of the stability and guarantees offered by the Argentine government. These funds permitted imports of capital goods, particularly railroad stock, which was purchased principally from Britain. If the funds were spent in Argentina, credit was still available from abroad, in the form of bills of exchange that could be used for further imports. The increase in imports, then, was faster than that in exports, and led to an increasing gap between them. One might expect that in an economy of this type exports would determine income and, in turn, the demand for imports. No gap, then, would exist between imports and exports. But the sequence of events in Argentina was different, since the characteristics of the economy at that time required an increase in imports first, in order to promote exports later, and foreign credit made the imports possible. The gap was closed with loans, which contributed to a continuous pressure to import. Eventually the debt service became greater than the available new credits. When it became impossible to obtain additional credits, there was a crisis because the government could no longer import and neither could it meet its debt-servicing payments. This situation immediately led to a decline in exports. It also meant that:

1. Now government revenue was derived principally from import duties.
2. Import duties were collected only on certain taxable items—not, for example, on exempted railroad material.
3. Duties were collected in local currency that had depreciated relative to the increased price of gold. This was also a result of the difficulties in the foreign sector.

Consequently, the government faced contradictory alternatives:

1. It could increase exports by changing the exchange rate so that it favored exports and made imports more expensive—that is to say, by devaluing the local currency relative to foreign exchange.
2. However, if the government adopted this policy, it would decrease its own revenues, since (a) its revenues were in local currency, which was constantly depreciating; and (b) imports, which were the principal source of revenue, would decrease.
3. Moreover, if the government did not maintain a fixed rate of exchange, the confidence of foreign investors would crumble, and with it the likelihood of obtaining further credits from abroad. Therefore, the situation was such that the government was faced with choosing between equally contradictory policies.

Composition of the Foreign Debt. Thus the government was depending on foreign trade, and import duties in particular, in order to finance its public works, support the currency, and pay for its operating expenses. Clearly, in order to tax imports, goods had to be imported, and in order to pay for them, goods had to be exported. But in order to be able to export, public works programs—principally railroad expansion—were essential, and the problem was precisely how to pay for this expansion before the potential revenue from exports became available. As we have seen, the government borrowed from abroad.

Three things are clear:

1. There were no other internal resources that could provide foreign exchange.
2. Social overhead capital had to be completed before exports could generate foreign exchange.
3. Foreign investors were not very interested in direct investments in Argentina.

Faced with these limitations, and a shortage of available capital on the international market, the government negotiated various forms of foreign bonds to cover the public debt. In the generalized disorder of the late 1880s many of these bonds were imprudent, unnecessary, even risky. However, the vast majority were negotiated in response to needs that could not have been met in any other way.

Table 17 shows the composition of Argentina's foreign debt, from the first loan in 1824 until 1913, according to the uses the funds were put to. It is noteworthy that more than 50 percent of the funds were spent on infrastructure. (Also see Table 18).

The Railroad: Immigration and Agriculture

Although the railroad network had expanded to permit the settlement of new territories, before 1880 the total length of railroad track was only 900 km. By 1890 there were 4500 km. of track, and the railroads crossed the entire Pampa region. The spread of railroads permitted settlements in remote areas of southern and western Buenos Aires province, in the south of Santa Fe province, in Córdoba, and later in the province of La Pampa. The railroads not only carried immigrants from the port of Buenos Aires to the interior; they also permitted long-distance internal migrations. Migrants moved first to neighboring provinces, and later to more remote provinces where there was a greater demand for labor. Finally, railroad stations eventually became population centers.

The railroad was very important in the development of urban centers during this period. Railroad centers were added to the already existing administrative cities along the colonial routes, and to the port cities of the Creole era. Rural products were shipped to the railroad centers, and these centers soon became the nuclei for other activities, including warehousing, commerce, and provisioning for the agriculturalists. In a short time the railroad centers assumed urban functions. A variety of general stores developed that provided the colonists with merchandise and acted as intermediaries in commercial and financial transactions.

The railroad also played an important role in the development process by incorporating previously unused resources, because land that was not served by the railroads generated no revenues.[36]

The Cost of Railroad Construction: Railroad Guarantees. The first track laid by the Western Railroad in 1857 went from the center of Buenos Aires to the suburb of Flores, 6 miles away. By 1892 the line had extended 7,000 miles at a cost of 75.6 million pounds sterling (393 million gold pesos). The total capital invested in railroads in relation to population was higher in Argentina (21 pounds sterling per inhabitant) than in more densely populated countries like France or Germany (where the cost of a kilometer of railroad track was 15 pounds sterling and 10 pounds sterling respectively). But it was less than in Australia (24 pounds sterling per kilometer) and the United States (35 pounds sterling per kilometer).

In Argentina, by 1890, according to Mulhall, 5,700 miles of track represented a capital investment of 68.8 million gold pesos. The railroads showed profits of 3.4 million pesos (5 percent annually). Most were built with private capital, except for the Western line, which was constructed with funds from the province of Buenos Aires and the Tucumán line, drawing on the public works loans of 1870. Around 1890 the extent of the railroads was as follows:

> *The Western Railroad.* Between 1866 and 1890 the Western Railroad laid 756 miles of track. It was sold to English concerns in 1890 because the province of Buenos Aires was in financial difficulty.
>
> *The Great Southern Railroad.* Construction began in 1864 on the Great Southern Railroad. The government guaranteed the company a 7 percent profit on the capital invested in construction. By the 1890s, after twenty years, the Great Southern had paid out 180 percent in dividends, at a 9 percent annual average. Because of these high profits, the Great Southern Railroad Company was able to dispense with the guarantees offered by the state.

By 1865 the Great Southern Railroad had laid 72 miles of track; it had by 1891 934 miles. The Central Argentine Railroad had been guaranteed 7 percent on invested capital. The cost per mile was estimated at 6400 pounds sterling. At the same time, the Central Argentine Railroad was also offered 3 million acres on the Rosario-Córdoba line. By 1892 the government had paid the railroad companies almost 3 million pounds in guarantees (15 million gold pesos). In 1891 alone, it paid 921,000 pounds sterling. By 1913 total capital invested in private lines was 1,210 million pesos (532 million gold pesos in 1891). (See Table 18)

However, what was paid in guarantees during the last years of the 1880s appears high.[37] In 1889 the payment of railroad guarantees corresponded to 3 percent of export revenues, but we should emphasize that this figure, for the reason already mentioned—namely the overvaluation of exports—is understated. The amount paid in guarantees corresponded to 6.2 percent of the interest paid on foreign loans. If we use corrected figures, the figure for the guarantees increases to 5 percent of the value of export revenue in 1890.

When the government assumed the task of building the railroad network by itself, it sought funding abroad to pay for the needed imports of equipment and construction material. In the case of the Western Railroad, when a difficult balance-of-payments situation combined with the impossibility of continuing imports, the government sold the line. It seems, therefore, that for a time the net entry of capital for railroads was a factor that permitted continued imports without aggravating the already difficult balance-of-payments situation. In short, it seems that the *way* in which the funds were obtained was more important than the sum total of invested capital, since it was becoming increasingly difficult to continue negotiating new credits abroad. However, the obligations contracted by the guarantees were most burdensome precisely during those years when credits were restricted.

On another level, the lowered costs of transportation meant higher profits for producers because of the relation between international market prices and production costs, of which transportation made up a substantial proportion. For example, in 1883 wagon transportation cost 7.5 gold pesos per ton per 100 km. In 1884 the Department of Engineers estimated that railroad transport cost 1.50 gold pesos per ton per 100 km.[38] Shipping costs, however, were even lower: 1.40 pesos per ton per 100 km. This gave the riverine provinces a great comparative advantage before the appearance of the railroads.

To a great extent, the investments in railroads that permitted an increase in producer profits were paid for by the population at large, at least during the early periods when the volume of freight moved was insufficient to generate the minimum profits that had been guaranteed to the railroad companies. The producers themselves paid for their transportation costs only when the volume of freight reached a point at which the minimum earnings expected by the railroad companies could be maintained at the going rates. Thus by guaranteeing the profits of investors, the government contributed in an important way to the development of a market for the railroads. On the other hand, it also contributed to a substantial reduction in the cost of production, especially in agriculture, which depended above all on cheap transportation.

Population: Immigration. The improved transportation and the economic expansion promoted by the railroads and public works attracted a great mass of people to the country during the 1880s. Table 19 shows immigrant arrivals between 1880 and 1889. The immigrants had special characteristics: a high proportion (about 70 percent) were male, and over 80 percent were of economically active age. This meant that immigrants entered the labor force in numbers out of proportion to their representation in the population, and consequently they made a relatively greater contribution both to the labor force and to the increase in the national product.

Most of the immigrants came from Italy, or from Spain. A high proportion described themselves as farmers, because farmers were especially protected by the immigration law. Despite this self-description, many of them settled in the cities because the economic expansion of the 1880s was based on the development of infrastructure and urban construction. The demand for urban labor in the 1880s was a powerful incentive, drawing immigrants to the city. It resulted in urban expansion, especially in Buenos Aires, whose growth rate in 1880 was considerably greater than that of rural areas (see Table 20). This was not the case after 1890.

The city had various "pull" effects, chief among them being decreased social distance and increased possibilities for social mobility. However, Mark Schuszchman's study suggests the limitations and rigidities in such mobility.[39] Yet another view sees the politics of land as responsible for the failures of colonization: Donald Castro argues that the immigrant was not able to acquire land, and therefore remained in the cities.[40]

Immigrants did move to the agrarian provinces, where they occupied previously uninhabited areas in Santa Fe and southern Córdoba. Although production did not increase as much as it would later, immigrants concentrated primarily on produce for the internal market and on fodder production. Already the preconditions for the impressive agricultural development of the 1890s were present. The agricultural growth between 1881 and 1888 was just the beginning of a process that accelerated after the crisis of 1890, and which from then on was marked by rapidity of development.

Changes in the 1890s, Export Expansion, and Developments between 1890 and 1914

Important changes occurred after 1890. For a number of reasons, the restrictions of the preceding two decades—which were based on the need to acquire foreign credits for building the infrastructure for exports—had disappeared.

In the next few years foreign capital was still needed and the demand for imports rose again, but after 1890 the volume of exports increased to the point where the revenues collected were sufficient both to pay for imports and to service the debt. Whereas in the 1880s exports had undergone only a slight increase, in the 1890s they expanded significantly (see Table 21). From 103 million gold pesos in 1891, the value of exports increased to 134 million in 1898 and to 185 million gold pesos in 1899.[41] At least during this period the increase was not the result of any change in international prices, for these remained unfavorable—especially for agricultural products—until almost the end of the century. Rather, the value of exports increased because of an unprecedented expansion in the volumes exported, particularly in a category that had been of minor importance at the end of the 1880s: grains—first wheat, and later corn.

A number of factors were responsible for the increase in exports.

First, the earlier policy of investing in infrastructure—principally rail-roads—had, as Ford[42] has pointed out, a delayed effect that only became apparent years later. Second, the fluctuating exchange policy made Argentine products competitive on the international market (see Table 23 below). Abandoning the gold standard had favorable consequences after 1890, especially since other grain-exporting nations like the United States still adhered to it. Other contributing forces, like the failure of the Russian harvest, also favored Argentine exports in the 1890s. On the one hand, the devaluation of the paper peso, the local currency, made imports more expensive, and thus protected domestic production of previously im-ported items. On the other hand, since the volume of currency in circula-tion was not tied to the availability of gold—that is to say, to exportable surpluses—internal demand was sustained, where it might otherwise have declined significantly because of the restrictions in the foreign sector.

These devaluationist policies also contributed to the development of domestic industries. Although employment in the public sector did not expand, employment in the private sector—except during the first years of the crisis—returned to the level of the 1880s. It is important to note that there was a significant decline in urban employment in the period right after the crisis, but this decline was absorbed by an important increase in rural employment. If the relation of prices to rural wages is considered, it seems clear that the policy of fluctuating exchange reversed the effects of declining international prices, which were only seriously felt during the first years of the 1890s. In any case, it is certain that the principal charac-teristic of the first period of expansion was the decline of transportation costs.

Between 1891 and 1919 the value of exports increased at an annual rate of 5.7 percent (gold pesos). Per capita exports also increased, which had not been the case during the previous decade. Exports rose from 30 gold pesos per capita at the beginning of the 1890s to 34 gold pesos by the end of the decade. By 1905 the value of exports was 61 gold pesos per person. Per capita imports were reduced, in turn, from 42 gold pesos in 1890 to 24.6 in 1900. After that, per capita imports rose again. What is significant is that while in the previous period capital goods had been imported, resulting in a heavy import burden relative to the total popula-tion, during this period there was a surplus of export earnings sufficient to cover not only the debts created by the imports of the earlier period but also current imports.

Agricultural Development: Agricultural Expansion in the Province of Buenos Aires and Changes in Land-Use Patterns. During the crisis, and in spite of its depressive effects, the best-informed contemporary observers were aware that the country was undergoing one of its most dynamic moments of development. This was the conclusion that Minister López reached on the basis of the excellent study that he presented to Congress in response to its request for a survey of the country's productive capacities.[43]

After 1890, and especially after 1891, grain prices, which had been low, rose unexpectedly because of the failure of the Russian harvest. In addition, the adherence of the United States to the gold standard facilitated the entry of Argentine wheat on the European market. From then on, Argentina became one of the principal grain suppliers on the world market. The growth of grain exports was surprising, since two decades earlier they had been altogether insignificant, but by the end of the century they equaled those of the livestock industry. After that the composition of Argentine exports was equally weighted between crop and livestock products. Variations in this structure were simply efficient responses to price fluctuations. Thus, although Argentina continued to export agricultural products, important changes had taken place in the composition of exports. They had shifted from traditional products with low labor inputs, such as hides and jerked beef, to wool, then to grains, and after 1900 to beef and mutton. From 1890 on, it was crop production that would define modern Argentina (see Table 24).

Crop production was to characterize Argentina not only because grain became the principal export commodity, or because of its implications for modern cattle raising, but also because crops meant a larger use of labor, which, therefore, created additional demands. When twentieth-century technological advances made the transportation of chilled and frozen beef possible, beef became another modern Argentine export. Livestock breeding for the production of beef also required increased labor inputs which required transportation facilities and the production of fodder in order to feed the cattle during the winter. In addition to corn, alfalfa was introduced as fodder during the first decade of the twentieth century; this permitted significant increases in beef production per hectare. Alfalfa reached the herding regions at the same time that agriculture and crop rotation were being introduced.

Meat Production—Price Changes. Just as cereal exports, especially wheat, had been the principal factor in the economic recuperation of the 1890s, so meat exports were responsible for the new export boom at the beginning of this century. Cattle had been exported on the hoof since the 1890s, but from 1900 frozen and chilled beef and mutton were also exported. Argentine exports doubled in a decade and the share of meat in the export totals was outstanding.

Frozen beef exports rose from a value of 2 million gold pesos in 1900 to 33 million in 1934. Chilled beef increased from a value of 600,000 gold pesos in 1908 to 4 million in 1914. The value of exported frozen mutton, which in the 1890s had been the most heavily exported frozen meat, remained between 4 and 5 million gold pesos.[44] Besides increased meat and cereal exports, agricultural prices also contributed to the export boom of the first decade of this century. After declining from 1880 to 1900, world market prices began to rise again. Between 1899 and 1914 the price of wheat rose 67 percent in gold pesos. The price of beef rose 90 percent, corn 80 percent, and wool 23 percent.[45]

It is clear that the expansion was much greater than that of the preceding period. To the greater physical volume of exports were added the effects of the rising prices, which contributed to a greater increase in revenues. Whereas until 1895 export expansion had resulted from an increase in the physical volume of exports—which had compensated for and even surpassed the effect of declining prices—export expansion after 1900 resulted from increases in both volume and prices.

These changes had other specific effects: remote areas were populated, and transportation networks and urban centers were developed. The need for food, clothing, and shelter for settlers created incentives for other activities. Finally, to the extent that these new economic activities also required more labor inputs, the distribution of income was affected. Of course income distribution was not entirely equitable, but labor did receive a greater proportion of the income generated than it had previously.

The situation was no longer simply that an increase in production was a result of the incorporation of unused factors of production, such as land or labor. Now increased production was due as well to technological improvements in crop production and cattle raising.

The Railroads and Freight Transport. We should point out that the ratio of passengers and freight to kilometers of railroad track was low until 1890; after that it increased significantly. The number of passengers and the volume of freight practically doubled between 1890 and 1910. The volume of freight rose from 574 tons per kilometer in 1890 to 764 tons per kilometer in 1900, and to 1,255 tons per kilometer in 1910. The number of passengers remained steady around 1,000 per kilometer between 1890 and 1900, but by 1910 it had reached 2,000 persons per kilometer.

The result was a greater use of the railroads, which had probably been operating at less than capacity since their construction. This shows that the railroads did more than simply respond to a preexisting demand. They played a pioneer role in incorporating lands and taking settlers to the areas where they were able to produce goods that were then shipped back along the railroads. The most important product shipped was grains, which constituted about 30 percent of all shipments. In 1904 the wheat shipped by rail was 83.7 percent of the nation's total production, and the corn shipped by rail was 53.7 percent of total corn production. Both cases indicate the extent to which the marketing of grain depended on the railroad.[46]

In addition to grain and the fuel necessary for consumption by settlers and by the railroad itself, the railroads also shipped significant quantities of industrial products and construction materials (see Table 25). This reveals the existence of an internal market with a growing demand. Later on, winter shipments of cattle sent by railroad to the processing plants to avoid weight loss became an important element of total railroad freight.

By 1914 the railroad network had reached its present configuration, and it was the principal carrier of export products. Furthermore, it had displaced the old fluvial shipping lines by linking, for example, Buenos Aires and Rosario by land. These cities had previously been linked by river transport, and the appearance of the railroads consequently undercut the importance of the port of San Nicolás. Finally, the realignments that followed the railroads promoted ports on the Atlantic coast as the new subregional agricultural centers, at the expense of the older river ports.

The Towns. During this period it was the recently settled central zone that underwent the greatest urban development, not the older northern zone along the coast and around the port of Buenos Aires. This was already noticeable between 1881 and 1895, but became significantly so by 1914. Wheat growing spread throughout this area, especially after 1900.[47]

The importance of the development of agriculture for urban growth is perfectly clear in the case of Rosario, with its links to the surrounding farmlands. Between 1890 and 1895 Rosario's urban population grew at a rate even greater than that of Buenos Aires. Rosario's growth during those years was linked to the increase in land brought under cultivation, the growing number of farms, and increased exports.[48] In contrast, the rapid growth of Buenos Aires during the previous period, before 1890, was related to higher import rates, public expenditures, and public works.

The Crisis of 1890—Policies. The crisis of 1890 proceeded as follows:

1. First it became impossible to continue payments abroad because of the acute imbalance between the country's obligations and its ability to pay, as determined by the revenues acquired from exports.
2. As a result, gold reserves declined and the price of gold rose.
3. Finally, banks were unable to meet the demands of their customers, who withdrew their deposits when faced with strong depreciation of the paper currency and its inconvertibility. The fear of depreciation was followed by the fear of bankruptcy.

In facing these problems, the government adopted policies that sought to solve the problem of the foreign debt. A moratorium was negotiated in London, and in the absence of new credits there was a drastic cut in imports. For its own part, the government attempted to curtail its expenditures and find new sources of revenue. State expenditures, which were 95 million paper pesos in 1890, fell to 46 million in 1891 and to 48 million in 1892. The reduction in real terms was even greater than these figures suggest. Additional duties were placed on imports, with the proviso that 50 percent had to be paid in gold. Minister López also placed a tax on all foreign bank deposits, which provoked an irate reaction in some banking circles. Public works were reduced by 72 percent between 1890 and 1891.

In a crisis such as this one, when the government did not have enough foreign exchange (gold), any effort on the government's part to buy gold on the open market would increase its price, and consequently increase the difficulty of making payments in gold. In spite of its budget cuts, the government's difficulties in making payments abroad increased because the peso had been devalued. The foreign exchange problem was solved by postponing payments, first with the de la Plaza moratorium and later with the Romero agreement. Exports also increased rapidly, growing between 1890 and 1895 by 74 percent, an annual rate of 12 percent.

The currency in circulation varied erratically between 1880 and 1890 because of the abandonment of the gold standard, and also because of the large issues authorized by the guaranteed banks. After 1890 the issue of money was much more restrained. Since the currency was no longer tied to the gold standard, the negative trade balances did not translate into strong falls in currency, and therefore the recessive effects on the economy were lighter. Between 1884 and 1890 the currency in circulation grew by 30 percent annually. Between 1890 and 1893 it grew at an annual rate of 7 percent, after which it became stable and remained so until 1902.

An important aspect of the differences between official policies in the crises of 1874 and 1890 is that until 1890 Argentina had neither a single monetary system nor a developed banking system.

The Tax System. As we have seen, government resources depended almost entirely on customs house collections. It might be argued that this system was not the most satisfactory, and that other alternatives existed—for example, sales or income taxes. However, in a sparsely populated country whose people had low incomes there was not a broad enough market to ensure continuous and substantial collection of funds through a sales tax. Nor could an income tax based on the earnings of a population dependent on wage labor provide a more or less continuous and secure source of funds, since a mass of wage laborers did not yet exist. These were the conditions that made foreign trade almost the only sure source of income for the treasury. Historical circumstances limited the possible alternatives.

The New Export Pattern. The production of primary goods for export, such as hides or jerked beef and, to a lesser degree, tallow, had responded to the available factors of production in Argentina during the first half of the nineteenth century. This pattern of agricultural production had required little labor, limited capital, and no transportation networks. The income generated by these exports did not lead to growth in demand in other areas—roads, housing, transportation, clothing, and so on—and therefore did not promote an expansion in the economy as a whole.

The new pattern was distinctive. Although, like the earlier patterns, it was based on the export of primary goods, it allocated the factors of production in different proportions. The production of grains and meat required more labor, as well as transportation networks and population centers in the rural areas to provide for the needs of the new settlers. In addition to the needs of the inhabitants, other demands generated by the processes of production and distribution had to be met, and this required the development of a whole series of activities.

Consequently the new pattern, although also export oriented and based on the production of primary goods, had different effects from the previous export pattern on:

1. The composition and distribution of the population.
2. The population of rural areas.
3. The development of transportation networks.
4. The growth of urban centers.
5. The development of local industries to supply the needs of the population as well as the demands created by the new productive activities.

The characteristics of this export pattern were:

1. The formation of a mass of wage earners in urban as well as rural areas. Agricultural wage labor developed in the rural areas on a permanent or seasonal basis, and in the regional population centers it developed in the tertiary (service) sector.
2. A sizable number of rural producers also emerged. These were not landowners. They were nonsalaried, or only partially salaried, and they worked the land under contracts, without ownership.
3. Finally, the labor force was more mobile a result of the new transportation facilities and the contractual characteristics of its ties to the land, as well as the opening up of new areas.

All these factors contributed to the formation of a national market that had never before existed, and consequently boosted the demand for goods and services, which increasingly were locally supplied.

Linkages: Industrial Development

It has sometimes been argued that unrestricted international trade with no protective barriers, which is required for specialization in the export of primary goods, is an obstacle to the development of local industry. Conversely, it has been argued that exports generate demands that are sometimes met by imports, but may also be met by local industries, especially those with a comparative advantage. The most obvious example of a local industry with a comparative advantage is the construction industry, for which geographical placement is a critical factor. Other examples are industries using local raw materials, when the cost of transporting imported merchandise makes local production more economic. This is also the case with prepared food and beverages, as well as with textiles.

The import statistics that we will examine indicate an increase in imports of nondurable goods: food and beverages, for example, as a consequence of the population increase and the increase in incomes. Furthermore, it is possible to see that the increase in these imports tapered off, not because of a decline in population or income, but rather because of the development of domestic industries that supplied the demand. Shifts in the composition of imports permit us to identify the most important changes in demand and to specify to what degree the new demands were met from within the country.

Demand not only increased, it diversified. Immigrants preferred to maintain their customary diet, and they needed clothes and housing. In addition to these necessities, an expanding population with rising incomes demanded the less basic goods as well, but it is clear that the bulk of the items imported were for popular consumption.

After a while imports of consumer goods declined, indicating not that demand among the growing population had fallen, but rather that the demand was being supplied by local industries. This can be demonstrated with data on industrial production.

The decline was most evident in imports of staple foods (which fell from 22.5 percent of total imports in 1880 to 8.6 percent in 1914) and beverages (14.1 percent in 1880 and 3 percent in 1914). Sugar and wine imports declined the most, as these were being produced in Mendoza and Tucumán.

There was an increase in textile imports (but a decline in ready-made clothing) until 1890, when they reached 39.4 percent of imports, and then a sharp drop to 17.4 percent in 1914.

The production of raw materials such as wood and other materials used in local construction and housing activities remained stable. The food, beverage, textile, and construction industries grew the most. While the relative proportion of imported consumer goods declined, raw materials, capital goods, and fuel imports remained high, and even increased. Railroad material was relatively more important before 1890.

Changes in the composition of imports suggest that the increases in wealth generated by exports were not derived solely from the countries abroad that were receiving the exports; nor did the wealth remain solely in the hands of a small export sector.

Population, employment, and income increases generated demand for a variety of goods. If in the beginning these were supplied by imports, local producers quickly took over. Perhaps the most important effect of the increase of income provided by exports was the creation of incentives for local production. This was most marked in those sectors where there was a comparative advantage for local production.

First to develop were the less capital-intensive activities involving the processing of raw materials to satisfy an immediate demand. The exchange policies of 1885 and 1899 protected local production because devaluation made imports more expensive. If we cannot specify, as we can in the case of the United States, which of the exporting activities had the backward linkages that provided incentives for domestic production of specific goods,[49] it is clear that the demand linkages discussed by Watkins were very important.[50]

Let us see, then, how this is reflected in the development of the industrial sector.[51]

Industry. Except for the years for which there is a national census (1895 and 1914, and the economic census of 1908), figures on industry (number of plants, capital, employees, and production) are dispersed, unsystematic, and incomplete—especially with regard to production. Also, the data are not always comparable. We have attempted to pull together the available information at the national, provincial, and municipal levels (including, for example, the provincial censuses and those for the city of Buenos Aires) when it refers to production either for export or for domestic consumption. (See Table 26). The first immediate generalization we can make is that there was no particular preference for the production of goods for the domestic or export market. What determined the growth of a particular industry was the availability of raw materials within the country. In constant terms, industrial capital grew by 6.8 percent per annum between 1895 and 1914 (at current prices this would have been 7.1 percent per annum).[52] If we compare the figures for 1895 with those of 1914, it seems that growth was much greater in the last five-year period.

However, the figures for 1910 do not seem sufficiently reliable, so we prefer to draw comparisons between the two national censuses, for 1895 and for 1914.

Industrial Production. Figures on industrial production are even more limited, since the census of 1895 did not include the whole country. Perhaps the only temporal comparisons that can be made are for the Federal Capital between 1887 and 1909; for the province of Buenos Aires between 1905, 1909, and 1913; or for the whole country between 1909 and 1914. In Table 27 figures on industrial production are deflated according to the export price index. There is little more to add, for the reasons already given. However, for the four years between 1909 and 1913 industrial production increased in constant prices, reaching a cumulative annual rate of 8.1 percent (greater than that of exports). In the Federal Capital industrial production increased in constant prices at an annual rate of 5.5 percent between 1887 and 1913. In the province of Buenos Aires the rate of growth was 14.6 percent between 1906 and 1913; between 1909 and 1913 it was 14 percent. In the city of Buenos Aires the annual rate of growth of industrial production was even higher, 23 percent. As impressive as these figures seem in relative terms, they say nothing about the effect of industrial production on the economy as a whole. In view of the characteristics of the export economy, the most reliable comparison that can be made is between the value of industrial production and the value of exports in a given year (even when part of the production is also exported). The value of industrial production in 1913 was very low relative to the value of exports in that year.

Population: Regional Displacements, Immigration, and Internal Migrations

According to the regional classification of the 1914 census, the eastern provinces were the fastest growing areas in the country between 1895 and 1914. But by 1914 this was no longer true.

To some extent, Entre Ríos and Corrientes lagged behind the growth in the new regional alignment around the Pampa. Southern Córdoba, on the other hand, which until 1914 had been oriented toward the central-north zone, became decisively integrated into the new Pampa region when the Central Argentine Railroad crossed the southern part of the province. The economy of the northern part of the province remained unchanged.

Between 1894 and 1914 the greatest population growth took place in the old Littoral: in the Federal Capital 137.3 percent; in Buenos Aires 124.3 percent; and in Santa Fe 126.5 percent. In the interior central-western areas Córdoba grew by 109.4 percent and Mendoza by 138.9 percent; the latter was the highest growth rate in the whole country. Curiously Santiago del Estero grew only by 62.1 percent; Tucumán by 54.3 percent; and Jujuy by 54.1 percent. The provinces with the least population growth were Entre Ríos, at 45.6 percent; Corrientes at 44.8 percent; San Luis at 42.7 percent; La Rioja at 14.7 percent; and Catamarca at 11.3 percent. In short, regional displacements favored the new Pampa center, Buenos Aires, southern Santa Fe, Córdoba, and La Pampa, as well as the provinces of Cuyo in the west and Tucumán in the north. The country had extended itself from the Littoral zones into a new interior region consisting of the Pampa and the central-western regions. Although the proportion of foreigners among the total population of the Federal Capital, Santa Fe, and Entre Ríos remained high, it diminished somewhat, as did the proportion of natives of other provinces. This was the result of a nationalization process among the immigrants who had arrived decades before and who now had Argentine-born children.[54] However, the proportion of foreigners increased in the more recently developed regions of Córdoba, La Pampa, San Juan, and even Tucumán and Mendoza. The proportion of natives from other provinces in Tucumán and Mendoza decreased compared to that recorded in 1895.

Figures on the relative growth rates of the principal urban centers reveal a little-known picture. The city that grew most between 1895 and 1914 was Avellaneda, a suburb of Buenos Aires. This anticipated a process that would become more important several decades later: the fabulous development of the industrial belt surrounding the city of Buenos Aires. Bahia Blanca, in the far south of Buenos Aires Province, and not the Federal Capital, followed Avellaneda in growth. In third place was Salta; then came La Plata, Santa Fe, Tucumán, Rosario, Córdoba, and the Federal Capital. These cities were followed by Santiago del Estero and Mendoza.

CONCLUSIONS

This chapter has described the evolution of an export economy over the course of a century. It has outlined the circumstances and factors that contributed to the different impacts of exports on the Argentine economy. Even though during the second half of the nineteenth century Argentina did not initiate a process of industrialization oriented toward the domestic market, but rather continued to export raw materials and food, important changes took place that had decisive effects on the pattern of subsequent economic development. Until 1850 the export of products for which there was no domestic demand—hides and jerked beef—grew out of a mode of cattle raising that was consonant with the existent resources, transportation, and markets. Extensive cattle raising developed in response to abundant lands, scarce population, and enormous distances. Although extensive cattle raising had limited economic effects, it resulted in the use of factors of production that would otherwise have remained unused.

An alternative strategy of development might have promoted the expansion of activities that until 1810 had been oriented toward the internal and regional markets of Alto Perú. This strategy would have necessitated the use of a scarce factor of production, such as population, or it would have required technological change, which, in turn, would have required an even scarcer resource, capital. The conditions under which colonial craft production took place did not yield a significant economic surplus. However, the technological conditions of extensive cattle raising did not create additional demands or incentives in other areas of the economy: extensive transportation networks were not necessary, since this mode of cattle raising required neither a large labor force nor the settling of empty spaces, and the cattle were able to move themselves. For many decades after the first expansion in exports, therefore, overland transportation was as scarce and difficult as it had been at the beginning of the nineteenth century. The settlements were sparse, and most were in the fluvial area. The limited number of economic activities linked to extensive cattle raising, coupled with political factionalism and further complicated by enormous distances, prevented the development of a domestic market at the national level. Distance and the cost of transport meant that until the appearance of the railroads the peripheral economies in the north and Cuyo remained limited to the local markets linked to the neighboring countries of Chile and Bolivia. Finally, distance and transportation also limited the amount of land that could be used for export production. As a result, after the Rosas campaign the amount of available land became stable. Finally, except for isolated years in which blockades caused exports to fluctuate violently, the volume of exports remained more or less at earlier levels.

Toward the end of the Rosas period exports were expanded by the addition of sheep products. Overgrazing resulted in a need for additional land, and the limits of the existing supply of land became increasingly evident.

Toward the end of the 1850s new exports were gradually added to the traditional ones: wool, then cereals and grains, and later meat. This occurred partly because of natural conditions, but also because problems that had been limiting development had been resolved. The development of a transportation network and the massive incorporation of population provided the basis for the new expansion in exports. Thus wool, and later grains and meats, entered foreign markets, and a new and sustained export expansion developed.

We have shown that the increase in export volume was tied to changes in the composition of exports, and that these changes modified the structure of production, with profound effects on the Argentine economy. What caused the increase in production and supply? The claim that it was the result of an almost mechanical response to increased European demand appears unfounded if one considers that it occurred just at the time that agricultural prices—especially for cereals—were in decline. These low prices were a response to the increased supply from new export countries: the United States, India, and Canada. If this was the case, and if we assume that after a while a producer cannot continue sowing if he does not receive sufficient returns, there must have been a substantial decline in the costs of production, so that in spite of the low prices, profits actually increased.

We have seen that the building of the railroads resulted in a drastic reduction in transportation costs. The railroads also opened access to lands which were cheaper than those in the already populated coastal areas. Thus it was the availability of fertile lands accompanied by the drastic fall in transportation costs that permitted the shipment of grain from Argentina to the European market.

In addition, the government played a decisive role—for example, in the mobilization of the labor force, which enabled 20 million hectares to come under cultivation. This was done in a number of ways. First, legislation was passed giving foreigners security and various guarantees. It was notably liberal with regard to cultural practices and traditions (legal rights, marriage and civil registry, freedom of religion, etc.). Second, immigrants' passages to Argentina were financed. Finally, the railroad lines permitted the new settlers to reach the most distant areas.

Government policies were equally important in other areas. Flexible exchange rates contributed to the maintenance or even rise in the profits of producers. Although cereal prices on the international market were declining, their prices in paper currency rose after inconvertibility was declared in 1885. However, this action would have contributed to the stability of profits only if domestic prices and costs did not rise in proportion to the devaluation of the currency. When we compare the relation of grain prices to rural wages, it is noteworthy that prices rose more than wages until 1895. After 1895 wages rose more than prices, which reduced profits once again. With the 1899 reform and the return to convertibility, wages remained practically at the same level as prices. The "gap" between prices and wages was really important only between 1885 and 1895. This was precisely the period when the first increase in cereal exports took place, just as railroad networks were expanding. Therefore the gap between prices and wages was less important than is frequently thought because the overriding factor was the lowering of transportation costs.

Government policy favoring exports consisted of a strong undervaluation of the Argentine peso. This is made clear in Table 23, which compares the price of gold and the relationship between prices in the United States and Argentina. The percentage of the undervaluation of the paper peso in relation to the dollar, comparing the purchasing power of both currencies, appears in the last column.

Argentine products, then, were incorporated into the world market as a result of lowered production costs, and not as a result of high prices and increased demand, at least until the 1890s.

If these were the expansion mechanisms, what were the mechanisms that diffused the effects of increased income from exports throughout the economy?

Cultivation entailed a different allocation of resources. In the first place, it was more labor intensive and income distribution was much more equitable than had been the case for cattle raising or hide production. Concomitantly, in contrast to the ratio of one worker per 1,000 hectares for cattle raising, now an average of between 100 to 400 hectares supported a family as well as seasonal workers. These agricultural families needed a multiplicity of services: transportation, housing, clothing, and various consumer goods. Thus urban centers developed in previously deserted rural areas, and they became the first nuclei of the transportation system, as well as centers of production, distribution, and supply for the surrounding population. All these factors contributed to the enlargement of the domestic market (Watkins's "demand linkages") and to the development of a national market. Finally, this situation stimulated other productive activities, as well as production for export. In addition, a relatively large amount of capital was invested in agriculture, and later in cattle raising. To the extent that these linkages existed, therefore, an important proportion of the income generated by exports remained in the country and was transferred to the rest of the economy by the creation of new demands that promoted investment in new areas to satisfy them.

In this sense, it is not simply the primary or export character of an economy that determines whether or not that economy will develop as an enclave.[55] Rather, it is, on the one hand, the technological conditions of production and the allocation of resources (land, labor, and capital), and on the other, the institutional and social conditions, and the characteristics of the population, including its educational level, that will determine the population's participation in political decisions and income distribution.

If the expansion of supply was a response not to price incentives but rather to a substantial decrease in costs that increased profits, and if this was due *principally* to the construction of the railroad networks, ports, and general infrastructure that preceded the spurt in exports, how was this important capital formation financed?

Here we must note the following points:

1. Argentina did not then produce capital goods, railroads, machinery, etc.
2. The surplus of domestic production that was not exported was small. Without any exports it would have been impossible to obtain the foreign exchange to acquire capital goods.
3. There was thus no alternative but to import the capital goods and to export in order to obtain the foreign exchange to pay for them.
4. In order to export, however, the prior construction of a social infrastructure of railroads, roads, and ports was essential.
5. Therefore capital goods had to be imported in order to develop a subsequent export capacity. The difference between the value of imports and exports was covered by credits obtained from abroad.
6. These circumstances repeatedly placed the Argentine economy in an extremely delicate position.

As we have seen, every period of expansion entailed an important increase in imports, which to a large degree were paid for by foreign credits. Crises occurred when exports were insufficient to pay for both imports and the debt service, and these crises led to reduced imports and a consequent reduced rate of capital formation. It was this structural situation in relation to the foreign sector that was responsible for the stop-go cycles and instability that have characterized the Argentine economy for so long.

With regard to the first point listed—that Argentina did not produce capital goods—it might be argued that it did not need to in order to industrialize, that the industrialization process could begin without acquiring such heavy and sophisticated equipment. For example, industrialization might have begun with the domestic production of textiles. This is true. In fact, this was the industrialization pattern in other parts of the world. However, this argument does not acknowledge that regional differences and distances in Argentina made it impossible to develop a national market without a transportation network. In fact, most arguments about the feasibility of alternative strategies of development for Argentina implicitly refer to the European experience, where markets developed first on the local, then on the regional, and finally on the national level. The United States' experience, like Argentina's, was based on the development of national markets by way of integration into the world market. That is to say, the formation of the national market was made possible by its being linked to the world market.

The development of agriculture entailed a different proportional allocation of resources, specific kinds of settlement patterns, transportation networks, and urban centers, as well as a more balanced income distribution. Consequently, the use of an abundant resource (land), which permitted the powerful expansion in exports, generated a significant surplus. Although at first capital goods were obtained by means of foreign indebtedness, or from foreign investments, the proportion of the foreign debt, which until 1890 had been the dynamic element in financing, became less important as exports replaced borrowing as a means of obtaining funds to import capital goods.

This not only permitted the construction of the great social overhead capital that made the development of modern Argentina possible. It also allowed for the capitalization of the countryside and for the provision of capital goods to a growing industrial sector. Although this sector was practically nonexistent at the end of the century, by 1914 it was supplying an important part of domestic consumption (90 percent in food products, 88 percent in clothing, 80 percent in construction, 4 percent in chemical products, and 33 percent in metals).

Another important factor was the government's educational policy, which provided compulsory and free primary education, paid for by the state, for every inhabitant of Argentina. This policy affected not only the native population, which was largely illiterate, but also the immigrant population, a high proportion of whom had come from countries with high rates of illiteracy. Education, therefore, helped to integrate the immigrants into Argentine society both by diffusing national symbols, and also, in many cases, by teaching Spanish and reading and writing. The government's educational policy, then, was an important investment in developing the quality of the nation's native as well as immigrant human capital. It also had important effects on income distribution. On the one hand, an improvement in the quality of labor permitted an increase in the workers' incomes. On the other hand, a mass of laborers who at least knew how to read and write were in a better position to claim a greater share of the national wealth.

Another factor that has been emphasized throughout this chapter has to do with the regional distribution of the income generated by exports. Observers have insisted for years that the development of the 600 km. around Buenos Aires took place at the expense and impoverishment of the interior. They have claimed that this resulted in a highly unequal regional distribution of wealth that has lasted to this day.

It is important to specify which area of the interior one is referring to.

There is no doubt that the old Northwest, which had been oriented toward the markets in Alto Perú during the eighteenth century, failed to find substitute markets for its local production in the Littoral during the nineteenth century. But it is not equally certain that the riverine provinces had not undergone significant development by the 1880s.

Clearly the most important aspect of the new regional realignment after 1880 was the integration of much of the interior with the coastal Pampa region, while the Mesopotamian provinces, which had been part of the riverine Littoral, entered a long period of decline. Córdoba, Tucumán in the north, and Mendoza in the far west, as well as the new regions south and east of Buenos Aires and the province of La Pampa, were integrated into the new regional economy of the pampa area.[56] The riverine provinces were bypassed. The nation's economy developed around the port, and regions that had been previously linked to other markets became integrated into a national market.

This development was accompanied by the decline of specific provinces in the old interior, not so much as a consequence of the growth of the region immediately surrounding the port of Buenos Aires, but rather because of the growth of the neighboring provinces. Thus the local economies of Catamarca and Rioja were absorbed by Tucumán, Mendoza, and Córdoba; and Santiago del Estero's by Tucumán, Córdoba, Jujuy, and Salta. But this does not mean that the whole interior became impoverished. As we have seen, the provinces that entered a long period of decline were the Mesopotamian provinces, which lost the advantage of river transport with the appearance of the railroads. And these provinces had undergone a period of significant—although not very lasting—growth toward the middle of the nineteenth century.

TABLE 1
VALUE OF EXPORTS, IMPORTS, AND REVENUES OF THE
BUENOS AIRES CUSTOMS HOUSE, 1748–1833
(IN MILLIONS OF HARD PESOS)*

Year	Exports	Imports	Buenos Aires Gov't. Revenues	Buenos Aires Customs Revenues***
1748–1753	1.6	—	—	—
1792	4.5	—	—	0.5
1793	3.7	—	—	0.4
1794	5.7	—	—	0.4
1795	5.1	—	—	0.3
1796	5.5	—	—	—
1797	—	—	—	0.4
1819	—	3.7[1]**	—	—
1822	5.0	9.9[2]**	2.5	1.9
1823	—	—	2.8	1.6
1824	—	—	2.6	2.0
1825	5.5	7.8[3][4]	3.2	2.3
1829	5.2	7.4[3]**	1.6[3]**	1.3[3]**
1830	—	—	1.6[3]**	1.2[3]**
1833	—	—	1.6[3]**	1.2[3]**
1836	3.4**	—	—	—
1837	5.6	6.9[3]**	—	1.1[3]**
1838	2.9**	2.8[3]**	—	—
1839	1.6**	1.3[3]**	—	0.1[3]**
1840	—	—	0.3[3]**	0.2[3]**
1842	7.2	—	1.9[3]**	1.8[3]**
1843	8.3	—	2.2[3]**	2.0[3]**

SOURCES:
Except in the cases marked by notes 1–4, all figures draw on the following general sources: Francisco Latzina, "El comercio argentino antaño y hogaño," in *Tercer Censo Nacional, 1914* (Buenos Aires: Rasso, 1917), p. 9 (annual average) and Ricardo Levine, *Investigaciones acerca de la historia económica del Virrlinato del Plata*, 2nd ed. (Buenos Aires: Editorial El Ateneo, 1952).

1. Datum from W. Parish in R. A. Humphreys, *British Consular Reports on Trade and Politics of Latin America, 1824–1826* (London: Offices of the Royal Historical Society, 1940) p. 56. The figure was in pound sterling; the conversion rate was 1 pound sterling = 5 gold pesos.
2. Francisco Latzina, "El comercio argentino antaño y hogaño" pp. 3–54.
3. Miron Burgin, *Economic Aspects of Argentine Federalism, 1820–1852*, (Cambridge, Mass.: Harvard University Press, 1946), pp. 66, 81, 222, 242, 254, 347. The data for 1829, 1830, 1833, 1837, 1838, 1839, 1840, 1842, 1843, 1845, 1849, and 1850 were in paper pesos and were converted according to Latzina's price quotations in "El comercio argentino antaño y hogaño," p. 267.
4. Woodbine Parish, *Buenos Aires y las Provincias del Río de la Plata* (Buenos Aires: Librería Hachette, 1958), pp. 526–527.

NOTES:
*The different monetary denominations are indicated in this chapter exactly as they appear in their respective sources, and their relationships to one another are listed in Appendix I.

**Data in gold pesos.

***The revenues of the Buenos Aires Customs House during the years 1837–1851 include port rights. These rights do not represent a significant amount. Between 1822 and 1834 they were around 1 percent of the Province's revenues.

TABLE 2
AVERAGE ANNUAL EXPORTS OF LIVESTOCK PRODUCTS FROM THE
PORT OF BUENOS AIRES, 1811–1860
(THOUSANDS OF UNITS OR TONS)

Goods	1810s	1820s	1830s	1840s	1850s
Cattle hides (units)	575	624	800	2,304	1,762
Salted meat (tons)	1	2	10	21	19
Raw wool (tons)	—	—	2	6	10
Tallows, fats (tons)	1	—	2	10	8

SOURCE: Jonathan Brown, *A Socio–Economic History of Argentina, 1776–1860* (Cambridge: Cambridge University Press, 1979), p. 80.

TABLE 3
POPULATION BY REGION, 1809–1869
(PERCENTAGES OF NATIONAL TOTALS)

Region	1809	1869
Littoral		
Buenos Aires	22.7	28.7
Sante Fe	3.2	5.1
Entre Ríos	4.2	7.7
Corrientes	3.2	7.4
Littoral, subtotal		
without Buenos Aires	10.6	20.2
Total	33.3	48.9
Center North		
Córdoba	14.8	12.1
Santiago del Estero	10.1	7.7
La Rioja	3.2	2.8
Catamarca	5.9	4.6
Tucumán	8.4	6.3
Salta	6.4	5.1
Jujuy	2.9	2.3
Total	51.7	40.9
Cuyo		
Mendoza	5.2	3.8
San Juan	5.4	3.5
San Luis	3.9	2.8
Total	14.5	10.1

SOURCE: *Primer censo de la República Argentina verificado los días 15, 16 y 17 de Septiembre de 1869, bajo la dirección de Diego G. de la Fuente* (Buenos Aires : Imprenta del Porvenir, 1872).

TABLE 4
POPULATION OF CATTLE AND SHEEP, 1864–1884
(MILLIONS OF HEAD)

	1864	1884	Percentage Increase
Cattle	10.2	14.1	38
Sheep	23.1	70.0	203

SOURCE: M. G. Mulhall, *Handbook of the River Plate, Comprising the Argentine Republic, Uruguay and Paraguay* (Buenos Aires: M. G. and E. T. Mulhall, Standard Court; London: Kegan Paul, Trench and Co., 1892).

TABLE 5
EXPORTS OF PRINCIPAL PRODUCTS, 1854–1883
(MILLIONS OF DOLLARS)

Product	1854	1863	1873	1883
Wools	3	10	21	31
Sheepskins	—	1	5	5
Cattle hides	4	7	6	9
Fats and Tallows	4	6	8	2
Meats	3	3	4	5
Grains and Cereals	—	—	—	5
Miscellaneous	1	1	2	3
Total	15	28	46	60

SOURCE: Mulhall, *Handbook of the River Plate,* p. 24. Values differ according to the sources. Those of the *Anuarios* agree with official values; those of Mulhall and Cortés Conde et al., *El comercio exterior argentino,* have been revised.

TABLE 6
LAND AREA DEDICATED TO CULTIVATION, 1854–1884

Year	Hectares	Acres	Acres per Person
1854	156,000	375,000	0.36
1864	211,000	506,000	0.33
1874	344,000	825,000	0.38
1884	1,730,000	4,260,000	1.48

SOURCE: Mulhall, *Handbook of the River Plate,* p. 30.

TABLE 7
RAILROAD EXPANSION, 1857–1880
(ALL UNITS IN THOUSANDS PER YEAR)

Year	Railroads (cumulative km.)	Passengers Transported	Cargo Transported (tons)	No. of Immigrants
1857	0.0	—	—	—
1865	0.2	747.6	71.7	4.9
1870	0.7	1,948.5	274.5	11.7
1875	1.4	2,597.1	660.9	42.0
1880	2.3	2,751.5	772.7	41.6

SOURCES: Alois E. Fliess, *La producción agrícola y ganadera de la República Argentina en el año 1891* (Buenos Aires: Imprenta de la Nación, 1892), p. 117; Emilio Rebuelto, *Medio siglo de estadística ferroviaria, 1880–1930* (Buenos Aires: Biblioteca Ferroviaria Argentina, 1930), p. 23; and Ernesto Tornquist, *The Economic Development of the Argentine Republic in the Last Fifty Years,* (Buenos Aires, 1919), p. 15.

TABLE 8
COASTAL TRADE FROM THE PORT OF BUENOS AIRES, 1856–1880
(IN THOUSANDS)

Year	Arrivals		Departures	
	Number of Vessels	*Tonnage*	*Number of Vessels*	*Tonnage*
1856	0.6	137.5	—	—
1865	3.9	107.9	4.3	111.9
1868	1.3	41.3	3.8	103.0
1880	5.2	201.4	5.3	193.1

SOURCES: *Registro estadístico del Estado de Buenos Aires 1856,* (Buenos Aires, 1856); and *Anuario estadístico de la República Argentina* corresponding to the years 1865, 1868, and 1880.

TABLE 9
GOVERNMENT REVENUES, 1873–1876
(IN MILLIONS OF HARD PESOS)

Year	Fiscal Revenues
1873	20.0
1874	15.9
1875	14.2
1876	13.5

SOURCE: *Extracto estadístico de la República Argentina correspondiente al año 1915,* (Buenos Aires Cía. Sudamericana de Billetes de Banco, 1916).

TABLE 10
NATIONAL PUBLIC DEBT, 1881–1885
(THOUSANDS OF GOLD PESOS)

Source	Nominal Value	Effective Value	Service
Banks and currency	26,561	22,258	1,487
Railroads	53,112	46,990	3,240
City of La Plata	21,517	19,892	1,566
Total	101,190	89,140	6,233

SOURCE: John H. Williams, *Argentine International Trade Under Inconvertible Paper Money, 1880–1900* (New York: Greenwood Press, 1969), p. 41.

TABLE 11
PUBLIC DEBT IN 1891
(THOUSANDS OF GOLD PESOS)

Source	Amount
National	205.0
Provincial	143.0
Municipal	25.0
Interest overdue	10.3
90% internal debt in gold	11.9
Guaranteed railroads	81.8
Total foreign debt	477.0

SOURCE: Williams, *Argentine International Trade*, p. 100.

TABLE 12
EXPORTS PER CAPITA, 1880–1890
(THOUSANDS OF GOLD PESOS)

Year	Corrected Values	Exports per Capita
1880	28.7	23.4
1885	25.0	29.1
1890	19.2	29.8

SOURCES: Cortés Conde et al., *El comercio exterior argentino,* and "Population Data" in *Anuario de la Sociedad Rural Argentina* (Buenos Aires, 1928–35). *Extracto estadístico de la República Argentina correspondiente al año 1915,* (Buenos Aires : Cía. Sudamericana de Billetes de Banco, 1916).

TABLE 13
IMPORTS PER CAPITA, 1880–1890
(THOUSANDS OF GOLD PESOS)

Year	Imports per Capita
1880	18.2
1885	32.2
1890	42.1

SOURCE: *Extracto estadístico de la República Argentina correspondiente al año 1915* (Buenos Aires : Cía. Sudamericana de Billetes de Banco, 1916).

TABLE 14

ARGENTINE FOREIGN TRADE: VALUE OF THE PRINCIPAL EXPORTS OF LIVESTOCK AND AGRICULTURE, AND THE TOTAL VALUE OF EXPORTS, 1880–1890

Year	(1) Jerked Beef (%)	(2) Frozen Meat (%)	(3) Dry Hides (%)	(4) Salted Meat (%)	(5) Sheep Skins (%)	(3–5) Total Hides (%)	(6) Wool (Untreated) (%)	(7) Fats, Tallows (%)	(1–7) Total Livestock Products (%)	(8) Wheat (%)	(9) Corn (%)	(10) Flax (%)	(8–10) Total Agricultural Products (%)	Total Livestock and Agricultural Products (%)	Total Value of Exports (millions of gold pesos) Corrected* Values	Total Value of Exports (millions of gold pesos) Official Values
1880	5.3	—	18.0	5.2	11.8	35.0	42.9	2.5	85.7	0.1	0.5	0.1	0.7	86.4	71.7	—
1881	5.6	—	17.1	5.4	8.5	31.0	47.9	2.7	87.2	—	0.8	1.0	1.8	89.0	59.6	58
1882	6.8	—	14.0	5.6	6.2	25.8	55.6	4.9	93.1	0.1	3.7	2.9	6.7	99.8	66.7	60
1883	3.9	—	12.0	4.1	8.1	24.2	51.2	4.0	83.3	3.3	0.7	1.7	5.7	89.0	66.5	60
1884	2.8	—	15.9	5.2	5.5	26.6	46.0	3.2	78.6	5.9	3.0	2.4	11.3	89.9	70.6	68
1885	4.3	0.1	16.5	8.0	4.6	29.1	42.7	4.9	81.0	3.1	3.9	3.5	10.5	91.5	72.0	84
1886	4.9	0.4	10.5	5.1	4.3	19.9	55.1	2.0	81.9	2.3	5.8	1.9	10.0	91.9	70.3	70
1887	3.7	0.9	12.8	6.2	6.3	25.3	40.5	0.8	70.3	10.2	7.6	3.8	21.6	91.9	76.1	84
1888	2.3	1.5	9.6	6.0	6.2	21.8	45.0	1.8	70.9	8.9	5.7	2.0	16.5	87.4	66.3	100
1889	5.1	1.1	8.0	6.6	9.3	23.9	44.5	2.3	76.8	1.2	10.3	1.4	12.9	89.7	65.4	123
1890	5.2	0.9	8.2	7.7	6.6	22.5	35.5	2.3	65.5	19.5	10.9	1.4	25.8	91.3	73.6	101

SOURCE: Cortés Conde et al., *El comercio exterior argentino*.
*Corresponds to the corrected values cited in the text. A comparison with "Official Values" column points up the differences mentioned in the text.

365

TABLE 15
BALANCE OF TRADE AND PAYMENTS, 1881–1885
(MILLIONS OF GOLD PESOS)

Year	Exports	Imports	Balance	New Loans	Interest	Balance	Credits (Exports + New Loans)	Debits (Imports + Interest)	Balance (Credits − Debits)
1881	57.9	55.7	+ 2.2	14.0	11.9	+ 2.1	72.0	67.6	+ 4.3
1882	60.3	61.2	− 0.8	25.2	15.7	+ 9.5	85.6	76.9	+ 8.7
1883	60.2	80.4	− 20.2	47.3	19.4	+ 27.9	107.6	99.9	+ 7.8
1884	68.0	94.0	− 26.0	39.7	27.5	+ 12.1	107.7	121.6	− 13.8
1885	83.8	92.2	− 8.3	38.7	22.6	+ 16.1	122.6	114.8	+ 7.7

SOURCE: Williams, *Argentine International Trade*, pp. 45, 46, 47.

TABLE 16
BALANCE OF PAYMENTS, 1886–1889
(MILLIONS OF GOLD PESOS)

Year	Credits			Debits			Balance of Payments (Total Credits − Total Debits)
	Exports	Foreign Loans	Total	Imports	Interest	Total	
1886	70	67	137	95	27	122	+ 15
1887	84	153	237	117	37	154	+ 83
1888	100	248	348	128	50	178	+170
1889	90	154	244	164	59	224	+ 19
1890	100	45	146	142	60	202	− 56
1891	103	8	111	67	32	98	+ 12

SOURCE: Williams, *Argentine International Trade*, p. 104.

TABLE 17
COMPOSITION OF THE ARGENTINE FOREIGN DEBT, 1894–1913
(THOUSANDS OF GOLD PESOS)

	Balance to Dec. 31, 1894	Balance to Dec. 31, 1913
Social Overhead Capital	138,1	165,0
Railroads	35,2	80,5
Others	103,0	84,1
Nonreproductive Investments	18,5	28,4
Financing	62,3	115,0
Total Foreign Debt	219,0	309,0

SOURCE: For 1894: *The Argentine Year Book* (Buenos Aires: John Grant and Son, 1902). For 1913: *The Argentine Year Book* (Buenos Aires: Robert Grant, 1914).

TABLE 18
GOVERNMENT-PAID RAILROAD GUARANTEES IN RELATION TO EXPORTS, FOREIGN DEBT, AND NATIONAL GOVERNMENT EXPENDITURES, 1874–1890
(MILLIONS OF GOLD PESOS)

Year	(1) Paid Railroad Guarantees	(2) Exports* Official Values (a)	(2) Exports* Corrected Values (b)	(3) Guarantees Paid as Percent of Exports Official Values $\frac{(1)}{(2a)} \times 100$	(3) Guarantees Paid as Percent of Exports Corrected Values $\frac{(1)}{(2b)} \times 100$	(4) Interest on Foreign Debt	(5) Guarantees Paid as Percent of Interest $\frac{(1)}{(4)} \times 100$	(6) National Government Expenditure	(7) Guarantees Paid as Percent of National Government Expenditure $\frac{(1)}{(6)} \times 100$
1874–1882	2.7	—	—	—	—	—	—	—	—
1883–1886	1.8	—	—	—	—	—	—	—	—
1887–1888	3.8	84.4	76.1	4.5	5.0	49.5	7.7	65[†] 76[‡]	5.8[†]
1889	3.1	90.1	65.4	3.6	4.9	59.8	5.2	107	2.9
1890	3.1	100.8	73.6	3.0	4.2	60.2	5.1	95	3.3
Total	14.5								

SOURCES: For column (1) Mulhall, *Handbook of the River Plate*, p. 26; for columns (2) to (6): Williams, *Argentine International Trade*, p. 101.

*Direct investment in railroad companies, even when guaranteed by the state, permitted imports of capital goods valued at 15 million pounds sterling by 1884 (75 million gold pesos), and at 68.8 million pounds sterling by 1890 (344 million gold pesos). See Mulhall, *Handbook of the River Plate*, p. 237. Since this was about five times the value of exports in a single year, it would not have been possible to obtain imports of that magnitude, through exports only, prior to 1890.

[†] These figures cover the year 1887 only.

[‡] This figure is for 1888 only.

TABLE 19
FIVE-YEAR AVERAGE OF IMMIGRANT ARRIVALS, 1880–1884 and 1885–1889
(THOUSANDS)

Years	Average
1880–1884	41
1885–1889	128

SOURCE: Argentine Republic, Ministerio de Hacienda, Dirección General de Estadística de la Nación, *La población y el movimiento demográfico de la República Argentina en los años 1939 y 1938 y síntesis de los anteriores,* Informe 78, Ser. D, No. 6 (Buenos Aires, 1940), pp. 146–147.

TABLE 20
DIFFERENCES IN THE RATE OF POPULATION GROWTH OF
BUENOS AIRES AND GROWTH OF CULTIVATED AREAS, 1855–1895

Population		Difference with Previous Period
Buenos Aires	1869–1890	0.1% (1855–1869)
	1890–1895	–1.6% (1869–1890)
Cultivated Areas	1888–1895	0.9% (1872–1888)

SOURCE: Cortés Conde, R., "Tendencias en el crecimiento de la población urbana en la Argentina" (*Verhandlungen des XXXVIII Internationalen Amerikanistenkongresses,* Stuttgart-Munchen, August 12–18, 1968,) p. 268.

TABLE 21
BALANCE OF INTERNATIONAL PAYMENTS, 1895–1900
(THOUSANDS OF GOLD PESOS)

Date	Balance of Borrowings			Balance of Trade			Balance of Payments (Cols. 3–6)
	(1) Borrowings	*(2)* Interest	*(3)* Balance (Cols. 1–2)	*(4)* Exports	*(5)* Imports	*(6)* Balance (Cols. 4–5)	
1895	17,197	38,149	– 20,952	120,068	95,096	+ 24,971	+ 4,019
1896	37,144	39,863	– 2,719	116,802	112,164	+ 4,638	+ 1,919
1897	38,295	43,985	– 5,690	101,169	98,289	+ 2,880	– 2,810
1898	46,063	50,530	– 4,467	133,829	107,429	+ 26,400	+ 21,934
1899	24,966	54,698	– 29,732	184,918	116,851	+ 68,067	+ 38,335
1900	27,540	58,575	– 31,035	154,600	113,485	+ 41,115	+ 10,082

SOURCE; Williams, *Argentine International Trade,* p. 152.

TABLE 22
AREA SOWN WITH WHEAT AND CORN, 1872–1888
(THOUSANDS OF HECTARES)

Province	Wheat			Corn		
	1872	*1881*	*1888*	*1872*	*1881*	*1888*
Buenos Aires	50	89	247	—	100	510
Sante Fe	36	184	402	1.7	41	61
Córdoba	13	—	56	36.6	—	79
Entre Ríos	8	—	67	—	—	49
San Juan	8	13	—	18.6	—	—
La Pampa	—	—	—	—	—	5
Mendoza	—	—	—	47.1	—	—
National Total	130	286	815	—	—	802

SOURCE: For 1872: *Segundo censo de la República Argentina, mayo 10 de 1895; censos complementarios,* Vol. III (Buenos Aires: Talleres Tipogfaficos de la Penitenciaría Nacional, 1898). For 1881: Alois E. Fliess, *La producción agraria y ganadera de la República Argentina en el año 1891; Estudio económico y estadístico* (Buenos Aires: Imprenta de la Nación, 1892); y Gabriel Carrasco, *Descripción geográfica y estadística de la Provincia de Santa Fé,* 4th Ed. (Buenos Aires: Stiller y Laas, 1886). For 1888: Latizna, F. *L'Agriculture et l'elevage dans la Republique Argentine d'aprés le recocement de la premiere quinzaine d'octobre de 1888* (Paris: P. Mouillot, 1889).

TABLE 23
ARGENTINE AND UNITED STATES PRICES: ARGENTINE PESO PARITY IN GOLD* AND THE RELATION OF THE PESO VIS-À-VIS THE DOLLAR, 1882–1907

Year	(1) Relative Prices, Argentina– United States (1882 = 1.0)	(2) Price of Gold in Paper Pesos	Percentage of Undervaluation: Paper Peso vis-a-vis Dollar $\left(\dfrac{2-1}{1} \times 100\right)$
1882	1.00	1.00	—
1883	0.98	1.00	2
1884	0.99	1.00	1
1885	0.91	1.37	50
1886	0.93	1.39	49
1887	1.31	1.35	3
1888	1.31	1.48	13
1889	1.36	1.91	40
1890	1.67	2.51	50
1891	1.89	3.87	105
1892	1.67	3.32	98
1893	1.53	3.24	111
1894	1.94	3.57	84
1895	2.16	3.44	59
1896	2.35	2.96	25
1897	2.14	2.11	−1
1898	1.77	2.58	45
1899	1.44	2.25	56
1900	1.61	2.31	43
1901	1.85	2.27	23
1902	1.83	2.27	24
1903	1.79	2.27	27
1904	1.77	2.27	28
1905	1.82	2.27	25
1906	1.98	2.27	15
1907	2.00	2.27	14

SOURCES: For Argentina: Roberto Cortés Conde, *El progreso argentino, 1880–1914* (Buenos Aires: Sudamericana, 1979); for United States: *Historical Statistics of the United States; Colonial Times to 1957*, prepared by the Bureau of the Census with the cooperation of the Social Science Research Council (Washington, D.C., 1960).
*The gold peso being almost equivalent to the dollar.

TABLE 24

**ARGENTINE FOREIGN TRADE: TOTAL EXPORTS AND VALUES OF
PRINCIPAL EXPORT ITEMS, 1891–1930**

Year	(1) Jerked Beef (salted meat) (%)	(2) Frozen Beef (%)	(3) Frozen Mutton (%)	(4) Cattle Hides (dry) (%)	(5) Cattle Hides (salted) (%)	(6) Sheep- skin (%)	(4–6) Total (%)	(7) Wool (%)
1891	4.1	—	0.6	5.7	6.9	4.7	17.3	35.0
1896	2.3	0.1	3.9	5.0	4.0	3.9	12.9	30.1
1901	1.6	3.3	4.5	5.0	3.1	4.0	12.1	25.8
1906	0.2	6.1	3.1	3.6	2.8	2.8	9.2	19.7
1911	0.5	10.0	3.6	4.5	5.8	2.1	12.4	15.0
1920	—	9.4	1.4	0.6	3.1	0.4	4.1	6.7
1930	—	2.9	2.4	1.0	5.3	0.7	7.0	6.7

SOURCE: Cortés Conde et al., *El comercio exterior argentino.*

(8) Fats & Tallows (%)	(1–8) Total Livestock (%)	(9) Wheat (%)	(10) Corn (%)	(11) Flax (%)	(9–11) Total Agriculture (%)	(1–11) Total Agriculture and Livestock (%)	Total Value of Exports (millions of gold pesos)
2.6	59.0	20.3	12.0	0.6	32.9	91.9	80.0
2.1	47.5	10.2	12.7	5.5	28.4	75.9	125.4
2.2	45.0	15.1	10.8	9.5	35.4	80.0	173.9
1.2	36.4	22.4	18.0	8.7	49.1	85.5	298.4
3.8	41.7	24.0	0.8	10.0	34.8	76.5	335.3
1.6	28.7	33.6	16.2	11.3	61.1	89.9	970.0
1.4	17.1	15.2	17.7	14.5	47.4	64.5	605.1

TABLE 25

RAILROAD SHIPMENTS:

PROPORTION OF THE TOTAL OF DIFFERENT CARGO CLASSES, 1901–1914

Year	(Cereals)	Total Agriculture	Foods	Livestock	Industry and Minerals	Construction Materials	Fuels, Misc. Merchandise
1901	(23.59)	27.34	2.65	8.04	11.46	11.22	39.29
1906	(29.85)	33.22	1.20	6.37	11.32	13.93	33.96
1911	(19.66)	34.37	1.04	12.20	11.74	16.18	34.47
1914	(25.67)	29.66	0.78	12.38	13.77	11.86	31.55

SOURCE: Rebuelto, *Medio siglo de estadísticas ferroviaria, 1880–1930*, p. 23.
*Including cereals.

TABLE 26
INDUSTRIAL CAPITAL DEFLATED BY INDEX OF IMPLICIT PRICES OF EXPORTS* 1881–1913
(THOUSANDS OF PESOS CORRIENTES)

	1881 (1.09)**	1887 (1.23)**	1895 (2.86)**	1904 (2.25)**	1908 (2.50)**	1909 (3.06)**	1910 (3.29)**	1913 (3.32)**
Capital	—	15,833	41,244	43,989	106,599	105,927	—	164,956
Buenos Aires	16,396	—	24,802	26,666	55,666	—	—	141,844
Santa Fe	—	15,357	11,552	—	—	—	15,079	56,632
Córdoba	—	—	2,799	—	—	9,087	—	22,610
Entre Ríos	—	—	8,143	—	—	7,008	—	21,769
Tucumán	—	—	—	—	—	—	—	26,866
La Pampa	—	—	31	—	—	396	—	1,019
Total	—	—	114,474	126,267	—	—	221,152	538,452

SOURCES: *Segundo censo de la República Argentina, mayo 10 de 1895* (Buenos Aires: Talleres Tipográficos de la Penitenciaría Nacional, 1898); *Censo industrial y comercial de la República Argentina, 1908–1914* (Buenos Aires: Ministerio de Agricultura, Dirección General de Comercio e Industria, 1915).

*Given the importance of exports in the GNP, we can assume that the index of the implicit prices of exports can be used as a proxy for the general price index. The index has been constructed by Héctor Dieguez, the figures on physical volume (in "Crecimiento . . .", in, *Desarrollo económico*) are divided by the export values from the series obtained by Cortés Conde et al., *El comercio exterior argentino*. Conversion to 1900 prices.

**Coefficients used for deflation taken from Héctor L. Dieguez, "Crecimiento e inestabilidad del valor y el volumen físico de las exportaciones argentinas en el período 1864–1963," in *Desarrollo económico*, Vol. XII, No. 46, Julio–Sept. 1972, pp. 333–49.

TABLE 27
INDUSTRIAL PRODUCTION DEFLATED BY INDEX OF IMPLICIT PRICES OF EXPORTS,* 1887–1913
(THOUSANDS OF PESOS CORRIENTES)

	1887 (1.23)**	1904 (2.25)**	1906 (2.91)**	1908 (2.61)**	1909 (3.06)**	1913 (3.22)**
Federal Capital	38,825	81,534	—	204,844	75,817	205,800
Buenos Aires	—	—	54,305	—	94,806	168,013
Santa Fe	—	—	—	—	—	60,199
Córdoba	—	—	—	—	—	23,046
Entre Ríos	—	—	—	—	—	21,998
La Pampa	—	—	—	—	—	1,248
Total in country	—	—	—	—	401,176	578,195

SOURCES: *Segundo censo de la República Argentina, mayo 10 de 1895* and *Censo industrial y comercial de la República Argentina, 1908–1914.*
*Given the importance of exports in the GNP, we can assume that the index of the implicit prices of exports can be used as a proxy for the general price index. As for Table 26, the index has been constructed by Dieguez "Crecimiento . . ." in *Desarrollo económico.*
**Coefficients used for deflation, taken from Dieguez, op. cit.

TABLE 28
REGIONAL DISTRIBUTION OF INDUSTRIES
(THOUSANDS)

Jurisdiction	Average Capital per Plant	
	1895	*1913*
Littoral		
Federal Capital	13.9	53.2
Buenos Aires	12.2	31.6
Sante Fe	11.9	32.2
Entre Ríos	15.7	30.3
Corrientes	.8	13.6
Total	13.1	37.7
Center		
San Luis	2.9	12.1
Córdoba	6.3	26.4
Santiago del Estero	9.5	25.3
Total	6.4	24.3
Andean		
Mendoza	15.8	67.2
San Juan	13.7	28.6
La Rioja	4.6	16.6
Catamarca	1.8	6.1
Total	12.3	37.9
North		
Tucumán	54.5	113.1
Salta	5.4	5.5
Jujuy	20.2	150.9
Total	33.7	40.1
Territories		
Misiones	9.7	24.2
Formosa	24.0	29.2
Chaco	33.3	130.1
La Pampa	2.4	8.7

TABLE 28 (continued)

Jurisdiction	Average Capital per Plant	
	1895	*1913*
Neuquen	.3	27.9
Rio Negro	2.9	5.6
Santa Cruz	—	34.7
Chubut	0.8	8.2
Tierra del Fuego	14.3	12.0
Los Andes	—	29.4
Total	11.8	31.0
Total for whole country	13.5	36.6

SOURCE: For 1895: *Segundo censo de la república Argentina, mayo 10 de 1895* (Buenos Aires : Talleres Tipográficos de la Penitenciaría Nacional, 1898); For 1913: *Tercer censo nacional levantado el 1° de junio de 1914* (Buenos Aires : Talleres Gráficos de L. J. Rosso, 1916–1917).

APPENDIX I
MONETARY CONVERSIONS, 1881–1899

1 peso fuerte (or hard peso) = 1.029 gold peso (1863–1875)
1 peso fuerte (or hard peso) = 1.033 gold peso (1876–1881)
1 peso moneda nacional = 0.44 gold peso (1899–1914)
1 pound sterling = 5.04 gold pesos
1 dollar = 1.036 gold peso (1881–1914)
1 gold peso equivalence in paper:

1881–1884 = 1	1892 = 3.29
1885 = 1.37	1893 = 3.24
1886 = 1.39	1894 = 3.58
1887 = 1.35	1895 = 3.44
1888 = 1.48	1896 = 2.96
1889 = 1.80	1897 = 2.91
1890 = 2.58	1898 = 2.57
1891 = 3.74	1899 = 2.25

SOURCE: J. Alvarez, *Temas de historia económica argentina* (Buenos Aires: El Ateneo, 1929).

NOTES

1. Exports from Buenos Aires in the seventeenth century did not surpass 100,000 silver pesos (valued at 1 gold peso in 1881), except in the ten–year period 1606–1615. Furthermore, they varied strongly, with spectacular lows between 1640 and 1655. Imports far surpassed exports, reflecting an outflow of silver and gold. Exports varied between 25,000 and 40,000 silver pesos, fiscal income between 20,000 and 200,000 silver pesos for the decade. All this gives some idea of the colony's poverty. Francisco Latzina, "El comercio argentino antaño y hogaño," in *Censo agropecuario nacional—La ganadería y la agricultura en 1908,* Vol. 3 (Buenos Aires: Talleres de Publicaciones de la Oficina Meteorológica Argentina, 1909), pp. 564 ff.

2. Ibid., p. 568.

3. Ibid., p. 573.

4. Tulio Halperín Donghi, *Revolución y guerra* (Buenos Aires: Siglo XXI, Editores S.A., 1972).

5. Miron Burgin, *The Economic Aspects of Argentine Federalism, 1820–1852* (Cambridge, Mass.: Harvard University Press, 1946). Halperín Donghi, *Revolución y guerra,* p. 80, writes that although these were the principal receipts for the state, they were not sufficient because of war costs.

6. Burgin, *Economic Aspects of Argentine Federalism,* p. 30.

7. Halperín Donghi, *Revolución y guerra,* p. 117.

8. Burgin, *Economic Aspects of Argentine Federalism,* p. 30.

9. Jonathan Brown, *A Socio–Economic History of Argentina, 1776–1860* (Cambridge: Cambridge University Press, 1979), p. 75.

10. Robert Baldwin, "Patterns of Development in Newly Settled Regions," in J. Friedman and W. Alonso, eds., *Regional Development and Planning* (Cambridge, Mass.: M.I.T. Press, 1946).

11. Alberto Rex González and José A. Pérez, *Argentina indígena—Vísperas de la conquista* (Buenos Aires: Editorial Paidós, 1972).

12. Halperín Donghi, *Revolución y guerra.*

13. The frontier recommended by Lieutenant Betbeze in 1779 and approved by Viceroy Vertiz in 1782. See R. Levene, *Investigaciones acerca de la historia económica del Virreinato del Plata,* 2nd ed. (Buenos Aires: Editorial El Ateneo, 1952).

14. See P. Randle, *La ciudad pampeana* (Buenos Aires: Eudeba, 1969), p. 11.

15. *Censo general de la Provincia de Buenos Aires, 1881* (Buenos Aires: Imprenta de El Diario, 1883); and *Segundo censo de la República Argentina, mayo 10 de 1895* (Buenos Aires: Talleres Tipográficos de la Penitenciaría Nacional, 1898).

16. According to Johan Jakob von Tschudi, *Reisen durch Sudamerika* (Leipzig, 1866), in 1857 a voyage from Hamburg to Rio de Janeiro lasted one month and six days.

17. Francisco de Aparicio, *La Argentina: Suma de geografía,* Vol. 3 (Buenos Aires: Ediciones Peuser, 1961), p. 57.

18. Ibid., p. 60.

19. Tulio Halperín Donghi, "Expansión de la frontera de Buenos Aires," in A. Jara, ed., *Tierras nuevas* (Mexico City: El Colegio de Mexico, 1973), p. 85.

20. Hla Myint, "The Classical Theory of International Trade and the Underdeveloped Countries," *The Economic Journal,* 68, No. 270 (1958): 317–337.

21. Baldwin, "Patterns of Development in Newly Settled Regions."

22. M. G. Mulhall, *Handbook of the River Plate,* (Buenos Aires: M. G. and E. T. Mulhall, Standard Court, 1892), p. 43 for year 1850 and Roberto Cortés Conde, Tulio Halperín Donghi, and Haydée Gorostegui de Torres *El comercio exterior argentino,* Vol. I "Exportaciones" (mimeo), n.d. for 1875. The figures in the text are not the figures published in the *Anuarios,* but the revised figures from the above publication of Roberto Cortés Conde et al. *El comercio exterior.*

23. Mulhall, *Handbook of the River Plate,* p. 43.

24. Ibid.

25. H. Gibson, "La evolución ganadera," in *Censo agropecuario nacional—La ganadería y la agricultura en 1908,* Vol. 3 (Buenos Aires, 1909).

26. Mulhall, *Handbook of the River Plate,* p. 11.

27. R. Cortés Conde et al., *El comercio exterior argentino,* provides export values for 1864, 1870, and 1873.

28. *Extracto estadístico de la República Argentina correspondiente al año 1915* (Buenos Aires: Compañía Sudamericana de Billetes de Banco, 1916) Gold pesos and hard pesos are almost equivalent (see Monetary Conversion Table in Appendix I at the end of this Chapter). Imports and exports are expressed in the source in gold pesos and revenues and expenses in hard pesos.

29. The devaluation in the 1890s was less and for a shorter period.

30. See *Segundo censo de la República Argentina, 1895,* Vol. 3, pp. CLVIII, CLIX.

31. Cargo moved through the port of Buenos Aires in 1880 was as follows:

	Tons
Overseas	733,755
Coasting trade	201,485
Total	935,240

(Figures from Ernesto Tornquist, *Economic Development of the Argentine Republic in the Last Fifty Years* (Buenos Aires, 1919), pp. 190–191.

32. A careful study of the new patterns of regionalization in the province of Buenos Aires is in Cristina San Román de Franco, *La Provincia de Buenos Aires en la década del 70: aspectos demográficos, económicos y políticos* (Tucumán: Primeras Jornadas de Historia por Centros de Investigación de Nivel Universitario, 1979).

33. Juan Alvarez, *Temas de historia económica argentina* (Buenos Aires: Editorial El Ateneo, 1929), p. 208.

34. Ibid., p. 213.

35. The correction was made by Cortés Conde et al., *El comercio exterior argentino,* Vol. I.

36. Guido di Tella and Manuel Zymelman, *Las etapas del desarrollo económico* (Buenos Aires: Eudeba, 1967), p. 8. Paul B. Goodwin, Jr., argues that railroads *responded* to demand rather than initiated the increase in demand in "The Central Argentine Railway and the Economic Development of Argentina, 1854–1881," *Hispanic American Historical Review* 57 (November 1977), pp. 613 ff. On railroads, see also Paul B. Goodwin, Jr., *The British Owned Railroads and the Unión Cívica Radical: A Study on the Political Issues of Foreign Capital, 1916–1930* (Ann Arbor: University of Massachusetts, 1971), microfilm; and Eduardo Zalduendo, *Libras y rieles* (Buenos Aires: Editorial El Coloquio, 1975).

37. On the important problem of guarantees, see Winthrop Wright's important book, *British-Owned Railways in Argentina: Their Effect on Economic Nationalism, 1864–1948* (Austin: University of Texas Press, 1974).

38. Juan Alvarez, *Estudio sobre las guerras civiles argentinas* (Buenos Aires: Juan Roldán, 1914).

39. Mark D. Szuchman, "The Limits of the Melting Pot in Urban Argentina: Marriage and Integration in Córdoba, 1868–1905," *Hispanic American Historical Review* (February 1977), pp. 24. See also Samuel L. Baily's interesting work on marriage patterns and the effects of assimilation in "Marriage Patterns and Immigrant Assimilation in Buenos Aires, 1882–1923," *Hispanic American Historical Review* 60 (February 1980), pp. 321.

40. Donald Castro, *The Development of Argentine Immigration Policy, 1892–1914* (Ann Arbor: University of Michigan, microfilm, 1972), p. 221.

41. Cortés Conde et al., *El comercio exterior argentino,* and "Population Data" in *Anuario de la Sociedad Rural Argentina,* (Buenos Aires, 1928). (See also note 35 in this chapter).

42. Alex George Ford, *The Gold Standard, Britain and Argentina* (Oxford: Clarendon Press, 1962).

43. Alois E. Fleiss, *La producción agrícola y ganadera de la Republica Argentina en el año 1891* (Buenos Aires: Imprenta de la Nación, 1892).

44. Simon G. Hanson, *Argentine Meat and the British Market* (Stanford, Calif.: Stanford University Press; London: Oxford University Press, 1938).

45. Alvarez, *Temas de historia económica argentina,* p. 208.

46. R. Cortés Conde, "Patrones de asentamiento y explotación agropecuaria en los nuevos territorios argentinos (1890–1910)," in *Tierras nuevas, expansión territorial y ocupación del suelo en América (siglos XVI–XIX)* (Mexico City: El Colegio de México, 1973), p. 109.

47. R. Cortés Conde and N. L. de Nisnovich, "El desarrollo agrícola en el proceso de urbanización," in Richard Schaedel et al., eds., *Urbanización y proceso social en América* (Lima: Instituto de Estudios Peruanos, 1972).

48. See Roberto Cortés Conde, "Tendencias en el crecimiento de la población urbana en Argentina," *Verhandlungen des XXXVIII Internationalen Amerikanistenkongresses* (Stuttgart-Munchen, August 1968), Band IV.

49. Albert Fishlow, *American Railroads and the Transformation of the Antebellum Economy* (Cambridge, Mass.: Harvard University Press, 1965); Robert Fogel, *Railroads and American Economic Growth* (Baltimore: The John Hopkins Press, 1964); Carlos Díaz-Alejandro, *Essays on the Economic History of the Argentine Republic* (New Haven, Conn.: Yale University Press, 1970).

50. Melville H. Watkins, "A Staple Theory of Economic Growth," *The Canadian Journal of Economic and Political Science,* 29 No. 2 (May 1963).

51. An interpretation that does not see agrarian expansion in opposition to industrialization, but rather considers them complementary, is in Ezequiel Gallo, "Agrarian Expansion and Industrial Development in Argentina, 1880–1930," in Raymond Carr, ed., *Latin American Affairs* (London: Oxford University Press, 1970), pp. 54 ff. Another contribution to the debate on industrialization argues that the issue has been distorted by the assumption that industrial development depends on tariff protection. See John Foggarty, "Australia y Argentina en el período 1914–1923," in John Foggarty, Ezequiel Gallo and Héctor L. Diegue, eds., *Argentina y Australia* (Buenos Aires: Instituto Torcuato di Tella, 1979), p. 38.

52. See Héctor L. Dieguez, "Crecimiento e inestabilidad del valor y el volumen físico de las exportaciones argentinas en el período 1864–1963," *Desarollo económico,* Vol. XII, No. 46, Julio–Sept. 1972, pp. 333–349 (compare 1895 with 1914).

53. See Baily, "Marriage Patterns and Immigrant Assimilation in Buenos Aires."

54. Albert O. Hirschman, *The Strategy of Economic Development,* (New Haven, Conn.: Yale University Press, 1960), Chapter 1.

55. Balán points to the development of sugar and wine industries in Tucumán and Mendoza as instances of integration into the national market where the transformations extended their scope from local to national markets, despite provincial locations. Regarding less successful cases in other provinces, he recognizes that lack of resources and greater distance may, among other reasons, have been responsible. Jorge Balán, "Una cuestión regional en la Argentina: burguesías provinciales y el mercado nacional en el desarrollo agro–exportador," *Desarrollo económico* (April–June 1978), pp. 49 ff.

INDEX